Vicarious Liability in Tort

Vicarious liability is controversial: a principle of strict liability in an area dominated by fault-based liability. By making an innocent party pay compensation for the torts of another, it can also appear unjust. Yet it is a principle found in all Western legal systems, be they civil law or common law. Despite uncertainty as to its justifications, it is accepted as necessary.

In our modern global economy, we are unlikely to understand its meaning and rationale through study of one legal system alone. Using her considerable experience as a comparative tort lawyer, Paula Giliker examines the principle of vicarious liability (or, to a civil lawyer, liability for the acts of others) in England and Wales, Australia, Canada, France and Germany, and with reference to legal systems in countries such as the United States, New Zealand and Spain.

PAULA GILIKER is Professor of Comparative Law at the University of Bristol, where she specialises in comparative tort law. She has previously taught at the University of Oxford and Queen Mary, University of London. She is also a qualified barrister and visiting lecturer at the Universities of Hong Kong and Valencia.

CAMBRIDGE STUDIES IN INTERNATIONAL AND COMPARATIVE LAW

Established in 1946, this series produces high quality scholarship in the fields of public and private international law and comparative law. Although these are distinct legal sub-disciplines, developments since 1946 confirm their interrelation.

Comparative law is increasingly used as a tool in the making of law at national, regional and international levels. Private international law is now often affected by international conventions, and the issues faced by classical conflicts rules are frequently dealt with by substantive harmonisation of law under international auspices. Mixed international arbitrations, especially those involving state economic activity, raise mixed questions of public and private international law, while in many fields (such as the protection of human rights and democratic standards, investment guarantees and international criminal law) international and national systems interact. National constitutional arrangements relating to 'foreign affairs', and to the implementation of international norms, are a focus of attention.

The Board welcomes works of a theoretical or interdisciplinary character, and those focusing on the new approaches to international or comparative law or conflicts of law. Studies of particular institutions or problems are equally welcome, as are translations of the best work published in other languages.

General Editors	James Crawford SC FBA
	Whewell Professor of International Law, Faculty of Law, and Director, Lauterpacht Research Centre for International Law, University of Cambridge
	John S. Bell FBA
	Professor of Law, Faculty of Law, University of Cambridge
Editorial Board	Professor Hilary Charlesworth *Australian National University*
	Professor Lori Damrosch *Columbia University Law School*
	Professor John Dugard *Universiteit Leiden*
	Professor Mary-Ann Glendon *Harvard Law School*
	Professor Christopher Greenwood *London School of Economics*
	Professor David Johnston *University of Edinburgh*
	Professor Hein Kötz *Max-Planck-Institut, Hamburg*
	Professor Donald McRae *University of Ottawa*
	Professor Onuma Yasuaki *University of Tokyo*
	Professor Reinhard Zimmermann *Universität Regensburg*
Advisory Committee	Professor D.W. Bowett QC
	Judge Rosalyn Higgins QC
	Professor J.A. Jolowicz QC
	Professor Sir Elihu Lauterpacht CBE QC
	Judge Stephen Schwebel

A list of books in the series can be found at the end of this volume.

Vicarious Liability in Tort:
A Comparative Perspective

Paula Giliker

CAMBRIDGE UNIVERSITY PRESS
Cambridge, New York, Melbourne, Madrid, Cape Town, Singapore,
São Paulo, Delhi, Dubai, Tokyo, Mexico City

Cambridge University Press
The Edinburgh Building, Cambridge CB2 8RU, UK

Published in the United States of America by Cambridge University Press, New York

www.cambridge.org
Information on this title: www.cambridge.org/9780521763370

© Paula Giliker 2010

This publication is in copyright. Subject to statutory exception
and to the provisions of relevant collective licensing agreements,
no reproduction of any part may take place without
the written permission of Cambridge University Press.

First published 2010

A catalogue record for this publication is available from the British Library

Library of Congress Cataloging-in-Publication Data
Giliker, Paula.
  Vicarious liability in tort : a comparative perspective / Paula Giliker.
    p. cm. – (Cambridge studies in international and comparative law)
  ISBN 978-0-521-76337-0 (Hardback)
  1. Respondeat superior. 2. Third parties (Law) I. Title. II. Series.
  K962.G55 2010
  346.03–dc22
                                                                    2010017639

ISBN 978-0-521-76337-0 Hardback

Cambridge University Press has no responsibility for the persistence or
accuracy of URLs for external or third-party internet websites referred to
in this publication, and does not guarantee that any content on such
websites is, or will remain, accurate or appropriate.

For Keith and Jasper

'I have never been able to see why the law should be so – why a man should be liable for the negligence of his servant, there being no relation constituted between him and the party complaining.'

(Lord Bramwell)[1]

'*Respondeat superior* is an argument which, like David, has slain its tens of thousands. Its seeming simplicity conceals in fact a veritable hornet's nest of stinging difficulties. It is the merest dogma, and in no sense explanation. For while everyone can see that the master ought to answer for acts he has authorised, why should he be liable either where no authorisation can be shown, or where express prohibition of an act exists?'

(Harold Laski)[2]

'[T]here is now a consensus among those ... who think about tort law that vicarious liability is an essential element in the tort system. Any idea of repealing vicarious liability would seem to us preposterous, inconceivable.'

(Gary T. Schwartz)[3]

---

[1] Before the Parliamentary Committee of 1876 (1887) Cd 285, p. 46.
[2] 'The basis of vicarious liability', *Yale Law Journal*, 26 (1916), 105 at 106–7.
[3] 'The hidden and fundamental issue of employer vicarious liability', *Southern California Law Review*, 69 (1996), 1739 at 1745.

Table of contents

List of diagrams — page xv
Table of cases — xvi
Table of legislation — xxxiv
Preface — xli

1 What is vicarious liability? — 1
  1.1 Introduction — 1
  1.2 Vicarious liability: an historical overview — 6
  1.3 The legal basis for vicarious liability — 13
      1.3.1 Distinguishing primary from vicarious liability — 16
  1.4 Conclusion — 18

2 Establishing a general framework for liability — 21
  2.1 Introduction — 21
  2.2 Identifying a general framework for liability — 21
      2.2.1 Key terminology and codal provisions in English, French and German law — 22
      2.2.2 The requirement of a wrongful act — 27
      2.2.3 The right to an indemnity — 30
      2.2.4 A common law problem: vicarious liability for exemplary damages? — 39
  2.3 Liability for the acts of others in other areas of law — 43
      2.3.1 Contract law — 44
      2.3.2 Company law — 46
      2.3.3 Public law — 50
      2.3.4 The relevance of French criminal law — 53
  2.4 Conclusion — 54

TABLE OF CONTENTS

3	The employer/employee relationship: identifying the contract of employment		55
	3.1	Introduction	55
	3.2	The control test	57
	3.3	Doubts as to the control test	60
		3.3.1 Control and doctors: who is liable for the negligent surgeon?	61
		3.3.2 Response	65
	3.4	Alternative approaches to the control test	66
		3.4.1 A more flexible interpretation of the control test	66
		3.4.2 The organisation and composite tests	69
	3.5	Application of the 'totality of the relationship' test: owner-drivers and bicycle couriers	73
		3.5.1 The owner-driver	73
		3.5.2 The bicycle courier	74
		3.5.3 Distinguishing factors	75
	3.6	Conclusion	77
4	Special difficulties: borrowed employees and temporary workers		81
	4.1	Introduction	81
	4.2	Lending employees: the 'borrowed servant' problem	83
		4.2.1 Dual liability?	89
	4.3	Temporary workers: vicarious liability for casual or agency staff?	93
		4.3.1 Finding liability	95
		4.3.2 A less technical approach?	97
	4.4	Conclusion	98
5	Other relationships giving rise to liability		101
	5.1	Introduction	101
	5.2	Relationships giving rise to vicarious liability beyond the contract of employment: statute	103
	5.3	Relationships giving rise to vicarious liability beyond the contract of employment: case law	106
		5.3.1 Civil law systems	106
		5.3.2 Common law 'relationships': using agency and non-delegable duties to extend strict liability for the torts of others	108

	5.4	A new model to meet contemporary needs: representative agents or liability arising out of the ability to direct, control and manage the activities of another?	127
		5.4.1 The 'representative agent'	127
		5.4.2 The power to organise, direct and control the activities of another: the development of *Blieck* and Article 1384(1) of the French Civil Code	133
	5.5	An appraisal: a new model to meet contemporary needs?	140
	5.6	Conclusion	143
6	Acting in the course of one's employment/functions/assigned tasks: determining the scope of vicarious liability		145
	6.1	Introduction	145
	6.2	Limiting the scope of liability: acting in the course of employment/one's functions/assigned tasks	147
	6.3	Determining the test for 'course of employment', 'les fonctions auxquelles ils les ont employés', 'in Ausführung der Verrichtung'	150
		6.3.1 The significance of policy	150
		6.3.2 Prohibited conduct	153
		6.3.3 The common law test: 'course of employment'	157
		6.3.4 Deliberate wrongdoing and the search for a new 'course of employment' test in the common law world	160
		6.3.5 A different test for fraud?	175
		6.3.6 The civil law test: the French example of 'les fonctions auxquelles ils les ont employés'	181
	6.4	Appraisal: what does 'close connection' or 'dans les fonctions' mean? Can a workable definition be found?	188
7	Parental liability for the torts of their children: a new form of vicarious liability?		196
	7.1	Introduction	196
	7.2	Parental responsibility at common law	197
		7.2.1 Parental liability to their child	198
		7.2.2 Parental liability to third parties injured by their child	200
	7.3	Finding a framework for parental responsibility in tort law	203

		7.3.1	Model One: fault-based liability – English and German law	206
		7.3.2	Model Two: vicarious or strict liability – English, Spanish and French law	210
		7.3.3	Strict liability – French law after 1997	213
	7.4	Which model should a legal system utilise?		217
	7.5	Conclusion: a common law doctrine of strict parental liability?		223

8	Understanding vicarious liability: reconciling policy and principle			227
	8.1	Introduction		227
	8.2	Theoretical justifications for vicarious liability in common and civil law		228
		8.2.1	Fault: *culpa in eligendo/in vigilando* and the theory of identification	231
		8.2.2	Victim compensation and loss distribution	234
		8.2.3	Risk and deterrence	237
	8.3	Balancing policy objectives: the modern approach to justifying vicarious liability		243
		8.3.1	Prioritising risk: the fair allocation of the consequences of the risk and deterrence	245
		8.3.2	A proportionate response: what is 'fair and just'?	247
		8.3.3	Conclusions	251
	8.4	General conclusion		252

9	A postscript: a harmonised European law of vicarious liability?			255
	9.1	Two frameworks for liability: Article 6:102, PETL (liability for auxiliaries) and Book VI, Article 3:201, DCFR (accountability for damage caused by employees and representatives)		258
		9.1.1	The relationship giving rise to liability: for whom is the employer liable?	259
		9.1.2	'Within the scope of their functions' and 'course of employment or engagement': to what extent is an employer liable?	262
	9.2	Conclusion: practicality and principle		263

Appendix: Key provisions of the French and German Civil Codes   267
Index   273

Diagrams

Diagram 1	The borrowed servant	*page* 83
Diagram 2	The agency worker	94
Diagram 3	Liability in tort/delict of the employer	245

Table of cases

Cases
Australia
Albrighton v Royal Prince Alfred Hospital [1980] 2 NSWLR 542   62, 118
Astley v Austrust Ltd [1999] HCA 6, 197 CLR 1   44
Boral Resources (Qld) Pty Ltd v Pyke (1989) 93 ALR 89   33
Bugge v Brown (1919) 26 CLR 110   155
Burnie Port Authority v General Jones Pty Ltd [1994] HCA 13, (1994) 179 CLR 520   120, 123
CML v Producers and Citizens' Co-operative Co. (1931) 46 CLR 41   176
Colonial Mutual Life Assurance Society Ltd v Producers and Citizens Co-operative Assurance Co. of Australia Ltd [1931] HCA 53, (1931) 46 CLR 41   128, 155
Commonwealth, The v Introvigne [1982] HAC 40, (1982) 150 CLR 258   120, 124
Darling Island Stevedoring and Lighterage Co. Ltd v Long [1957] HCA 26, (1956–1957) 97 CLR 36   14
Deatons Pty Ltd v Flew (1949) 79 CLR 370   158, 172, 173, 174
Deutz Australia Pty Ltd v Skilled Engineering Ltd [2001] VSC 194   84
Ellis v Wallsend District Hospital (1989) 17 NSWLR 553   62, 118
Henson v Board of Management of Perth Hospital (1939) 41 WALR 15   62
Gray v Fisher [1922] SASR 246   210
Gray v Motor Accident Commission [1998] HCA 70, (1998) 196 CLR 1, 158 ALR 485   40
Gutman v McFall [2004] NSWCA 378   114
Healing (Sales) Pty Ltd v Inglis Electrix Pty Ltd [1968] HCA 60, (1968) 121 CLR 584   41
Hollis v Vabu [2001] HCA 44, (2001) 207 CLR 21, 181 ALR 263   74, 75, 76, 77, 127, 128, 131, 133, 143, 234, 249, 250, 251
Kondis v State Transport Authority (formerly Victorian Railways Board) [1984] HCA 61, (1984) 154 CLR 672   84, 120

Leichhardt Municipal Council v Montgomery [2007] HCA 6, (2007) 230 CLR 22, (2007) 233 ALR 200   117, 123, 125, 144
McDonald v The Commonwealth (1946) 46 SR (NSW) 129   84, 89
McHale v Watson [1966] HCA 13, (1966) 115 CLR 199   202
Morgan v Kittochside Nominees Pty Ltd (2002) 117 IR 152   91
Nationwide News Pty Ltd v Naidu [2007] NSWCA 377   174
New South Wales v Ibbett [2006] HCA 57, (2007) 231 ALR 485   18, 42
New South Wales v Lepore; Samin v Queensland; Rich v Queensland [2003] HCA 4, (2003) 212 CLR 511, 195 ALR 412   xxxv, 2, 19, 120, 124, 161, 172, 173, 174, 190, 195
Northern Sandblasting Pty Ltd v Harris [1997] HCA 39, (1997) 188 CLR 313   125, 140, 162, 249, 251, 262
Oceanic Crest Shipping Co. v Pilbara Harbour Services Pty Ltd [1986] HCA 34, (1986) 160 CLR 626   91
Ryan v Ann St Holdings [2006] QCA 217   174
Sandstone DMC Pty Ltd v Trajkovski [2006] NSWCA 205   174
Scott v Davis [2000] HCA 52, (2000) 204 CLR 333, (2000) 175 ALR 217   109, 120, 128, 131, 132
Smith v Leurs [1945] HCA 27, (1945) 70 CLR 256, [1945] ALR 392   200, 201
Soblusky v Egan [1960] HCA 9, (1960) 103 CLR 215   111, 112
Sprod v Public Relations Orientated Security Pty Ltd [2007] NSWCA 319   174
Starks v RSM Security Ltd [2004] NSWCA 351   174
Stevens v Brodribb Sawmilling Co. Pty Ltd [1986] HCA 1, (1986) 160 CLR 16, 63 ALR 513   70, 71, 123
Sweeney v Boylan Nominees Pty Ltd [2006] HCA 19, (2006) 226 CLR 161, (2006) 227 ALR 46   70, 129, 131, 132, 133
Transfield Services (Australia) v Hall; Hall v QBE Insurance (Australia) [2008] NSWCA 294   123
Transtate Pty Ltd v Rauk [2002] NSWCA 222   84
Uren v John Fairfax & Sons Pty Ltd (1966) 117 CLR 118   39
Zorom Enterprises Pty Ltd v Zabow [2007] NSWCA 106   174
Zuijs v Wirth Brothers Proprietary Ltd [1955] HCA 73, (1955) 93 CLR 561   66, 127

Canada

3464920 Canada Inc v Strother [2007] 2 SCR 177, (2007) 281 DLR (4th) 640   165
671122 Ontario Ltd v Sagaz Industries Canada Inc. [2001] 2 SCR 983, 204 DLR (4th) 542   69, 71, 72, 79
BG Checo International Ltd v British Columbia Hydro and Power Authority [1993] 1 SCR 12, (1993) 99 DLR (4th) 577   44

TABLE OF CASES

Bazley v Curry [1999] 2 SCR 534, (1999) 174 DLR (4th) 45   xxxv, 2, 19, 76, 92, 129, 161, 162, 163, 164, 165, 166, 169, 172, 173, 174, 189, 191, 193, 194, 197, 238, 241, 246, 247, 249, 251, 262

Blackwater v Plint [2005] 3 SCR 3, (2005) 258 DLR (4th) 275   18, 42, 92, 93, 124, 165

British Columbia Ferry Corp. v Invicta Security Service Corp. (1998) 167 DLR (4th) 193, [1998] 4 WWR 536   184, 191

Canadian Pacific Railway Company v Lockhart [1942] AC 591   155, 172

EB v Order of the Oblates of Mary Immaculate (British Columbia) [2005] 3 SCR 45, (2005) 258 DLR (4th) 385   164, 165, 189, 193

EDG v Hammer [2003] 2 SCR 459, (2003) 230 DLR (4th) 554   124, 165

Fullowka v Pinkerton's of Canada Ltd [2010] SCC 5   107

G (BM) v Nova Scotia (Attorney-General) 2007 NSCA 120   164

Gramak v O'Connor (1974) 41 DLR (3d) 14   111

H (SG) v Gorsline [2004] 2004 ABCA 186, [2005] 2 WWR 716   165

Hamilton v Farmers' Ltd [1953] 3 DLR 382   236

Hill v Church of Scientology of Toronto [1995] 2 SCR 1130, (1995) 126 DLR (4th) 129   42

Jacobi v Griffiths [1999] 2 SCR 570, (1999) 174 DLR (4th) 71   2, 161, 163, 164, 165, 189, 194, 240, 247

James Street Hardware & Furniture Co. v Spizziri (1985) 33 CCLT 209; affd (1987) 43 CCLT9   84

John Doe v Bennett [2004] 1 SCR 436, (2004) 236 DLR (4th) 577   165

KLB v British Columbia [2003] 2 SCR 403, 230 DLR (4th) 513   79, 162, 164, 189

Lewis (Guardian ad litem of) v British Columbia [1997] 3 SCR 1145, (1997) 153 DLR (4th) 594   121

Lockhart v Canadian Pacific Railway Co. [1942] AC 591   157

London Drugs Ltd v Kuehne & Nagel International Ltd [1992] 3 SCR 299, (1993) 97 DLR (4th) 261   35, 241, 245

MB v British Columbia [2003] 2 SCR 477, (2003) 230 DLR (4th) 567

McKee v Dumas (1976) 70 DLR (3d) 70   84, 88

McKee v Reid's Heritage Homes Ltd [2009] ONCA 916   127

Montreal v Montreal Locomotive Works Ltd [1947] 1 DLR 161   71, 72, 74

Pawlak v Doucette [1985] 2 WWR 588   112

Peeters v Canada [1994] 1 FC 562, (1993) 108 DLR (4th) 471   41

Plains Engineering Ltd v Barnes Securities Services Ltd (1987) 43 CCLT 129   184

The Queen v Levy Bros [1961] SCR 189, (1961) 26 DLR (2d) 760   176

Sisters of St Joseph of the Diocese of London v Fleming [1938] SCR 172   62

Whiten v Pilot Insurance Company [2002] 1 SCR 595, (2002) 209 DLR (4th) 257   39, 42

Wiebe Door Services Ltd v MNR [1986] 3 FC 553   60

WW Sales Ltd v City of Edmonton [1942] SCR 467   158

England and Wales

A v Ministry of Defence [2004] EWCA Civ 641, [2005] QB 183   17, 119
A (A Child) v Ministry of Defence [2004] EWCA Civ 641, [2005] QB 183   62
Airfix Footwear Ltd v Cope [1978] ICR 1210   95
Armagas Ltd v Mundogas SA (The Ocean Frost) [1986] AC 717 (HL and CA)   176, 178, 179, 180
Armory v Delamirie Ltd (1722) 1 Stra 505, 93 ER 664   57
Ashworth v Stanwix (1860) 3 E & E 701, 121 ER 701   104
Attorney-General of the British Virgin Islands v Hartwell [2004] UKPC 12, [2004] 1 WLR 1273   167, 170, 193
Balfron Trustees Ltd v Petersen [2001] IRLR 758   175
Bank voor Handel en Scheepvaart NV v Slatford [1953] 1 QB 248   69
Barnes v Hampshire CC [1969] 1 WLR 1563   204
Barrett v Enfield LBC [1999] UKHL 25, [2001] 2 AC 550   199, 200
Barwick v English Joint Stock Banking Co. (1867) LR 2 Exch 259   109, 132, 148, 176
Bayley v Manchester, Sheffield and Lincolnshire Ry Co. (1873) LR 8 CP 148   149, 154
Beard v London General Omnibus Co. [1900] 2 QB 530   154
Bebee v Sales (1916) 32 TLR 413   201
Bernard v Attorney-General of Jamaica [2004] UKPC 47, [2005] IRLR 398   167, 168, 171, 193, 251
Bickman v Smith Motors Ltd [1955] 5 DLR 256   155
Biffa Waste Services Ltd v Maschinenfabrik Ernst Hese GmbH [2008] EWCA Civ 1257, [2009] QB 725   85, 124
Black v Christchurch Finance Co. [1894] AC 48   121
Booth v Mister (1835) 7 C & P 66, 173 ER 30   110
Boson v Sandford (1691) 2 Salk 440, 91 ER 382   12, 149
Bottomley v Todmorden Cricket Club [2003] EWCA Civ 1575, [2004] PIQR P18   124
Bower v Peate (1876) 1 QBD 321   122
Brook Street Bureau (UK) Ltd v Dacas [2004] EWCA Civ 217, [2004] ICR 1437   96, 99, 142
Broom v Morgan [1953] 1 QB 597   14, 27
Brown v Robinson [2004] UKPC 56   169, 171
Buchan v Secretary of State for Employment [1997] IRLR 80
Burfitt v Kille [1939] 2 KB 743   204
Bygraves v Dicker [1923] 2 KB 585   104
Cable & Wireless plc v Muscat [2006] EWCA Civ 220, [2006] ICR 975   96
Candler v Thomas (t/a London Leisure Lines) [1998] RTR 214   110, 111

TABLE OF CASES

Caparo Industries plc v Dickman [1990] 2 AC 605   169
Carmarthenshire CC v Lewis [1955] AC 549   198, 201, 204, 222
Carmichael v National Power plc [1999] 1 WLR 2042   93
Carty v Croydon LBC [2005] EWCA Civ 19, [2005] 1 WLR 2312   51, 199
Cassidy v Ministry of Health [1951] 2 QB 343   17, 60, 62, 64, 118, 122
Century Insurance Co. Ltd v Northern Ireland RTB [1942] AC 509   151, 152, 159
Chandler v Broughton (1832) 1 C & M 29, 149 ER 301   110
Chester v Bailey [1905] 1 KB 237   168
Chowdhary v Gillot [1947] 2 All ER 541   111
Clelland v Edward Lloyd Ltd [1938] 1 KB 272   57
Clements v London & North Western Railway Co. [1894] 2 QB 482   210
Collins v Hertfordshire County Council [1947] KB 598   62
Colour Quest Ltd v Total Downstream UK plc [2009] EWHC 540 (Comm)   85
Connolly v Sellars Arenascene Ltd [2001] EWCA Civ 184, [2001] ICR 760   47
Conway v George Wimpey & Co. Ltd [1951] 2 KB 266   155
Crédit Lyonnais Bank Nederland NV (now Generale Bank Nederland NV) v Export Credits Guarantee Department [2000] 1 AC 486   27, 156
Croft v Alison (1821) 4 B & Ald 590, 106 ER 1052   149, 168
Dadourian Group International Inc. v Simms [2009] EWCA Civ 169, [2009] 1 Lloyd's Rep 601   177
Dalton v Henry Angus & Co. (1881) 6 App Cas 740   122
Daniels v Whetstone Entertainments Ltd [1962] 2 Lloyd's Rep 1   168, 170
De Francesco v Barnum (1890) 45 Ch D 430   210
Denham v Midland Employers' Mutual Assurance Ltd [1955] 2 QB 437   98
Derry v Peek (1889) LR 14 App Cas 337   177
Donaldson v McNiven [1952] 2 All ER 691   201, 210
The Druid (1842) 1 Wm Rob 391, 166 ER 619   168
Dubai Aluminium Co. Ltd v Salaam [2002] UKHL 48, [2003] 2 AC 366   3, 105, 167, 171, 178, 179, 194, 248
Duncan v Findlater (1839) 6 Cl & Fin 894, 7 ER 934   228
Dyer v Munday [1895] 1 QB 742   168, 192
Eastham v Eastham and Eastham [1982] CLY 2141   198
Edgington v Fitzmaurice (1885) LR 29 Ch D 459   177
Ellis v Sheffield Gas Consumers Co. (1853) 2 El & Bl 767, 118 ER 955   116
Ellis v Turner (1800) 8 TR 531, 101 ER 1529   12, 149
Etheridge v K (a minor) [1999] Ed CR 550   202
Evans v Liverpool Corp. [1906] 1 KB 160   61, 118
Farah v MPC [1998] QB 65   104
First Energy (UK) Ltd v Hungarian International Bank Ltd [1993] 2 Lloyd's Rep 194   180

Fisher v Oldham Corp. [1930] 2 KB 364   104
Frank v Reuters Ltd [2003] EWCA Civ 417, [2003] ICR 1166   96
Frans Maas (UK) Ltd v Samsung Electronics (UK) Ltd [2004] EWHC 1502 (Comm), [2004] 2 Lloyd's Rep 251   152
Gates v Bill [1902] 2 KB 38   104
General Engineering Services Ltd v Kingston and Saint Andrew Corp. (Jamaica) [1989] 1 WLR 69   190
Gibb v United Steel Companies [1957] 1 WLR 668   86
Gold v Essex CC [1942] 2 KB 293   62
Gorely v Codd [1967] 1 WLR 19   201, 210
Gough v Thorne [1966] 1 WLR 1387   202
Gravil v Carroll [2008] EWCA Civ 689, [2008] ICR 1222   168, 171
Gray v Pullen (1864) 5 B & S 970, 122 ER 1091   121
Greatorex v Greatorex [2000] 1 WLR 1970   199
Green v New River Co. (1792) 4 TR 589, 100 ER 1192   31
Groves v Lord Wimborne [1898] 2 QB 402   121
Gwilliam v West Hertfordshire Hospitals NHS Trust [2002] EWCA Civ 1041, [2003] QB 443   124
HL Bolton (Engineering) Co. Ltd v TJ Graham & Sons Ltd [1957] 1 QB 159   47
HSBC Bank plc v 5th Avenue Partners Ltd (also known as *So v HSBC Bank plc*) [2009] EWCA Civ 296, [2009] 1 CLC 503   179
Hall (Inspector of Taxes) v Lorimer [1994] 1 WLR 209   73
Hancke v Hooper (1835) 7 C & P 81, 173 ER 37   57
Hardaker v Idle District Council [1896] 1 QB 335   121
Harvey v O'Dell [1958] 2 QB 78   33
Hawley v Luminar Leisure Ltd [2006] EWCA Civ 18, [2006] PIQR P17   85, 86
Heasmans v Clarity Cleaning Co. Ltd [1987] ICR 949   187, 189
Hedley Byrne v Heller and Partners [1964] AC 465   179
Henderson v Merrett Syndicates Ltd [1994] UKHL 5, [1995] 2 AC 145   44
Hern v Nichols (1708) 1 Salk 289, 91 ER 256   180, 234
Hewitt v Bonvin [1940] 1 KB 188   111
Hillyer v The Governors of St Bartholomew's Hospital [1909] 2 KB 820   51, 58, 61, 64, 118
Hobbs (Farms) Ltd v Baxenden Chemical Co. Ltd [1992] 1 Lloyd's Rep 54   121
Holliday v National Telephone Co. [1899] 2 QB 392   121, 122
Honeywill and Stein Ltd v Larkin Bros Ltd [1934] KB 191   121
Hosking v De Havilland Aircraft Co. Ltd [1949] 1 All ER 540   121
Houldsworth v City of Glasgow Bank (1880) 5 App Cas 317   109
Hughes v Percival (1882–83) LR 8 App Cas 443   117
Hutchinson v York etc. Railway Co (1850) 5 Exch 343, 155 ER 150   228

xxii TABLE OF CASES

Huzzey v Field (1835) 2 CM & R 432, 150 ER 186   149
Ilkiw v Samuels [1963] 1 WLR 991   159
Imperial Chemical Industries Ltd v Shatwell [1965] AC 656   15, 27, 233
Interlink Express Parcels Ltd v Night Trunkers Ltd [2001] EWCA 360, [2001] RTR 338   85
Iqbal v London Transport Executive (1973) 16 KIR 329   154
JD v East Berkshire Community Health NHS Trust [2005] UKHL 23, [2005] 2 AC 373   199
JJ Coughlan Ltd v Ruparelia [2003] EWCA Civ 1057, [2004] PNLR 4   171, 177
J (A Child) v North Lincolnshire CC [2000] 1 WLR 1082   199
James v Greenwich LBC [2008] EWCA Civ 35, [2008] ICR 545   96
Jauffur v Akhbar The Times, 10 February 1984   198
Joel v Morison (1834) 6 C & P 501, 172 ER 1338   149, 184
John Laing Construction v Ince [2001] CLY 4543   114
Jones v Hart (1699) 2 Salk 441, 91 ER 382   12
Jones v Manchester Corp. [1952] 2 QB 852   33
Jones v Scullard [1898] 2 QB 565   90
Jones v Staveley Iron and Chemical Co. Ltd [1955] 1 QB 474 (CA)   14
Jones v Tower Boot Co. Ltd [1997] ICR 254   145
KR v Royal & Sun Alliance plc [2006] EWCA Civ 1454, [2007] 1 All ER (Comm) 161   47
Kay v ITW Ltd [1968] 1 QB 140   154
Keen v Henry [1894] 1 QB 292   104
Keppel Bus Co. v Sa'ad bin Ahmad [1974] 1 WLR 1082   169
Klein v Caluori [1971] 2 All ER 701   111
Kooragang Investments Pty v Richardson & Wrench [1982] AC 462   179
Kuddus v Chief Constable of Leicestershire Constabulary [2001] UKHL 29, [2002] 2 AC 122   17, 40, 42
Lancashire County Council v Municipal Mutual Insurance Ltd [1997] QB 897   42
Lane v Shire Roofing Co. (Oxford) Ltd [1995] PIQR P417   56, 70
Laugher v Pointer (1826) 5 B & C 547, 108 ER 204   12, 26, 90, 149
Launchbury v Morgans [1971] 2 QB 245 (CA)   113
Lee Ting Sang v Chung Chi-Keung [1990] 2 AC 374   70, 71
Lennard's Carrying Co. Ltd v Asiatic Petroleum Co. Ltd [1915] AC 705   47
Limpus v London General Omnibus Co. (1862) 1 H & C 526; 158 ER 993   149, 154, 228
Lindsey County Council v Marshall [1937] AC 97   62
Lister v Hesley Hall Ltd [2001] UKHL 22, [2002] 1 AC 215   xxxv, 2, 3, 18, 19, 132, 145, 158, 160, 161, 162, 166, 169, 172, 173, 175, 178, 180, 186, 189, 193, 194, 197, 242, 248, 249, 250, 262, 263

Lister v Romford Ice and Cold Storage Co. [1957] AC 555   31, 32, 33, 159
Lloyd v Grace, Smith & Co. [1912] AC 716   105, 109, 132, 148, 151, 168, 176, 179
London County Council v Cattermoles (Garages) Ltd [1953] 1 WLR 997   155, 168
MCA Records Inc v Charly Records Ltd (No 5) [2001] EWCA Civ 1441, [2003] 1 BCLC 93   48
M'Manus v Crickett (1800) 1 East 106, 102 ER 43   12
McDermid v Nash Dredging & Reclamation Co. Ltd [1987] AC 906   120, 122
McMeechan v Secretary of State for Employment [1997] ICR 549   96
Maga v Birmingham Roman Catholic Archdiocese Trustees [2010] EWCA Civ 256   169
Mahmud v BCCI [1998] AC 20   23
Majrowski v Guy's and St Thomas's NHS Trust [2005] EWCA Civ 251, [2005] QB 848, [2006] UKHL 34, [2007] 1 AC 224   2, 158, 167, 190, 249
Man Nutzfahrzeuge AG v Freightliner Ltd [2005] EWHC 2347 (Comm)   178
Market Investigations v Minister of Social Security [1969] 2 QB 173   70
Matania v National Provincial Bank [1936] 2 All ER 633   122
Mattis v Pollock (t/a Flamingo's Nightclub) [2003] EWCA Civ 887, [2003] 1 WLR 2158   167, 169, 170, 193
Mead v Hamond (1722) 1 Stra 505, 93 ER 663   57
Meekins v Henson [1964] 1 QB 492   105
Meridian Global Funds Management Asia Ltd v Securities Commission [1995] 2 AC 500   47
Mersey Docks and Harbour Board v Coggins and Griffith (Liverpool) Ltd [1947] AC 1   64, 83, 84, 85, 88, 244
Middleton v Fowler (1698) 1 Salk 282, 91 ER 247   12
Miller v Falconer (1808) 1 Camp 251, 170 ER 947   31
Milligan v Wedge (1840) 12 Ad & E 737, 113 ER 993   58
Mitchell v Crassweller (1853) 13 CB 237, 138 ER 1189   149, 228
Mitchell v Tarbutt (1794) 5 TR 649, 101 ER 362   14
Montgomery v Johnson Underwood Ltd [2001] EWCA Civ 318, [2001] ICR 819   96
Moon v Towers (1860) 8 CB (NS) 611, 144 ER 1306   202, 210
Morgans v Launchbury [1973] AC 127 (HL)   113
Morris v Ford Motor Co. Ltd [1973] QB 792   31, 33, 239
Morris v CW Martin & Co. [1966] 1 QB 716   18, 122, 152, 168, 175, 193
Mullin v Richards [1998] 1 WLR 1304   202
N v Chief Constable of Merseyside Police [2006] EWHC 3041 (QB), [2006] Po LR 160   170
Nethermere (St Neots) Ltd v Taverna and Gardiner [1984] ICR 612   95, 99
Newton v Edgerley [1959] 1 WLR 1031   201

North v Wood [1914] 1 KB 629   201
Norwood v Navan [1981] RTR 457   114
Nottingham v Aldridge [1971] 2 QB 739   111
Oceangas (Gibraltar) Ltd v Port of London Authority (The Cavendish) [1993] 2 Lloyd's Rep 292   104
O'Kelly v Trusthouse Forte [1984] 1 QB 90   142
Orchard v Lee [2009] EWCA Civ 295, [2009] PIQR P16   202
Ormrod v Crosville Motor Services Ltd [1953] 1 WLR 409 (QB), [1953] 1 WLR 1120 (CA)   112
Osborn v Gillett (1873) LR 8 Exch 88   15, 27
Padbury v Holliday and Greenwood Ltd (1912) 28 TLR 494   122
Palmer v Lawley [2003] CLY 2976   201
Parker v Miller (1926) 42 TLR 408   111
Pasley v Freeman (1789) 3 Term Rep 51, 100 ER 450   177
Performing Right Society Ltd v Mitchell & Booker (Palais de Danse) [1924] 1 KB 762   58
Phelps v Hillingdon London Borough Council [2001] 2 AC 619   51, 199
Photo Production Ltd v Securicor Transport Ltd [1980] AC 827   184
Pickard v Smith (1861) 10 CB (NS) 470, 142 ER 535   121, 122
Plumb v Cobden Flour Mills Co. Ltd [1914] AC 62   154
Poland v John Parr and Sons [1927] 1 KB 236   160, 168, 178, 192
Quarman v Burnett (1840) 6 M & W 499, 151 ER 509   116
R v Crown Diamond Paint Co. Ltd [1983] 1 FC 837   155
R v H (Assault of Child: Reasonable Chastisement) [2001] EWCA Crim 1024, [2002] 1 Cr App R 7   200
R v JJB [2004] EWCA Civ 14, [2004] 2 Cr App Rev (S) 41   202, 203
R v Walker (1858) 27 LJMC 207   58
R (on the application of M) v Inner London Crown Court [2003] EWHC 301, [2003] 1 FLR 994   203
Rambarran v Gurrucharran [1970] 1 WLR 556   111
Razzel v Snowball [1954] 1 WLR 1382   63
Ready Mixed Concrete (South East) Ltd v Minister of Pensions and National Insurance [1968] 2 QB 497   58, 70, 73, 74, 76, 94
Reedie v London and North Western Ry (1849) 4 Ex 244, 154 ER 1201   116, 229
Ricketts v Erith BC [1943] 2 All ER 629   204, 210
Roe v Minister of Health [1954] 2 QB 66   62, 118
Rogers v Night Riders [1983] RTR 324   104
Rogers v Wilkinson The Times, 19 January 1963   201
Rookes v Barnard [1964] AC 1129   39, 40, 42
Rose v Plenty [1976] 1 WLR 141   155

Rossano v Swan Hunter & Wigham Richardson Ltd (The Arum) [1921] P12   104
Rowe v Herman [1997] 1 WLR 1390   123
Rowlands v Chief Constable of Merseyside Police [2006] EWCA Civ 1773, [2007] 1 WLR 1065   18, 41
Ryan v Fildes [1938] 3 All ER 517   31, 168
S v Walsall MBC [1985] 1 WLR 1150   130, 199
Sadler v Henlock (1855) 4 E & B 570, 119 ER 209   58
Salsbury v Woodland [1970] 1 QB 324   58, 121, 123
Samson v Aitchison [1912] AC 844   110
Secretary of State for Trade and Industry v Bottrill [2000] 1 All ER 915   47
Semtex v Gladstone [1954] 2 All ER 206   31
Sharrod v London and North Western Rly Co. (1849) 4 Ex 580, 154 ER 1345   13, 228
Short v J & W Henderson Ltd (1946) 79 Ll L Rep 271   66
Simmons v Heath Laundry Co. [1910] 1 KB 543   58
Slade v Metrodent [1953] 2 QB 112   210
Smith v Cammell Laird and Co. Ltd [1940] AC 242   121
Smith v Chadwick (1881–82) LR 20 Ch D 27   177
Smith v Stages [1989] AC 928   151, 152
Speed v Thomas Swift & Co. [1943] KB 557   119
Standard Chartered Bank v Pakistan National Shipping Corp. (No 2) [2002] UKHL 43, [2003] 1 AC 959   48
Staton v National Coal Board [1957] 1 WLR 893   159
Staveley Iron and Chemical Co. Ltd v Jones [1956] AC 627 (HL)   14, 15, 27, 233
Stevenson Jordan & Harrison Ltd v MacDonald & Evans [1952] 1 TLR 101   69
Storey v Ashton (1869) LR 4 QB 476   159
Surtees v Kingston upon Thames RBC [1992] PIQR P101, [1991] 2 FLR 559   199
TA v DPP [1997] 1 Cr App R (S)   203
Tarry v Ashton (1876) 1 QBD 314   121, 123
'Thelma' (owners) v University College School [1953] 2 Lloyd's Rep 613   112
Thomas v Quartermaine (1887) 18 QBD 685   119
Thompson v Commissioner of Police of the Metropolis [1998] QB 498   41
Todd v Adams (The Maragetha Maria) [2002] EWCA Civ 509, [2002] 2 Lloyd's Rep 293   74
Trotman v North Yorkshire County Council [1999] LGR 584   3, 160
Turberville v Stampe (1698) 1 Ld Raym 264, 91 ER 1072   12, 148, 149
Twine v Bean's Express Ltd [1946] 1 All ER 202, (1946) 62 TLR 458 (CA)   13, 14, 155, 156
Uxbridge Permanent Benefit Building Society v Pickard [1939] 2 KB 248   109, 176
Vandyke v Fender [1970] 2 QB 292   111

Vasey v Surrey Free Inns plc [1996] PIQR 373   168
Viasystems (Tyneside) Ltd v Thermal Transfer (Northern) Ltd [2005] EWCA Civ 1151, [2006] QB 510   85, 90, 91, 93, 98
Vowles v Evans & Welsh Rugby Union [2003] EWCA Civ 318   136
W v Commissioner of Police of the Metropolis [2000] 1 WLR 1607   119
WHPT Housing Association Ltd v Secretary of State for Social Services [1981] ICR 737   70
Ward v Hertfordshire CC [1969] 1 WLR 790   204
Warren v Henlys Ltd [1948] 2 All ER 935   169, 170
Watson v BBBC [2001] QB 1134   136
Wattleworth v Goodward Road Racing Co. Ltd [2004] EWHC 140, [2004] PIQR P25   136
Weir v Bettison [2003] EWCA Civ 111, [2003] ICR 708   171
Whatman v Pearson (1868) LR 3 CP 422   159
Wheatley v Patrick (1837) 2 M & W 650, 150 ER 917   110
Whittaker v Minister of Pensions and National Insurance [1967] 1 QB 156   69
Williams v Natural Life Health Foods Ltd [1998] 1 WLR 830, [1998] 2 All ER 577   48
Wilsher v Essex AHA [1987] QB 730 (CA), [1988] AC 1074 (HL)   16, 17, 62, 119
Wilsons & Clyde Coal Co. Ltd v English [1938] AC 57   17, 119
Yewens v Noakes (1880) 6 QBD 530   58

France

Req 19 February 1866 S 1866.1.214   27
T. confl. 8 February 1873 (*Blanco*) D 1873.2.20   52
T. confl. 30 July 1873 (*l'affaire Pelletier*) Rec. CE, p.117; DP 1874, 3, p.5, concl. David   52
Req 12 July 1887 S 1887.1.384   107
Cass civ 16 June 1896, S 1897.1.17 note A. Esmein, D. 1897 1.433 concl L. Sarut, note R. Saleilles   133
Civ 16 June 1896 (*Teffaine*) S 1897.1.17 note A Esmein, D 1897.1.433 concl Sarrut, note Saleilles
Crim 25 February 1907 DP 1907.1.413   182
Civ 8 May 1908 DP 1909.1.135   58
Crim 15 March 1923 D 1923.1.157   58
Ch réun 13 February 1930 (*Jand'heur*) DP 1930.1.57 concl Matter, rapport Le Marc'hadour, note G. Ripert, S 1930.1.121 note P. Esmein   133
Paris 14 March 1930 D 1930.2.115 note Besson   58
Req 1 May 1930 DP 1930.1.137 note R. Savatier   107
Crim 24 February 1934, Gaz Pal 1934.1.654   102

Civ 20 May 1936 (*arrêt Mercier*) DP 1936.1.87 note EP   63
Civ 30 December 1936 DP 1937.1.5 note R. Savatier   27
Civ 4 May 1937 (*Veuve Meyer*) DH 1937.363   58
Civ 8 November 1937 Gaz Pal 1938.1.43   107
Req 24 January 1938 DP 1938.1.50 note signed EP   86
Req 3 November 1942 D 1947.145 note A. Tunc   86
Crim 18 October 1946 S 1947.1.39   6, 156, 182
Req 21 July 1947 D 1947.486   62, 64
Civ 15 July 1948D 1948.471   86
Paris 16 Jan 1950 D 1950.169   62
Crim 25 January 1951 S 1951.1.298 1 June 1954 JCP 1954 II 8435 note R. Rodière   86
Req 20 April 1953 JCP 1953 II 7663 note R. Savatier   62, 64
Crim 5 November 1953 JCP 1953 II 7818 bis   182
Civ 2, 1 July 1954 (two cases) D 1954.628   182
Civ 2, 28 April 1955 Bull civ II N° 219, p.132   107
Civ 2, 20 July 1955 D 1956 somm 151, JCP 1956 II 9052 note R. Savatier   87
Civ 2, 12 October 1955 JCP 1955 II 9003 note P. Esmein; D 1956.301 note R. Rodière   213
Civ 15 November 1955 D 1956.113 note R. Savatier, JCP 1956 II 9106 note R. Rodière   64
CE 3 February 1956 (*Thouzellier*) D 1956.596 note J. M. Auby, JCP 1956 II 9608 note D. Lévy   134
Civ 2, 11 May 1956 D 1957.121 note R. Rodière   86
Crim 20 March 1958 Bull crim N° 280, p.484   182
Crim 28 October 1958 D 1959.somm 21   86
Ch réun 9 March 1960 D 1960.329 note R. Savatier, JCP 1960 II 11559 note R. Rodière, Gaz Pal 1960.1.313   183
Crim 27 December 1961 Bull crim N° 563, p.1074; D 1962 somm 75; JCP 1962 II 12652   107
Civ 2 17 July 1962 Bull Civ 2 N°599   87
Civ 2, 17 December 1964 Bull civ 2 N° 830; JCP 1965 II 14125 note R. Rodière   68, 87
Com 16 June 1966 JCP 1968 II 15330 note J. Bigot   86
Civ 2, 9 February 1967 Gaz Pal 1967.1.224   91
CE 13 July 1967 (*Département de la Moselle*) Rec p.341, D 1967.675 note F. Moderne   134
Civ 2, 17 July 1967 Gaz Pal 1967.2.236   48
Civ 2, 9 November 1967 Bull civ II N° 321, JCP 1972 II 17159 note D. Mayer   59
Crim 7 November 1968 D 1969 somm 34   66

Civ 1, 12 November 1968 D 1969.96, JCP 1969 II 15864 note R. Savatier   64
Civ 20 July 1970 Gaz Pal 1970 2 somm 57   107
Crim 25 May 1971 D 1971 somm 168   106
Crim 15 February 1972 D 1972.368; JCP 1972 II 17159 note D. Mayer   66
Civ 2, 9 November 1972 Bull civ II N° 275   66
Civ 29 November 1973 D 1974.194 note B. Dauvergne   97
Civ 1, 11 December 1974 D 1975 IR 67   28
Com 26 January 1976 D 1976.449 rapp J. Mérimée   66, 86
Civ 2, 15 March 1976 Bull civ II N° 100, D 1977.27   88
Crim 10 May 1976 D 1976 IR 175   97
Crim 20 May 1976 Gaz Pal 1976.2.545 note Y. M.   107
Civ 2, 12 January 1977 D 1977 IR 330 obs C. Larroumet   66
Crim 15 February 1977 D 1977 IR 330 obs C. Larroumet   97, 185
Paris 25 February 1977 D 1977 IR 329 obs C. Larroumet.   62
Civ 2, 27 April 1977 Bull civ II N° 108   48
Ass plén 10 June 1977 D 1977.465 note C. Larroumet, JCP 1977 II 18730 concl P. Gulphe   183
Civ 2, 1 December 1977 D 1978 IR 407 obs C Laurroument   87
Crim 18 July 1978 Bull Crim N° 237, page 627   183
Civ 21 February 1979 D 1979 IR 350   107
Civ 2, 11 July 1979 JCP 1979 IV 317; D 1980 IR 36 obs C. Larroumet   156, 183
Civ 1, 17 July 1979 D 1980 IR 114   107
Soc 9 November 1982 D 1982.621 and D 1983.531 note H. Sinay   107
Crim 14 March 1983 Bull crim N° 78, p. 175   86
Ass. plén 17 June 1983 JCP 1983 II 20120 concl P. A. Sadon, note F. Chabas, D 1984.134 note D. Denis   184
Crim 13 December 1983 Bull crim 1983 N° 342, D 1984 IR 459 obs J. Penneau   67
Ass plén 9 May 1984 (*Fullenwarth*) (2nd case) D 1984.525 concl J. Cabannes, note F. Chabas, (1st case) JCP 1984 II 20255 note N. Dejean de la Bâtie
Crim 15 January 1985 Bull crim N° 24, p.59   30, 98, 136, 214, 215, 240
Com 5 February 1985 Bull Civ 1985 IV N° 47   86
Ass plén 15 November 1985 D 1986.81 note J.-L. Aubert, JCP 1986 II 20568 note G. Viney   185
Cass crim 15 May 1986 Gaz Pal 1986.2.682   186
Soc 21 July 1986 Bull civ 1986 V N° 421 p. 320   107
CE 29 April 1987 (*Ministère de la Justice*) JCP 1988 II 20920 note B. Pacteau   134
Crim 20 October 1987 (*Suteau*) Bull crim 1987 N° 359 p. 960   87, 88

Ass plén 13 November 1987 Bull ass plén N° 5   34
Crim 22 March 1988 Bull crim N° 142, p. 369   67, 107
Ass plén 19 May 1988 (*Héro*) D 1988.513 note C. Larroumet; Gaz Pal 1988.2.640 concl M. Dorwling-Carter   180, 187, 246, 262
Crim 23 June 1988 Bull crim 1988 N° 289 No 4   152
Crim 14 June 1990 Bull crim 1990 N° 245   66
CE 4 July 1990 Leb1990.972, D 1991 Somm 291   68
Soc 17 July 1990 Bull Civ V N° 375 page 324   107
Civ 5 December 1990 Bull civ II No 257, p.132, RTD civ. 1991.348 obs P. Jourdain   27
Ass plén 29 March 1991 (*Blieck*) D 1991.324 note C. Larroumet, JCP 1991 II 21673, concl H. Dontenwille, note J. Ghestin   20, 30, 134, 135, 137, 186, 223
Civ 1, 4 June 1991 Bull civ 1991 N° 185 p. 122, JCP 1991 II 21730 note E. Savatier   63
Crim 14 October 1991 Rev. sociétés 1992.782 obs B. Bouloc   49
Crim 5 March 1992 Bull crim 1992 N° 101, p. 255, JCP 1993 II 22013 note F. Chabas   67, 68
Civ 2, 7 July 1993 Bull civ II N° 249, p. 137; JCP 1993 IV 2325   67, 180
Com 12 October 1993 (*l'arrêt Rochas*) Bull civ IV N° 338; D 1994.124 note G. Viney, JCP 1995 II 22493 note F. Chabas   36
Civ 2, 22 May 1995 Bull civ II N° 155; JCP 1995 II 22550 note J. Mouly   136, 139, 187
Civ 2, 18 Sept 1996 Bull civ II N° 217; D 1998.118 note J. Rebourg   135
Crim 4 January 1996 JCP 1996 IV 1028   185
Crim 10 October 1996 Bull crim N° 357; JCP 1997 II 22833 note F. Chabas; D 1997.309 note M. Huyette   135
Civ 2, 11 December 1996 Resp civ et assur 1997 comm N° 84   107
Civ 2, 19 February 1997 (*SAMDA*) Bull civ 1997 II N° 55; Gaz Pal 1997, 2, 575 note F. Chabas   136, 214, 215, 216
Civ 2, 19 February 1997 (*Bertrand*) Bull civ II N° 56 p.32; JCP 1997 II 22848 concl R. Kessous, note G. Viney, D 1997.265 note P. Jourdain   24, 136
Crim 26 March 1997 JCP 1997 II 22868 rapp F. Desportes; D 1997.496 note P. Jourdain   135
Civ 2, 21 May 1997 Bull Civ II N° 154, page 89   188
Com 22 January 1998 Bull civ IV N° 48; D 1998.605 note D. Gibirila   49
Civ 2, 25 February 1998 D 1998. 325 Concl R. Kessous   135
Com 28 April 1998 Bull civ IV N° 139   49
Civ 2, 2 December 1998 (*Sté Aube-Cristal*) Bull civ II N° 292, p. 176; D 1999 IR 29; JCP 1999 II 10165 note M. Josselin-Gall   215

Civ 1, 26 May 1999 JCP 1999 II 10112 rapp P. Sargos   63, 67
Civ 2, 20 January 2000 (*Schott*) Bull civ II N° 14; D 2000 somm 469 obs D. Mazeaud; JCP 2000 II 10374 note A. Gouttenoire-Cornut   217
Civ 2, 20 January 2000 Bull civ II N° 15; D 2000.571 note M. Huyette   135
Cass ass plén, 25 February 2000 (*Costedoat*) Bull Ass plén N° 2; JCP 2000 II 10295 concl R. Kessous, note M. Billiau; JCP 2000 I 241, p. 1244 obs G. Viney, D 2000.673 note Ph. Brun   36, 37, 38, 48, 241, 246, 247
Civ 2, 3 February 2000 JCP 2000 II 10316 note J. Mouly   136
Crim 28 March 2000 Bull crim N° 140; JCP 2001 II 10457 note C. Robaczewski   135
Civ 2, 28 June 2000 Bull crim N° 256; D 2001 somm 2792 obs L. Dumaine; JCP 2000 I 280 obs G. Viney   220
Civ 2, 26 October 2000 JCP 2000 IV 2834   66
Civ 2, 16 November 2000 Bull civ II N° 69; JCP 2001 I 340 obs G. Viney   222
Civ 2, 29 March 2001 Bull civ II N° 69; JCP 2002 II 10071 note S. Prigent   222
Civ 2, 10 May 2001 (*Levert*) Bull civ II N° 96; D 2001 Jur 2851 rapp P. Guerder, note O. Tournafond; JCP 2001 II 10613 note J. Mouly   215
Ass plén 14 December 2001 (*Cousin*) Bull Ass plén N° 17; JCP 2002 II 10026 note M. Billiau, D 2002.1230 note J. Julien   38
Civ 2, 6 June 2002 D 2002.2750 note M. Huyette; JCP 2003 II 10068 note A. Gouttenoire-Cornut et N. Roget   135
Crim 29 October 2002 Bull crim 2002 N° 197 p. 733; D 2003 Jur 2112 note L. Mauger-Vielpeau   217, 220, 222
Civ 1, 13 November 2002 Bull civ 1 No 263, D 2003.580 note S. Deis-Beauquesne; JCP 2003 II 10096 note M. Billiau   36
Civ 2, 12 December 2002 (*Drum majorette*) Bull civ II N° 289, JCP 2003 IV 1220   137
Ass Plén 13 December 2002 Bull Ass plén N° 4, p. 7; JCP 2003 II 10010 note A. Hervio-Lelong; D 2003 Jur 231 note P. Jourdain   136, 214
Civ 2, 6 February 2003 JCP 2003 II 10120 note C. Castets-Renard   188
Civ 2, 6 February 2003 Bull Civ 2003 II N° 33, D 2004.som 1341 obs P Jourdain   89
Civ 2, 7 May 2003 D 2003.2256 note M. Huyette   135
Rouen 7 May 2003 Res civ et assur Oct 2003 comm 54 par Ch. Radé   220
Com 20 May 2003 D 2003.2623 note B. Dondéro 49
Civ 2, 22 May 2003 Bull civ 2003 II N° 156 p. 132, Banque et droit 2003.76 N° 91   186

Civ 2, 3 July 2003 Bull civ 2003 II N° 230 p. 191; JCP 2003 II 10009 note R. Desgorces   216
Civ 2, 5 February 2004 Bull Civ II N° 50, page 41   217
Crim 7 April 2004 Bull crim N° 94; D 2004 IR 1563   38
Civ 2, 8 April 2004 D 2004.2601 note Y.-M. Serinet, JCP 2004 II 10131 note Imbert   30
Civ 2, 29 April 2004 Bull civ 2004 II N° 202 p. 170; D 2004 IR 1429   216
Crim 18 May 2004 Bull Crim N° 123, page 470   222
Civ 2, 3 June 2004 Bull civ 2004 II N° 275, p. 233; JCP 2005 I 132 N° 5; Gaz Pal 2004.2.3857 note F. Gréau   186
Civ 2, 21 October 2004 D 2005.40 note J.-B. Laydu   30, 136
Civ 1 9 November 2004 Bull civ 1 N° 262; D 2005.253 note F. Chabas; JCP 2005 II 10020 rapp D. Duval-Arnould, note S. Porchy-Simon   36
Crim 8 February 2005 Bull crim N° 44, p. 131; D 2005 IR 918; JCP 2005 I 149 obs G. Viney and II 10049 note M.-F. Steinlé-Feuerbach   217, 222
Civ 2 16 June 2005 Bull civ II N° 158, p. 141; D 2005 IR 1806   186
Crim 28 March 2006 Bull crim N° 91; JCP 2006 II 10188 note J. Mouly   38
Civ 2, 19 October 2006 Bull civ II N° 275   87
Civ 2, 26 October 2006 Bull civ II N° 299; JCP 2007 II 10004 note J. Mouly; D 2007.204 note J.-B. Laydu   139
Ass plén 29 June 2007 D 2007.2455 note J. François   137, 139
Civ 1, 12 July 2007 Bull civ 2007 I N° 270; JCP 2008 I 125 obs P. Stoffel-Munck   37
Civ 2, 20 December 2007 Bull civ 2007 II N° 274; D 2008.1248 note J. Mouly   38
Civ 2, 21 February 2008 Resp civ et assur 2008 comm 124 note H. Groutel; D 2008.2125 note J.-B. Laydu; JCP 2008 I 186 obs P. Stoffel-Munck   38

Germany
RG 7 December 1911 RGZ 78, 239 (linoleum case)   45
BGH 25 October 1951 BGH24, 1 = NJW 1952, 418   11
BGH 4 November 1953 BGHZ 11, 151 = NJW 1954, 505   153
BGH 2 February 1955 Vers R 1955, 205   153
BGH 23 February 1955 Vers R 1955, 214   153
BGH 15 February 1957 LM §823 BGB (Hb) 5   261
BGH (GS) 4 March 1957 BGHZ 24, 21 NJW 1957, 785 (the *Straßenbahn* case)   28
BGH 30 October 1959 Vers R 1960, 134   153
BGH 15 December 1959 BGHZ 31, 358, 366 = NJW 1960, 669   154

BGH 26 January 1960 VersR 1960, 355, 356   208
BGH 27 October 1965 VersR 1965, 48   208
BGH 30 June 1966 BGHZ 45, 311 = NJW 1966, 1807   66
BGH 20 September 1966 VersR 1966, 1074   152, 262
BGH 30 October 1967 BGHZ 49, p. 19   50
BGH VersR 1967, 353, 354   184
BGH 28 February 1969 MDR 1969, 564   208
BGH Vers R 1983, 734   208
BGH 29 May 1990 BGHZ 11, 282   208
OLG Dusseldorf, 23 December 1994 NJW-RR 1995, 1430   88, 97
BGH 21 September 1971 NJW 1972, 334   50
BGH VersR 1975, 520 (*Rausschmeisser*)   67
BGH 17 May 1983 NJW 1983, 2821   208
BGH NJW 1986, 776   65
BGH 1 July 1986 NJW-RR 1987, 13   208
BGH 14 February 1989 NJW-RR 1989, 723   156
BGH VersR 1992, 844   108
BGH 26 January 1995 NJW-RR 1995, 659   88, 92
BGH 14 February 1995, BGHZ 129. 6 = NJW 1995, 1611 (*Belegarzt*)   1
BGH 12 July 1996 NJW 1996, 3205   29
BGH NJW-RR 1998, 250   67
OLG Frankfurt 28 March 2001 MDR 2001,752   208

Ireland
Moynihan v Moynihan [1975] 1 IR 192   112
O'Keeffe v Hickey [2008] IESC 72   112

New Zealand
A v Bottrill [2003] 1 AC 449   39
Dollars & Sense Finance Ltd v Nathan [2008] NZSC 20, [2008] 2 NZLR 557   130, 131
McCallion v Dodd [1966] NZLR 710   198
Pettersson v Royal Oak Hotel Ltd [1948] NZLR 136   172
S v Attorney-General [2003] 3 NZLR 450   2, 19, 42, 129, 130, 161, 164

Scotland
Mulholland v William Reid & Leys Ltd 1958 SC 290   57

United States
Bing v Thunig (1957) 143 NE 2d 3   62
Gordon v SM Byers Motor Car Co. (1932) 309 Pa 453   91
Lashbrook v Patten 1 Duv 316 (Ky 1864)   113

Los Ranchitos v Tierra Grande Inc. 861 P 2d 263 (NM App 1993)   157
Mahar v Stone Wood Transp 823 A 2d 540 (Me 2003)   157
Monty v Orlandi 337 P 2d 861 (Cal App 1959)   157
Morgan v ABC Manufacturer 710 SO 2d 1077   91
Siidekum v Animal Rescue League of Pittsburg (1946) 353 Pa 408   91
US v Silk (1946) 331 US 704   70, 71, 74

Table of legislation

Australia
Australian Federal Police Act 1979 (Cwth)
s. 64B   104
Civil Liability Act 1936 (South Australia)
s. 59   34
Civil Liability Act 2002 (NSW)
s. 5Q   117
Employees Liability Act 1991 (NSW)
s. 2A   104
s. 3   34
Insurance Contracts Act 1984 (Cth)
s. 65   33
s. 66   33
Law Reform (Vicarious Liability) Act 1983 (NSW)
s. 9B   42
Partnership Act 1891
s. 10   105
Partnership Act 1891 (South Australia)
s. 10   105
Partnership Act 1963
ss. 14, 14A, 16   105

Canada
Negligence Act RSBC 1996, c. 333
s. 4   31
Ontario Labour Relations Act SO 1995
Sched. A, s. 1   127

Partnership Act RSBC 1996
s. 348   105
Police Act RSBC 1996, c. 367
ss. 11, 21   104

England and Wales

Animals Act 1971
s. 6(3)   224
Anti-Social Behaviour Act 2003
s. 19   203
s. 20   203
s. 25   203
s. 26   203
Companies Act 1985
ss 35(1), 35 (A)(1)   47
Crime and Disorder Act 1998
s. 8   203
s. 9   203
ss. 13A-13E   202
Children Act 1989
s. 2(1)(2)   198
Children Act 2004
s. 58(3)   200
Civil Liability (Contribution) Act 1978   31, 91
s. 2   41, 200
Congenital Disabilities (Civil Liability) Act 1976
s. 2   200
Crown Proceedings Act 1947
s. 2   50
Employers' Liability (Compulsory Insurance) Act 1969   236
Family Law Reform Act 1969
s. 1   198
Fire Prevention (Metropolis) Act 1774   121
Human Rights Act 1988   50
Law Reform (Personal Injuries) Act 1948
s. 1   119
London Hackney Carriage Act 1843 (London)   104
Partnership Act 1890
s. 10   104
Married Women's Property Act 1882
s. 12   14

Pilotage Act 1913
s. 15   104
Pilotage Act 1987
s. 16   104
Police Act 1964
s. 48   104
Police Act 1996
s. 88   42, 104
Powers of Criminal Courts (Sentencing) Act 2000
s. 137   202, 203
s. 150(2)   203
Protection from Harassment Act 1997
s. 3   167
Race Relations Act 1976
s. 32(1)   145
Road Traffic Act 1988
Serious Organised Crime and Police Act 2005   202
s. 143   115, 200
Town Police Clauses Act 1847   104
Workmen's Compensation Act 1897   66, 235

European legislation
Directive 72/166/EEC
Article 3(1)   115
Second Council Directive 84/5/EC   115
European Convention on Human Rights
Art. 8   203

France
French Civil Code/Code civil (C civ)
Article 371-1   215
Article 372   216
Article 388   192
Article 489-2   212
Article 1147   63
Articles 1350-1360   241
Article 1355   241
Article 1355(2)   30
Article 1356   217
Article 1359(1)   37

Article 1360   78, 138, 241
Article 1382   1, 2, 27, 48, 214, 223, 232
Article 1383   27, 48
Article 1384   8, 23, 24, 53, 103, 140, 147, 188, 213, 231, 250
Article 1384(1)   8, 23, 25, 27, 30, 103, 108, 136, 137, 138, 139, 141, 144, 189, 215, 247
Article 1384(2)   8, 24
Article 1384(3)   8, 24
Article 1384(4)   8, 23, 24, 29, 30, 186, 189, 214, 216, 240, 241
Article 1384(5)   8, 25, 27, 30, 35, 45, 48, 52, 53, 54, 55, 57, 67, 68, 87, 97, 98, 101, 102, 103, 106, 107, 108, 137, 138, 139, 141, 144, 145, 181, 182, 184, 185, 186, 188, 232, 238, 246
Article 1384(6)   23, 24
Article 1384(7)   23, 24
Article 1384(8)   24
Article 1385   9
Article 1386   9
Article 1733   24
Article 1734   24
Commercial Code
Article L225-251   48
Article L225-256   48
Code of Criminal Procedure
Article 2   53
Articles 706-3ff   220
Code of Education
Article L911-4   24
Code of Insurance
Article L121-2   188, 220, 221, 250
Article L121-9   103
Article L121-12(3)   33, 35
Article L211-1   183
Article L511-III   103
Code of Judicial Organisation
Article L431-5   54
Article L431-6   54
Code of Public Health
Article L1142-2   64
Article R4127-5   61

Consumer Code
Article L121-9   103
Criminal Code
Article 121-3   38
Social Security Code
L451-1   52
L452-5   52
Sporting Code
Articles L321-1ff   139
loi of 4 June 1970   213
loi of 20 July 1899   182
loi of 5 April 1937   213
loi 5 July 1985 *(loi Badinter)*   183
loi of 4 March 2002   213, 216
loi of 15 December 2005   103

Germany
German Civil Code/Bürgerliches Gesetzbuch (BGB)
§ 2   198
§ 30   49
§ 31   11, 12, 49, 51, 65, 66, 148
§ 34   11
§ 89   49, 51
§ 253 (II)   64
§ 276   63
§ 276(2)   11
§ 278   11, 45, 57, 63, 148
§ 426   49
§ 823   2, 49, 50, 65
§ 823 (I)   11, 12, 28, 46, 232, 262
§ 823 (II)   28
§ 826   28
§ 828   209
§ 828(1)   212
§ 828(2)   212
§ 829   209
§ 831   9, 11, 27, 28, 44, 45, 46, 49, 50, 57, 65, 67, 88, 97, 101, 103, 144, 146, 148, 152, 207, 231, 232
§ 831(1)   26, 55, 231, 245

§ 831(2)   11
§ 832   28, 206, 207, 209
§ 833   19, 103
§ 834   103
§ 839   11, 51, 57
§ 840   28, 49
§ 1626(1)   207
§ 1631(1)   207
§ 1672   207
§ 1793   207
§ 1797   207
§ 1800   207
§ 1909   207
§ 1915   207
German Basic Law/Grundgesetz
Article 34   51
Article 34GG   52
Imperial Law of Liability 1871 (*Reichhaftpflichtgesetz*)   232
Road Traffic Act of 19 December 1952 (*Straßenverkehrsgesetz* StVG)   11, 156
Liability Act of 4 January 1978 (*Haftpflichtgesetz* HPflG)   11, 46

New Zealand
Accident Compensation Act 2001   252

Spain
Spanish Civil Code/ Código Civil español
Article 1903   211, 245
Article 1903 II   211
Article 1903 VI   211
Organic Act on Criminal Liability of Minors (Ley Orgánica 5/2000, Reguladora de responsabilidad penal de los menores)
Article 61.3   210

United States
Federal Tort Claims Act, 28 USC §§ 2671–2680   35
§ 2679(d)(2)   35
United States: Restatement (3d) of Agency (2006)
§ 1.01   109
§ 7.01 Agent's Liability to Third Party   22, 108
§ 7.07 Employee Acting Within Scope Of Employment   71, 108, 145, 157, 192

United States: Restatement (2d) of Agency (1958)
§ 220(2)   70, 72
§ 401   31
United States Restatement of Agency (1933)
§ 220(1)   58

Preface

Like most lawyers, I first came across the doctrine of vicarious liability in tort as a student. I found it somewhat of an oddity: a principle of strict liability in an area of law dominated by fault, notably the tort of negligence. Vicarious liability seemed to be the cuckoo in the nest; imposing liability without fault on innocent parties (usually employers) regardless of their attempts to exercise reasonable care. I soon learnt that whilst the doctrine was regarded as an indispensable element of the law of torts, my textbooks could provide no clear rationale for its existence and that, in practice, uncertainty seemed to arise at each stage of its operation: was there a relationship giving rise to vicarious liability? What connection had to exist between the employee's (it is in most cases the employee) misconduct and the job he was supposed to perform? Frustratingly, later, as a teacher and lecturer in law, these problems continued to trouble me and, dare I say, intensified in the face of cases arising from the Supreme Courts of leading common law jurisdictions in 1999,[1] 2001[2] and 2003[3] in which the most learned judges of each jurisdiction struggled both to provide an explanation for vicarious liability and a legal framework in which the doctrine could be applied. Further, as a comparative lawyer, I came to realise that this was not just a common law problem. Civil lawyers equally experienced difficulties in delineating both a role and workable legal framework for its equivalent doctrines (usually termed 'liability for the acts of others').[4] Comparative law produced two immediate insights, however. First, that the basic

[1] *Bazley v Curry* (1999) 174 DLR (4th) 45.
[2] *Lister v Hesley Hall Ltd* [2001] UKHL 22, [2002] 1 AC 215.
[3] *New South Wales v Lepore; Samin v Queensland; Rich v Queensland* (2003) 212 CLR 511.
[4] See, generally, B. Koch (ed.), *Unification of tort law: liability for damage caused by others* (The Hague: Kluwer International, 2003).

xli

legal framework was similar in all systems and raised similar interpretative difficulties. Secondly, that despite the German Civil Code refusing to accept a strict liability principle in its Civil Code of 1896, the courts had nevertheless found ways of imposing strict liability in circumstances similar to that found in the common law and non-Germanic civil law systems. There is therefore something fundamental about this doctrine, arising in some form in all Western legal systems.

This, in essence, is the inspiration for this book: trying to understand the doctrine which we will call for convenience 'vicarious liability'. Although the term derives from the common law, it is used here to signify a concept, not a particular legal system. 'Vicarious liability' is used thus in a trans-systemic way, as equivalent to the French doctrine of *responsabilité du fait d'autrui* under Article 1384 of the Civil Code (C civ.) and compared with the German doctrine of *Haftung für den Verrichtungsgehilfen* under § 831 of the Civil Code (BGB). The term 'liability for the acts of others', preferred in civil law, is too inclusive: it can include primary liability for the acts of others and also, potentially, liability for non-tortious actions. 'Vicarious liability' is used here to signify the strict liability of one person for the tortious/wrongful acts of the other.

To reach an understanding of this doctrine, the prism of comparative law is utilised, looking at not only common law systems such as Canada, Australia and, to a more limited extent, New Zealand and the United States, but also considering liability in France – which in its 1804 Civil Code had already imposed strict liability on employers for the torts of their employees – and Germany, as representative civil law systems. The aim is to go beyond the technicalities of individual legal systems to examine the key constituents of a vicarious liability claim more broadly and to gain a deeper understanding of its operation and its potential development, whilst highlighting areas where reform is needed. The structure of the book therefore follows this pattern. After a brief introduction, I will examine the general framework of liability in common and civil law jurisdictions, then move on to its key elements:

- relationships giving rise to vicarious liability (employer/employee; borrowed employees and temporary workers; other relationships giving rise to liability) *and*
- the limits to the scope of liability: acting in the course of one's employment/ functions/assigned tasks.

Consideration will also be given to the potential for vicarious liability to be extended into other areas of law, for example, parental liability for their children's torts.

Such a study leads to a number of fundamental questions. Can we identify a clear rationale for this doctrine? Are clear and simple tests identifiable for the issues discussed above? How do twenty-first century developments, for example, attempts to find unified principles of European tort law, impact on our common understanding of this doctrine? In writing this book and considering the answers to all these questions, I have gained a deeper understanding and awareness of the nature and character of this doctrine and I hope, in this book, to share that with my readers.

A book such as this is not written without support and I must thank both my colleagues and comparative law students at the University of Bristol for their interest and support in this endeavour. I would also like to thank Cambridge University Press, in particular Finola O'Sullivan, and Harold Luntz, Keith Stanton, Claudina Richards, Friedrich Schulenburg and Colm McGrath for their assistance. I must also thank the long-suffering Keith and Jasper for whom the two words 'vicarious' and 'liability' have become impossible to avoid in the last two years and who now know far more about this subject than, in their opinions, they ever needed to know!

Paula Giliker
Bristol

1 What is vicarious liability?

1.1 Introduction

The doctrine of vicarious liability lies at the heart of all common law systems of tort law. It represents not a tort, but a rule of responsibility which renders the defendant liable for the torts committed by another. The classic example is that of employer and employee: the employer is rendered strictly liable for the torts of his employees, provided that they are committed in the course of the tortfeasor's employment. In such circumstances, liability is imposed on the employer, not because of his own wrongful act, but due to his relationship with the tortfeasor. The claimant is thus presented with *two* potential defendants: the individual tortfeasor and a third party, likely to be with means and/or insured and usually clearly identifiable in circumstances where it may be difficult to identify the actual culprit in question. Any study of vicarious liability cannot therefore avoid consideration of its role in determining who ultimately bears the burden of paying compensation.

Nevertheless, it is a principle at odds with tort's traditional focus on general principles of individual responsibility. Traditionally described as 'the law of civil wrongs', a basic formulation of tort law may be summed up as rendering the tortfeasor liable for committing a wrong which has caused harm to another.[1] A more sophisticated analysis may be stated in terms of corrective justice: 'Corrective justice is the idea that liability rectifies the injustice inflicted by one person on another.'[2] Vicarious

---

[1] As succinctly captured by the French Civil Code in Article 1382: 'Any act which causes harm to another obliges the person whose fault caused the harm to make reparation.'
[2] E. J. Weinrib, 'Corrective justice in a nutshell', *University of Toronto Law Journal*, 52 (2002), 349, who refers to its classic formulation in Aristotle's treatment of justice in *Nicomachean Ethics*, Book V. See also A. Beever, *Rediscovering the law of negligence* (Oxford: Hart Publishing, 2007) who argues that the law of negligence is best understood in terms

liability breaks this causal link. It is, as Lord Nicholls commented in the House of Lords, 'at odds with the general approach of the common law. Normally common law wrongs, or torts, comprise particular types of conduct regarded by the common law as blameworthy. In respect of these wrongs the common law imposes liability on the wrongdoer himself. The general approach is that a person is liable only for his own acts.'[3] Neither is it consistent with the core principles of fault found in civilian systems. Article 1382 of the French Civil Code imposes liability on the basis of proof of fault (*faute*) by the defendant.[4] Equally, the German Civil Code imposes liability in damages on 'a person who, intentionally or negligently, unlawfully injures the life, body, health, freedom, property or another right of another person'.[5] In all these systems, fault is seen as the core basis for liability. Clearly the existence of and justification for vicarious liability require some explication.

Yet, this is a topic which has attracted surprisingly little theoretical interest, despite the fact that it runs counter to the basic principle of tort law which maintains that a person should only be held accountable for the wrongs he or she commits against another. In recent years, this lack of theoretical understanding has become increasingly problematic. During the last ten years, the House of Lords (from 2010 the Supreme Court) of England and Wales, the Supreme Court of Canada, the High Court of Australia and the New Zealand Court of Appeal have, in leading cases, sought to understand and explain the nature of this doctrine, with mixed success.[6] The extension of the doctrine in these cases, which has in some cases resulted in the imposition of strict liability on faultless defendants for acts of sexual abuse and violent assaults by those for whom they are held responsible, has led many to question the current operation of this doctrine and how far innocent parties should be expected to bear the burden of the harm caused by miscreants whose conduct they may strongly abhor.

---

of a relatively small set of principles which represent an aspect of morality called corrective justice.

[3] *Majrowski v Guy's and St Thomas's NHS Trust* [2006] UKHL 34, [2007] 1 AC 224 at para. 8.

[4] G. Viney and P. Jourdain, *Traité de droit civil: les conditions de la responsabilité*, 3rd edn (Paris: LGDJ, 2006), N° 439.

[5] § 823, German Civil Code/*Bürgerliches Gesetzbuch* (hereafter BGB). Translations of the BGB are taken from the German Ministry of Justice website: www.gesetze-im-internet.de/englisch_bgb/englisch_bgb.html

[6] See, notably, *Lister v Hesley Hall Ltd* [2002] 1 AC 215 (UK); *Bazley v Curry* (1999) 174 DLR (4th) 45; and *Jacobi v Griffiths* (1999) 174 DLR (4th) 71 (Canada); *New South Wales v Lepore* (2003) 212 CLR 511, 195 ALR 412 (Australia); and *S v Attorney-General* [2003] 3 NZLR 450 (New Zealand).

The English case of *Lister v Hesley Hall Ltd*[7] provides an excellent illustration of the tension in existing law. Here the defendants, a private company, owned and managed a school and boarding annexe dealing with children who, in the main, had emotional and behavioural difficulties. The institution was run by a warden, Mr Grain, who was responsible for discipline and for supervising the boys when they were not at school. The claimants were boys resident at the home between 1979 and 1982, who had been systematically sexually abused by Grain. Grain was subsequently sentenced to seven years' imprisonment for multiple offences involving sexual abuse, but the victims sought civil compensation. A claim for negligence against the defendants had been rejected at first instance and was not appealed. The House of Lords was therefore asked whether the defendants should be held vicariously liable for Grain's acts. In finding such acts to be covered by vicarious liability,[8] the House of Lords accepted that the doctrine could extend to wilful misconduct which was the very antithesis of the duties for which Grain had been employed and regardless of the absence of any evidence that the employer should have detected misconduct or that greater preventative measures could have stopped the abuse. In extending the doctrine beyond previously accepted limits,[9] one might expect that the House of Lords would provide a detailed explanation of the nature of vicarious liability, thereby fulfilling its role of providing guidance to the lower courts in future cases. Instead, five opinions were delivered, which not only blurred the distinction between primary and vicarious liability, but gave limited and, at times, contradictory advice to future courts. The result is a doctrine which seems harsh, difficult to justify and problematic to apply. Lord Nicholls in *Dubai Aluminium Co Ltd v Salaam*[10] commented that the decision 'provides no clear assistance' and subsequent case law has sadly demonstrated the truth of this statement, both in England and Wales and in the Commonwealth generally.[11]

Such concerns are not confined to common law systems. French law demonstrates an increasing willingness to utilise ideas of vicarious

---

[7] [2002] 1 AC 215.
[8] Notably by confirming that such acts were in the course of Grain's employment: see Chapter 6.
[9] See *Trotman v North Yorkshire County Council* [1999] LGR 584.
[10] [2002] UKHL 48, [2003] 2 AC 366 at para. 25. See also A. Dugdale and M. A. Jones (gen. eds.), *Clerk & Lindsell on torts*, 19th edn, (London: Sweet & Maxwell, 2006), 6-01: 'rather vague test'.
[11] See, in particular, Chapter 6.

liability to ensure that victims obtain access to compensation. Indeed, the breadth of the French doctrine of liability for the acts of others may be startling to a common lawyer, but has not been achieved without considerable doctrinal debate. The French Supreme Court has struggled for many years to establish clear principles of vicarious liability and its most recent attempts have not escaped considerable criticism from the Commission appointed to reform the French Civil Code.[12] German law provides an obvious contrast. In its Civil Code, vicarious liability is rejected in preference for fault-based principles. Subsequently, however, the courts have devised a variety of means to circumvent the relevant provisions, leading to many calls (as yet unheeded) for reform of the Code.

The uncertainty created by such judgments renders a study of the operation of the modern doctrine of vicarious liability increasingly important. This book seeks to explain the operation of the doctrine, setting out not only its application but examining its theoretical basis. At present, it is a doctrine which, like so many principles of the common law, is more relied upon than understood. In re-examining the rationale and practical application of vicarious liability in modern law, the book will focus on English law, but utilise comparative law as a means of both criticising and re-evaluating the law. English law, by virtue of its long history and ongoing influence on Commonwealth law, provides an obvious focus for the study. However, in view of the current muddled state of English law, there is much to be gained from a study of other legal systems, which provide alternative perspectives of the application and role of vicarious liability in a modern market economy. A study of other legal systems gives one access to a wealth of research, case law and analysis which is capable of throwing fresh light on the operation of this doctrine.

Indeed, traditionally, a study of this kind would utilise comparative examples, but limit its focus to the common law. The leading monograph of Professor Atiyah adopts the conventional approach of analysing English law in its common law context.[13] However, much has changed since 1967. The United Kingdom is part of the European Union and the

---

[12] P. Catala, *Avant-projet de réforme du droit des obligations et de la prescription* (Paris: La Documentation française, 2006): translation by S. Whittaker and J. Cartwright: www.justice.gouv.fr/art_pix/rapportcatatla0905-anglais.pdf

[13] P. S. Atiyah, *Vicarious liability in the law of torts* (London: Butterworths, 1967). Baty, however, in his 1916 work examined both civil and common law systems: see T. Baty, *Vicarious liability* (Oxford: Clarendon Press, 1916), ch. IX, Scotland and foreign countries.

laws of contract and tort are increasingly influenced by European law. As will be discussed in Chapter 9, proposals for harmonisation of European private law in both these fields indicate a growing convergence of common and civil law systems which a modern text should not ignore. Despite the apparent perils of common and civil law comparative work,[14] it would be arrogant to neglect legal systems which have, despite obvious structural differences, much in common both economically and politically with English law. What is immediately striking in examining comparative perspectives of vicarious liability (or, in civil law terms, liability for the acts of others) is the similarity of the formulations adopted in both common and civil law jurisdictions. To ignore such sources in a modern examination of vicarious liability would be to neglect an area of scholarship which, we will see, is both challenging and thought-provoking.

This book will therefore examine the three major legal families of Western law: the common law (including Canada, Australia, New Zealand and, to a limited extent, the United States), the Romanistic (here, France) and Germanic (here, Germany). This is a doctrine which crosses legal boundaries and an area of law where the most obvious examples of the Romanistic and Germanic systems provide the most fruitful studies.

In examining the role of vicarious liability in these post-industrialised States, a number of points should be noted. First, it is important to clarify the question of terminology. The term 'vicarious liability' derives from the common law, and civilian systems will generally refer to 'liability for the acts of others'. This latter term is, however, more inclusive and will extend to strict liability in both contract and tort, and even liability for actions not amounting to torts. On this basis, this book will use the term 'vicarious liability' in a neutral transsystemic sense to signify rendering one person/body strictly liable for the *torts* of another in the law of tort. Liability in contract law will not be covered, except where it is necessary to distinguish it from the law of tort. Chapter 5, for example, will consider the law of agency which renders the principal liable for the *torts* of its agent in order to distinguish such liability from that arising in the law of tort. Reference to contractual liability for the torts of others may be found in general texts on contract law. Secondly, less attention will be given to the German legal system, which, as will be seen, still

---

[14] See J. Stapleton, 'Benefits of comparative tort reasoning: lost in translation', *Journal of Tort Law*, 3 (2007).

retains in its Code the provision that 'vicarious' liability is based on fault, albeit fault is presumed against the defendant. In contrast, the common law and French legal systems have embraced a strict liability principle and the focus of this book will be primarily on the scope of this strict liability principle in a system based fundamentally on fault-based liability. Finally, the aim of this book is to identify core legal principles which underlie vicarious liability and gain from the interpretative experience of the courts covered by this survey. It is not therefore to present a practitioners' guide to each legal system, but to use comparative law to explain the current legal position and help the reader understand the perplexing doctrine which is vicarious liability.

This first chapter will provide a basic introduction to the nature of vicarious liability in terms of its legal characteristics, relationship with primary liability and its significance in modern legal systems. It will commence with a brief outline of the historical background to vicarious liability, although a more detailed discussion of the relevant case law will be undertaken in later chapters. The book will then focus on its practical operation: providing a general framework for liability (Chapter 2), describing its operation in relation to employers (Chapters 3 and 4) and other defendants (Chapter 5) and the degree of connectedness needed between the parties' relationship and the tort committed (Chapter 6). Chapter 7 will consider whether English law should, in line with its European counterparts, impose a special form of liability on parents for the torts of their children: a category not yet acknowledged by the common law courts. Chapter 8 will finally examine the rationale for the doctrine, considering the justifications given for the existence of this rule of strict liability at the heart of the law of civil wrongs, drawing together the conclusions reached in earlier chapters. Finally, Chapter 9 will examine proposals for the harmonisation of vicarious liability in European Union Member States, assessing the potential impact of such proposals on the future development of European private law.

1.2 Vicarious liability: an historical overview

The idea of liability for the torts of others may be traced back to Roman law. Although Roman lawyers did not consider this problem as a whole nor reach any general statement of principle,[15] specific examples of

---

[15] K. Zweigert and H. Kötz, *Introduction to comparative law*, 3rd rev. edn (Oxford: Clarendon Press, 1998), p. 630.

liability of a superior for the wrongful acts of an inferior may be found. The most significant is the personal liability of the head of the family (the paterfamilias) for the delicts of his child or slave. If the child or slave committed a tort (delict), the paterfamilias would be liable to pay damages on their behalf unless he chose to hand over the culprit to the victim (the doctrine of noxal surrender).[16] It is questionable, however, to what extent Roman law has, in fact, influenced the modern doctrine of vicarious liability.[17] Lawson comments that 'the whole notion of a master's liability for the wrongs of his free servant committed in the course of his employment is alien to Roman ideas'[18] and the broad principles of vicarious liability found in modern law bear no relation to such specific provisions.[19]

The background history of vicarious liability is therefore best understood in the context of nineteenth-century codifications. Although historians have traced the common law doctrine back to medieval times,[20] the nineteenth century represents a time of significant development. Economic and technological advances indicate the growing importance of the employer/employee relationship, distinct from an earlier focus on craftsmen and apprentices as seen in the (pre-industrial) French Civil Code of 1804. The rise of corporations, the impact of the Industrial

---

[16] The noxal surrender of daughters became obsolete in the Republic, but continued for sons until its abolition by Justinian: A. Borkowski and P. du Plessis, *Textbook on Roman law*, 3rd edn (Oxford University Press, 2005), p. 115. See, generally, J. A. C. Thomas, *Textbook on Roman law* (Amsterdam: North-Holland, 1976), ch. XXXIII.

[17] Even Zimmermann concedes that 'Vicarious liability provides an example of a vigorous modern institution created on extremely slender Roman foundations': R. Zimmermann, *Roman law, contemporary law, European law: the civilian tradition today* (Oxford University Press, 2001), p. 123. Holdsworth also notes some influence filtering into the common law through the court of Admiralty and mercantile custom, but acknowledges that this was not a major influence on the law: W. S. Holdsworth, *A history of English law* (London: Methuen, 1966 reprint), vol. VIII, pp. 475–6.

[18] F. H. Lawson, 'Notes on the history of tort in the civil law', *Journal of Comparative Legislation and International Law*, 22 (1940), 136 at 139. Holmes notes, however, that innkeepers and shipowners were made answerable for their free servants by the praetor's edict: see O. W. Holmes, 'Agency' *Harvard Law Review* 4(1891), 345 at 350. Holmes is noticeably far more forthright on the influence of Roman law on modern principles of agency and vicarious liability.

[19] David Johnston, for example (see 'Limiting liability: Roman and the civil law tradition' *Chicago-Kent Law Review*, 70 (1995), 1515, 1528–32), argues that the idea of a functional limit on employers' liability was developed by Roman jurists only in the case of contractual agency and was introduced into delict by subsequent commentators such as Pothier in his *Traité des obligations* (Paris: Chez Debure, 1768).

[20] See D. J. Ibbetson, *A historical introduction to the law of obligations* (Oxford University Press, 1999), pp. 69–70.

8   WHAT IS VICARIOUS LIABILITY?

Revolution (both in terms of accident causation and the anonymity of the actual culprit) and political change render the question of liability of interested and, towards the end of the nineteenth century, insured third parties more and more relevant. As will be seen in Chapter 8, such factors impact not only on the growth of vicarious liability, but on its underlying rationale, thereby changing its role and significance in the law of tort.

Although the drafters of the French Civil Code were influenced by natural law ideas favouring a general notion of fault,[21] some provision was made for vicarious liability in the 1804 Code, albeit linked to presumptions of fault. Article 1384, since amended, stated that:

(1) A person is liable not only for the damages he causes by his own act, but also for that which is caused by the acts of persons for whom he is responsible, or by things which are in his custody.
(2) The father, and the mother if the father is deceased, are liable for the damage caused by their minor children who live with them.
(3) Masters and employers, for the damage caused by their servants and employees in the functions for which they have been employed.
(4) Teachers and craftsmen, for the damage caused by their pupils and apprentices during the time when they are under their supervision.
(5) The liability above exists, unless the father and mother, teachers or the craftsmen prove that they could not prevent the act which gives rise to that liability.

Express provision is thus made for the imposition of liability on parents, masters, employers, teachers and craftsmen for the acts of persons under their care or tutelage.[22] Liability is based on a presumption of fault. All, bar employers,[23] may rebut the presumption of negligence by showing that they exercised reasonable care. In this way, fault is maintained as the central principle. The preparatory works to the Civil Code assist our understanding of the motives of the drafters. Liability on one party for the acts of another was explained as a principle of justice: 'those on whom it is imposed can blame themselves, at the very least, for weakness, others

---

[21] See J. Domat, *Les loix civiles dans leur ordre naturel* (1689) (Paris: David, 1756).
[22] Article 1384, French Civil Code.
[23] Although Eörsi reports that the preliminary draft of the Civil Code contained a possibility for exemption in Article 19(5), which allowed the employer a due diligence defence, this was subsequently rejected on the basis that if the exemption was upheld, the employer might avoid liability for damages caused during his absence; described by Eörsi as 'rather irrelevant reasoning': G. Eörsi, 'Private and governmental liability for the torts of employees and organs' in A. Tunc (chief ed.), *International encyclopedia of comparative law* (Tübingen: Mohr, 1983), vol. XI, ch. 4, para. 4–8.

VICARIOUS LIABILITY: AN HISTORICAL OVERVIEW   9

for bad choices, all for negligence'.[24] This presumed negligence thus justifies imposing liability on specified parties; the most significant being that imposed on employers which, in the pursuit of profit, have wrongfully placed confidence in employees who have harmed others.[25] On this basis, an irrebuttable presumption of fault is imposed on employers, justified by the assumption that fault must exist for such an event to occur.[26]

Two points should be noted. First, the French Civil Code does not impose a general head of liability for the acts of others. Specific categories are stated, which are supplemented by strict liability for damage caused by animals (Article 1385)[27] and collapsing buildings (Article 1386).[28] Secondly, liability is justified by reference to fault in all cases. As will be discussed in later chapters, this early focus on presumed fault has since been lost. This reflects a movement in tort law generally towards a more objective interpretation of fault based on ideas of social risk. Although the wording of the Civil Code has changed little since 1804, its interpretation today bears little resemblance to the intentions of its drafters, whose objectives were influenced by natural law and the age of reason.

In contrast, the German Civil Code (BGB) of 1896 rejected any notion of responsibility without fault. § 831 of the Code thus provides that:

(1) A person who uses another person to perform a task is liable to make compensation for the damage that the other unlawfully inflicts on a third party when carrying out the task. Liability in damages does not apply if the principal exercises reasonable care when selecting the person deployed and, to the extent that he is to procure devices or equipment or to manage the business activity, in the procurement or management, or if the damage would have occurred even if this care had been exercised.

---

[24] Treihard, who contributed to the drafting of the Civil Code, whose comments of 1803 are reported in P. A. Fenet, *Recueil complet des travaux préparatoires du code civil* (1827) (Osnabrück: O. Zeller, 1968), vol. XIII, p. 468.

[25] See Bertrand de Greuille, *rapporteur* to the *Tribunat*, whose statement of 1803 is also reported in Fenet, *Recueil complet*, p. 476.

[26] Carbonnier notes that the provision was initially read as based on an assumption of fault by the employer for his negligent choice or supervision of employee: J. Carbonnier, *Droit civil 4, les obligations*, 22nd edn (Paris: Presses Universitaires de France, 2000), p. 243.

[27] 'The owner of an animal, or the person using it, during the period of usage, is liable for the damage the animal has caused, whether the animal was under his custody, or whether it had strayed or escaped.'

[28] 'The owner of a building is liable for the damage caused by its collapse, where it happens as a result of lack of maintenance or of a defect in its construction.'

(2) The same responsibility is borne by a person who assumes the performance of one of the transactions specified in subsection (1) sentence 2 for the principal by contract.

This imposes a rebuttable presumption of fault on the principal – liability is assumed unless the principal can prove that he is not at fault or could not have prevented the injury. Paragraph 2 seeks to deal with the hierarchical organisation of a large enterprise and provides that the presumption of fault will also apply to the 'immediate boss' of the tortfeasor, for example, a foreman instructed to select personnel. Although such provision may seem to resemble the early French interpretation of the Code, outlined above, it should be remembered that even in 1804 the French were not prepared to allow employers to avoid liability so easily. Whilst it may seem extraordinary that a Code, promulgated on the first day of the twentieth century, should reject vicarious liability, Zweigert and Kötz note opposition by nineteenth-century theorists to the notion of liability without fault and that, although specific statutory provision was made for accidents deriving from industrialisation,[29] this view survived to influence the draftsmen of the German Civil Code.[30] Brüggemeier notes that a debate did indeed occur during the drafting process, but that despite arguments in favour of rendering industry liable for the risks caused by its activities, the majority of the Second Drafting Commission, consisting of older officials, predominantly scholars of the *Gemeines Recht*[31] who favoured the principle of no liability without fault, was not convinced.[32] Concern of overburdening small businesses in a developing economy in the face of strong lobbying from trade, industry and agriculture, combined with the fault-based reasoning of the influential legal theorists, the pandectists,[33] thus led the codifiers to question the need for a general principle of vicarious liability.[34]

---

[29] For example, the Imperial Law of Liability of 1871 (*Reichhaftpflichtgesetz*): strict liability on railway companies for death or personal injury caused through the operation of the railways.

[30] Zweigert and Kötz, *Introduction to comparative Law*, pp. 630–1.

[31] German common law based on the sixth-century codification of Roman law put in force by the emperor Justinian: Encyclopædia Britannica online: www.britannica.com/EBchecked/topic/228063/gemeines-Recht

[32] G. Brüggemeier, *Haftungsrecht: Struktur, Prinzipien, Schutzbereich* (Heidelburg: Springer, 2006), p. 121.

[33] So-called because of their use of the Digest. See H. Coing, 'German "Pandektistik" in its relationship to the former "ius commune"', *American Journal of Comparative Law*, 37 (1989), 9.

[34] See H. H. Seiler, 'Die deliktische Gehilfenhaftung in historischer Sicht', *JuristenZeitung* (1967) 525 and MünchKommBGB/Wagner, 5th edn (Munich: C. H. Beck, 2009), § 831, para. 1.

Nevertheless, as will be discussed in subsequent chapters, German law today does impose vicarious liability despite the express wording of its Code. In addition to specific strict liability provisions outside the BGB,[35] the courts have turned to contract law. Zimmermann has remarked that '§ 831 BGB has turned out to be a major source of embarrassment'[36] and the resort of the German courts to contract law[37] and other provisions of the BGB[38] serves not only to demonstrate the strategic error of the decision in 1896 to adhere to fault-based liability, but also the ability of the courts to adapt codified law to meet contemporary social and economic needs. Nevertheless, the reforms of the BGB in 2002 did not include any changes to § 831. Equally, an earlier proposal for change in 1967 was not adopted. Wagner suggests that concerns still exist as to the burden which vicarious liability in tort would impose on small businesses and private households.[39] § 831(2) has additionally met considerable criticism for, in the context of large business organisations, permitting the main employer to exempt himself from liability by showing that the lower intermediate employee, who in fact selected and was supervising the tortfeasor, had been properly chosen and supervised. This leaves the victim with a claim against the hapless manager or foreman, who may be incapable of paying (the doctrine of 'decentralised exoneration' or '*dezentralisierter Entlastungsbeweis*').[40] Markesinis and

---

[35] For example, the Road Traffic Act of 19 December 1952 (BGBl. I, 837) (as amended) (*Straßenverkehrsgesetz* StVG) and Liability Act of 4 January 1978 (BGBl. I, 145) (as amended) (*Haftpflichtgesetz* HPflG): for translations into English, see www.utexas.edu/law/academics/centers/transnational/

[36] R. Zimmermann, *The law of obligations: Roman foundations of the civilian tradition* (Oxford: Clarendon Press, 1996), pp. 1125–6. See also B. S. Markesinis, *The German law of obligations, vol. II: the law of torts: a comparative introduction*, 3rd edn (Oxford: Clarendon, 1997), pp. 686–90.

[37] See, in particular, § 278 BGB (responsibility for persons employed in performing obligation): 'A debtor is responsible for the fault of his legal representative and of persons whom he employs in performing his obligation, to the same extent as for his own fault. The provision of § 276(2) does not apply.'

[38] Note also the development of *Organisationsverschulden* (duty to organise one's enterprise) under § 823(I) and § 31 BGB (liability of association for the damage to third parties by executive committee, member of the executive committee or another constitutionally destined representative). Special rules also exist for public servants under § 839 (liability for breach of official duty) and under § 34 sub. 1 of the Constitution. These developments will be discussed in more depth in later chapters.

[39] MünchKommBGB/Wagner, §831, para. 4.

[40] See Eörsi, 'Private and governmental', para. 4–56; MünchKommBGB/Wagner, §831, para. 42; J. von Standinger, D. W. Belling, C. Eberl-Borges, *Kommentar zum Bürgerlichen Gesetzbuch* (Berlin: De Gruyter, 2008), §831, paras. 120ff, and BGH 25 October 1951, BGHZ 4, 1 = NJW 1952, 418 = VersR 1952, 166, following the earlier decisions of the Reichsgericht.

Unberath describe it as 'undesirable both economically and in terms of labour-management relations' and note that it has unsurprisingly not been followed by other systems such as the Swiss.[41] In practice, the Supreme Court has sought to render the employer directly liable for breach of its organisational duty (*Organisationpflicht*) under § 823(I) BGB or, if a corporation, strictly liable for the acts of its organs under § 31 BGB.[42]

In contrast, the common law development of vicarious liability can be traced back to early medieval ideas of identification of a master with the acts of their servants or notions of agency, although Pollock claims to have invented the phrase in the 1880s.[43] In these early examples, including liability of an innkeeper for goods stolen in the inn, of a householder for the escape of fire started by a servant or guest, and of shipmasters for goods wrongfully taken by mariners, the servant's acts are attributed to the master.[44] However, truly vicarious liability arises only by the end of the seventeenth century at a time of expansion in commerce and industry. Holt CJ promulgated a test of implied command and set down the foundations for the modern doctrine in a number of judgments.[45] In *Boson v Sandford* in 1691, Holt CJ famously stated that 'for whoever employs another is answerable for him, and undertakes for his care to all that make use of him'.[46] Although there are signs that liability was, even in the time of Chief Justice Holt, limited to where the employee was going about his master's business,[47] from the 1800s the courts started to develop the course of employment test.[48] Ibbetson notes tension arising

---

[41] B. S. Markesinis and H. Unberath, *The German law of torts: a comparative treatise*, 4th edn (Oxford: Hart, 2002), p. 700.

[42] MünchKommBGB/Wagner, §831, paras. 43–4.

[43] See O. W. Holmes, *Holmes–Pollock letters* (Cambridge University Press, 1941), vol. I, p. 233.

[44] See Ibbetson, *A historical introduction*, pp. 69–70; and Holmes, 'Agency', 358–60.

[45] J. H. Baker, *An introduction to English legal history*, 4th edn (London: Butterworths, 2002), p. 410; J. H. Wigmore, 'Responsibility for tortious acts: its history', *Harvard Law Review*, 7 (1894), 383. Holdsworth describes Holt as 'a lawyer who, by reason both of his technical equipment and his knowledge of the commercial needs and conditions of the day, was eminently qualified to do for this branch of the law what he had done for many other branches of commercial law': *A history of English Law*, p. 474.

[46] *Boson v Sandford* (1691) 2 Salk 440, 91 ER 382. See also *Turberville v Stampe* (1698) 1 Ld Raym 264, 91 ER 1072; *Middleton v Fowler* (1698) 1 Salk 282, 91 ER 247; *Jones v Hart* (1699) 2 Salk 441, 91 ER 382.

[47] See Holdsworth *A history of English Law*, p. 475.

[48] See Lord Kenyon's judgment in *Ellis v Turner* (1800) 8 TR 531 at 533, 101 ER 1529 at 1531: 'The defendants are responsible for the acts of their servant in those things that respect his duty under them, though they are not answerable for his misconduct in those things that do not respect his duty to them.' See also *Laugher v Pointer* (1826) 5 B & C 547, 108 ER 204 and *M'Manus v Crickett* (1800) 1 East 106, 102 ER 43 (this case is also significant for establishing

from the 1790s as to the conflict between vicarious liability and a movement towards a moral concept of personal fault.[49] Doubts as to the principled basis of the doctrine led the courts to consider other means – the introduction of non-delegable duties or reliance on agency principles – in order to legitimise the imposition of liability for the acts of another. The impact of such devices will be examined in more detail in later chapters, but what appears is a lack of theoretical coherence which survives to this day. English law, a system based on a strong notion of precedent, has inherited a legacy which is muddled doctrinally and lacks a clear theoretical justification for the law applied by the courts.

1.3 The legal basis for vicarious liability

While civil law talks simply of 'liability for the acts of others', an ongoing debate exists at common law as to the legal basis for vicarious liability. The common law has developed two alternative legal bases for the doctrine. The first and most popular explanation is that it is indeed liability imposed on one person for the wrongful act of another. This is sometimes termed the 'servant's tort' theory. The second (known as the 'master's tort' theory) holds that the master is liable for the torts of the servant by reason of the attribution of the servant's acts to the master. The law thereby deems the master to have committed the wrongful act.

Despite its historical origins, the master's tort theory has received some support in modern law. In 1956, Glanville Williams argued strongly in its favour, terming it a fiction, justified by its results.[50] It has also been relied upon in a number of cases. In *Twine v Bean's Express Ltd*,[51] for example, Twine had been given a lift in a van driven by the defendants' employee, who had been expressly prohibited from taking passengers. Twine was aware of this. As a result of the negligent driving of the employee, Twine was killed and his widow brought an action against the driver's employers. Uthwatt J, at first instance, approved

---

that cases in future would be pleaded in case only and not trespass, confirmed by Parke B in *Sharrod v London and North Western Rly Co* (1849) 4 Ex 580, 154 ER 1345).

[49] See Ibbetson, *A historical introduction*, pp. 181–4.

[50] See G. Williams, 'Vicarious liability: Tort of the master or the servant?', *Law Quarterly Review*, 72 (1956), 522 at 545 and *Crown proceedings* (London: Stevens, 1948), p. 43.

[51] [1946] 1 All ER 202. Approved by the Court of Appeal, but on other grounds, namely that the negligence of the driver was not committed in the course of his employment: (1946) 62 TLR 458.

the defendants' decision to argue the case not on the basis as to whether the driver owed a duty to the passenger to take care, but whether the employers owed that duty. In his view, 'the law attributes to the employer the acts of a servant done in the course of his employment and fastens upon him responsibility for those acts'.[52] Additionally, in a number of decisions, Denning LJ argued that liability should not be seen as vicarious, but as personal to the master.[53] Reliance was placed on case law reference to the maxim '*qui facit per alium facit per se*', which can be translated as 'He who acts through another, acts for himself'. It is questionable whether, in using this phrase, the courts did, in fact, intend to approve its literal meaning. The phrase has been frequently used by the courts to explain vicarious liability without any real discussion of its significance.[54] Lord Reid in *Staveley Iron and Chemical Co v Jones*[55] was critical of reliance on such maxims which he found to be 'rarely profitable' and 'often misleading':

> The maxims *respondeat superior* and *qui facit per alium facit per se* are often used, but I do not think that they add anything or that they lead to any different results. The former merely states the rule baldly in two words, and the latter merely gives a fictional explanation of it.

Academics such as Newark were equally severe: '[t]he general principle enunciated in *Twine's* case ... is erroneous and is inconsistent with the essential nature of vicarious liability'.[56] Subsequent case law has agreed.[57] The House of Lords in *Staveley Iron and Chemical*

---

[52] [1946] 1 All ER at 204.
[53] See *Broom v Morgan* [1953] 1 QB 597 at 607–9 and *Jones v Staveley Iron and Chemical Co. Ltd* [1955] 1 QB 474, 480. Kitto J in *Darling Island Stevedoring and Lighterage Co. Ltd v Long* (1956-7) 97 CLR 36, 60-5 equally argued for the master's tort theory, relying upon the work of Glanville Williams and Denning LJ, although Fullagar J strongly disagreed.
[54] For example, Lord Kenyon CJ in *Mitchell v Tarbutt* (1794) 5 TR 649 at 651, 101 ER 362 at 363 commented merely that 'it is immaterial whether the tort were committed by the defendant or his servant, because the rule applies *qui facit per alium, facit per se*'. Similar criticism may be directed at the phrase '*respondeat superior*' (let the principal answer). Holmes cynically remarks that 'It certainly has furnished us with one of the inadequate reasons which have been put forward for the law as it is': Holmes, 'Agency', 357.
[55] [1956] AC 627 at 643.
[56] F. H. Newark, '*Twine v Bean's Express Ltd*', *Modern Law Review*, 17 (1954), 102 at 118.
[57] An apparent exception is *Broom v Morgan* [1953] 1 QB 597 where the plaintiff was able to sue the defendant employer for the negligence of her own husband. In the case itself, the wife had faced the obstacle of s. 12 of the Married Women's Property Act 1882 (since repealed) which barred a claim against her husband. In such circumstances, any claim would have to be brought against a third party for negligence. Interpreting the section as merely providing a procedural bar to the claim does not, however, prevent the

Co Ltd v Jones[58] and *Imperial Chemical Industries Ltd v Shatwell*[59] strongly supported the servant's tort theory of vicarious liability. Lord Morton remarked in *Staveley* that:

> Cases such as this, where an employer's liability is vicarious, are wholly distinct from cases where an employer is under a personal liability to carry out a duty imposed upon him as an employer by common law or statute. In the latter type of case the employer cannot discharge himself by saying: 'I delegated the carrying out of this duty to a servant, and he failed to carry it out by a mistake or error of judgment not amounting to negligence.' ... These words, however, are, in my view, incorrect as applied to a case where the liability of the employer is not personal but vicarious.[60]

It cannot be denied that this view represents the most straightforward view of vicarious liability. It is a rule of responsibility, not attributed fault. It is highly artificial to attribute to one person the wrongdoing of another simply on the basis of a pre-existing relationship in the absence of some form of consent or legal necessity.[61] Legal fictions should be discouraged whenever possible in the law in that they tend to undermine confidence in the openness and legitimacy of the legal process. More importantly, the master's tort theory blurs the whole notion of individual responsibility. Primary liability exists for one's own wrongdoing. Secondary liability logically represents liability for the acts of others. The 'master's tort' doctrine fits naturally within neither category and thereby undermines the clarity of tort law in general. Further, it neglects an important aspect of vicarious liability. As will be seen, vicarious liability generally renders both the tortfeasor and the person deemed at law responsible jointly liable to the victim. The master's tort theory renders solely the master liable. The level of accountability existing within vicarious liability is thus lost.[62]

The dominant view is thus that the 'servant's tort' theory prevails. Nevertheless, one author went so far recently as to comment, 'The (modern) language of "vicarious liability" presupposes that what is being

---

existence of a tort by the husband for which the employer could be held vicariously liable: see *Osborn v Gillett* (1873) LR 8 Exch 88.

[58] [1956] AC 627.   [59] [1965] AC 656.

[60] [1956] AC 627 at 639. See also Lord Reid at 643: 'an employer, though guilty of no fault himself, is liable for the damage done by the fault or negligence of his servant acting in the course of his employment.'

[61] For example, it is necessary to identify the acts of directors with that of the company which clearly cannot act by itself.

[62] The 'master's indemnity' will be examined in Chapter 2.

imputed is liability for the harm and not the act itself... Unfortunately, orthodoxy is wrong and Glanville Williams was right.'[63] This suggests that the debate is far from over.

Whilst some authors have doubted whether much in fact rests on a study of the true basis of vicarious liability,[64] the tensions between a theory based on primary liability and secondary liability continue to provide uncertainty in modern law. It also illustrates the difficulty that the courts sometimes experience in distinguishing between primary and vicarious liability. This issue will be examined further below.

1.3.1 Distinguishing primary from vicarious liability

The distinction between primary and vicarious liability is fundamental. From an individual's perspective, liability may be imposed primarily, that is, by means of proof that the individual has committed a tort, or vicariously, that is, by means of proof that another person has committed a tort for which he will be held responsible. The rationale for the imposition of liability will differ in each case, as will the impact on the individual. Generally, there will be less an individual can do to avoid the latter form of liability. One might also crudely draw a divide in terms of corrective and distributive justice. The former serves to correct the individual's behaviour, whilst the latter imposes an obligation on the individual deemed most appropriate to bear the risk of injury to the victim.

The Court of Appeal decision in *Wilsher v Essex AHA*[65] provides a good example of this division in practice. Here, a premature baby, placed in a special care baby unit in a hospital managed by the defendants, received negligent treatment from his doctors. Lord Browne-Wilkinson VC noted two possible claims against the Area Health Authority arising from the doctors' negligence:[66]

> (i) Direct liability: that is, the Area Health Authority will be liable if it so conducts its hospital that it fails to provide doctors of sufficient skill and experience to give the treatment offered at the hospital.
> (ii) Vicarious liability: namely where the Area Health Authority is held liable when one of its doctors is found personally to be at fault.

---

[63] R. Stevens, 'Vicarious liability or vicarious action', *Law Quarterly Review*, 123 (2007), 30. See also R. Stevens, *Torts and rights* (Oxford University Press, 2009), pp. 259–67.
[64] See Atiyah, *Vicarious liability*, p. 7.
[65] [1987] QB 730, CA (not raised in HL: [1988] AC 1074). [66] [1987] QB at 778.

Thus expressed, the claims are distinct and based on different duties of care. The *Wilsher* case is useful, also, in helping us understand one of the points of confusion in this area of law. Few would dispute that where X commits a tort which injures W, the resultant liability of X is primary, not vicarious. The facts of *Wilsher* were, however, more complicated. In claim (i), the Area Health Authority (AHA) commits a tort by failing to provide a doctor of sufficient skill with the result that the doctor provided (let us call him Z) injures W. Here, the immediate injury to W is caused by Z. Z has been negligent. Nevertheless, the action will be brought against the AHA on the basis of primary liability.

The cause of this confusion is the concept of the non-delegable duty. Here, the duty is imposed on one party to ensure that reasonable care is taken to protect another.[67] Although this duty can be delegated, responsibility cannot.[68] Hence, the AHA is under a non-delegable duty to see that a reasonable standard of care is provided to those treated at the hospital and, where this does not occur, it is held primarily responsible for breach of its non-delegable duty.[69]

Despite this clear conceptual division, the courts have not always avoided this potential source of confusion. The recent English debate as to the recoverability of exemplary (or punitive) damages under the doctrine of vicarious liability illustrates this point. Such damages are peculiar to the common law, providing claimants with an additional sum of damages whose goal is to punish the defendant for his misconduct and deter him and others from undertaking such conduct in future. As will be discussed in more detail in Chapter 2, the common law courts have struggled to deal with the question of whether the person vicariously liable should be required to pay exemplary, in addition to compensatory, damages. For Lord Scott in *Kuddus v Chief Constable of Leicestershire Constabulary*, the answer was simple: a person should only be required to pay exemplary damages when he has committed punishable behaviour, that is, he is personally at fault.[70] However, as the Law

---

[67] This is distinct from principles of agency whereby the principal (X) may be found liable for the torts of his agent (Z) if the act in question is authorised or ratified by him. Agency will be dealt with in Chapter 5.

[68] The classic example is that of an employer for the safety of his employees: see *Wilsons & Clyde Coal Co. v English* [1938] AC 57.

[69] *Cassidy v Ministry of Health* [1951] 2 QB 343. See also *A v Ministry of Defence* [2004] EWCA Civ 641; [2005] QB 183.

[70] [2002] 2 AC 122 at para. 131. The question was not argued and such comments are thus obiter.

Commission noted in 1997,[71] despite these reservations, the courts have consistently assumed that vicarious liability would extend to exemplary damages.[72] It was only in 2006 that the Court of Appeal finally resolved that the arguments in favour of vicarious liability justified the imposition of exemplary damages on the employer.[73]

What this debate illustrates – and it is one with which there is Commonwealth disagreement[74] – is the failure until recently to conceptualise the question in terms of the primary/vicarious distinction. Only in the last ten years have the common law courts been asking themselves the obvious question: why should a party without fault be liable for a punitive award of damages in circumstances when the actual culprit avoids payment? The attempts to resolve this crucial question will be evaluated in Chapter 2.

This failure to recognise and address the distinction between primary and vicarious liability continues to cause uncertainty in modern law.[75] While, on a theoretical level, the primary/vicarious distinction is relatively clear, applying this division to the law has proven, in practice, to be more difficult.

1.4 Conclusion

Vicarious liability, as a doctrine, is thus problematic. It does not fit into the dominant concept of fault underlying the law of tort and focuses not on individual responsibility for one's actions, but on responsibility for

[71] Law Commission Report No. 247 (1997), *Aggravated, exemplary and restitutionary damages*.
[72] Ibid., at 5:209: '[a]lthough it has consistently been assumed that vicarious liability extends to exemplary or punitive damages on the same basis as compensatory damages, we cannot find any case in which the application of vicarious liability has been challenged in an English court.' Note also Atiyah, *Vicarious liability*, p. 435.
[73] *Rowlands v Chief Constable of Merseyside Police* [2006] EWCA Civ 1773, [2007] 1 WLR 1065. See comment by H. Gow, 'A sorry tale', *New Law Journal*, 157 (2007), 164. See also the comments of Lord Hutton in *Kuddus* [2002] 2 AC 122 at para. 79.
[74] Contrast *New South Wales v Ibbett* [2006] HCA 57, (2007) 231 ALR 485 (vicarious liability) and *Blackwater v Plint* (2005) 258 DLR (4th) 275 (vicarious liability for exemplary damages rejected), discussed in more detail in Chapter 2.
[75] One notable source of this confusion lies in the judgments of the Court of Appeal in *Morris v Martin* [1966] 1 QB 716, relied upon by the House of Lords in *Lister v Hesley Hall Ltd* [2002] 1 AC 215. As will be discussed in later chapters, their Lordships in *Lister* demonstrated a surprising lack of clarity as to the division between primary and vicarious liability; most evident in the judgment of Lord Hobhouse (see, for example, at para. 57) but also in other judicial references to duties 'entrusted' or 'delegated' (see Lords Steyn, Clyde and Millett) – the terminology of non-delegable duties, not vicarious liability. The practical impact of this uncertainty will be addressed in detail in later chapters (notably in Chapter 6).

others in the absence of proof of fault on one's part. German law, in refusing to accept a general principle of vicarious liability, sought to retain an underlying basis of fault and to confine any such liability to specific instances governed by statute.[76] It is significant that, despite such intentions, German law today does recognise strict liability for the torts of others. As will be discussed in later chapters, it uses a variety of techniques to find such liability and the emphasis on fault has been dismissed as an 'embarrassment' and a 'mistake'. This example indicates clearly that there is a demand in any modern legal system for rules of vicarious liability and that fault will not, by itself, provide an adequate explanation for the compensatory structure of the law. Indeed, vicarious liability rests at the heart of the modern law of tort, despite its status as a cuckoo in the nest of corrective justice. It provides a solvent target for claims and, supported by the defendant's ability to insure or self-insure, is perceived as a means by which everyday risk may be spread within various sectors of society. Yet, notably in the common law world, it has been under-theorised. Eighteenth- and nineteenth-century judges troubled themselves little to provide an adequate explanation for the imposition of vicarious liability; Latin maxims helpfully filling a gap where such reasons might be required. In contrast, civil law has addressed the basis for liability for the acts of others, although, as will be seen, without necessarily finding an obvious solution or adopting a consistent approach. Whilst such concerns might be dismissed as those of an academic seeking conceptual nicety in a law which works perfectly well in practice, recent case law has highlighted the dangers of imprecision. Decisions such as *Lister v Hesley Hall Ltd*,[77] *Bazley v Curry*,[78] *New South Wales v Lepore*,[79] *S v Attorney-General*[80] and even civil law cases such as

---

[76] Indeed there is only one example of strict liability in the tort section of the BGB, namely § 833 BGB (liability of the animal keeper for animals: *Haftung des Tierhalters*): 'If a human being is killed by an animal or if the body or the health of a human being is injured by an animal or a thing is damaged by an animal, then the person who keeps the animal is liable to compensate the injured person for the damage arising from this.' Interestingly, even this Roman-based principle is restricted in the second paragraph to pets: 'Liability in damages does not apply if the damage is caused by a domestic animal intended to serve the occupation, economic activity or subsistence of the keeper of the animal and either the keeper of the animal in supervising the animal has exercised reasonable care or the damage would also have occurred even if this care had been exercised.'
[77] [2002] 1 AC 215 (UK). [78] (1999) 174 DLR (4th) 45 (Canada).
[79] (2003) 212 CLR 511; 195 ALR 412 (Australia). [80] [2003] 3 NZLR 450 (New Zealand).

l'affaire Blieck[81] in France demonstrate real uncertainty as to the scope of vicarious liability and the extent to which parties tangentially linked to the wrongful acts of another may find themselves liable to pay compensation to the victim. The modern view seems to be that insurance represents a universal panacea to the problem of funding full compensation to victims, without detailed consideration of how the parties liable are, without clear and discernible rules, to insure against a risk which is difficult, if not impossible, to determine with any great accuracy.

The next three chapters (2 to 6) will undertake a detailed study of the case law, noting how the doctrine is applied and to what extent the courts have adhered to particular policy reasons for imposing liability. Particular attention will be paid to recent case law and whether it is capable of giving guidance to future litigants. The final three chapters (7 to 9) will address concerns for the future development of the doctrine: the possibility of a specific common law head of parental liability, proposals for a harmonised European doctrine of vicarious liability and, fundamentally, the many and varied justifications for the doctrine and the extent to which they provide clear and credible explanations for the doctrine. The aim is to identify more clearly the nature and operation of the doctrine of vicarious liability across legal systems and, in so doing, enhance the reader's understanding of this vital component of the working mechanism of the modern law of tort.

---

[81] (*Association des centres éducatifs du Limousin et autre c/ Consorts Blieck*) Ass plén 29 March 1991 D 1991.324 note C. Larroumet, chr G. Viney p. 157, JCP 1991 II 21673, concl H. Dontenwille, note J. Ghestin.

2 Establishing a general framework for liability

2.1 Introduction

Before examining in detail the conditions for vicarious liability in modern legal systems, it is important, especially in a comparative study, to identify the basic legal framework for such claims. As stated in Chapter 1, the doctrine of vicarious liability, by which we mean strict liability for the *tortious acts* of another, possesses a similar legal framework whether derived from case law or code. This chapter will therefore examine the fundamental elements of any such claim and clarify the key terminology used, the role of fault and the extent to which the person held strictly liable may require the tortfeasor to indemnify him for compensation paid to the victim. It will conclude with a brief overview of the relationship between liability in tort for the wrongful acts of others and other areas of private law liability, such as contract and criminal law. This is particularly relevant in the context of civilian systems where the relationship between tort and other areas of private law may surprise common lawyers, who take for granted the existence of concurrent liability in contract and tort law, that public authorities should be subject to the ordinary principles of tort law, and that a clear division exists between criminal and civil liability. Whilst in all modern legal systems there is an obvious overlap between tort law and the provisions of social security and insurance law, an understanding of the structure of civilian systems will help the reader understand the legal developments described elsewhere in this book.

2.2 Identifying a general framework for liability

Using comparative analysis, a common framework may be identified across legal systems for imposing vicarious liability. Eörsi describes two basic types of solutions which have emerged under capitalist systems and which are represented in the three key systems (common law; Romanistic; Germanic) examined in this book. The first solution is that of strict liability: liability of the employer arising from the fact that the torts of the employee are committed in the course of employment (the common law and Romanistic model). The second model retains the centrality of fault: liability of the employer presumed to be at fault (the Germanic model including Germany, Switzerland and Austria).[1] In both these solutions, three common factors may be found: the need for a specific type of relationship, a wrongful act and that the victim is harmed in the course of a specific task or in the course of employment. Chapters 3 to 5 will examine the types of relationships giving rise to liability and Chapter 6 the scope of liability arising within the course of a task or employment. This chapter will focus on the role of fault as the trigger for liability, first identifying the terminology used in practice to identify vicarious liability and later the extent to which a right to indemnity still exists in modern law where the policy goals of employee protection and loss distribution via the person (usually the employer) most able to spread the losses has led many to question whether an employer (or his insurance company) *should* be able to recover damages paid from the errant employee. It will also address a peculiarly common law problem: should vicarious liability extend beyond liability for compensatory damages to include exemplary or punitive damages imposed in common law systems to punish the tortfeasor? While it might seem unjust to impose such damages on an employer, as we shall see, there are nevertheless policy arguments which indicate that vicarious liability should extend to all damages awarded in favour of the claimant.

2.2.1 Key terminology and codal provisions in English, French and German law

As stated in Chapter 1, 'vicarious liability'[2] is the term employed by the common law[3] and is used as shorthand throughout this book to signify strict liability for the tortious acts of others. At common law, vicarious liability has traditionally been described as the liability of the master for

---

[1] G. Eörsi, 'Private and governmental liability for the torts of employees and organs' in A. Tunc (chief ed.), *International encyclopedia of comparative law* (Tübingen: Mohr, 1983), vol. XI, ch. 4, para. 4–20.

[2] Although von Bar has criticised the term as inappropriate in that it suggests liability by agency rather than liability supplementing that of the original tortfeasor: C. von Bar, *A common European law of torts* (Oxford University Press, 1998), p. 337.

[3] However, note the continued use of 'agency' in the United States: see Restatement (3d) of Agency, § 7.01 Agent's Liability to Third Party.

his servants, although the terms 'employer/employee' are now more frequently used in practice.[4] The employment relationship provides the primary example of vicarious liability and, in holding an employer strictly liable for the torts of his employees acting in the course of their employment, the courts draw a fundamental distinction between the 'contract of service' (or employment) and the 'contract for services' (by which an independent contractor is hired to work for the employer). Only the former is capable of giving rise to vicarious liability. The distinction between the employer/employee relationship and that of employer and independent contractor thus represents a basic limitation on the scope of the doctrine of vicarious liability. As will be seen in Chapter 6, the doctrine is further confined to acts committed 'in the course of employment', although the common law courts continue to struggle to find a satisfactory test to determine when this has occurred.

It is noticeable that the common law focus on the employment relationship is not shared by continental civil codes which prefer less precise formulae. Article 1384 of the French Civil Code, in fact, contains a number of provisions which impose a form of strict liability, although in its original form only the liability of *commettants* (employers) could be described as vicarious liability.

Vicarious liability

- Article 1384(5): liability of employers for employees (absorbing that of masters and servants); and
- Article 1384(1): in recent years interpreted to impose liability for the wrongful acts[5] of others under one's organisation, management and control.

Strict liability for acts causing harm to others

- Article 1384(4): liability of father and mother, so far as they exercise parental authority, for acts of their minor children who live with them.

Presumed liability subject to proof that reasonable care would not have prevented the act in question[6]

- Article 1384(6) and (7): liability of craftsmen for their apprentices during the time when they are under their supervision.

---

[4] See *Mahmud v BCCI* [1998] AC 20 at 45.

[5] There is some debate as to the nature of the act required to give rise to liability under Article 1384(1): see 5.4.2.

[6] Article 1384(7) states that: '(Act of 5 April 1937). The above liability exists, unless the father and mother or the craftsmen prove that they could not prevent the act which gives rise to that liability.'

Parental liability, discussed in detail in Chapter 7, imposes the broadest form of liability. As a result of case law intervention,[7] liability under Article 1384(4), previously interpreted in the same manner as craftsmen liability under Article 1384(6), is now deemed to impose strict liability for all acts of children causing harm to others, subject only to proof of *force majeure* or contributory negligence. In view of this development, it has been questioned whether Article 1384(6) should now be interpreted similarly. Although there is no recent case law on this, a number of commentators suggest that craftsmen should likewise be held strictly liable subject to the defences of *force majeure* or fault of the victim.[8]

Teachers were also originally subject to the same regime as craftmen, that is, presumed liable for damage caused by their pupils during the time when they were under their supervision, unless they could prove under Article 1384(7) that the correct exercise of their duties of supervision would not have prevented the accident. However, the suicide of a schoolteacher (Leblanc) found liable under Article 1384, led to the *loi* of 20 July 1899 rendering the State liable in place of all public sector teachers, later replaced by the *loi* of 5 April 1937 which determined that *all* teachers could only be liable on proof of fault.[9] Article 1384(8) now states that 'As to teachers, the faults, imprudence or negligent conducts invoked against them as having caused the damaging act must be proved by the plaintiff at the trial, in accordance with the general law.'[10]

---

[7] Notably the *Bertrand* case of 1997 (Cass civ 2, 19 February 1997 Bull civ II N° 56 p. 32; Jurisclasseur Périodique, 1997 II 22848 concl R. Kessous, note G. Viney, D 1997.265 note P. Jourdain, chron 297 par Ch. Radé).

[8] See F. Terré, P. Simler and Y. Lequette, *Droit civil: les obligations*, 10th edn (Paris: Dalloz, 2009), N° 825 and, generally, C. Meyer-Royère, 'La responsabilité du fait des apprentis', *Les petites affiches*, 8 and 9 May 2000.

[9] It still remains the case that the State will be substituted as defendant for teachers in the public sector: see Terré, Simler and Lequette, *Droit civil*, N° 812 and Code of Education, Article L911-4. See, generally, V. P. Dabezies, 'La loi de 1937 et les orientations nouvelles en matière de responsabilité des membres de l'enseignement public', *Actualité Juridique–Droit Administratif* (1969), 391.

[10] Note other statutory limitations of liability, which form Articles 1384(2) and (3). Article 1384(2): '(Act of 7 Nov. 1922) However, a person who possesses, regardless of the basis thereof, all or part of a building or of movable property in which a fire has originated is not liable towards third parties for damages caused by that fire unless it is proved that the fire must be attributed to his fault or to the fault of persons for whom he is responsible.' Article 1384(3): '(Act of 7 Nov. 1922) This provision may not apply to the landlord and tenant relationship, which remains governed by Articles 1733 and 1734 of the Civil Code.'

Article 1384(1) is perhaps the most interesting provision. Originally treated as a general introductory provision – it simply states that 'A person is liable not only for the damages he causes by his own act, but also for that which is caused by the acts of persons for whom he is responsible, or by things which are in his custody' – it has, since 1991, been interpreted to provide for a general rule of liability for the acts of others. An active debate, which will be discussed at the end of Chapter 5, exists as to whether, logically, Article 1384(1) will ultimately absorb the other provisions to form one head of liability for the acts of others, although this has yet to occur.[11] At present, however, these provisions remain distinct and bear different characteristics.

In terms of vicarious liability, the main provision is still that of Article 1384(5), despite the recent growth of case law under Article 1384(1). In the original version of the 1804 Code, only this provision imposed truly strict liability, that is, without any possibility of rebuttal on proof of absence of fault.[12] Bertrand de Greuille, writing in 1803, justified this result by virtue of the fact that employers would be acting in pursuit of profit and must be deemed to have wrongfully placed confidence in employees who have harmed others.[13] In determining liability, Article 1384(5) focuses on the relationship between the '*commettant*' and his '*préposé*' who is acting in the functions for which he has been employed.

Article 1384(5) thus provides:

Masters and employers [will be strictly liable] for the damage caused by their servants[14] and employees in the functions for which they have been employed.

Les maîtres et les commettants [sont responsables] du dommage causé par leurs domestiques et préposés dans les fonctions auxquelles ils les ont employés.

As will be seen in Chapter 6, the term '*les fonctions auxquelles ils les ont employés*' has proved difficult to interpret in practice. For the moment, it is worthwhile highlighting that the terms '*commettant*' and '*préposé*',

---

[11] See, for example, M. Josselin-Gall, 'La responsabilité du fait d'autrui sur le fondement de l'article 1384, alinéa 1. Une théorie générale est-elle possible?' JurisClasseur Périodique (JCP) 2000.1.2011.

[12] See Ch. Radé, *JurisClasseur responsibilité civile et assurances*, Fasc 143: *Droit à réparation – responsabilité du fait d'autrui – domaine: responsabilité des commettants* (Paris: LexisNexis, 2007), who remarks, at para. 1, on the remarkable longevity of this provision.

[13] Bertrand de Greuille, *rapporteur* to the *Tribunat*, also reported in P. A. Fenet, *Recueil complet des travaux préparatoires du code civil* (1827) (Osnabrück: O. Zeller, 1968), vol. XIII, p. 476.

[14] The master/servant relationship is now deemed to be included in that of *commettant/préposé* and will therefore not be considered independently.

which can be translated as 'principal' and 'employee',[15] expressly indicate that the relationships under Article 1384(5) are not confined to the employer/employee relationship, but may extend to other relationships where one party is employed to undertake certain functions on behalf of another. On this basis, the terms '*commettant*' and '*préposé*' will be used throughout this book. The German Civil Code of 1896, additionally, utilises more generic terms than that of employer and employee in its provision for vicarious agents carrying out a task for another (*Haftung für den Verrichtungsgehilfen*). § 831(1) provides:

A person who uses another person to perform a task is liable to make compensation for the damage that the other unlawfully inflicts on a third party when carrying out the task. Liability in damages does not apply if the principal exercises reasonable care when selecting the person deployed and, to the extent that he is to procure devices or equipment or to manage the business activity, in the procurement or management, or if the damage would have occurred even if this care had been exercised.

(1): *Wer einen anderen zu einer Verrichtung bestellt, ist zum Ersatz des Schadens verpflichtet, den der andere in Ausführung der Verrichtung einem Dritten widerrechtlich zufügt. Die Ersatzpflicht tritt nicht ein, wenn der Geschäftsherr bei der Auswahl der bestellten Person und, sofern er Vorrichtungen oder Gerätschaften zu beschaffen oder die Ausführung der Verrichtung zu leiten hat, bei der Beschaffung oder der Leitung die im Verkehr erforderliche Sorgfalt beobachtet oder wenn der Schaden auch bei Anwendung dieser Sorgfalt entstanden sein würde.*

The use of terminology in civilian systems is revealing. While all systems adopt loose definitions as to the scope of the doctrine (course of employment/functions for which they are employed/when carrying out the task), the relationship giving rise to liability is tightly defined in the common law, whereas civilian systems have chosen to utilise broader terms, such as '*commettant/préposé*' and '*Geschäftsherr/Verrichtungsgehilfe*', which indicate that liability will not be confined to the employment contract. As will be seen in Chapter 5, the common law approach has rendered it difficult to extend the doctrine of vicarious liability outside the employment context in the absence of express statutory provision. Judges, attempting to do so by invoking instead the doctrine of agency, have left confusion in their wake. It should not be thought, however, that the more flexible language of the civil law renders the contract of employment less important in this context. As will be seen in Chapter 3,

---

[15] But note that the term '*employé*' is not used.

the contract of employment continues to provide the primary example of liability under Article 1384(5) and § 831.

2.2.2 The requirement of a wrongful act

This requirement lies at the heart of the doctrine of vicarious liability: liability will not arise unless the victim can prove the commission of a specific tort, for example negligence or trespass to the person.[16] As stated by the House of Lords in *Crédit Lyonnais Bank Nederland NV (now Generale Bank Nederland NV) v Export Credits Guarantee Department*,[17] the common law doctrine of vicarious liability demands that the wrong committed by the employee (for which the employer would be held liable) constitutes an actionable tort which occurs in the course of the employee's employment. It will not suffice that a tort may only be proved if combined with other acts which were not performed in the course of his employment. Equally, if the employee has a valid defence – for example, that the defaulting employee would have been able to raise the defence of *volenti non fit injuria*[18] – vicarious liability will not arise.[19] Similarly in France, liability under Article 1384(5) has traditionally arisen for the faults of employees, although it is not expressly required in the wording of Article 1384(5).[20] The claimant must therefore show the existence of a wrongful act satisfying Articles 1382 or 1383 (intentional fault or negligence).[21] If he cannot establish that the employee

---

[16] See Lord Morton in *Staveley Iron and Chemical Co. v Jones* [1956] AC 627 at 639: 'what the court has to decide in the present case is: Was the crane driver negligent? If the answer is "Yes," the employer is liable vicariously for the negligence of his servant. If the answer is "No," the employer is surely under no liability at all.'

[17] [2000] 1 AC 486.

[18] See *Imperial Chemical Industries Ltd v Shatwell* [1965] AC 656.

[19] In contrast, however, a mere procedural bar to an action against the employee personally will not bar vicarious liability: see *Osborn v Gillett* (1873) LR 8 Exch 88; *Broom v Morgan* [1953] 1 QB 597.

[20] Article 1384(5) provides only that 'Masters and employers [are liable] for the damage caused by their servants and employees in the functions for which they have been employed.' The requirement can be traced back to a decision of the *chambre des Requêtes* of 1866: Cass req 19 February 1866 S 1866.1.214.

[21] It is less likely that an employee will be held liable for injuries due to objects under the defendant's control (based on Article 1384(1)) as the employer, not the employee, is likely to be found to have ultimate control over the object: see M.-A. Péano, 'L'incompatabilité entre les qualités de gardien et de préposé' D 1991 chron 51, Civ 30 December 1936 DP 1937.1.5. rapp L. Josserand, note R. Savatier, and Civ 5 December 1990 Bull civ II N° 257, p. 132, Revue trimestrielle de droit civil 1991.348 obs P. Jourdain. See, generally, G. Viney, 'La responsabilité personnelle du préposé' in P. Conte et al. (eds.), *Mélanges Lapoyade-Deschamps* (University of Bordeaux, 2003), pp. 83ff.

would be personally liable, for example there is an unforeseeable and unpreventable external event (*cause étrangère*) (that is, an act of God, act of a third party or the victim himself), then the employer cannot be held liable.[22] Where, however, only contributory negligence may be shown by the victim, the *commettant* will remain partially liable.[23]

In Germany, however, the fault in question is that of the employer, not the employee. § 831 BGB provides that the employer is presumed to be at fault when his employees unlawfully inflict harm on a third party when carrying out their duties unless he can show otherwise. Proof of intentional or unintentional fault by the employee (*Verschulden*) is not required,[24] although it must still be shown that the employee has unlawfully caused harm to the victim (requirement of *Rechtswidrigkeit*).[25] In practice, however, concern has been expressed that an innocent act which harms another might give rise to liability. The modern approach is to require some form of wrongful conduct, such that lack of reasonable care should be seen as part of 'unlawfulness' itself.[26] The decision of the Great Senate in 1957 considered the application of this theory in the context of the presumption of fault under § 831.[27] Here, the claimant had fallen whilst trying to board a tram and had been run over by a car. It was unclear whether the accident had been caused by the fault of the driver and the conductor of the tram, or was simply due to the

---

[22] Civ 1, 11 December 1974 D 1975 IR 67, Cass civ 2, 13 November 1992 Resp civ et assur 1993 comm 110.

[23] See, generally, Ch. Radé, *JurisClasseur responsabilité civile et assurances*, Fasc 143, *Droit à réparation – responsabilité du fait d'autrui – domaine: responsabilité des commettants* (Paris: LexisNexis, 2007) at paras. 56–9.

[24] Proof of fault by the employee will, however, lead to joint and several liability with the employer: see § 840: '(1) If more than one person is responsible for damage arising from a tort, then they are jointly and severally liable. (2) If besides the person who is obliged to make compensation for damage caused by another person under §§ 831 and 832 the other person is also responsible for the damage, then in their internal relationship the other is obliged alone, and in the case specified in § 829 the person with a duty of supervision is obliged alone.' All translations of the BGB are taken from the German Ministry of Justice website: www.gesetze-im-internet.de/englisch_bgb/englisch_bgb.html

[25] Defined by Markesinis as 'the violation of a legal norm in the absence of a legally recognized excuse': B. S. Markesinis and H. Unberath, *The German law of torts: a comparative treatise* (Oxford: Hart, 2002), p. 79. Such norms are set out in §§ 823(I) and (II) and 826.

[26] See Markesinis and Unberath, *German law of torts*, p. 81. Although this seems to merge the requirements of 'unlawfulness' and 'fault', it is argued that *Verschulden* remains distinct, signifying the imputation of fault.

[27] BGH (GS) 4.3.57 BGHZ 24, 21 NJW 1957, 785: the *Straßenbahn* case (translated in Markesinis and Unberath, *German law of torts*, pp. 778–83).

carelessness of the claimant. The Sixth Civil Senate was reluctant to accept that an employee acted unlawfully merely on evidence that harm had been caused to the victim without proof that the employee had acted in an objectively irregular way. On this basis, an act would only be unlawful if the claimant had shown an infringement of his legally protected rights and the employer was unable to prove that the employee had acted correctly in the circumstances (here conforming to road traffic rules). If the employer could not prove this, he would then be required to rebut the presumption of fault under § 831. Such reasoning has quite rightly been described as 'convoluted',[28] but demonstrates the ongoing influence of fault within the German system.

The fault requirement – be it the presumed fault of the employer in a fault-based system or the fault of the 'employee' in a strict liability system – is thus the basic trigger for liability. Nevertheless, it has not gone unchallenged. If, as will be discussed in Chapter 8, one chooses to justify the imposition of vicarious liability by reason of the level of risk created by the defendant's enterprise or simply its deeper pockets, why should liability be confined to acts which amount to torts or give rise to delictual liability? In reality, the commission of tort requirement is a condition limiting the application of the doctrine. To extend the defendant's burden beyond tortious acts to any harmful acts is a step which the common law courts have not been prepared to take. However, French law, in recent years, has shown a greater willingness to contemplate such an extension of liability. In the 1968 reform of the French Civil Code, the legislator rendered mentally handicapped persons liable in tort even in the absence of proof of subjective fault,[29] thus signifying recognition of the need to impose liability on the basis of objective risk rather than personal fault. More significantly, parental liability for the acts of their children under Article 1384(4)[30] was in 1984 extended to *all*

---

[28] Ibid., p. 699. See also B. Kupisch 'Die Haftung für Verrichtungsgehilfen', Juristische Schulung (JuS) [1984], 250. W. van Gerven, J. Lever and P. Larouche, *Tort law: ius commune casebooks for the common law of Europe* (Oxford: Hart, 2000), p. 485, note that despite criticism by commentators, the test was confirmed in 1996 (BGH 12 July 1996 NJW 1996, 3205 at 3207).

[29] Article 489–2: 'A person who has caused damage to another when he was under the influence of a mental disorder is nonetheless liable to compensation.' All translations are taken from *Légifrance*: www.legifrance.gouv.fr. See G. Viney, Revue trimestrielle de droit civil (RTD civ.) 1970.263 and J.-J. Burst, JCP, 1970 I 2307 N° 51.

[30] Article 1384(4): The father and mother, in so far as they exercise 'parental authority', are jointly and severally liable for the damage caused by their minor children who live with them.

harmful acts, regardless of the inability of the child to appreciate that the act in question was wrongful.[31] As discussed in Chapter 7, the French Supreme Court found Article 1384(4) to be satisfied on proof that the child, living with his parents, had committed an act which was the direct cause of the damage suffered by the victim. Such developments have led some commentators to question whether it should still be necessary under Article 1384(5) to require proof of a fault by the person for whom the defendant is held liable.[32] Such arguments are consistent with greater acceptance that those responsible for the creation of risks should bear the consequences of any harmful acts which result.[33] Nevertheless, there remains resistance to such a step; understandably as it would require a willingness to extend liability radically. In the 2005 proposals to reform the French Civil Code,[34] it was suggested that the fault requirement should be retained and, indeed, reimposed in relation to parental liability for children.[35] The fault requirement was reaffirmed by the French Supreme Court in 2004[36] and would therefore seem unlikely to disappear in the near future.

2.2.3 The right to an indemnity

Although vicarious liability renders one party strictly liable for the torts of another, this does not signify that the person at fault is not personally liable. Vicarious liability *supplements* this liability, giving the victim a

---

[31] Ass plén 9 May 1984 D 1984.525 concl J. Cabannes, note F. Chabas, JCP, 1984 II 20255 note N. Dejean de la Bâtie.

[32] See, for example, M. Billiau, JCP, 2000 II 10295, but *contra* P. Jourdain, RTD civ. 2000.584, H. Capitant, F. Terré and Y. Lequette, *Les grands arrêts de la jurisprudence civile*, 12th edn (Paris: Dalloz, 2008), vol. II at 491.

[33] See, notably, the extension of Article 1384(1) to impose strict liability more generally on persons controlling the acts of others, discussed in Chapter 5: (*l'affaire* Blieck (*Association des centres éducatifs du Limousin et autre c/ Consorts Blieck*) Ass plén 29 March 1991 D 1991.324 note C. Larroumet, chr G. Viney p. 157, JCP 1991 II 21673, concl H. Dontenwille, note J. Ghestin).

[34] P. Catala, *Avant-projet de réforme du droit des obligations et de la prescription* (Paris: La Documentation française, 2006). The report was presented to the Minister of Justice by the President of the Reform Commission, Professor Pierre Catala in September 2005. The project is also sometimes referred to as the *Avant-projet Catala*.

[35] Article 1355-2 proposes that liability should rest 'on proof of an action of a kind which would attract liability in a person who caused the harm directly', thereby reversing the case law applicable to parents and children (translation by S. Whittaker and J. Cartwright: www.justice.gouv.fr/art_pix/rapportcatatla0905-anglais.pdf).

[36] See Civ 2 8 April 2004 D 2004.2601 note Y.-M. Serinet, JCP 2004 II 10131 note Imbert, RTD civ. 2004.517 obs P. Jourdain, Civ 2 21 October 2004 D 2005.40 note J.-B. Laydu (liability under Article 1384(1)).

choice of defendants, who are together held jointly and severally liable.[37] It is a doctrine for the benefit of victims and, therefore, the person at fault must answer personally if sued directly. Correspondingly, the innocent party held vicariously liable may seek an indemnity from the wrongdoer to cover any damages paid out on his account.

Yet, this framework, which underlies the common law and civilian strict liability systems, must be examined in the light of the most common manifestation of vicarious liability: that of employer for the torts of his employees. Vicarious liability permits the victim to sue the employer, who will usually be insured and of greater means than the employee. In turn, the employer (or his insurer under the doctrine of subrogation) is entitled to bring an indemnity claim against the employee tortfeasor to recover the damages paid.[38] This, in the words of Finnemore J, is consistent with the demands of corrective justice: 'Justice, as we conceive justice in these courts, requires that the person who caused the damage is the person who must in law be called on to pay damages arising therefrom.'[39] Otherwise a negligent employee will be free from responsibility for his actions.[40]

In modern times, there are both practical and conceptual reasons to question the use of the indemnity in the employer/employee context. An employee, whom the victim may have elected not to sue due to lack of means, is unlikely to have the means to indemnify the employer. In practice, an employer is most likely simply to dismiss the employee as unfit for his position.[41] Equally, concerns as to employment relations may suggest that it would be unwise to pursue individual employees for negligence;[42] such liability also being inconsistent with the protection

---

[37] See, for example, Civil Liability (Contribution) Act 1978 (UK); Negligence Act, RSBC 1996, c. 333, section 4 (British Columbia).

[38] The leading common law case is *Lister v Romford Ice and Cold Storage Co.* [1957] AC 555 (indemnity based here on the ground that the employee has breached an implied term in the contract of employment to use reasonable care and skill). See also § 401, US Restatement (2nd) of Agency: 'An agent is subject to liability for loss caused to the principal by any breach of duty.' The right to an indemnity appears to be long established in the common law: see *Green v New River Co.* (1792) 4 TR 589, 100 ER 1192 and *Miller v Falconer* (1808) 1 Camp 251, 170 ER 947 (although the issue was competence of witnesses) and *Ryan v Fildes* [1938] 3 All ER 517.

[39] *Semtex v Gladstone* [1954] 2 All ER 206 at 212.

[40] See J. A. Jolowicz, 'Right to indemnity between master and servant', *Cambridge Law Journal*, 14 (1956), 101–111 at 101, who advises that such liability could be funded by the employers taking out a policy covering their employees and giving the employees the benefit of the policy.

[41] See Eörsi, *Private and governmental liability*, para. 4–115.

[42] *Morris v Ford Motor Co. Ltd* [1973] QB 792 at 798 per Lord Denning MR.

of employees in the labour law context. Further, it fails to pay sufficient regard to the actual insurance position. Employers will generally take out insurance to cover themselves for liability arising from their employees' actions. In reality, it will be the insurance company, not the employer, which is seeking to bring an action against the employee in the employer's name via the doctrine of subrogation.

Two primary means have been utilised to limit the application of the indemnity in practice: first, by confining the insurers' subrogation rights to intentional misconduct, and, secondly, the more radical means of preventing the victim or employer from pursuing an employee in the absence of intentional misconduct. As will be seen, the tension continues to exist between making a tortious employee accountable for his personal misconduct and broader social goals of victim protection and relieving employees from undue financial burdens when they are acting in the course of their employment.

2.2.3.1 Limiting the indemnity right: employers and insurers

Most modern legal systems have sought to find a means to limit the ability of the employer's insurance company to enforce this indemnity. In England and Wales, this was achieved by informal means. The *Lister v Romford Ice and Cold Storage Co.* decision of 1957[43] had provoked concern when an insurance company, contrary to the employer's wishes, had pursued a negligent employee to recover monies paid under the employer's insurance policy.[44] Glanville Williams, commenting on the decision, highlighted its consequences: 'It follows that the friendliest relation between the employer and his staff can now be disrupted, and the employee impoverished, by the action of an insurance company, which finds itself in the happy position of having received premiums for a risk that it does not have to bear.'[45] In response, an inter-departmental committee was set up by the Minister of Labour in 1957. In its 1959 report, it rejected the option of legislative reform in favour of evidence of voluntary agreement in the insurance sector restricting when insurers would enforce the indemnity.[46] English law therefore chose to

---

[43] [1957] AC 555.
[44] Although Jolowicz found it to have the 'wholesome' effect of rendering the employee liable as much as anyone else for the damage he caused by his negligent conduct: see Jolowicz, 'Right to indemnity' p. 111.
[45] G. Williams, 'Vicarious liability and the master's indemnity', *Modern Law Review*, 20 (1957), 220 at 221.
[46] See G. Gardiner, 'Report of committees', *Modern Law Review*, 22 (1959), 652.

rely on the 'gentleman's agreement' reached between employers' liability insurers not to pursue actions against employees, except where there has been evidence of collusion or wilful misconduct.[47] This solution has not commended itself to all commentators; Lord Gardiner remarking that 'it may be doubted whether on general grounds this rather peculiar method of law reform should be encouraged',[48] but survives to this day. *Morris v Ford Motor Co.*,[49] however, highlights the limits of this agreement, which did not apply to a third party firm of cleaners bound by contract to indemnify the employer.[50] Australia, in contrast, has introduced legislation to this effect; the Insurance Contracts Act 1984 (Cth), section 66, putting the gentleman's agreement into statutory form.[51] Equally in France from the 1930s, the insurers' ability to pursue the employee has been limited, save in cases of *'malveillance'*[52] (*malveillance* being

---

[47] Details of the agreement are set out in *Morris v Ford Motor Co. Ltd* [1973] QB 792.

[48] Gardiner, 'Report of committees', 656. See also R. Lewis, 'Insurers' agreements not to enforce strict legal rights: bargaining with government and in the shadow of the law', *Modern Law Review*, 48 (1985), 275, 281–2, who warns at 291 that 'Regulation by informal agreement with trade associations inevitably has fewer teeth than legislative control, which places responsibility directly upon the individual companies and for which the sanctions in the event of default are more apparent and more likely to be enforced.'

[49] [1973] QB 792.

[50] The majority of the Court of Appeal nevertheless, either on the basis of equity or an implied term, succeeded in avoiding the application of the indemnity on the facts of this case in circumstances where (per James LJ at 815) '[t]heir agreement was operative in an industrial setting in which subrogation of the third party to the rights and remedies of the defendants against their employees would be unacceptable and unrealistic'. See also *Harvey v O'Dell* [1958] 2 QB 78 (*Lister* distinguished on the somewhat questionable ground that the act in question was in the course of employment, but not a duty for which he was employed (here storekeeper involved in motorcycle accident)). The *Lister* implied term, additionally, does not apply where the employer is guilty of negligence (*Jones v Manchester Corpn* [1952] 2 QB 852), although, in such circumstances, the Civil Liability (Contribution) Act 1978 would apply.

[51] Section 66 provides that 'Where: (a) the rights of an insured under a contract of general insurance in respect of a loss are exercisable against a person who is the insured's employee; and (b) the conduct of the employee that gave rise to the loss occurred in the course of or arose out of the employment and was not serious or wilful misconduct; the insurer does not have the right to be subrogated to the rights of the insured against the employee.' ('Subrogation to rights against employees', Act No. 80 of 1984 as amended, discussed in *Boral Resources (Qld) Pty Ltd v Pyke* (1989) 93 ALR 89). Note also section 65 of the Insurance Contracts Act 1984 which further restricts the right of subrogation in relation to persons whom the insured might not have pursued due to a familial or personal relationship or where the third party causing the damage is not insured.

[52] Art 36(3) of *loi* 13 July 1930 (now L 121–12(3), *Code des assurances*): 'Notwithstanding the above provisions, the insurer shall have no recourse against the children, descendants, ascendants, relations in direct line, officials, employees, workers or servants and in

defined by insurance law as an intentional act committed against the insured, that is, an act intended to harm the insured).[53] There seems, therefore, to be a body of authority that insurance companies should not be permitted to 'have their cake (or premium) and eat it', and that in the interests of good industrial relations, such claims should be confined to circumstances where the conduct of the employee is so serious that he does not merit any such protection.

2.2.3.2 Protecting the employee from any claims in the absence of intentional misconduct

It is a more drastic step to prevent both victim and employer from bringing an action against the errant employee. The rationale is no longer simply that of industrial relations, but, more fundamentally, the notions of risk and loss distribution underlying vicarious liability in relation to accidents in the workplace. Faced with an insured employer and an insurance company accepting premiums to cover accidents caused by employees, it has been questioned whether it can be just and equitable to require employees to share the risks of accidents arising in the workplace.[54] The influence of this argument is most notable in the current French position,[55] but it is possible to identify some common law support for such ideas. In Australia, a number of States have legislated to abolish the indemnity itself and render the employer solely liable in certain circumstances.[56] Equally, in the

---

general any person normally living in the insured's home, except in the case of "*malveillance*" committed by one of such persons.'

[53] Cass ass plén 13 November 1987: Bull ass plén N° 5. In the employer/employee context, this is unlikely to be the case.

[54] For an early exponent of this view, see R. Steffen, 'The employers' "indemnity" action', *University of Chicago Law Review*, 25 (1957–8), 465.

[55] Note also the position of German law discussed in Markesinis and Unberath, *The German law of torts*, pp. 701, 705–9, in which recourse against the employee for a contribution or indemnity is equally limited, and, further, labour law has intervened to give the negligent employee, under certain circumstances, a right of indemnity against the employer when the conduct is sufficiently linked to his employment. As they comment (at p. 701), this is the very reverse of the situation arising in the common law.

[56] See Employees Liability Act 1991 (NSW), section 3 (but not where there is serious and wilful misconduct, or the tort did not occur in the course of, and did not arise out of, the employment of the employee) and Civil Liability Act 1936 (South Australia), section 59 (save where a person commits serious and wilful misconduct in the course of his employment and that misconduct constitutes a tort). Both sections render the employer liable to indemnify the employee in respect of liability incurred by the employee for the tort (unless the employee is otherwise entitled to an indemnity in respect of that liability).

United States, all government employees acting within the scope of their employment are protected from personal liability.[57] In Canada, La Forest J, in his powerful dissenting judgment in *London Drugs Ltd v Kuehne & Nagel International Ltd* discussing the theoretical foundations of vicarious liability, asserted that:

> In my view, not only is the elimination of the possibility of the employee bearing the loss logically compatible with the vicarious liability regime, it is practically compelled by the developing logic of that regime. In our modern economy, an employee's capacity to cause loss does not bear any relation to his salary... The employer will almost always be insured against the risk of being held liable to third parties by reason of his vicarious liability: the cost of such liability is thus internalized to the profitable activity that gives rise to it. There is no requirement for double insurance, covering both the employee and his employer against the same risk. Shifting the loss to the employee, either by permitting a customer to act against the employee or by permitting the employer to claim an indemnity against the employee, upsets the policy foundation of vicarious liability.[58]

Despite such arguments, such a view has not generally found favour in Canada,[59] or across common law jurisdictions. However, it has met a far warmer reception by the French courts.

In France, until the 1990s,[60] it was generally accepted that, although not expressly stated in Article 1384(5), the *commettant* would 'guarantee' the liabilities of the *préposé*, that is, would be strictly liable for damages, but with a right of indemnity[61] against the *préposé* himself.[62] In this way, innocent victims would be able to obtain compensation, whilst the employee would be answerable to his employer for his fault. In practice, this indemnity was rarely exercised, notably due to L121-12(3) of the Insurance Code mentioned above.

---

[57] Federal Tort Claims Act, 28 USC §§ 2671-80 (see also comparable State statutes). If the employee was acting within the scope of his employment, upon proper certification, the United States is to be substituted as defendant for the common law torts of its federal employees: 28 USC § 2679(d)(2).

[58] [1992] 3 SCR 299, (1993) 97 DLR (4th) 261 at 284.

[59] See L. Klar, *Tort Law*, 4th edn (Toronto: Carswell, 2008), p. 648.

[60] For earlier criticism of the treatment of employees committing merely ordinary acts of negligence in the course of their employment, see M.-T. Rives-Lange, 'Contribution à l'étude de la responsabilité des maîtres et commettants', JCP 1970.1.2309.

[61] The *action récursoire* (action for indemnity).

[62] G. Viney and P. Jourdain, *Traité de droit civil: les conditions de la responsabilité*, 3rd edn (Paris: LGDJ, 2006), N° 808.

However, in the 1990s, the idea of risk and loss distribution as an underlying reason for vicarious liability became increasingly influential, leading some commentators to question the indemnity.[63] The existence of the indemnity also contrasted with the position in labour law, which would only render the employee liable to the employer in cases of serious misconduct (*faute lourde*).[64] The influence of public law additionally appears particularly significant in this development.[65] Public sector employees are subject to a separate system of law in France with its own court structure and legal provisions. It is well established that a State employee will *not* be held personally responsible if he commits a '*faute de service*' (fault in service).[66] The State alone will be liable. Only where the employee has committed a '*faute personnelle*' (a serious personal fault) will he be rendered personally liable.[67]

From 1993,[68] the civil law courts moved towards reducing the employee's potential for liability in tort. This cumulated in 2000 in the (in)famous *Costedoat* case, which stated that a *préposé*, acting within the limits of the task assigned to him by the *commettant*, would no longer be liable to the third party victim.[69] This goes one step further than limiting the employer's indemnity and blocks a claim by the victim

---

[63] See ibid., 'the liability of the *commettant* is a means by which to attribute to the enterprise the risks which the actions of the *préposé* have created in its service' (my translation).

[64] See Radé, *Jurisclasseur responsabilité*, paras. 61 and 73.

[65] See B. Puill, 'Les fautes du préposé: s'inspirer de certaines solutions du droit administratif', JCP G 1996 I 3939.

[66] See M. Paillet, *Jurisclasseur administratif*, Fasc 818: *faute de service* (Paris: LexisNexis, 2008). See T. confl., 30 July 1873 (*l'affaire, Pelletier*): Rec. CE, p. 117; DP 1874, 3, p. 5, concl. David, n° 2). This signifies that the victim will almost always be assured of compensation from the administration.

[67] J. Waline, *Droit administratif*, 22nd edn (Paris: Dalloz, 2008), paras. 507–11, discussed in more detail at the end of this chapter.

[68] *l'arrêt Rochas* (Com 12 October 1993 Bull civ IV N° 338; D 1994.124 note G. Viney, JCP 1995 II 22493 note F. Chabas, Def 1994.812 obs J.-L. Aubert, RTD civ. 1994.111 obs P. Jourdain), although doubts were expressed at the time as to its scope: see Chabas's note.

[69] '*que n'engage pas sa responsabilité du préposé à l'égard des tiers le préposé qui agit sans excéder les limites de la mission qui lui a été impartie par son commettant*': Cass ass plén, 25 February 2000 Bull Ass plén N° 2; JCP 2000 II 10295 concl R. Kessous, note M. Billiau; JCP 2000 I 241, p. 1244 obs G. Viney, D 2000.673 note Ph. Brun and somm 467 obs Ph. Delebecque; RTD civ. 2000.582 obs P. Jourdain. After some doubts (Civ 1 13 November 2002 Bull civ 1 No 263, D 2003.580 note S. Deis-Beauquesne; JCP 2003 II 10096 note M. Billiau), the Cour de cassation expressed its willingness to allow salaried doctors and midwives to take advantage of this principle: Civ 1 9 November 2004 Bull civ 1 N° 262; D 2005.253 note F. Chabas; JCP 2005 II 10020 rapp D. Duval-Arnould, note S. Porchy-Simon, RTD civ. 2005.143 obs P. Jourdain. See C. Riot, 'L'exercise "subordonné" de l'art médical' D 2006 chron 111.

himself. In so doing, the French Supreme Court in 2000 brought the civil jurisdiction in line with the solution already reached in public law: unless the employee commits a *faute personnelle*, he will not be personally liable and the victim may only bring an action against the employer.

The 2000 *Costedoat* decision would appear to mark a firm step away from the perception of employer as mere guarantor towards the notion of employer as the bearer of the social risk of employment. In confirming that in future, in the absence of *faute personnelle*, the employer will bear the burden of liability, the court accepted the arguments of risk-based liability: the employer should bear the risk of the employee's tort and compensate for any consequential harm he causes (such losses to be borne via the mechanism of insurance). This does not mean, however, that there is no requirement of fault to trigger liability under Article 1384(5) – recent case law has shown that *Costedoat* acts as a procedural bar to claims against the employee, but does not abolish the requirement of fault.[70] Yet, some commentators have expressed concern as to where this leaves one of the key justifications of vicarious liability: the protection of innocent victims. What happens if, as in *Costedoat* itself, the employee is sued because the employer is insolvent and no insurance cover exists? In such circumstances, French law now reduces the protection of victims.[71] The recent reform proposals for the French civil code suggest a possible compromise.[72] Article 1359–1 provides that:

> Employees who, without committing an intentional fault, have acted within the limits of their functions, for purposes which conform to their roles and without disobeying their employers' orders, cannot incur personal liability towards their victims unless the latter on their side establish their inability to obtain reparation for their harm from the employer or his insurer.[73]

On this basis, the employees' personal liability is subsidiary to that of the employer and can be invoked should the employers' 'guarantee' fail. Victim protection is thus reasserted as the primary goal of

---

[70] See Civ 1 12 July 2007 Bull civ 2007 I N° 270; JCP 2008 I 125 obs P. Stoffel-Munck.

[71] M. Fabre-Magnan, *Droit des Obligations, 2 Responsabilité civile et quasi-contrats* (Paris: PUF, 2007), N° 130: 'Cette jurisprudence semble ainsi marquer un retrait par rapport à l'objectif de garantie des victimes qui semblait jusque-là le seul guide de l'évolution du droit de la responsabilité civile.'

[72] See n. 34.

[73] For translation, see www.justice.gouv.fr/art_pix/rapportcatatla0905-anglais.pdf. See also RTD civ. 2000.582 obs P. Jourdain and G. Durry, 'Plaidoyer pour une révision de la jurisprudence Costedoat (ou: une hérésie facile à abjurer) in D. Mazeaud (ed.) *Mélanges Gobert* (Paris: Economica, 2004) p. 495 at pp. 549ff.

liability, whilst, in the view of the reformers, ensuring sufficient protection for employees.[74]

There remains, however, the problem of defining the key limit on the employee's immunity: *'faute personnelle'*.[75] It is not defined in *Costedoat* and subsequent case law has yet to establish a clear definition.[76] The notion is not clear in public law and it remains a matter of contention in civil law. A 2001 decision found that where the employee has deliberately committed a criminal act, even under the orders of his employer, he remains liable.[77] This has led commentators to conclude that the personal liability of the employee will depend not only on the relationship of the acts with his employment, but also the nature and seriousness of the acts in question.[78] The position remains uncertain.

The right of indemnity thus raises many of the issues which render vicarious liability controversial: the role of fault, the protection of the vulnerable, and the extent to which modern legal systems deem it *just* that employers should be required to absorb risks associated with workplace accidents. A number of comments may be made. First, the attempts outlined above which protect the tortfeasor from indemnity claims arise in the employment context. Consistent with developments

---

[74] Catala, *Avant-projet de réforme*, at p. 180.
[75] See I. Gallmeister, 'L'incidence de la faute du préposé sur la responsabilité de son commettant', *Gazette du Palais* (18–20 Sept 2005), doctr. 8.
[76] See J. Mouly, 'Quelle faute pour la responsabilité civile du salarié?' D 2006 chron 2756 and E. Ayissi Manga, 'Préposé et responsabilité' Revue de la Recherche Juridique (RRJ) 2002-2, 715, spéc.
[77] *L'arrêt Cousin*: Ass plén 14 December 2001 Bull Ass plén N° 17; JCP 2002 II 10026 note M. Billiau, JCP 2002 I 124 N° 7 par G. Viney, D 2002.1230 note J. Julien and somm 1317 obs D. Mazeaud, RTD civ. 2002.109 obs P. Jourdain. See also Crim 7 April 2004 Bull crim N° 94; D 2004 IR 1563 (all the elements of the criminal offence must be shown, but it is not necessary that the criminal court imposes its own sanction). In 2006, this was extended to unintentional criminal acts satisfying Article 121-3 of the Criminal Code (i.e. the deliberate endangering of others, and recklessness, negligence, or failure to observe an obligation of due care or precaution imposed by any statute or regulation, where it is established that the offender has failed to show normal diligence, taking into consideration where appropriate the nature of his role or functions, of his capacities and powers and of the means then available to him), here involuntary homicide: Crim 28 March 2006 Bull crim N° 91; JCP 2006 II 10188 note J. Mouly; RTD civ. 2007.135 obs P. Jourdain.
[78] Fabre-Magnan, *Droit des Obligations*, N° 130. Note, however, recent case law which suggests that a criminal act or *'faute intentionnelle'* will render the employee personally liable, which suggests an extension of the employee's personal liability: see Civ 2 20 December 2007 Bull civ 2007 II N° 274; D 2008.1248 note J. Mouly and Civ 2 21 February 2008 Resp civ et assur 2008 comm 124 note H. Groutel; D 2008.2125 note J.-B. Laydu; JCP 2008 I 186 obs P. Stoffel-Munck.

elsewhere to protect employees, many legal systems have sought to limit employee exposure to compensatory claims arising in the course of employment and, importantly, in the absence of intentional misconduct. Moreover, all systems demonstrate that, in practice, few indemnity claims will be brought, be it due to limits on the insurers' ability to subrogate the employer's claim or simply the impracticability and undesirability in terms of industrial relations of pursuing the tortfeasor. Secondly, the attempts of, notably, the French courts to extend employee protection by obstructing claims by the victims themselves go further and demonstrate the force of risk-based reasoning, whereby the employer alone is rendered liable to the victim in the absence of serious personal misconduct by the employee. However, the problems which have arisen – what is meant by *'faute personnelle'*? What happens when the victim cannot sue the employer due to his insolvency? – have led many commentators to suggest that the case law has gone too far. Equally, proponents of corrective justice have questioned where this leaves the accountability of employees, rendered 'irresponsible' by such developments.[79] Such a debate is likely to continue as long as the fault of the employee remains a condition for liability, raising the inevitable question why the employee should not also be held personally accountable for his torts.

2.2.4 A common law problem: vicarious liability for exemplary damages?

This final section deals with a matter peculiar to the common law: the award of exemplary (or punitive) damages in addition to compensatory damages. In *Rookes v Barnard*,[80] Lord Devlin sought to restrict exemplary damages to three kinds of cases: where there has been oppressive, arbitrary or unconstitutional actions by government servants; where the conduct is calculated by the defendant to make a profit, which may well exceed any compensation payable to the claimant; and where such damages have been expressly authorised by statute. Whilst other Commonwealth countries have adopted a more generous approach to exemplary damages,[81] all agree on the aim of such damages, namely

---

[79] For example, Mazeaud questions on what textual authority the personal liability of the *préposé* can be dispensed: H. and L. Mazeaud, *Leçons de droit civil. Obligations: théorie générale*, 9th edn (Paris: Montchrestien, 1998), N° 482.

[80] [1964] AC 1129. See P. R. Ghandhi, 'Exemplary damages in the English law of tort', *Legal Studies*, 10 (1990), 182.

[81] See *Uren v John Fairfax & Sons Pty Ltd* (1966) 117 CLR 118 (Australia); *Whiten v Pilot Insurance Company* (2002) 209 DLR (4th) 257 (Canada); and *A v Bottrill* [2003] 1 AC 449 (Privy Council for New Zealand).

that they seek to punish defendants for their misconduct, and attempt to deter them and others from undertaking such conduct in future. As Lord Devlin acknowledged in *Rookes*, such damages are essentially different from ordinary compensatory damages. Their object is to punish and deter and in so doing, risk confusing the civil and criminal functions of the law.[82] The English Law Commission in 1997 nevertheless felt that exemplary damages still played a valuable role and that they should be available for all torts or equitable wrongs[83] where the defendant, in committing the tort, or by his subsequent conduct, has deliberately and outrageously disregarded the claimant's rights.[84]

Such emphasis on punishment for wrongdoing and deliberate and outrageous disregard for another's rights sits uneasily with the concept of vicarious liability. Clearly in relation to primary liability, it represents a judgement of the defendant's conduct for which he or she must personally pay. It requires a further step to justify rendering an innocent third party liable to pay a sum in addition to compensation for the victim's injury. At face value, it appears to be inconsistent with the very rationale given for the imposition of exemplary damages – the innocent party pays, whilst the guilty party may go unpunished.[85] As Lord Scott comments in *Kuddus v Chief Constable of Leicestershire Constabulary*, '[t]he objection to exemplary damages awards in vicarious liability cases seems to me to be fundamental. The only acceptable justification of exemplary damages awards in cases . . . is that the conduct complained of has been so outrageous as to warrant a punitive response. . . . The other side of the coin is, in my opinion, equally valid: the defendant should not be liable to pay exemplary damages unless he has committed punishable behaviour.'[86]

However, *Kuddus* represents a rare discussion of this issue in practice. The Law Commission in 1997 observed that '[a]lthough it has

---

[82] See [1964] AC at 1221.   [83] Excluding breach of contract.
[84] Law Commission Report No. 247 (1997), *Aggravated, Exemplary and Restitutionary Damages*, para. 6.3. See also the High Court of Australia in *Gray v Motor Accident Commission* [1998] HCA 70, (1998) 196 CLR 1 at para. 14: because the kinds of cases in which exemplary damages might be awarded are so varied, a single formula might be difficult, but the majority of cases may be justified by 'conscious wrongdoing in contumelious disregard of the plaintiff's rights' (per Gleeson CJ, McHugh, Gummow and Hayne JJ).
[85] If not called upon to indemnify the third party: see 2.2.3. See S. Todd, 'Tort actions by victims of sexual abuse', *Tort Law Review*, 12 (2004), 40.
[86] [2002] 2 AC 122 at para. 131. The question was not argued and such comments are thus obiter. Nevertheless, Stevens uses such arguments to support his contention that vicarious liability is based on attribution of actions, not liability, to the employer: R. Stevens, *Torts and rights* (Oxford University Press, 2009), p. 266.

consistently been assumed that vicarious liability extends to exemplary or punitive damages on the same basis as compensatory damages, we cannot find any case in which the application of vicarious liability has been challenged in an English court'.[87] The courts have thus awarded exemplary damages without any real consideration of the implications of the primary/vicarious liability divide.[88] The Law Commission took the view that, on balance, a person should be vicariously liable to pay punitive damages in respect of another's conduct.[89] Vicarious liability provides an indirect method of encouraging employers to control and educate their workforces and discourage potential wrongdoers: one of the objectives of exemplary damages.[90] Further, it assists claimants seeking exemplary damages of a significant size and where it is difficult to identify the culpable member of the employers' workforce.

The Court of Appeal in December 2006 agreed. It held in *Rowlands v Chief Constable of Merseyside Police*[91] that 'since the power to award exemplary damages rests on policy rather than principle',[92] as a matter of policy, the courts should be able to make exemplary damages awards against an employer. In the court's view, vicarious liability was necessary to ensure that an adequate sum of damages would be paid to the

---

[87] Law Commission Report No. 247 (1997), *Aggravated, Exemplary and Restitutionary Damages*, para. 5.209. Note also P. S. Atiyah, *Vicarious liability in the law of torts* (London: Butterworths, 1967), p. 435.

[88] See *Thompson v Commissioner of Police of the Metropolis* [1998] QB 498; *Peeters v Canada* (1993) 108 DLR (4th) 471; *Healing (Sales) Pty Ltd v Inglis Electrix Pty Ltd* (1968) 121 CLR 584. A further interesting question arises in relation to Lord Devlin's comment in *Rookes v Barnard* [1964] AC 1129 at 1228, that the means of the defendant are relevant. In terms of vicarious liability, whose means are relevant? In *Thompson v Commissioner of Police of the Metropolis* [1998] QB 498 at 517, Lord Woolf MR found it 'wholly inappropriate to take into account the means of the individual officers except where the action is brought against the individual tortfeasor'. Logically, this must be the case if vicarious liability is permitted on the 'deeper pockets' basis. This raises, however, the prospect of potentially draconian consequences if the employer is later permitted to exercise his right of indemnity against the actual tortfeasor. In his Lordship's view, this could be resolved by the court exercising its power under s. 2 of the Civil Liability (Contribution) Act 1978 to limit any reimbursement.

[89] Draft Bill Clause 11(1).

[90] It also distinguished vicarious liability from its general treatment of joint and several liability due to the peculiar nature of the relationship between the tortfeasor and person who is vicariously liable for his acts: Law Commission Report No. 247 (n. 87 above), paras. 5.222–4.

[91] [2006] EWCA Civ 1773, [2007] 1 WLR 1065. Comment H. Gow, 'A sorry tale', *New Law Journal*, 157 (2007), 164.

[92] [2006] EWCA Civ 1773 at para. 47 per Moore-Bick LJ. Such a statement emphasises the need to understand the relevant policy arguments, dealt with in Chapter 8.

claimant by the person who bears public responsibility for the conduct of the officers concerned – in other words, the deepest pocket should pay.[93] However, the argument goes further than this, as recognised by Lord Hutton in *Kuddus*[94] and the High Court of Australia in *State of New South Wales v Ibbett*.[95] Both cases focus on the same context: exemplary damages for oppressive, arbitrary or unconstitutional actions by police officers for which the relevant authority is made liable.[96] If exemplary damages seek to deter as well as punish, Lord Hutton[97] argued that this is best dealt with by rendering the Chief Constable liable in circumstances where he has the power to bring home to all officers that such conduct will not be tolerated[98] and where it may be difficult to identify the particular officer in question.[99] In contrast, the Supreme Court of Canada in *Blackwater v Plint*,[100] despite that court's generally more generous treatment of exemplary damages,[101] has refused to find an employer vicariously liable for exemplary damages awarded in a sexual abuse case. It is disappointing that no attempt is made to explain

---

[93] Ibid. More contestable is the comment at para. 48 that 'I think that in a matter of this kind this court should be slow to disturb an understanding of the law that has existed for over 40 years and on the basis of which many decisions at the highest level have proceeded'. A failure to understand the difficulties in imposing punitive damages on an innocent party for over 40 years is hardly a justification for its continuation. Note also that there is no principle of public policy preventing insurance cover for exemplary damages arising vicariously: *Lancashire County Council v Municipal Mutual Insurance Ltd* [1997] QB 897.

[94] See [2002] 2 AC 122 at para. 79.   [95] [2006] HCA 57, (2007) 231 ALR 485.

[96] In both *Kuddus* and *Ibbett*, the liability of the police service was governed by statute: s. 88 of the Police Act 1996 and s. 9B of the Law Reform (Vicarious Liability) Act 1983 (NSW). It is interesting to note that, while the New Zealand Court of Appeal in *S v Attorney-General* [2003] 3 NZLR 450 refused to find the Crown liable for exemplary damages when the Department in question was not directly at fault, Blanchard J (at 474-5) reserved the position where a police officer deliberately or recklessly inflicted personal injury on the claimant. Arguably, under *Rookes v Barnard* [1964] AC 1129, the most significant category of vicarious liability claims would be category 1 police claims.

[97] [2002] 2 AC 122 at para. 79.

[98] Atiyah in 1967 also agreed that the deterrent aspect of exemplary damages could, in particular for claims of false imprisonment and in relation to police officers, be justified in terms of the deterrent effect: Atiyah, *Vicarious liability*, p. 435.

[99] This may be due to the anonymity of uniform or simply that the miscreant officer is unlikely to identify himself.

[100] (2005) 258 DLR (4th) 275. The Court dealt with the point in only one paragraph, commenting that 'The trial judge . . . correctly stated that punitive damages cannot be awarded in the absence of reprehensible conduct specifically referable to the employer': para. 91.

[101] *Hill v Church of Scientology of Toronto* (1995) 126 DLR (4th) 129 and *Whiten v Pilot Insurance Company* (2002) 209 DLR (4th) 257. See M. Graham, 'Exemplary and punitive damages in contract and tort', *Lloyd's Maritime and Commercial Law Quarterly* (2002), 453.

why the rationale used by Lord Hutton – deterrence, ability to take preventative measures, anonymity of employees, deeper pockets – should not also apply in this context.[102]

It would therefore appear that the common law world is moving towards acceptance of exemplary or punitive damages in vicarious liability. In terms of English law, the limited categories of claims identified in *Rookes* do serve to minimise the impact of this ruling and the case law has clearly focused on the particular context of abusive conduct by the police force. The natural objection to the imposition of punitive damages on a body, which is not personally at fault, has been overcome by acceptance of the deterrence rationale of vicarious liability, discussed in more depth in Chapter 8. Such developments are additionally consistent with a move towards greater reliance on vicarious liability to ensure full compensation for victims and an assumption that it will, in any event, be covered by insurance or self-insurance by the body rendered liable. Recent case law does highlight, however, that exemplary damages have been awarded in the past without any real thought to the primary/vicarious liability distinction. This has led the courts to impose damages without any consideration of the absence of fault by the individual employer. Recognition of the vicarious nature of such liability is, however, merely a first step. Liability can only be imposed by examining the rationale underlying the modern doctrine of vicarious liability and assessing whether there are indeed clear and persuasive reasons for rendering an innocent party liable for punitive, in addition to compensatory, damages. As will be seen in Chapter 8, doubts as to the effectiveness of the deterrence rationale may indeed lead us to question whether Moore-Bick LJ in *Rowlands* accurately adjudged the balance to tip in favour of liability on the faultless employer.

2.3 Liability for the acts of others in other areas of law

It is inevitable that the question of liability for the acts of others will arise in contexts outside that of tort law. Excluding statutory intervention, the most obvious examples in private law are those of contract and company law. This final section will examine briefly the nature of such liability and how it interacts with tort law. As will be seen, these areas of law are most important in German law where they serve to circumvent

---

[102] See J. W. Neyers, 'Joint vicarious liability in the Supreme Court of Canada', *Law Quarterly Review*, 122 (2006), 195 at 199–200.

the limitations of § 831 BGB and are arguably the reason why this fault-based provision has survived to this day. Common lawyers, familiar with the concept of concurrent liability, view such liability as supplementary, but in systems, such as French law, where concurrent liability does not exist, commentators are nevertheless likely to raise concern if the position in contract law is significantly different from that existing in the law of tort. This section will also address two aspects of the French legal system of which non-French lawyers may be unaware: the ability of the criminal courts to award damages in tort and the separate treatment of tort claims against State and public authorities which are not governed by the French Civil Code and indeed are heard by a different court system: the administrative courts. Although this book is concerned with the private law of tort, mention must be made of the special treatment of public sector employees in French law – a concept at odds with the common law concept of equality before the law, as advocated by Dicey. This will be undertaken in two ways: by dealing with the law generally in this chapter and by considering the impact of administrative law case law on liability for the acts of others on the development of French law generally throughout this book.

2.3.1 Contract law

Contractual disputes will often arise due to the non-performance or defective performance of the defendant's employees – the defendant here being held accountable for their faulty performance. Modern commercial life would be unable to function if contracting parties were only held liable for their own personal faults. In dealing solely with tort liability, this book will not attempt to cover all areas of the law of obligations in which liability for the faults of others arise, but an appreciation of the relationship between tort and contract liability in this context is helpful. As stated above, the common law permits the concurrence of liability in tort and contract in respect of the same conduct;[103] the task of the court being to reconcile the two parallel claims. In contrast, French law does not have a doctrine of concurrent liability. The doctrine of *non-cumul* (non-accumulation of actions) requires parties to bring their claim in either contract *or* tort law, and claims cannot be brought in the alternative. This potentially has a

---

[103] See *Henderson v Merrett Syndicates Ltd* [1994] UKHL 5, [1995] 2 AC 145 (England and Wales); *BG Checo International Ltd v British Columbia Hydro and Power Authority* [1993] 1 SCR 12, (1993) 99 DLR (4th) 577 (Canada); *Astley v Austrust Ltd* [1999] HCA 6, 197 CLR 1 (Australia).

significant impact on claims based on the tortious acts of employees acting under a contract of employment: the contractual context suggesting that all claims should be governed by contract law alone, rendering the law of tort irrelevant. However, this is not how the law operates in practice. Professor Viney notes that the courts will often apply Article 1384(5) to contract claims on the basis that there is little difference between the general principle of contractual liability imposing liability for auxiliaries and the tort provisions.[104] In particular, the criminal courts, dealing with claims for compensation, also seem to favour reliance on Article 1384(5) rather than contract law, regardless of the context.[105]

However, contract law does possess greater importance in examining the provisions of German tort law. In placing liability under § 831 on the basis of presumed fault, German tort law does not recognise vicarious liability. Such liability, however, may be found elsewhere in German private law, notably under the contractual provisions of the Code. § 278 BGB (Responsibility of the obligor for third parties) provides that:

The obligor is responsible for fault on the part of his legal representative, and of persons whom he uses to perform his obligation, to the same extent as for fault on his own part.

Der Schuldner hat ein Verschulden seines gesetzlichen Vertreters und der Personen, deren er sich zur Erfüllung seiner Verbindlichkeit bedient, in gleichem Umfang zu vertreten wie eigenes Verschulden.

In providing for strict liability for the faults of persons used to perform his contractual obligations (liability for *Erfüllungsgehilfe*), § 278 provides an alternative basis for liability which the employer cannot avoid by demonstrating absence of fault.[106] As noted by Markesinis and Unberath, it provides a means of evading § 831, 'invoking the adaptable law of contract in order to remedy the deficiencies of the law of tort'.[107] Although this is limited to non-performance of contractual obligations, the German courts have been willing to extend contract law to cover pre-contractual accidents[108] and to protect identifiable third parties to the

---

[104] Viney and Jourdain, *Traité de droit civil*, N° 791–2.
[105] van Gerven, Lever and Larouche, *Tort law*, 499/3–4.
[106] MünchKommBGB/Grundmann, 5th edn (Munich: C. H. Beck, 2009), § 278, para. 7.
[107] Markesinis and Unberath, *The German law of torts*, p. 703.
[108] As in the famous linoleum case: RG 7 December 1911 RGZ 78, 239 (claimant and child hit by falling roll of linoleum whilst shopping in a department store due to negligence of shop assistant: department store found liable for sales assistant's fault under § 278).

contract (contracts with protective effects towards third parties/*Vertrag mit Schutzwirkung für Dritte*).[109] Whilst this represents only one of the many techniques used by German law to circumvent the fault basis of § 831 – the use of company law and specific provisions for public servants is addressed at 2.3.2 and 2.3.3, but note also alternative claims in tort for organisational fault (*Organisationverschulden*) under § 823(I) BGB[110] and the imposition of strict liability by statute[111] – such use of contract law demonstrates that despite the failure to reform § 831, strict liability for the wrongs of others is also an important part of German law and the fault basis for § 831 represents only part of the picture of potential liability.[112] Indeed, Wagner claims that contract, company law and *Organisationverschulden* have proved so successful in providing a means of circumventing the limits of § 831 that, in practice, German law differs little from that found in France or England.[113] For this reason, German law can only give limited assistance in a study based on the incidence of vicarious liability in *tort* law, and reference to systems based on the Germanic model thus forms only a subsidiary concern of this book.

2.3.2 Company law

In every system examined in this book, special provisions exist whereby corporations, as legal persons, are deemed to act through their organs for whom they will be held strictly liable.[114] These respond to an obvious difficulty in that a company, as an artificial legal entity, may only act through the medium of its officers. The tortious acts of its officers will therefore, by law, be attributed to the company itself. Whilst this may

---

[109] See B. S. Markesinis, H. Unberath and A. Johnston, *The German law of contract: a comparative treatise*, 2nd edn (Oxford: Hart, 2006), pp. 204–16.

[110] '(1) A person who, intentionally or negligently, unlawfully injures the life, body, health, freedom, property or another right of another person is liable to make compensation to the other party for the damage arising from this.'

[111] See, for example, Liability Act of 4 January 1978 (BGBl. I, 145) (as amended) (*Haftpflichtgesetz* HPflG) § 3. '*Liability of other entrepreneurs:* Anyone who operates a mine, quarry, pit, or factory is liable to compensation if an authorized agent or representative or anyone employed in the direction or supervision of the undertaking or of the workmen causes by a fault in the carrying out of the service arrangement, death or bodily injury to a human being.' Brüggemeier notes the significance of these special statutes in responding to the risks produced from industrialisation: see G. Brüggemeier, *Haftungsrecht: Struktur, Prinzipien, Schutzbereich* (Heidelburg: Springer, 2006), pp. 137–41.

[112] See ibid., at 119–37.

[113] MünchKommBGB/Wagner, 5th edn (Munich: C. H. Beck, 2009), § 831, para. 2.

[114] Eörsi reports that all legal systems impute the acts of organs to the legal entity: Eörsi, 'Private and governmental liability' para. 4–32.

resemble vicarious liability – strict liability for the torts of another – it is clearly an example of *primary* liability and so will be dealt with briefly in this section. In practice, there is little difference in common and French law between the effect of vicarious or primary liability in this context. Its main significance lies in German law where, in common with the provisions for strict liability in contract law, it has been used by the courts to extend the scope of strict liability for the wrongful acts of others and thereby circumvent the fault basis of § 831.

As one might expect, the authority for the strict liability of corporations for their organs derives from case law in the common law, code in German law and in the pre-industrialisation French Civil Code by case law development by the courts, supplemented by more recent legislation. In the common law, Viscount Haldane LC famously stated in *Lennard's Carrying Co. Ltd v Asiatic Petroleum Co. Ltd*[115] that 'a corporation is an abstraction. It has no mind of its own any more than it has a body of its own; its active and directing will must consequently be sought in the person of somebody who for some purposes may be called an agent, but who is really the directing mind and will of the corporation, the very ego and centre of the personality of the corporation.'[116] The rules of agency will therefore generally be sufficient to establish liability.[117] It should be noted, however, that the option still exists to find the company liable for even its senior officers on the ordinary principles of vicarious liability. In *Secretary of State for Trade and Industry v Bottrill*,[118]

---

[115] [1915] AC 705 at 713. See also Denning LJ in *HL Bolton (Engineering) Co. Ltd v TJ Graham & Sons Ltd* [1957] 1 QB 159 at 172.

[116] Somewhat more recently, the Privy Council in *Meridian Global Funds Management Asia Ltd v Securities Commission* [1995] 2 AC 500 has suggested that in some cases a more flexible test will be needed in preference to the somewhat artificial search for the company's 'directing mind and will'. Attribution will be viewed as a question of construction in each case, with regard to the language, content and policy of the particular rule of law in question. For some rules, therefore, it may be possible to attribute the acts and thoughts of lesser employees if indicated by the language and policy of the law in question. See also *KR v Royal & Sun Alliance plc* [2006] EWCA Civ 1454, [2007] 1 All ER (Comm) 161.

[117] Note that arguments based on ultra vires do not operate in the tort context: F. Reynolds and P. Watts (eds.), *Bowstead & Reynolds on Agency*, 18th edn (London: Sweet and Maxwell, 2006), para. 8–188; Companies Act 1985, sections 35(1), 35A(1).

[118] [2000] 1 All ER 915. See also *Connolly v Sellars Arenascene Ltd* [2001] EWCA Civ 184, [2001] ICR 760. Note that these were both cases where directors were seeking the protection awarded to employees and vicarious liability will raise different policy issues. On the need to monitor the ability of directors to obtain employee protection, see K. Wardman, 'Directors and employee status: an examination of the relevant company law and employment law principles', *Company Law*, 24 (2003), 139.

for example, the Court of Appeal held the controlling shareholder of a company to be its employee. Much will depend on the facts of each case. In terms of personal liability, where the director is acting for the company, the House of Lords in *Standard Chartered Bank v Pakistan National Shipping Corp (No. 2)* held that the director in question may also be held personally liable for his fraud.[119] The officer's liability in tort will thus depend on the ordinary principles of tort law rather than any provisions of company law.[120]

French law has equally developed a body of case law whereby legal persons of all kinds will be held strictly liable for their corporate organs. As in English law, much will depend on the level of employee. Low-level employees will be covered by Article 1384(5). Where the individual cannot be said to be subordinate to the company and therefore within Article 1384(5),[121] the courts may nevertheless find the company liable for the torts of individuals who are in charge of representing it to the outside world, such as board members, executive officers, trustees in bankruptcy etc.[122] Liability will arise where the individual (i) acts on behalf of the corporation, and (ii) breaches obligations, for example, commits a fault within Articles 1382 or 1383, whilst acting on the corporation's behalf.[123] There has been a debate, similar to that in English law, as to the extent to which an officer should be held personally liable for wrongs committed on behalf of the company. A position has been reached similar to that applied to employees in the *Costedoat* case discussed above: the victim will be confined to bringing a claim against the company unless the wrongful

---

[119] For deceit, see *Standard Chartered Bank v Pakistan National Shipping Corp (No. 2)* [2002] UKHL 43, [2003] 1 AC 959, notably Lord Hoffmann at para. 22 and Lord Rodger at para. 40. For negligent misstatement, see *Williams v Natural Life Health Foods Ltd* [1998] 2 All ER 577, [1998] 1 WLR 830 (director only personally liable where he has assumed responsibility to the claimant who reasonably relied upon him). Hannigan notes, at 3–78, that perhaps due to the clarity brought to the issue by *Standard Chartered* or the increasing availability of directors' and officers' liability insurance or simply hard times, there appears to be an increase in claims in deceit against individual directors: B. Hannigan, *Company law*, 2nd edn (Oxford University Press, 2009).

[120] P. L. Davies, *Gower & Davies' principles of modern company law*, 8th edn (London: Sweet & Maxwell, 2008), para. 7–25. For a clear statement of the principles governing the liability of a director as a joint tortfeasor with the company, see Chadwick LJ in *MCA Records Inc v Charly Records Ltd (No. 5)* [2001] EWCA Civ 1441, [2003] 1 BCLC 93 at paras. 48–52.

[121] Civ 2, 17 July 1967 Gaz Pal 1967.2.236; RTD civ. 1968.149 obs G. Durry, Civ 2, 27 April 1977 Bull civ II N° 108.

[122] See Viney and Jourdain, *Traité de droit civil*, N° 850, who comment that there is not a very precise definition of this category.

[123] Note also specific legislative provisions dealing with corporate officers contained within the new Commercial Code, for example, Articles L 225–251 and L 225–256.

act is distinct from the officer's functions (*faute séparable ou détachable*), rendering him personally liable.[124]

It is in German law that this form of liability is most significant. In contrast to the protection given to employers in § 831, § 31 BGB provides:

> The association is liable for the damage to a third party that the board, a member of the board or another constitutionally appointed representative causes through an act committed by it or him in carrying out the business with which it or he is entrusted, where the act gives rise to a liability in damages.[125]

§ 31 Haftung des Vereins für Organe

Der Verein ist für den Schaden verantwortlich, den der Vorstand, ein Mitglied des Vorstands oder ein anderer verfassungsmäßig berufener Vertreter durch eine in Ausführung der ihm zustehenden Verrichtungen begangene, zum Schadensersatz verpflichtende Handlung einem Dritten zufügt.

On its face, this provision mirrors that in French and English law and appears uncontroversial: a legal person is held strictly liable for the wrongful acts of its organs. Liability will be joint and several:[126] the individual will be liable under ordinary fault principles (see § 823ff) and the corporation under § 31. However, in practice, the courts have come to adopt a broad interpretation of 'constitutionally appointed

---

[124] See Com 22 January 1998 Bull civ IV N° 48; JCP 1998.1.187 N° 25 obs G. Viney; D 1998.605 note D. Gibirila, Com 28 April 1998 Bull civ IV N° 139; RTD civ. 1998.688 obs P. Jourdain. It is clear that a criminal conviction for an intentional offence will satisfy this test: Crim 14 October 1991 Rev. sociétés 1992.782 ob B. Bouloc; 14 December 1999 RTD civ. 2000.342. The Cour de cassation in 2003 gave a more precise definition which associated personal fault with intentional and serious misconduct (*lorsque le dirigeant commet intentionnellement une faute d'une particulière gravité incompatible avec l'exercise normal des fonctions sociales*): Com 20 May 2003 D 2003.2623 note B. Dondéro; RTD civ. 2003.509 obs P. Jourdain. Viney and Jourdain comment that whilst this is not the most certain of definitions, it does indicate a movement in favour of a limited and controlled extension of personal liability: Viney and Jourdain, *Traité de droit civil*, N° 857.

[125] For companies under public law, see § 89 BGB: '(1) The provision of § 31 applies with the necessary modifications to the treasury and to corporations, foundations and institutions under public law.' These provisions also cover the various types of partnerships, for example OHG/*Offene Handelsgesellschaft* (general partnership) and KG/*Kommanditgesellschaft* (limited partnership) and have been recently extended to the BGB *Gesellschaft* (see MünchKommBGB/Reuter, 5th edn (Munich: C.H. Beck, 2009), § 31, para. 16). See also § 30 BGB (Special representatives/*Besondere Vertreter*): 'It may be provided by the articles of association that, in addition to the board, special representatives are to be appointed for particular transactions. In case of doubt, the power of agency of such a representative extends to all legal transactions that the sphere of business allocated to him normally entails.'

[126] See §§ 840 426 BGB.

50 ESTABLISHING A GENERAL FRAMEWORK FOR LIABILITY

representatives' (*anderer verfassungsmäßig berufener Vertreter*) to include representatives who have the right to make independent decisions in their own sphere of work, subject only to general instructions.[127] It is irrelevant that their powers are not defined in the articles of association. This will therefore include not only chief executives and board members, but management, such as branch directors and department heads.[128] As stated by the German Supreme Court in 1967:

> It is enough that the representative is charged, through the general operational guidelines and practices of the business in question, with the autonomous execution of significant and essential functions of the legal person.[129]

Whilst there are obviously limits to the use made of this provision, it does extend strict liability to the torts of senior staff in circumstances where the common law and French law would resort to vicarious liability. As such, it represents another means of circumventing § 831.[130]

2.3.3 Public law[131]

As is well known, the common law has no separate system of administrative law and the starting point is that all defendants, be they private individuals or public authorities, should be subject to the same private law principles of tort law.[132] The position in English law in relation to vicarious liability was clearly stated by the Court of Appeal in 1909: 'It is now settled that a public body is liable for the negligence of its servants in the same way

---

[127] See Markesinis and Unberath, *The German law of torts*, p. 701; MünchKommBGB/Wagner, 5th edn (Munich: C.H. Beck, 2009), §831, para. 18.

[128] See, for example, BGH 21 September 1971 NJW 1972 p. 334 (senior hospital consultant); BGH 30 October 1967 BGHZ 49, p. 19 (branch manager). There is also authority that where the tortfeasor should have been appointed as a representative, but was not, this may be regarded as an organisational fault giving rise to liability under § 823: see van Gerven, Lever and Larouche, *Tort law*, 488 and J. von Standinger, D. W. Belling and C. Ebert Borges, *Kommentar zum Bürgerlichen Gesetzbuch* (Berlin: De Gruyter, 2008), § 831, para. 42.

[129] BGH 30 October 1967, BGHZ 49, 19 at 21. Translation taken from van Gerven, Lever and Larouche, *Tort law*, 488.

[130] See Brüggemeier, *Haftungsrecht*, 120; MünchKommBGB/Wagner, §831, para. 2; von Staudinger et al., *Kommentar*, § 831, para. 42.

[131] See, generally, D. Fairgrieve, M. Andenas and J. Bell (eds.), *Tort liability of public authorities in comparative perspective* (London: British Institute of International and Comparative Law, 2002).

[132] Subject, in the United Kingdom, to the provisions of the Crown Proceedings Act 1947, section 2, the Human Rights Act 1998 and specific public body torts such as misfeasance in public office. See, generally, W. V. H. Rogers, *Winfield & Jolowicz on tort*, 18th edn (London: Sweet and Maxwell, 2010), para. 5-45 ff.

as private individuals would be liable under similar circumstances, notwithstanding that it is acting in the performance of public duties, like a local board of health, or of eleemosynary and charitable functions, like a public hospital.'[133] Allowance is nevertheless made for discretion often awarded to public bodies in the execution of their statutory duties and powers. As Lord Slynn noted in *Phelps v Hillingdon London Borough Council*:[134]

> The professionalism, dedication and standards of those engaged in the provision of educational services are such that cases of liability for negligence will be exceptional. But though claims should not be encouraged and the courts should not find negligence too readily, the fact that some claims may be without foundation or exaggerated does not mean that valid claims should necessarily be excluded.

In German law, the liability of civil servants is governed by the private law provision § 839 BGB (liability for officials) and claims for damages in tort will be heard in the civil courts:

> (1) If an official intentionally or negligently breaches the official duty incumbent upon him in relation to a third party, then he must compensate the third party for damage arising from this. If the official is only responsible because of negligence, then he may only be held liable if the injured person is not able to obtain compensation in another way.[135]

This must be read in conjunction with Article 34 of the Basic Law, which renders the State liable where the breach has taken place in the exercise of the public office of the civil servant.[136] As a result, State liability may be described as resting on two pillars – private and public law – which

---

[133] *Hillyer v The Governors of St. Bartholomew's Hospital* [1909] 2 KB 820 at 825 per Farwell LJ.

[134] [2001] 2 AC 619 at 655. See also *Carty v Croydon LBC* [2005] EWCA Civ 19, [2005] 1 WLR 2312. The English Law Commission recently undertook a project to review the law in relation to redress from public bodies for substandard administrative action: see Law Commission, *Administrative redress: public bodies and the citizen* (Law Com. No. 322, May 2010): impractical to pursue reform of State liability at this time.

[135] Note also the remaining provisions of § 839: '(2) If an official breaches his official duties in a judgment in a legal matter, then he is only responsible for any damage arising from this if the breach of duty consists in a criminal offence. This provision is not applicable to refusal or delay that is in breach of duty in exercising a public function' and '(3) Liability for damage does not arise if the injured person has intentionally or negligently failed to avert the damage by having recourse to appeal.'

[136] 'If any person, in the exercise of a public office entrusted to him, violates his official obligations to a third party, liability rests in principle on the State or the public authority which employs him. In the case of wilful intent or gross carelessness the right of recourse is reserved. With respect to the claim for compensation or the right of recourse, the jurisdiction of the ordinary courts must not be excluded.' Note that this does not include fiscal liability, which will be dealt with under § 831 or, for corporations, §§ 31 89 BGB.

are interrelated and influence each other.[137] These provisions render the State employer indirectly liable for the tortious acts of its officials. Unlike § 831, these provisions contain no *Entlastungsbeweis*/exculpatory provision by which the employer can avoid liability by demonstrating lack of fault.[138] By virtue of Article 34 GG, it will apply to every public servant (as defined by administrative law) which will include public workers, employees and civil servants who are exercising a function which is part of the sovereign activities of the public body.[139]

In contrast, the French administrative law courts have developed their own principles of liability in relation to public sector employers.[140] Article 1384(5) will therefore *not* apply to public sector employers.[141] A specific regime is applicable to public sector workers, governed by public, not private, law.[142] In the absence of any overarching substantive code,[143] French administrative law relies heavily on judge-made law, deriving from the case law of the *Conseil d'Etat* and the lower administrative courts.[144] Administrative law has developed its own principles of tort law which will apply to public body defendants.[145] The key concept in this context is that of *faute de service* (fault in service), which is defined broadly as a failure in the normal functioning of the public

---

[137] See G. Brüggemeier, 'From individual tort for civil servants to quasi-strict liability of the State: governmental or state liability in Germany' and R.-A. Summa, 'A comparative study of the English and German liability of public bodies in negligence' in Fairgrieve, Andenas and Bell (eds.), *Tort liability*; Brüggemeier, *Haftungsrecht*, 157–60; and von Staudinger et al., *Kommentar*, § 831, para. 41.

[138] RGZ 139, 149, 151.

[139] See Summa, 'A comparative study' p. 367; and Brüggemeier, *Haftungsrecht*, p. 573, who notes a trend towards no-fault liability based on these provisions and the imposition of direct enterprise liability on the State.

[140] As established by the famous *Blanco* decision of 1873: TC 8 February 1873 (*Blanco*) D 1873.2.20. For an Anglo-French comparison, see D. Fairgrieve, *State liability in tort: a comparative law study* (Oxford University Press, 2003).

[141] Other exclusions from private law exist. For example, the Social Security Code (L451–1) generally excludes civil claims for accidents at work or occupational illnesses which are dealt with by social security provisions, but note the exclusion in case of intentional fault by the employer or one of his employees (L452–5).

[142] This is well illustrated by medical law where a visit to a general practitioner would be seen as a matter for the private law of contract, whilst a claim against a public service hospital (obviously distinct from a private clinic) would be brought under the principles of administrative law.

[143] Apart from certain codes which consolidate specific principles and rules. There are, of course, numerous statutes which regulate public administration activities.

[144] For a description in English, see N. L. Brown and J. S. Bell, *French administrative law*, 5th edn (Oxford University Press, 1998).

[145] See, generally, J. Waline, *Droit administratif*, 22nd edn (Paris: Dalloz, 2008), N° 458ff.

service.[146] An objective link must also exist between the *faute* of the public servant and his position. State employers will not be liable for faults '*sans rapport avec le service*'/outside the scope of employment, for example, in one case a postman attacking the person to whom he was supposed to be delivering a registered parcel.[147] The civil servant will not, however, be held personally responsible unless he commits a serious personal fault (*faute personnelle*) which is typified by malicious conduct or gross fault.[148]

Claims against public bodies, be it the local authority or public hospital, for liability for the torts of their employees will therefore arise in public law, where a parallel system of liability exists, as developed by the French administrative courts. As this section illustrates, the basic structure is the same: a relationship is required between institution and public servant, who commits a fault which is within the scope of his employment. Despite this clear jurisdictional divide, the private law courts, as we will see, are often influenced by developments in public law in their interpretation of liability under Article 1384 of the French Civil Code and will often attempt to avoid any major doctrinal differences between the treatment of claims in private and public law.

2.3.4 *The relevance of French criminal law*

Although this book will not address vicarious liability in criminal law, it should be noted that Article 1384(5) of the French Civil Code has been interpreted by both the French civil and criminal courts and a brief explanation of the ability of the criminal courts to hear civil claims may be helpful at this stage. French criminal law provides for the victim to bring a claim for damages (the *partie civile*) at the criminal trial.[149] Article 2 of the Code of Criminal Procedure provides that 'The *action civile* for compensation for damage caused by a *crime* (felony), *délit* (misdemeanour) or *contravention* (petty offence) may be brought by those who have personally suffered damage, directly caused by the criminal action.'[150]

---

[146] Ibid., N° 475: '*la faute du service est un manquement aux obligations du service c'est-à-dire une défaillance dans le fonctionnement normal du service.*'
[147] TC 21 December 1987 AJDA 1988.364, noted in J. Bell, S. Boyron and S. Whittaker, *Principles of French law*, 2nd edn (Oxford University Press, 2008), p. 191.
[148] Waline, *Droit administratif*, N° 509.
[149] See Bell, Boyron and Whittaker, *Principles*, pp. 368–9. The commission of a criminal offence is considered to amount to a civil fault, which entitles the victim to sue for civil compensation.
[150] My translation. Modified by Ordonnance N° 58-1296 of 23 December 1958, in force 2 March 1959. See also P. O. Lapie, 'The *partie civile* in the criminal law of France', *Journal of Comparative Legislation and International Law*, 10 (1928), 33.

On this basis, both the criminal and civil courts will interpret Article 1384 (5) to establish liability to pay damages. Yet, it should be noted that it is not uncommon, in practice, for the civil and criminal chambers of the French Supreme Court to adopt different reasoning. It should therefore not be automatically assumed that both jurisdictions will interpret Article 1384(5) in the same way, although inconsistencies between different chambers of the French Supreme Court may ultimately be resolved by the *Chambre mixte* (mixed chamber of the Cour de cassation)[151] or *Assemblée plénière* (plenary assembly of the Cour de cassation).[152]

2.4 Conclusion

This chapter has sought to establish a basic framework for the operation of the doctrine of vicarious liability across legal systems. It is premised on the commission of a tort – a noticeable divide existing between systems rendering one person strictly liable for the tort of another and systems which still impose liability on the basis of the presumed fault of the person in charge. While the continued existence of fault-based systems may suggest limited acceptance of the strict liability model, it is clear from German law that this has led to the development of exceptions, be they statutory or based on the interpretation of existing tort provisions or other areas of law such as company and contract law. The need for such developments indicates general recognition of the need for some form of strict liability, notably in the employment context.

The next four chapters will examine the other key elements of the vicarious liability framework in more depth. Chapters 3 to 5 will examine the relationships which give rise to vicarious liability, whilst Chapter 6 will describe the tortuous process by which legal systems have determined the scope of vicarious liability and when the tort will be deemed to take place 'in the course of employment' or within the functions or tasks assigned to the tortfeasor himself.

---

[151] Dealing with questions relating to the jurisdiction of different chambers, or where the question has been answered (or is likely to be answered) differently in different chambers: Code of Judicial Organisation, Art. L 431–5. See also A. Perdriau, 'La chambre mixte et l'assemblée plénière de la Cour de cassation', JCP 1994 I 3798 and J. Gordley and A. von Mehren, *An introduction to the comparative study of private law* (Cambridge University Press, 2006), p. 101.

[152] Dealing with cases raising questions of principle, notably where there is a divergence between the decisions of the lower court judges or the lower court judges and the Supreme Court: Code of Judicial Organisation, Art. L 431–6.

3   The employer/employee relationship: identifying the contract of employment

3.1   Introduction

The next three chapters will address the first element of any vicarious liability claim: the need for a particular relationship between the defendant and the person for whom he is rendered strictly liable. The most common example of this relationship is that of the employer/employee (or, to use civilian terminology, the *commettant/préposé*[1] or *Geschäftsherr/ Verrichtungsgehilfe*[2]). From the nineteenth century onwards, industrialisation has rendered this particular relationship of increasing significance in terms of the damage which could be caused by employees and, with the advent of insurance, the financial ability of the employer to provide compensation. At the very heart of this doctrine, in both common and civil law, therefore, lies the employer/employee relationship.

In examining the scope of this relationship across common and civil legal systems, a common starting point may be identified: control. Whether interpreted as the ability to control, instruct or exert authority over the employee, all the systems surveyed in this book perceive this element as the key characteristic of the employment relationship. Nevertheless, as will be seen, changes in employment practices, the rise of the professional and increased use of technology have diminished the utility of this test and led to its reappraisal in relation to modern employment relations. It can no longer be assumed that an employee will act under the absolute control of his superior. Employees will often be expected to act independently, show initiative, and make on-the-spot decisions

[1] The test used under Article 1384(5) of the French Civil Code, which can be translated as 'principal' and 'employee', but note that the term *'employé'* is not used.
[2] The test used under § 831(1) of the German Civil Code, loosely translated as 'principal or master'/'principal/person employed to perform the obligation'.

without recourse to their superior. It is equally more likely that employees will be immediately answerable to their line-manager rather than their ultimate employer. Faced with such developments, this chapter will examine the tests used by the courts and the extent to which they are capable of adapting to socio-economic change. Utilising the specific example of claims against physicians operating on patients within the defendant hospital, this chapter will consider the tests used to identify the contract of employment and the difficulties arising in practice.

The following two chapters will take this analysis a step further. Chapter 4 will consider the particular problem of temporary work placements, either in relation to employees sent to work for another employer (the borrowed servant problem) or workers hired by agencies to work for another. Neither fits easily into the traditional employer/employee test. Chapter 5 will then consider other non-traditional relationships, such as non-contractual agency relationships and partners in a firm and the extent to which this primary requirement of a relationship linking tortfeasor and defendant has been extended *beyond* the employment context to permit an extension of vicarious liability principles.

Before considering the tests used to identify the employment relationship, however, it is important to commence with a warning. The common law courts continue to refer indiscriminately to cases arising in the field of taxation, workmen's compensation, social security law, health and safety legislation and discrimination law in determining the existence of a contract of employment.[3] The case law is not confined to a vicarious liability context. Certain authors have questioned whether this practice should continue, bearing in mind the very different policy considerations and legal framework governing each particular area of law,[4] and it would, indeed, seem preferable to recognise the distinct

[3] See D. Howarth, *Textbook on tort* (London: Butterworths, 1995), p. 636: 'cases about social security law and unfair dismissal are cited freely and without embarrassment in tort cases without regard to the importance of the questions of what social security and tax law are trying to achieve and whom unfair dismissal law is trying to protect'. The need for caution was, however, discussed in *Lane v Shire Roofing Co.* [1995] PIQR, p. 417 at 421 per Henry LJ.

[4] See E. McKendrick, 'Vicarious liability and independent contractors – a re-examination', *Modern Law Review*, 53 (1990), 770 and R. Kidner, 'Vicarious liability: for whom should the employer be liable?', *Legal Studies*, 15 (1995), 47, who both argue that the courts should recognise that the status of workers may vary according to the context in question. See also L. Friedlander, 'What has tort law got to do with it? Distinguishing between employees and independent contractors in the federal income tax, employment insurance, and Canada pension plan contexts', *Canadian Tax Journal*, 51 (2003), 1467.

needs of each context, but this practice continues. In contrast, in German law, the liability of the *Geschäftsherr* under § 831 is treated as distinct from contractual liability arising under § 278 of the Code (liability for *Erfüllungsgehilfe*), which is different in scope and, in practice, far more generous.[5] Reference to the *Geschäftsherr* in this book should therefore be taken solely to designate liability under § 831 of the German Civil Code, that is, delictual liability.[6] In France, the terms *commettant/préposé* are also confined to the context of Article 1384(5), although the interpretation of these terms has been influenced by the rules applying to public sector employees developed in French public law.

We will start with an examination of the 'control' test, before proceeding to consider the ability and willingness of legal systems to respond to new modes of employment, the increasing independence of workers and the complexity and diversity of modern employment relations.

3.2 The control test

In defining the relationships giving rise to vicarious liability, the starting point has generally been that of control and the ability to exert authority over the employee.[7] Sir William Blackstone, in his *Commentaries on the laws of England* (1765–1769), noted that 'the master is answerable for the act of his servant, if done by his command, either expressly given, or implied'.[8] The employment relationship was thus characterised as one where the employer could control the employee's work and instruct the employee what work to undertake and how it should be

---

[5] 'The obligor is responsible for fault on the part of his legal representative, and of persons whom he uses to perform his obligation, to the same extent as for fault on his own part.' See MünchKommBGB/Wagner, 5th edn (Munich: C.H. Beck, 2009), §831, para. 14 and J. von Staudinger, D. W. Belling and C. Eberl-Borges, *Kommentar zum Bürgerlichen Gesetzbuch*, (Berlin: De Gruyter, 2008) §831, paras. 23–4.

[6] Delictual liability may also be found under § 839 BGB (claims in tort against officials) and §823(1) BGB (organisational fault/*Organisationverschulden*).

[7] Vicarious liability of masters for their apprentices features strongly in earlier law but there is little recent authority. In the common law, liability for apprentices has been assimilated into the law relating to employees due to the close analogy between the contract of service and the apprenticeship contract. In *Clelland v Edward Lloyd Ltd* [1938] 1 KB 272 and *Mulholland v William Reid & Leys Ltd* 1958 SC 290, for example, the courts simply applied the rules relating to employers and employees to determine whether the negligent apprentice could be said to be acting in the course of his employment for the defendant. See also *Hancke v Hooper* (1835) 7 C & P 81, 173 ER 37; *Mead v Hamond* (1722) 1 Stra 505, 93 ER 663; *Armory v Delamirie Ltd* (1722) 1 Stra 505, 93 ER 664.

[8] W. Blackstone, *Commentaries on the laws of England* (W. Morrison ed.) (London: Cavendish, 2001), vol. I, p. 429.

done.[9] Control, direction and authority are all seen as necessary conditions for liability. Control includes the power of deciding the thing to be done, the way in which it shall be done, the means to be employed in doing it, and the time when and the place where it shall be done.[10] Early French law deduced that, as a result, an employer should not be liable for employees he had not personally chosen,[11] although this restriction was subsequently abandoned.[12]

Control also serves to distinguish an employer from an independent contractor.[13] An employee, working under, to use the language of the common law, a 'contract of service' or 'contract of employment', must submit to the orders and instructions of his employer. An independent contractor, acting under a 'contract for services', is deemed to possess greater autonomy, taking him outside the persons for whom the employer will be held liable. This employee/independent contractor distinction represents to this day a fundamental limitation on the scope of the doctrine of vicarious liability.[14]

Looking across the common law and French and German law, the logic of the control test was initially deemed irrefutable. Bramwell LJ in *Yewens v Noakes* in 1880 stated that: 'A servant is a person subject to the command of his master as to the manner in which he shall do his work'.[15] This test was to dominate the common law during the nineteenth and first part of the twentieth century. The 1933 US Restatement of Agency provided at § 220(1) that 'A servant is a person employed to perform service for another in his affairs and who, with respect to his physical conduct in the performance of the service, is subject to the other's control or right to control'. In the classic French case of 1937,[16] the French Supreme Court

---

[9] See, for example, *Simmons v Heath Laundry Co.* [1910] 1 KB 543; *Hillyer v St Bartholomew's Hospital* [1909] 2 KB 820; *Performing Rights Society Ltd v Mitchell & Booker (Palais de Danse)* [1924] 1 KB 762. See, generally, *Pollock on Torts*, 12th edn (London: Stevens, 1923), p. 79.

[10] See MacKenna J in *Ready Mixed Concrete (South East) Ltd v Minister of Pensions and National Insurance* [1968] 2 QB 497 at 515.

[11] Civ 8 May 1908 DP 1909.1.135; 7 April 1924 DH 1924.373.

[12] Crim 15 March 1923 D 1923.1.157 and Paris 14 March 1930 D 1930.2.115 note Besson.

[13] See *Salsbury v Woodland* [1970] 1 QB 324 at 336 per Widgery LJ.

[14] The nature of this distinction will be considered in more detail in Chapter 5.

[15] (1880) 6 QBD 530 at 532–3. See also *R v Walker* (1858) 27 LJMC 207. Crompton J in *Sadler v Henlock* (1855) 4 E & B 570 at 578, 119 ER 209 at 212, arguably provided the starting point of the control test: see G. M. Stevens, 'The test of the employment relation', *Michigan Law Review*, 38 (1939), 188, 199. Distinct callings were distinguished: see *Milligan v Wedge* (1840) 12 Ad & E 737, 113 ER 993 (licensed drover exercises distinct calling and no master and servant relationship with butcher for whom he is acting).

[16] Civ 4 May 1937 (*Veuve Meyer*) DH 1937.363.

also recognised the test to be one of authority and subordination, characterised by 'the right to give the employee (*préposé*) orders or instructions as to the manner in which he shall undertake the functions for which he is employed',[17] thus placing a reciprocal relationship of authority and subordination at the heart of this test. German law equally focused on the right to give instructions (*Weisungsrecht*), thereby identifying the employee as a person subject to these instructions (*Weisungsabhängig*).[18]

The control test is appealing due to the fact that it possesses a dual role: it determines *for whom* the defendant will be liable and *why*. This is particularly persuasive in systems where fault-based liability remains a dominant feature of the tort system and is indeed suggestive of the continuing influence of concepts such as *culpa in eligendo* (fault in the choice/selection of the employee).[19] As Atiyah observed, 'one of the reasons for the persistence of the control test is that control has been seen not merely as a test of the existence of the conditions for liability but as a justification for imposing it'.[20] Fault may, at the very least, be presumed when an actor controlled by the defendant harms the victim. Bertrand de Greuille, writing in 1803, justified the imposition of strict liability on the employer as follows: 'Shouldn't he reproach himself for placing confidence in malicious, clumsy or negligent staff?'[21] Alternatively, in the words of leading French authors, 'it is because the employer has the power to order that he is held liable for the acts of his employee who is required to obey him'.[22]

---

[17] 'Le droit de donner au préposé des ordres ou des instructions sur la manière de remplir les fonctions auxquelles il est employé.' My translation.

[18] See MünchKommBGB/Wagner, 5th edn (Munich: C.H. Beck, 2009), §831, Rn 14; von Staudinger et al., *Kommentar*, §831, paras. 59ff.

[19] Eörsi observes its ongoing influence in French law, despite its rejection as a requirement during the preparatory works on the Code Civil: see G. Eörsi, 'Private and governmental liability for the torts of employees and organs' in A. Tunc (chief ed.), *International encyclopedia of comparative law* (Tübingen, Mohr, 1983), vol. XI, para. 4–8. Alternatively, Mazeaud has argued that liability can by analysed as based on fault if one accepts that the fault of the *préposé* is attributed to the *commettant*: see F. Chabas, 'Lesson 24' in H. and L. Mazeaud (eds.), *Leçons de droit civil. Obligations: théorie générale*, 9th edn (Paris: Montchrestien, 1998).

[20] P. S. Atiyah, *Vicarious liability in the law of torts* (London: Butterworths, 1967), p. 40.

[21] Bertrand de Greuille, *rapporteur* to the *Tribunat*, also reported in P. A. Fenet, *Recueil complet des travaux préparatoires du Code civil* (1827) (Osnabrueck: O. Zeller, 1968), vol. XIII, p. 476 (my translation).

[22] H. Capitant, F. Terré and Y. Lequette, *Les grands arrêts de la jurisprudence civile*, 12th edn (Paris: Dalloz, 2008), vol. II, p. 461 (my translation). See also 9 Jan 1931 DP 1931.1.171 note G. Daillan, Civ 2, 9 Nov 1967 Bull civ II N° 321, JCP 1972 II 17159 note D. Mayer.

3.3 Doubts as to the control test

By the latter half of the twentieth century, however, changes in work practices and market conditions had rendered the test less helpful, save in the most straightforward cases. Kahn-Freund observed in 1951 that the control test was:

> ... based upon the social conditions of an earlier age: it assumed that the employer of labour was able to direct and instruct the labourer as to the technical methods he should use in performing his work. In a mainly agricultural society and even in the earlier stages of the Industrial Revolution the master could be expected to be superior to the servant in the knowledge, skill and experience which had to be brought to bear upon the choice and handling of the tools ... The technical and economic developments of all industrial societies have nullified these assumptions.[23]

In a post-industrial age, advances in technology signify that employees are frequently expected to be able to exercise discretion and initiative in their performance without direct supervision. Professionals or workers with some particular skill would not expect to be told what to do and how to act during each working day. For example, one would not expect an accountant to be told how to proceed with an audit or a mechanic how to repair a car. Somervell LJ in *Cassidy v Ministry of Health*[24] gave the example of a certified master of a ship. The master may be employed by the owners under what is clearly a contract of employment, and yet the owners have no power to tell him how to navigate his ship. As stated by MacGuigan JA in the Canadian case of *Wiebe Door Services Ltd v MNR*:

> A principal inadequacy [with the control test] is its apparent dependence on the exact terms in which the task in question is contracted for: where the contract contains detailed specifications and conditions, which would be the normal expectation in a contract with an independent contractor, the control may even be greater than where it is to be exercised by direction on the job, as would be the normal expectation in a contract with a servant, but a literal application of the test might find the actual control to be less. In addition, the test has broken down completely in relation to highly skilled and professional workers, who possess skills far beyond the ability of their employers to direct.[25]

---

[23] O. Kahn-Freund, 'Servants and independent contractors', *Modern Law Review*, 14 (1951), 504, 505–6. See also R. Kidner, 'Vicarious liability: for whom should the "employer" be liable?', *Legal Studies*, 15 (1995), 47.
[24] [1951] 2 KB 343 at 352.   [25] [1986] 3 FC 553 at 558–9.

3.3.1 Control and doctors: who is liable for the negligent surgeon?

The classic example, which has troubled all legal systems, is that of the position of the doctor or surgeon in relation to the hospital in which they work, providing healthcare to patients. Physicians will be subject to other influences apart from that of an employer, for example their professional oaths (Hippocratic oath) and codes of practice (for example, that of the General Medical Council (UK), *Code de déontologie médicale* (France, Québec),[26] German Medical Association (*Bundesärztekammer*),[27] Canadian Medical Association, American Medical Association). Equally, the exercise of their profession is characterised by personal autonomy and discretion in the treatment of patients. A test of control, direction and authority bears little relation to the practice of the medical profession. Can a professional, who is expected to act independently, observe professional ethics and may work for a number of institutions, be deemed to satisfy the control test?

The answer is, logically, 'No' and, for some time, this led to a denial of employee status for physicians and surgeons at common and civil law. In the leading common law case of *Hillyer v Governors of St Bartholomew's Hospital*,[28] the English Court of Appeal held that the only duty undertaken by the governors of a public hospital towards a patient who is treated in the hospital by physicians and surgeons is to use due care and skill in their selection of such staff. Vicarious liability, on this basis, would only exist in relation to purely ministerial or administrative duties, such as, for example, attendance by nurses in the wards.[29] Denning LJ has suggested that the unwillingness to impose vicarious liability in such circumstances might be due to a desire to relieve charitable hospitals from liabilities which they could not afford (a matter becoming irrelevant when the State took responsibility for

---

[26] The status of the French *Code de déontologie médicale* should be noted in that it is not simply a matter of self-regulation by the profession, but the *Ordre des médecins* is charged with drafting a text which is presented to the government, which must be consistent with the existing legal framework and which is ultimately published in the Official Journal signed by the Prime Minister: see www.conseil-national.medecin.fr. Article 5 of the Code (Article R.4127-5 du code de la santé publique) states that: *Le médecin ne peut aliéner son indépendance professionnelle sous quelque forme que ce soit* (the doctor cannot give up his professional independence in any form whatsoever).

[27] See www.bundesaerztekammer.de and M. Stauch, *The law of medical negligence in England and Germany* (Oxford: Hart, 2008), pp. 4–5.

[28] [1909] 2 KB 820. See also *Evans v Liverpool Corpn* [1906] 1 KB 160.

[29] [1909] 2 KB at 829 per Kennedy LJ.

hospital provision),[30] but blame must primarily lie with the narrowness of the control test and its inability to adapt to the needs of the liberal professions. As professional men, exercising personal judgement and autonomy, physicians were classified as independent contractors; their independence and skills acting to exclude 'employee' status.[31] In the words of the 1950 Paris Court of Appeal, '[the hospital] is with regard to surgeons, doctors or interns without authority or control concerning the practice of their professional skills'.[32]

By the 1940s, the common law courts had recognised the need to modify the rule. In four key cases, the English courts held that professional skill should not prevent a person working full-time for the hospital from being treated as an employee.[33] In parallel, the courts also developed the primary liability of hospitals to patients in terms of negligence and a non-delegable duty. Denning LJ in *Cassidy* held that, in any event, hospitals have a non-delegable duty to undertake to treat patients and to select, appoint and employ the professional men and women who are to give the treatment, and will be primarily liable for negligence by any of those persons who treat the patient.[34] It remains the case, however, that it has never been clearly resolved whether visiting or consulting physicians and surgeons should now be regarded

---

[30] *Cassidy v Ministry of Health* [1951] 2 KB 343 at 361. See also P. O. Osode, 'The modern hospital and responsibility for negligence – pointing Canadian courts in the right direction', *Anglo-American Law Review*, 22 (1993), 289, 290–2 and A. L. Goodhart, 'Hospitals and trained nurses', *Law Quarterly Review*, 54 (1938), 533, who comments at 575 that: 'This attempt to protect charitable hospitals by judicial legislation has not had a happy result, for it is illogical and has introduced confusion into the law.'

[31] See Req 21 July 1947 D 1947.486; 20 April 1953 JCP 1953 II 7663 note R. Savatier. Generally, J. Ambialet, *Responsabilité du fait d'autrui en droit medical* (Paris: LGDJ, 1965).

[32] Paris 16 January 1950 D 1950.169 (my translation).

[33] *Gold v Essex CC* [1942] 2 KB 293 (radiographer); *Collins v Hertfordshire County Council* [1947] KB 598 (resident junior house surgeon); *Cassidy v Ministry of Health* [1951] 2 KB 343 (assistant medical officer and house surgeon); and *Roe v Minister of Health* [1954] 2 QB 66 (anaesthetist). Note also criticism by Lord Wright in the earlier decision of *Lindsey County Council v Marshall* [1937] AC 97 at 124 in which all the law lords refrained from relying upon *Hillyer* and confined the decision to the dangerous condition of the premises. Note similar developments across the Commonwealth and the United States during this period: *Sisters of St Joseph of the Diocese of London v Fleming* [1938] SCR 172 (SCC); *Henson v Board of Management of Perth Hospital* (1939) 41 WALR 15 (Australia); and *Bing v Thunig* (1957) 143 NE 2d 3 (US).

[34] See *Cassidy v Ministry of Health* [1951] 2 KB 343 at 365. See also *Wilsher v Essex Area Health Authority* [1987] QB 730 (CA); *Albrighton v Royal Prince Alfred Hospital* [1980] 2 NSWLR 542; *Ellis v Wallsend District Hospital* (1989) 17 NSWLR 553; and *A (A Child) v Ministry of Defence* [2004] EWCA Civ 641, [2005] QB 183. See M. Brazier, and J. Beswick, 'Who's caring for me?', *Medical Law International*, 7 (2006), 183.

as employees, despite the comments of Denning LJ that, since the advent of the National Health Service, no distinction should be made between hospital staff.[35] Such issues may be circumvented, however. For example, in the UK, the question is rendered irrelevant due to the fact that the NHS indemnity scheme covers all such staff, regardless of their technical status.[36]

In contrast, the French and German courts have maintained their loyalty to tests of authority and direction. The unwillingness of the courts to modify their definitions of *commettant* and *Geschäftsherr* may be explained by the context in which claims arise. In both jurisdictions, treatment by a doctor is usually governed by *contract* law,[37] and will be subject to the contractual provisions of the Code (Article 1147, *Code Civil* and §§ 276–278 BGB). § 278 provides for strict liability for the acts of employees. Equally, the development of the concept of liability for the acts of others in contract law in France[38] has permitted the courts to find a clinic liable in contract law for mistakes by a physician classified as a *salarié*;[39] the action arising from the clinic's breach of contract for which the existence or not of a *commettant/préposé* relationship is irrelevant.[40] Physician liability will, therefore, generally be determined by the law of contract and thus the provisions of the law of tort are irrelevant.

---

[35] *Razzel v Snowball* [1954] 1 WLR 1382 at 1386.

[36] See NHS Circular: HSG (96) 48: *NHS indemnity arrangements for handling clinical negligence claims against NHS staff* (1996) and K. Syrett, 'Institutional liability' in A. Grubb, J. McHale and J. Laing (eds.), *Principles of medical law*, 3rd edn (Oxford University Press, 2010), ch. 7.

[37] In France, the key case to this effect is Cass civ 20 May 1936, DP 1936.1.87 rapp L. Josserand, concl P. Matter, note EP (*arrêt Mercier*). See, generally, the 2007 Annual Report of the Cour de cassation, Etude: *La santé dans la jurisprudence de la Cour de cassation*, pp. 241ff; www.courdecassation.fr/IMG/pdf/rapport_annuel_2007.pdf

[38] '*Responsabilité contractuelle du fait d'autrui*': see G. Viney and P. Jourdain, *Traité de droit civil: les conditions de la responsabilité*, 3rd edn (Paris: LGDJ, 2006), N° 813.

[39] That is, in circumstances where there is no contract between the physician and the patient: the patient contracting solely with the clinic: see Civ 1, 26 May 1999 JCP 1999 II 10112 rapp P. Sargos, RTD civ. 1999.634; Civ 1, 4 June 1991 Bull civ 1991 N° 185 p. 122, JCP 1991 II 21730 note E. Savatier, RTD civ. 1992.123 obs P. Jourdain. Where the physician is not a *salarié* of the clinic, but a visiting physician who contracts directly with the patient, the contractual action will still be brought, but against the physician; the clinic only being liable for its own contractual obligations, e.g. the provision of accommodation, food or paramedical services.

[40] It should also be noted that, in France, a distinction must also be drawn between the public and private law contract regimes. Whilst a visit to a general practitioner would be seen as a matter for the private law of contract, a claim against a public service hospital (obviously distinct from a private clinic) would be brought under the principles of administrative law: see Chapter 2. Our focus in this book will be on private law claims.

It will therefore be rare for a claim to be brought in tort/delict. However, some case law does exist from which a comparison may be made. As mentioned in Chapter 2, despite the doctrine of *non-cumul* (non-accumulation of actions), the French criminal courts will often deal with the *action civile* (civil action raised during the criminal case) on the basis of tort principles. Equally, if there is no contract – for example, urgent medical care is given to an unconscious patient – the courts will be forced to utilise the law of delict.[41] Examining the case law which exists, a similar reaction may be identified to that of the earlier common law cases. Hospitals were not found to be the '*commettant*' of the doctor or surgeon, who were deemed to work for their own account.[42] Whilst nurses and other minor hospital staff are accepted as employees, the 'control/authority' test leads to the conclusion that if, in the course of an operation, the nurse commits a wrongful act, the person responsible would be the surgeon himself, under whose orders the nurse was acting, rather than the hospital.[43]

German law would appear to adopt a similarly restrictive interpretation of the '*Geschäftsherr/Verrichtungsgehilfe*' relationship, in excluding

---

[41] See C. Vilar, 'L'évolution des responsabilités du chirurgien et de l'anesthésiste' RTD civ. 1974.747 at N°s 21–9. Contrast German law where the difficulties raised by the treatment of children and unconscious or incompetent patients are dealt with either through a contract concluded by a proxy or *negotiorum gestio* (*Geschäftsführung ohne Auftrag*) under § 677ff. Although the inability to claim for non-pecuniary loss in contract law did, in the past, encourage injured patients to bring a concurrent claim in tort law, the reforms to the BGB (notably the new § 253(II) BGB) has rendered it likely that contract law will dominate patient claims in future: see Stauch, *The law of medical negligence*, p. 11.

[42] See Req 21 July 1947 D 1947.486; Paris 16 Jan 1950 D 1950.169; 20 April 1953 JCP 1953 II 7663 note R. Savatier.

[43] Civ 15 Nov 1955 D 1956.113 note R. Savatier, JCP 1956 II 9106 note R. Rodière; Civ 1, 12 Nov 1968 D 1969.96, JCP 1969 II 15864 note R. Savatier (liability for intern). Compare with the English case of *Hillyer v Governors of St Bartholomew's Hospital*: 'But although [nurses] are such servants for general purposes, they are not so for the purposes of operations and examinations by the medical officers . . . The nurses and carriers, therefore, assisting at an operation cease for the time being to be the servants of the [hospital authorities], inasmuch as they take their orders during that period from the operating surgeon alone, and not from the hospital authorities' [1909] 2 KB 820 at 826 per Farwell LJ The surgeon was therefore deemed to have assumed responsibility for controlling and directing the assistant surgeons and nurses during the operation. Goodhart, 'Hospitals and trained nurses', 566 denied, however, that this ever signified that the surgeon would be treated as the employer, but this is not the view of Denning LJ in *Cassidy v Ministry of Health* [1951] 2 KB 343 at 361, although his lordship acknowledged that this argument had become untenable following *Mersey Docks and Harbour Board v Coggins & Griffith (Liverpool) Ltd* [1947] AC 1 and that there could now be no doubt that nurses would remain the employees of the hospital authorities, even when they are under the direction of the surgeon in the operating theatre.

senior consultants (*Chefarzt*)[44] and private physicians and midwives (*Belegarzt* and *Beleghebamme*) from § 831. In a 1995 case of the Supreme Court,[45] a private hospital was found not to be liable under either §§ 278 or 831 for the doctor, who had used its facilities to treat a private patient. Here, negligence was alleged against both an obstetrician and a midwife for failing to detect signs of eclampsia which, it was alleged, if noted would have prevented the claimant being born in a state of asphyxia leading to permanent brain damage. As an external physician, the court ruled that the *Belegarzt* was not covered by the contractual obligations of the hospital. However, having the right to give the midwife instructions (*Weisungsrecht*), the *Belegarzt* himself would be deemed liable for the faults of the midwife whilst under his control.[46]

3.3.2 Response

By the second half of the twentieth century, perceived difficulties with a strict application of the control test led the judiciary to question whether the factor of control could still be considered decisive. Two reactions may be identified in the systems surveyed: amending the control test to render it more flexible and responsive to modern employment practices, or treating the issue of control as only one factor, of many, governing identification of the contract of employment.[47] Generally, civil systems have favoured the former option and common law systems the latter. In practice, this seems to have resulted in similar decisions, although a growing body of criticism is appearing in civil law as to the fiction of the 'control' or 'subordination' test, which, it is argued,[48] amounts to a mere incantation which hides the real reasons for the courts' decisions.

---

[44] Although liability may be imposed under company law (§31 BGB) by treating the Chefarzt as the 'organ' of the clinic, as discussed in Chapter 2: see BGHZ 77, 74 = NJW 1980, 1901, MünchKommBGB/Wagner, §831, para. 45; von Staudinger et al., *Kommentar*, §831, para. 66.

[45] BGH 14 Feb 1995, BGHZ 129. 6 = NJW 1995, 1611 (*Belegarzt*), noted von Staudinger et al., *Kommentar*, §831, para. 66 and K. Müller, *Medizinrecht* (1996), 208.

[46] A claim under § 823 for organisational fault by the hospital was also rejected (contrast BGH NJW 1986, 776 (overtired doctors on night shift), noted by G. Spindler in *Beck'scher Online-Kommentar BGB*, 13th edn (2009) §823, para. 702).

[47] An intermediary category may also be noted: looking at a number of factors but treating the question of control as most important.

[48] See, notably in French law, Viney and Jourdain, *Traité de droit civil*, N° 792 and Brun, who describes the test as 'abstract, even divinatory': P. Brun, 'L'évolution des regimes particuliers de responsabilité du fait d'autrui', Resp civ et assur November 2000 No hors série 12, N° 18.

3.4 Alternative approaches to the control test

3.4.1 A more flexible interpretation of the control test[49]

The French test remains that of *'subordination juridique'*, that is, identifying who has the right to give orders or instructions to the employee as to how to do their job (*le droit de donner à un subordonné des ordres ou des instructions sur la manière de remplir ses fonctions*). Although the test based on authority and subordination remains (and such authority must be real and not merely apparent),[50] more recent case law has moved to a more flexible interpretation.[51] The power to give instructions need not have a contractual[52] or legal basis, but may simply exist as a matter of fact. Indeed, it is no longer necessary to prove that such a power has been exercised, provided that the *commettant* is deemed to possess authority over the *préposé*.[53] Further, and importantly, one can have authority over a subordinate, despite the absence of technical knowledge.[54]

Similarly in German law, the case law no longer requires a detailed right of control: 'it is sufficient that the employer can at any time determine the scope and duration of the tasks of the employee, restrict them or terminate them'.[55] As noted by van Gerven, Lever and Larouche,

---

[49] See, generally, H. Slim, 'Recherches sur la responsabilité du fait d'autrui en droit comparé', Resp civ et assur November 2000 No hors série 52, esp N°s 3-8.
[50] Cass crim 15 February 1972 D 1972.368; JCP 1972 II 17159 note D. Mayer; RTD civ. 1973.350 obs G. Durry.
[51] See, for example, Crim 7 November 1968 D 1969 somm 34. For a similar attempt in the common law to 'liberalise' the control test, see the fourfold test suggested by Lord Thankerton in *Short v J & W Henderson Ltd* (1946) 79 Ll L Rep 271 at 277: '(a) the master's power of selection of his servant; (b) the payment of wages or other remuneration; (c) the master's right to control the method of doing the work; and (d) the master's right of suspension or dismissal' (case under Workmen's Compensation Act), and cases such as *Zuijs v Wirth Brothers Proprietary Ltd* (1955) 93 CLR 561, 571 where an acrobat engaged in a trapeze act was found to be the employee of the circus; the High Court of Australia finding that control need only exist as to incidental or collateral matters.
[52] The existence of remuneration is not a condition (Civ 2, 9 November 1972 Bull civ II N° 275; Crim 14 June 1990 Bull crim 1990 N° 245), but may nevertheless be indicative of the existence of a *lien de préposition*: Civ 2, 26 October 2000 JCP 2000 IV 2834.
[53] See, for example, Com 26 January 1976 D 1976.449 rapp J. Merimée; Civ 2, 12 January 1977 D 1977 I.R. 330 obs C. Larroumet: '*il suffit qu'il ait eu la* **possibilité** *de donner au préposé des ordres ou des instructions sur la manière de remplir ses fonctions*'. (emphasis added)
[54] Civ 2, 12 January 1977 D 1977 I.R. 330 obs C. Larroumet.
[55] BGH 30 June 1966 BGHZ 45, 311 = NJW 1966, 1807, 1808 (translation from W. van Gerven, J. Lever and P. Larouche, *Tort law: ius commune casebooks for the common law of Europe* (Oxford: Hart Publishing, 2000), p. 497). Although the 1966 case itself would be decided differently today (due to changes in the availability of damages for non-material injury in contract law and the extension of §31 BGB to partnerships pursuant

the focus of the test is no longer on the fact of instructing the employee how to do his job, but the *possibility* of being able to control the employee's actions.[56] On this basis, liability may be extended to independent contractors and traders, depending on the circumstances under which they work and whether a general right to give instructions has been retained.[57] Legeais notes that, despite the different wording, the French and German courts in fact utilise similar criteria to determine the existence of an employer/employee relationship.[58]

There is even a move towards adopting a more liberal approach to the liability of physicians in French law, who, as seen in 3.3.1, the courts have been reluctant to classify as '*préposés*' due to their professional independence. Whilst developing liability in contract law – the primary basis for liability – in its decision of 1992[59] the Criminal chamber of the Cour de cassation refused to accept that an anaesthetist hired by the Red Cross to provide holiday cover would not be treated as a *préposé* under Article 1384(5), despite his professional independence. This has been described as 'a radical change to the very notion of "*préposé*", that is to say the abandonment of the principle of the independence of physicians'.[60] Alternatively, it may be seen as recognition that a salaried doctor may be considered a part of the hospital staff, and thereby a 'subordinate', without relinquishing his or her professional

---

to §§705ff BGB in so far as they participate in legal business), it still remains good authority for the definition of *Verrichtungsgehilfe*. See also BGH NJW-RR 1998, 250, 251f; von Staudinger et al., *Kommentar*, §831, paras. 120ff; MünchKommBGB/Wagner, §831, para. 14; and M. Reimann and J. Zekoll, *Introduction to German law*, 2nd edn (The Hague: Kluwer Law International, 2005), p. 214: 'Although this does not necessarily require permanent and paid employment, it is required that the principal have the authority to determine the scope and duration of the employee's tasks and to restrict or terminate them as necessary.'

[56] Van Gerven, Lever and Larouche, *Tort law*, p. 497.
[57] See, for example, the case of a *Rausschmeisser* (bouncer) in a disco: BGH VersR 1975, 520.
[58] R. Legeais, 'L'évolution de la responsabilité civile des maîtres et commettants du fait de leurs préposés en droit français et en droit allemand' in P. Couvrat (ed.) *Ecrits en l'honneur du Professeur Jean Savatier* (Paris: Presses universitaires de France, 1992), 303, 305.
[59] Crim 5 March 1992 Bull crim 1992 N° 101, p. 255, JCP 1993 II 22013 note F. Chabas, RTD civ. 1993.137 obs P. Jourdain. See also Crim 13 December 1983 Bull crim 1983 N° 342, D 1984 IR 459 obs J. Penneau (midwife) and Crim 22 March 1988 Bull crim N° 142 (contractor working for department store installing goods purchased by customers, deemed to be acting according to the instructions or orders of the store). For contractual liability: see Civ 1, 26 May 1999 JCP 1999 II 10112 rapp P. Sargos, RTD civ. 1999.634 obs P. Jourdain.
[60] Note Chabas (n. 59 above) (my translation). See also Brun, 'L'évolution des regimes particuliers', N°s 19–20.

independence.[61] Van Gerven also suggests that the fact that liability would have arisen in contract law or, if it had been a public hospital, in public law,[62] might have encouraged the Cour de cassation to reach a similar result in the law of tort.[63] In practice, the *loi* of 4 March 2002 further diminishes the significance of any distinction between salaried doctors and ordinary hospital employees by rendering it compulsory for health establishments to obtain insurance covering all salaried staff acting in the course of their employment.[64]

Viney and Jourdain in their leading textbook go as far as to suggest that the more flexible approach demonstrated in recent case law reflects the fact that the courts are, in reality, focusing not on the power to give instructions, but on whether the performance in question was for the purposes of (and to the profit of) the *commettant*.[65] In reality, the reciprocal relationship of subordination and authority provides merely a formula; its interpretation to be determined by the courts. The courts have taken the opportunity to utilise this simple formula to impose liability under Article 1384(5) far beyond the traditional employer/employee relationship, as will be discussed in Chapter 5.

To speak in terms of 'authority', 'control' and 'subordination' is therefore to refer only to general guidance to the question whether the person deemed in authority should be held responsible for the wrongs of another whom he is deemed to control. What is clear is that, despite adherence to the 'authority/subordination' formula, the courts have nevertheless responded to changes in employment practices, even in the traditionally sensitive field of liability for physicians, but that as a result, the formula gives limited practical assistance as a test for determining the scope of liability.

---

[61] See Jourdain RTD civ. 1993 (n. 59 above), 140. This is additionally consistent with the more liberal definition of 'employee' used in French labour legislation and amendments to the *Code de déontologie médicale*, Arts. 95–9: *Exercice salarié de la medicine*.

[62] A public authority will be held liable for salaried physicians in public hospitals, in the absence of evidence of gross fault or malice: see CE 4 July 1990 Leb1990.972, D 1991 Somm 291.

[63] Van Gerven, Lever and Larouche, *Tort law*, para. 499/3.

[64] See Article L 1142–2 Code of Public Health: 'Insurance subscribed by institutions, services and organisations mentioned in the first paragraph covers the employees who have acted within the limits of their mission which is fixed for them despite the fact that they have independence in the practice of their medical skill.'

[65] Viney and Jourdain, *Traité de droit civil*, N° 792. But contrast Civ 2,17 December 1964 JCP 1965 II 14125 note R. Rodière: 'la notion de profit n'est pas déterminante'.

3.4.2 The organisation and composite tests

An alternative approach is to adopt a less rigid definition of 'employee' and examine the role of the worker in the defendant's organisation. This has received support from some French authors such as Viney and Jourdain (see 3.4.1), and such ideas gained favour in the common law from the 1940s. Two tests will be identified here: the organisation test and the composite test. Whilst the common law now generally favours the latter test, the influence of the organisation (or integration) test, primarily propounded by Lord Denning, has not totally disappeared.

3.4.2.1 The organisation (or integration) test

From 1940, courts began to look at how a worker was integrated into the company. Denning LJ in *Stevenson Jordan & Harrison Ltd v MacDonald & Evans*[66] suggested an alternative test for identifying 'employee' status, namely the degree to which the alleged employee had been integrated into the defendant's business:

> One feature which seems to run through the instances is that, under a contract of service, a man is employed as part of the business, and his work is done as an integral part of the business; whereas, under a contract for services, his work, although done for the business, is not integrated into it but is only accessory to it.[67]

While such a test marks a step away from the control test towards a more contextual analysis of the parties' relationship, it arguably does no more than restate the question. It is not clear that the enquiry 'is X integrated into the business or part and parcel of the business?' is easier to answer than 'is X an employee'? More worryingly, as indicated by the Supreme Court of Canada in its leading case of *671122 Ontario Ltd v Sagaz Industries Canada Inc*,[68] the question whether the worker's activity is integral to the employer's business will usually be answered in the

---

[66] [1952] 1 TLR 101. Applied by Mocatta J in *Whittaker v Minister of Pensions and National Insurance* [1967] 1 QB 156 (QBD).

[67] [1952] 1 TLR 101 at 111. See also the comments of Denning LJ in *Bank voor Handel en Scheepvaart NV v Slatford* [1953] 1 QB 248 at 295: 'I would observe that the test of being a servant does not rest nowadays on submission to orders. It depends on whether the person is part and parcel of the organization.'

[68] [2001] 2 SCR 983, 204 DLR (4th) 542 at para. 42 per Major J. See also Kidner, 'Vicarious liability', 60–1, who argues that the organisation test, to work, must have two parts: whether the worker's activities are essential to the organisation, and whether the worker is part of the organisation in terms of management structures or in business on his own account.

affirmative: for example, even the work of a contract cleaner may be said to be technically integral to sustaining the business. MacKenna J in *Ready Mixed Concrete (South East) Ltd v Minister of Pensions and National Insurance*[69] was equally dismissive of the test, regarding it as too generous and creating uncertainty: 'This raises more questions than I know how to answer. What is meant by being "part and parcel of an organisation?" Are all persons who answer this description servants? If only some are servants, what distinguishes them from the others if it is not their submission to orders?'[70] Lord Griffiths in *Lee Ting Sang v Chung Chi-Keung*[71] dismissed the test as merely emphasising the fact that persons working in a professional capacity, such as doctors or engineers, may in law be employees, despite the absence of control over their activities.

3.4.2.2 The composite or economic reality/entrepreneur test: examining the totality of the parties' relationship

In view of such criticism, the common law courts now generally favour a broader test in which control is only one factor, out of many, in determining whether a contract of employment exists.[72] As Cooke J commented in the leading English case of *Market Investigations v Minister of Social Security*,[73] 'the most that can be said is that control will no doubt always have to be considered, although it can no longer be regarded as

---

[69] [1968] 2 QB 497 at 524.
[70] Note, however, some indirect support by Kirby J dissenting in *Sweeney v Boylan Nominees Pty Ltd* [2006] HCA 19, (2006) 227 ALR 46, at para. 61.
[71] [1990] 2 AC 374 at 388 (PC (HK)).
[72] See, for example, *Ready Mixed Concrete (South East) Ltd v Minister of Pensions and National Insurance* [1968] 2 QB 497; *WHPT Housing Association Ltd v Secretary of State for Social Services* [1981] ICR 737; *Lane v Shire Roofing Co. (Oxford) Ltd* [1995] IRLR 493; *Stevens v Brodribb Sawmilling Co.* [1986] HCA 1, (1986) 160 CLR 16 at 49. Note also criticism from the United States: *United States of America v Silk* (1946) 331 US 704 and the Restatement (2nd) of Agency § 220(2) (published in 1958), which listed ten non-exhaustive criteria for identifying a master–servant relationship: (a) the extent of control which, by the agreement, the master may exercise over the details of the work; (b) whether or not the one employed is engaged in a distinct occupation or business; (c) the kind of occupation, with reference to whether, in the locality, the work is usually done under the direction of the employer or by a specialist without supervision; (d) the skill required in the particular occupation; (e) whether the employer or the workman supplies the instrumentalities, tools, and the place of work for the person doing the work; (f) the length of time for which the person is employed; (g) the method of payment, whether by the time or by the job; (h) whether or not the work is a part of the regular business of the employer; (i) whether or not the parties believe they are creating the relation of master and servant; and (j) whether the principal is or is not in business.
[73] [1969] 2 QB 173 at 185.

the sole determining factor'. In this case, finding that no comprehensive test could be found, his Honour stated:

> The observations of Lord Wright,[74] of Denning LJ and of the judges of the Supreme Court[75] suggest that the fundamental test to be applied is this: 'Is the person who has engaged himself to perform these services performing them as a person in business on his own account?' If the answer to that question is 'yes,' then the contract is a contract for services. If the answer is 'no,' then the contract is a contract of service. No exhaustive list has been compiled and perhaps no exhaustive list can be compiled of the considerations which are relevant in determining that question, nor can strict rules be laid down as to the relative weight which the various considerations should carry in particular cases. The most that can be said is that control will no doubt always have to be considered . . . and that factors which may be of importance are such matters as whether the man performing the services provides his own equipment, whether he hires his own helpers, what degree of financial risk he takes, what degree of responsibility for investment and management he has, and whether and how far he has an opportunity of profiting from sound management in the performance of his task.[76]

Lord Griffiths in the Privy Council has remarked that 'the matter had never been better put than by Cooke J'[77] and other Commonwealth courts have agreed. The High Court of Australia, for example, in *Stevens v Brodribb Sawmilling Co. Pty Ltd*[78] accepted the governing test not to be that of control, but that of the 'totality of the employment relationship'.[79] Recognition that the control test can no longer be an absolute test does not, however, exclude a finding that it is still relevant,[80] but in moving towards this multi-faceted test, greater emphasis

---

[74] In *Montreal v Montreal Locomotive Works Ltd* [1947] 1 DLR 161 at 169 (see text to n. 82 below).
[75] Reference being made to *United States of America v Silk* (1946) 331 US 704.
[76] [1969] 2 QB at 184–5.
[77] In *Lee Ting Sang v Chung Chi-Keung* [1990] 2 AC 374 at 382.
[78] (1986) 160 CLR 16, 63 ALR 513. Approval was also given by the Supreme Court of Canada in *671122 Ontario Ltd v Sagaz Industries Canada Inc* [2001] 2 SCR 983, 204 DLR (4th) 542 (SCC).
[79] (1986) 160 CLR at 29 per Mason J. His Honour noted at 24 that: 'Other relevant matters [apart from control] include, but are not limited to, the mode of remuneration, the provision and maintenance of equipment, the obligation to work, the hours of work and provision for holidays, the deduction of income tax and the delegation of work by the putative employee.'
[80] For example, the US Restatement (3rd) of Agency § 7.07 (Employee acting within scope of employment) (2006), continues to focus on the degree of control the principal exercises over the agent: '(1) An employer is subject to vicarious liability for a tort committed by its employee acting within the scope of employment . . . (3) For purposes

is placed on the ability of the independent contractor to work for his own account in comparison to the employee. Here, the 1947 Privy Council decision in *Montreal v Montreal Locomotive Works Ltd*[81] has proved influential. In this case, Lord Wright held that 'In the more complex conditions of modern industry, more complicated tests have often to be applied . . . a fourfold test would in some cases be more appropriate, a complex involving (1) control; (2) ownership of the tools; (3) chance of profit; (4) risk of loss. Control in itself is not always conclusive.'[82] The independent contractor is thus free to profit and spread his risks, but also more at risk of losses than the employee. Whilst the parties' intentions will be seen as relevant, they are by no means conclusive and are to be considered in the context of all other evidence. In the case itself, Cooke J held that part-time interviewers working under short-term contracts for a market research company were employees. Their employers exercised extensive control over their work and the limited discretion given to employees to decide when they would work, and the ability to work for others during the relevant period, were not inconsistent with the existence of a series of contracts of employment.

The Cooke approach has been described by the Supreme Court of Canada as 'a persuasive approach to the issue', identifying '[t]he central question [to be] whether the person who has been engaged to perform the services is performing them as a person in business on his own account'.[83] Major J in this case emphasised that 'It bears repeating that the above factors constitute a non-exhaustive list, and there is no set formula as to their application. The relative weight of each will depend on the particular facts and circumstances of the case.'[84] The common

of this section, (a) an employee is an agent whose principal controls or has the right to control the manner and means of the agent's performance of work, and (b) the fact that work is performed gratuitously does not relieve a principal of liability.' Note (f), however, confirms that the numerous factual indicia, previously expressly stated in § 220 of the 2nd Restatement (see n. 72), are still relevant.

[81] [1947] 1 DLR 161 at 169.
[82] See also the entrepreneur test stated by W.O. (later Justice) Douglas, 'Vicarious liability and administration of risk', *Yale Law Journal*, 38 (1929), 584 at 595, which posited four differentiating earmarks of the entrepreneur: control, ownership, losses, and profits. Flannigan reinterprets the Wright/Douglas entrepreneur test as one based on enterprise control, whereby in the absence of non-nominal employer control, the worker should be classified as an independent risk-taker, i.e. independent contractor: R. Flannigan, 'Enterprise control: The servant–independent contractor distinction', *University of Toronto Law Journal* (1987), 25.
[83] *671122 Ontario Ltd v Sagaz Industries Canada Inc* [2001] 2 SCR 983, 204 DLR (4th) 542 at para. 47 per Major J.
[84] Ibid., para. 47.

law courts thus accept that there can be no universal test to determine whether a person is an employee or an independent contractor, and that many different factors may have to be taken into account.[85] The net result, as will be shown in 3.5, is a degree of uncertainty in the law as an inevitable concomitant to the flexibility needed to classify modern employment relationships.

3.5 Application of the 'totality of the relationship' test: owner-drivers and bicycle couriers

Two common law decisions demonstrate the operation of this test in practice, showing its flexibility, but also the discretion given to courts in each factual scenario. The cases – one English and one Australian – involve a similar factual situation: the court being asked to determine the status of a worker who is delivering goods (ready-mixed concrete/ documents and parcels) using his own transport at the behest of a company operating a delivery service. In the first case, an owner-driver, delivering concrete, was found to be an independent contractor. In the second, a bicycle courier was found to be an employee. In both cases, the same test was used. The application of the test and the reasons for such divergent results will be examined below.

3.5.1 The owner-driver

Ready Mixed Concrete (South East) Ltd v Minister of Pensions and National Insurance[86] concerned the status, for tax purposes, of owner-drivers delivering goods for Ready Mixed Concrete. MacKenna J held that a contract of employments exists if three conditions are fulfilled:

- The employee agrees that, in consideration of a wage or other remuneration, he will provide his own work and skill in the performance of some service for his employer;
- He agrees, expressly or impliedly, that in the performance of that service he will be subject to the other's control in a sufficient degree to make that other master; and
- The other provisions of the contract are consistent with its being a contract of service.[87]

---

[85] See, for example, ibid., para. 46 per Major J, and *Hall (Inspector of Taxes) v Lorimer* [1994] 1 WLR 209 at 218 (Nolan LJ).
[86] [1968] 2 QB 497 (dispute about National Insurance contributions).
[87] Ibid., at 515.

What the *Ready Mixed Concrete* test provides is, in essence, a summary of the composite test, emphasising the need for mutuality and control in an employment relationship. McKenna J took the opportunity, however, to highlight the limitations of the control test, making express reference to Lord Wright's test in *Montreal v Montreal Locomotive Works Ltd*[88] and the economic reality test used in the United States.[89] On the facts, drivers in question had provided their own vehicles, which were maintained at their own expense, and were paid at mileage rates under a contract which expressly declared them to be independent contractors. The vehicles, however, were obtained via a finance organisation associated with the company, painted in company colours and the driver was to obtain the company's permission to hire a replacement driver. Further, the drivers were obliged to wear the company uniform, comply with the company rules and were prohibited from operating as a carrier of goods except under contract. Nevertheless, McKenna J determined the 'owner-drivers' to be independent contractors. His Honour regarded the drivers as 'small business men', who owned their own assets and incurred both the chance of profit and the risk of loss.[90] Although the company clearly exercised a high degree of control, this was not determinative and had to be considered in light of the other provisions of the contract as a whole.

3.5.2 *The bicycle courier*

In the Australian case of *Hollis v Vabu*,[91] vicarious liability was indeed in issue; the question being the status of a bicycle courier, who had negligently injured Mr Hollis whilst making a delivery. The courier was unidentifiable save for his uniform on which appeared the trading name of Vabu, owners of the courier business. Here, the majority[92] found the couriers to be employees of the company for whom it was vicariously liable. Again, there were factors supporting both independent contractor and employee status. The couriers were paid by fixed rates per job, required to use their own bicycles and were able to deal with the

---

[88] [1947] 1 DLR 161 at 169, PC.   [89] See *US v Silk* (1946) 331 US 704.
[90] See also *Todd v Adams (The Maragetha Maria)* [2002] EWCA Civ 509, [2002] 2 Lloyd's Rep 293 where the Court of Appeal held that an arrangement whereby remuneration of the crew of a fishing vessel depended solely on a share of the profits (or losses) of each trip should be characterised as a joint venture rather than a contract of service.
[91] (2001) 207 CLR 21.
[92] Gleeson CJ, Gaudron, Gummow, Kirby and Hayne JJ in a joint judgment. McHugh J concurred in the result but not the reasoning. Callinan J dissenting.

company as sole traders or members of a partnership. In contrast, they wore uniforms, were provided with radio equipment by the company and allocated jobs by radio. The company provided strict instructions concerning dress, appearance, language, delivery procedures and dealing with clients and undertook the provision of insurance for the couriers (deducting the amounts from their wages). The majority here focused on a number of factors in determining that the couriers were in fact employees:[93]

- The couriers were providing unskilled labour;
- The couriers had little or no control over the manner in which the work was performed;
- The uniform presented them to the public as emanations of Vabu and no measures were taken to render the couriers personally identifiable; and
- The couriers had no negotiating power in terms of remuneration or undertaking their own business enterprises.

The provision of their own equipment was not seen as determinative. Bicycles, the High Court found, were relatively cheap and could be used for purposes other than work.[94] In practice, the couriers were not running their own business or acting independently of Vabu, although a different conclusion might arise if greater investment in capital equipment was required and greater skill and training was required in its operation.[95]

3.5.3 Distinguishing factors

Although there are clear similarities between the cases, a number of observations may be made. First, the composite test means that no one factor will be determinative. A high level of control may argue in favour of employee status, but this is not automatic. Nevertheless, it remains an important concern: in *Hollis*, the High Court emphasised the high degree of control exercised by Vabu, which extended beyond incidental or collateral matters.[96] Secondly, in seeking signs of the small business man, the degree of investment appears significant – the purchase of a

---

[93] See (2001) 207 CLR 21, paras. 48–57.
[94] McHugh J ibid., para. 71 disagreed on this point on the basis that some couriers used their own motor vehicles, which indicated that they were *not* employees.
[95] Ibid., para. 47.
[96] 'Vabu's whole business consisted of the delivery of documents and parcels by means of couriers. Vabu retained control of the allocation and direction of the various deliveries. The couriers had little latitude': ibid., para. 57.

large truck being more suggestive of independent contractor status than the purchase of a bicycle, usable for leisure activities as well. Thirdly, evidence of independence, characterising independent contractor status, may at times seem forced. In *Ready Mixed Concrete*, for example, McKenna J relied upon the facts that the driver might (albeit with permission) use a replacement driver, choose another to maintain the vehicle and, perhaps weakest of all, choose where to purchase fuel for the lorry.[97] What this highlights, however, is the discretion awarded to judges in weighing up the different relevant factors. This is further highlighted in *Hollis* where the majority noted at the start of its judgment the 'important findings' that Vabu had known for some time prior to the accident that a number of couriers posed a danger to pedestrians due to their failure to obey traffic rules and that, although means were available, Vabu had failed to pursue a scheme rendering their couriers personally identifiable.[98] The relevance of this apparent reference to fault may appear questionable in a case related to vicarious liability. Nevertheless, this factor was later relied upon as a reason why a contract of employment should be found, namely that the policy ground of deterrence favoured the existence of an employer/employee relationship when it would encourage the introduction of greater safety measures to reduce the number of accidents and the risks to the community as a whole.[99] On this basis, Vabu's failure to take steps to reduce the risk of harm supported a finding of the employer/employee relationship.

Two further comments may be made. First, the majority in *Hollis* clearly utilise policy factors, such as deterrence, which go beyond a formal examination of the practicalities of the working relationship between the parties. In an open-ended test, examining a multitude of factors, it remains a moot point to what extent such policy factors should influence the determination of the employer/employee relationship. Secondly, one underlying theme of *Hollis* was the need for the law to evolve to accommodate contemporary notions of employment relations. This led McHugh J to suggest the more radical solution of redefining 'employees' as 'representative agents'.[100] This suggestion will be

---

[97] See [1968] 2 QB at 526. [98] (2001) 207 CLR 21, para. 3.
[99] Ibid., para. 53, ground 4, relying on McLachlin J's ruling in *Bazley v Curry* (1999) 174 DLR (4th) 45 at paras. 32–3.
[100] 'If the law of vicarious liability is to remain relevant in the contemporary world, it needs to be developed and applied in a way that will accommodate the changing nature of employment relationships. But any such developments or applications must be done consistently with the principles that have shaped the development of vicarious

discussed in Chapter 5 when we examine how far the courts are prepared to extend the vicarious liability relationship beyond that of the traditional employer and employee. For the majority in *Hollis*, however, it was enough that the courts sought to ensure that the common law tests continued to be sufficiently flexible to adapt to changing social conditions.[101]

3.6 Conclusion

The primary example of vicarious liability is that imposed on the employer for the torts of his employees. It may thus be said that the employer/employee relationship remains at the heart of all systems of vicarious liability. It serves to define the key relationship in which it is deemed justifiable to hold one party strictly liable for the torts of another. As Stevens recognised in 1939, 'The definition of servant or employee is, then, part of the general question of how the risk and cost of injuries should be borne.'[102] In determining *who* is liable, the courts are thus defining the boundaries of liability and who ultimately bears the burden of compensating victims.

Nevertheless, as seen in this chapter, the identification of a test to determine this relationship has become far from straightforward. The certainties of the past, where the labourer was told how to toil by his master, have become confused by the informalities of many modern employment relationships and the independence and initiative shown by an educated workforce in a modern technological age. Without a detailed written contract, it may be difficult to identify the nature of the relationship and this problem is exacerbated by deliberate evasion of such formalities, often to obtain tax advantages or, from the employers' perspective, to avoid protective legislation. To this must be added an unwillingness to exclude the liberal professional, trained and using his

---

liability and the rationales of those principles. They should also be done in a way that has the least impact on the settled expectations of employers and those with whom they contract': (2001) 207 CLR 21, para. 85.

[101] The majority view has been labelled 'relatively conservative' by one commentator in adhering to the traditional contract of employment analysis, although he does concede that some of the statements in *Hollis* may sow the seeds for an approach that is rooted more firmly in the economic realities of work relationships: A. Stewart, 'Redefining employment? Meeting the challenge of contract and agency labour', *Australian Journal of Labour Law*, 15 (2002), 235 at 245.

[102] G. M. Stevens, 'The test of the employment relation', *Michigan Law Review*, 38 (1939), 188 at 199.

own skills and knowledge to deal with specific tasks, from the scope of vicarious liability.[103] As a result, the courts have moved towards a far more flexible interpretation of the employer/employee relationship, either by adopting a looser interpretation of the need for control/the right to give instructions/authority, or by focusing on the totality of the relationship including economic factors such as risk, potential profit and investment and even policy concerns such as deterrence. A common law judge has concluded that 'it is impossible to devise a single foolproof test to accommodate both (a) the principle of certainty, which requires predictability of result and consistency of conclusion, and (b) the principle of justice, which requires space for the operation of circumstances in individual cases',[104] and this seems as true in civil law as in common law.

While the 'control' test provides a straightforward test, it is generally recognised that it can no longer be said to represent many employment relationships accurately and a more sophisticated test is required. It is submitted that a more flexible version of the 'control' test is not the answer. As seen in relation to the civilian systems which seek to maintain a test based on subordination or the right to give instructions, it may appear to avoid the uncertainties of the multi-faceted common law test, but changes in the workplace and increased use of technology have led the courts to interpret the tests loosely, requiring only the possibility of some form of control. It has been objected that this renders the test a formality, described as being simultaneously ambiguous and inadequate,[105] whilst raising difficulties in relation to professionals whom it is difficult to encompass within any test based solely on control. On this basis, despite its uncertainties, the 'totality of relationship' test is to be preferred. It highlights the complexities of modern employment practices, the key distinction between employees and independent

[103] For example, the recent proposal to reform the French Civil Code (P. Catala, *Avant-projet de réforme du droit des obligations et de la prescription* (Paris: La Documentation française, 2006)) suggests (at Article 1360) that 'a person is liable for harm caused by another person whose professional or business activity he regulates or organises and from which he derives an economic advantage where this occurs in the course of this activity. This includes notably the liability of healthcare establishments for harm caused by the doctors to whom they have recourse. The claimant must show that the harmful action results from the activity in question' (translation by S. Whittaker and J. Cartwright: www.justice.gouv.fr/art_pix/rapportcatatla0905-anglais.pdf).
[104] *Buchan v Secretary of State for Employment* [1997] **IRLR** 80 at 81 per Mummery P.
[105] See N. Molfessis, 'La jurisprudence relative à la responsabilité des commettants du fait de leurs préposés ou l'irrésistible enlisement de la Cour de cassation' in D. Mazeaud (ed.), *Mélanges Gobert* (Paris: Economica, 2004) 495 at 502.

contractors, and the economic framework within which employment operates. As such, it provides the best way of dealing with the topic of this chapter: identifying the contract of employment.

Therefore, whilst it is possible to identify factors which go to determine *when* the courts will find an employment relationship, the law has come to value flexibility over certainty, evidenced by the common law test and the broad civilian tests. As seen in the owner-driver/bicycle courier example, flexibility brings with it uncertainty, but it is hard to see how this may be avoided without retaining an unduly narrow and unrealistic test.

This leads one to a number of conclusions. First, that legal systems now adopt a broader view of the employer/employee relationship. Secondly, that this very conclusion informs us that the definition of the contract of employment does not exist in a vacuum. It acts as a preliminary condition for the application of the doctrine of vicarious liability, and, as a result, it should be considered in the light of the aims and objectives of the doctrine itself. In *671122 Ontario Ltd v Sagaz Industries Canada Inc*, for example, the Supreme Court of Canada found a direct connection between the main policy grounds justifying vicarious liability and the distinction between employees and independent contractors:

Vicarious liability is fair in principle because the hazards of the business should be borne by the business itself; thus, it does not make sense to anchor liability on an employer for acts of an independent contractor, someone who was in business on his or her own account. In addition, the employer does not have the same control over an independent contractor as over an employee to reduce accidents and intentional wrongs by efficient organization and supervision. Each of these policy justifications is relevant to the ability of the employer to control the activities of the employee, justifications which are generally deficient or missing in the case of an independent contractor.[106]

As such, the common law refusal to recognise the significance of the context in which vicarious liability arises, runs the real danger of failing to appreciate the underlying policy justifications which justify the imposition of strict liability on the employer. Finally, if the employer/ independent contractor distinction may be seen to be linked to the policy grounds underlying vicarious liability, then these policy goals may also justify extending liability beyond the traditional contract of employment into other relationships characterised by an inequality of

---

[106] [2001] 2 SCR 983, 204 DLR (4th) 542 at paras. 34 and 35 per Major J. See also McLachlin CJ in *KLB v British Columbia* [2003] 2 SCR 403, 230 DLR (4th) 513 at paras. 20–6.

power between tortfeasor and defendant, in circumstances where the tortfeasor is ostensibly acting to further the interests of the defendant.

The next chapter will examine how the doctrine has adapted to meet the 'borrowed servant' problem and the issue of temporary employees in general. A move towards 'contracting out' certain jobs in recent years, for example security or cleaning work, has rendered it difficult to determine whether a contract of employment exists at all and, if so, with whom. Chapter 5 will examine the more contentious question hinted at in this chapter – if the employer/employee relationship is to be interpreted broadly, how willing are the courts to extend this relationship to non-traditional relationships, where one person exerts economic power over the actions of another or may simply be working at the request of another?

4 Special difficulties: borrowed employees and temporary workers

4.1 Introduction

This chapter will address two particular issues arising from the requirement of an employer/employee relationship: *which* employer will be responsible for the wrongful acts of an employee currently on loan to a temporary employer, and *who*, if anyone, will be responsible for the wrongful acts of casual or agency staff. These raise distinct, if overlapping, concerns. In both situations, the worker is engaged in temporary work, often for a short period of time, and his relationship with the temporary employer does not bear the traditional hallmarks of a contract of employment. However, in the first situation, the question is not whether the worker is employed, but whether the general or temporary employer will be vicariously liable for his wrongful conduct. Here, the courts have sought to provide some degree of certainty by resort to presumptions of liability and, in more recent times, attempted to find a test consistent with the policy rationales underlying the imposition of vicarious liability. Atiyah in 1967 presented a more radical solution: rather than choosing between the general and temporary employer, policy would suggest that the best approach would be to render both employers liable, thus ensuring the victim compensation without having to predict which employer would be held liable at law.[1] This approach has not generally been adopted by the courts.

The second situation raises more fundamental problems in that the casual worker, supplying his labour on demand, either directly or via an employment agency, resembles an independent contractor, not an employee. In the absence of 'employee' status, neither the agency which supplies him nor the enterprise which uses his labour will be

[1] P. S. Atiyah, *Vicarious liability in the law of torts* (London: Butterworths, 1967), p. 164.

vicariously liable. Although this problem is not new – use of homeworkers and casual staff precedes the Industrial Revolution[2] – the growing 'vertical disintegration' of employment relations in recent years has led to employees, who previously would have been employed as permanent staff, being treated as self-employed.[3] The removal of 'employee' status has a potentially significant impact on the scope of vicarious liability, thereby depriving the victim of the ability to pursue an (insured) enterprise and leaving him to sue a worker, who is unlikely to be insured (unless this is required by contract) or to possess sufficient means to compensate for serious injuries.[4]

Workers supplied by an employment agency provide a good example of the difficulties arising from this move towards contracting-out staff. In terms of contract law, neither of the two contracts involved in this model (the contract for services between worker and agency and the contract for the supply of labour between agency and end-user) resembles a contract of employment. However, the courts have clearly been reluctant to deny the benefit of strict liability in favour of victims unlucky enough to be injured by temporary, rather than permanent staff, particularly when they are indistinguishable from permanent staff. More fundamentally, it has been questioned whether, in reality, such workers may be characterised as entrepreneurs, contracting out their services to the highest bidder and freely undertaking the risks and benefits of self-employment, or simply individuals taking the only work on offer.

Both these examples challenge the traditional view of what is meant by the contract of employment and its relationship with the doctrine of vicarious liability. The reality of modern employment practices signifies that many of the certainties of the past – 'who's your boss?' and 'where do you work?' – have become opaque. The struggle by legal systems to adapt to such modern developments will be examined in this chapter.

---

[2] See J. Schwarzkoff, 'The social condition of the working class' in S. Berger (ed.), *A companion to nineteenth century Europe, 1789–1914* (Oxford: WileyBlackwell, 2009).
[3] See H. Collins, 'Independent contractors and the challenge of vertical disintegration to employment protection laws', *Oxford Journal of Legal Studies*, 10 (1990), 353, and A. Stewart, 'Redefining employment? Meeting the challenge of contract and agency labour', *Australian Journal of Labour Law*, 15 (2002), 235.
[4] See R. Kidner 'Vicarious liability: for whom should the "employer" be liable?', *Legal Studies*, 15 (1995), 47, and E. McKendrick 'Vicarious liability and independent contractors – a re-examination', *Modern Law Review*, 53 (1990), 770.

4.2 Lending employees: the 'borrowed servant' problem

In Chapter 3, we focused on identifying the characteristics which indicate the existence of an employer/employee relationship. In this section, we address a different problem: the tortfeasor (Y) is employed by general employer (A), but sent to work for temporary employer (B) and, whilst working for B, commits a tort. In such circumstances, generally, A will continue paying Y's salary, although Y will be acting in the fulfilment of duties specified by B. If Y commits a tort, should A, B or both parties be liable under the doctrine of vicarious liability?[5]

The triangular relationship between general employer, temporary employer and employee is outlined in Diagram 1.

Such situations are not uncommon. For example, a contractor may hire skilled welders or plumbers to assist in a construction contract, or obtain equipment on a temporary basis which is supplied with its own driver or operator. When an accident is caused by the hired employee, the question arises as to the distribution of risk, or more bluntly, whose insurance company will pay.

The common law position is still that stated by the House of Lords in *Mersey Docks and Harbour Board v Coggins and Griffith (Liverpool) Ltd*.[6] Here, the harbour board had hired out a crane, together with its driver Newall, to a firm of stevedores. The contract of hire stated that Newall was to be regarded as an employee of the firm, although the board would continue

A (general employer) →→→→→→→→→→→ B (temporary employer)

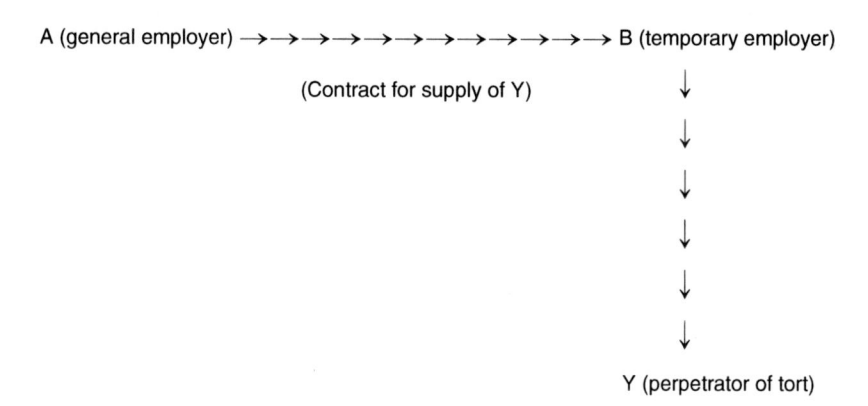

(Contract for supply of Y)   ↓
                                 ↓
                                 ↓
                                 ↓
                                 ↓
                                 ↓
                          Y (perpetrator of tort)

Diagram 1 The borrowed servant

---

[5] The common law traditionally has asked whether the effect of the loan is to render the employee '*pro hac vice*' (for an occasion/for the time being) the employee of the hirer.
[6] [1947] AC 1.

to pay his wages and retained a power of dismissal. In loading a ship, Newall negligently injured one of the firm's employees and the question was who was liable for his actions. The House of Lords held that the harbour board (that is, the general employer) remained liable. At the time of the accident, although the firm had instructed Newall what work to undertake, it had no control as to how Newall operated the crane. Looking at all the circumstances of the case, the facts that the harbour board retained authority to control how the crane was driven and paid the wages of Newall, indicated it was still his employer. Further, it was held that, in most cases, the courts would assume that the general or permanent employer would remain the employer of the tortfeasor. He would bear the burden of showing that responsibility should not remain with him and this burden was recognised to be a heavy one.[7] Only in exceptional circumstances would this heavy burden of proof be satisfied to render the hirer liable. Even where the contract of hire specifies that the employee is to be treated as an employee of the temporary employer, the courts will examine the substance of the relationship.[8]

This approach has been followed by the Commonwealth courts. In Australia, for example, Mason J in *Kondis v State Transport Authority (formerly Victorian Railways Board)*,[9] approved the test as stated in *Mersey Docks* and the earlier Australian case of *McDonald v The Commonwealth*,[10] examining whether the defendants in the circumstances could be said to be exercising control over Clissold, the hired crane driver. On the facts, the entire supervision and control of the operation of the crane was in the hands of Clissold and Mason J ruled that it could not be said that the temporary employer exercised any supervision or control at all over the employee at the relevant time. Equally, in the Canadian case of *McKee v Dumas*,[11] Dubin JA followed the lead of *Mersey Docks* in holding that the burden of transferring liability from the general employer would be a heavy one. In *McKee*, an experienced driver of a tractor-trailer, paid by the general employer which retained the right to hire, fire and discipline

---

[7] Ibid., at 10 per Viscount Simon; at 13 per Lord Macmillan; at 21 per Lord Uthwatt.
[8] Although the parties may agree as to an indemnity.
[9] [1984] HCA 61, (1984) 154 CLR 672 at para. 11.
[10] (1946) 46 SR (NSW) 129. See also *Deutz Australia Pty Ltd v Skilled Engineering Ltd* [2001] VSC 194, in particular paras. 109–14 per Ashley J, and *Transtate Pty Ltd v Rauk* [2002] NSWCA 222.
[11] (1976) 70 DLR (3d) 70 at 75 (Ont CA). See also *James Street Hardware & Furniture Co. v Spizziri* (1985) 33 CCLT 209 (Ont HC), aff'd on this point (1987) 43 CCLT 9 (Ont CA).

him, was found to remain the responsibility of the general employer, despite the fact that he had been driving the temporary employer's vehicle at the time of the accident.

A number of factors may be identified as influential: control (continuing to play a dominant role), who pays the worker's wages, who has power of dismissal, how long the alternative work lasts, the complexity of the machinery and the skill of the operator himself.[12] Hallett LJ in *Hawley v Luminar Leisure Ltd*[13] reiterated the relevance of control in the modern context:

> The question of control may not be wholly determinative, but, for as long as *Mersey Docks* remains the authoritative decision on when responsibility for an employee's tortious acts may pass from a general employer to a 'temporary deemed employer', the question of control remains at the heart of the test to be applied.[14]

In this case, a nightclub was found to be vicariously liable for a doorman hired under a contract for the provision of security services where the doorman could be shown to be acting under the orders of the nightclub manager. The court found that, in practice, it was the nightclub manager who took control and responsibility for staff: 'When she said jump, they jumped'.[15]

The continued dominance of control may, in the light of the doubts expressed in Chapter 3, appear questionable. In *Mersey Docks* itself, Newall, when asked who controlled his actions, responded 'I take no orders from anybody'. This 'sturdy' answer, according to Lord Simonds, demonstrated that he was a skilled man who knew his job and would carry it out his own way.[16] The weaknesses of the test in relation to skilled professionals are equally applicable here. A skilled professional will be expected to act at his discretion and not require constant supervision and direction. Control, in such circumstances, can only be one factor to be weighed against other relevant factors. Nevertheless, in the context of unskilled labour, control would still appear of particular relevance and

---

[12] [1947] AC 1 at 17 per Lord Porter. See also May LJ in *Viasystems (Tyneside) Ltd v Thermal Transfer (Northern) Ltd* [2005] EWCA Civ 1151 at para. 7.
[13] [2006] EWCA Civ 18, [2006] PIQR P17.
[14] Ibid., at para. 82. See also Arden LJ in *Interlink Express Parcels Ltd v Night Trunkers Ltd* [2001] EWCA 360, [2001] RTR 338, at para. 60: '... in the context of temporary deemed employment, the paramount test is that of control'; the Court of Appeal in *Biffa Waste Services Ltd v Maschinenfabrik Ernst Hese GmbH* [2008] EWCA Civ 1257, [2009] QB 725; and David Steel J in *Colour Quest Ltd v Total Downstream UK plc* [2009] EWHC 540 (Comm).
[15] [2006] EWCA Civ 18 at para. 76.   [16] [1947] AC 1 at 20.

it is perhaps not surprising that in cases where the presumption in favour of the general employer has been rebutted, the temporary employer has generally been found to have direction and control over unskilled labour.[17]

The question of control is similarly important in civil law. The French courts will examine who had authority over the employee when the tort took place.[18] Although, as commentators acknowledge, this is not always a straightforward matter,[19] the courts will consider a number of factors: any clear contractual allocation of responsibility, indicating the common intention of the parties,[20] who possesses the right to instruct the employee at the relevant time, the length of the loan and technical competence of the parties.[21]

In practice, French law leaves much to the findings of fact of the lower court judges (*les juges du fond*) against which appeal is limited.[22] Although the French courts have resisted any presumption against the general employer (in contrast to the common and German law), in the majority of cases, notably involving vehicles or machinery hired with drivers, the general employer will be held liable unless he can be shown to have given up all control over the employee.[23] If, however, the courts

---

[17] See *Hawley v Luminar Leisure Ltd* [2006] EWCA Civ 18 (bouncer at nightclub) and *Gibb v United Steel Companies* [1957] 1 WLR 668 (dock workers).

[18] Req 24 January 1938 DP 1938.1.50 note signed EP; 21 October 1942 Gaz Pal 1942.2.243; 3 November 1942 D 1947.145 note A. Tunc; Civ 15 July 1948 D 1948.471; Crim 25 January 1951 S 1951.1.298; 1 June 1954 JCP 1954 II 8435 note R. Rodière; Civ 15 November 1955 Gaz Pal 1956.1.32; Civ 2, 11 May 1956 D 1957.121 note R. Rodière; 2 June 1956 D 1956 somm 84; Crim 28 October 1958 D 1959.somm 21.

[19] See the leading article of F. Gaudu, 'La responsabilité civile du prêteur de main d'oeuvre', D 1988 chron 235.

[20] See Com 26 January 1976 D 1976.449 rapp J. Mérimée: clear and precise contractual provision specifying that the SNCF workers should be considered as the *préposés* of the temporary employer which acted to transfer to the temporary employer the right to give orders. See also Civ 3, 17 Nov 1976 D 1977 IR 99, JCP 1977 IV 3 and Soc 30 January 1985 Bull civ V N° 71; obs J. Huet RTD civ. 1986.132.

[21] F. Terré, P. Simler and Y. Lequette, *Droit civil: les obligations*, 10th edn (Paris: Dalloz, 2009), N° 831.

[22] See Cass crim 14 March 1983 Bull crim N° 78, p 175, although the Cour de cassation does control the actual definition of the *lien de préposition* and requires the *juges du fond* to state that the liability of the *commettant* is based on the exercise of direction and control over the *préposé* at the moment of injury: Cass com 5 February 1985 Bull civ 1985 IV N° 47.

[23] See Terré, Simler and Lequette, *Droit civil*, N° 831; G. Viney and P. Jourdain, *Traité de droit civil: les conditions de la responsabilité*, 3rd edn (Paris: LGDJ, 2006), N° 793; Com 16 June 1966 JCP 1968 II 15330 note J. Bigot; Com 18 June 1969 Bull civ IV N° 233, p. 221; Civ 2, 9 November 1976 D 1977 IR 107; Crim 28 Nov 1979 D 1980 IR 311; Com 13 May 1980 JCP 1980 IV 281.

find special circumstances which indicate that the temporary employer has total control over the employee, then the temporary employer will be liable.

The French approach, in practice, therefore resembles that of the common law. However, notably in the context of vehicles lent with their drivers or equipment with their operators, the courts have favoured a rather technical approach in determining whether the general or temporary employer exercises principal authority over the employee. For example in the 1987 *Suteau* case,[24] Carrières Gaillard had lent a tractor, low-platform trailer and driver (Suteau) to SARELO to assist it to move a digger. Driving on the route stipulated by SARELO, Suteau reached a level crossing where a road sign warned of a hazard to low-platform vehicles. Suteau nevertheless decided to cross and the trailer became struck between two tracks. The trailer was then struck by an oncoming train, injuring several people. In finding the general employer (Carrières Gaillard) liable for the actions of Suteau under Article 1384(5), the Supreme Court distinguished between the control exercised by the temporary employer in relation to its operations generally, for example matters such as speed, route or itinerary, and that exercised by the general employer in relation to the technical part of driving the vehicle: here, the question whether the vehicle could cross the level crossing successfully being a technical matter for which the general employer would be liable.[25] On this basis, the person responsible for the employee will depend on what exactly the employee gets wrong: does his fault relate to the operation and driving of the vehicle (general employer) or its general use as a means of transport (temporary employer)?[26] Radé has quite rightly termed it 'a subtle distinction'.[27]

---

[24] Cass crim 20 October 1987 Bull crim 1987 N° 359 p. 960.
[25] '*Gaillard n'a à l'évidence pas transféré à l'utilisateur son pouvoir de contrôle et de direction en ce qui concernait la partie technique de la conduite du véhicule ... confronté à une difficulté relevant de sa spécialité, Z ... avait repris la direction de l'opération et se trouvait toujours, pour cette partie de sa mission, sous la dépendance de son employeur habituel.*' (Ibid.)
[26] See Civ 2, 17 July 1962 Bull civ 2 N° 599, Gaz Pal 1962.2.309; Civ 2, 17 December 1964 Bull civ 2 N° 830, JCP 1965 II 14125 note R. Rodière; Paris 1 December 1977 D 1978 IR 407 obs C. Larroumet, who argues that it ensures that the person with actual authority over the particular action is held responsible; Civ 2, 19 October 2006 Bull civ 2 N° 275, RTD civ. 2007.133 obs P. Jourdain. Note, however, criticism in Civ 2, 20 July 1955 D 1956 somm 151, JCP 1956 II 9052 note R. Savatier: '*une distinction arbitraire, sans se référer aux conventions intervenues entre les parties*'.
[27] Ch. Radé, *Jurisclasseur responsabilité civile et assurances, Fasc 143: Droit à réparation – responsabilité du fait d'autrui – domaine: responsabilité des commettants* (Paris: LexisNexis, 2007), para. 28. It is, however, consistent with the treatment of nurses assisting a

Gaudu has questioned how such a division assists our understanding of the relevant law.[28] It is over-technical and may give rise to arbitrary distinctions.[29] In his view, it is far more useful to retain the general test outlined above to identify who is responsible. This seems sensible and consistent with the common law approach which, in applying the 'control' test, examines the extent to which the general employer may be deemed to retain control over the employee's actions in the circumstances of each case.[30]

The technicalities of the French position may also be contrasted with the leading German case of 1995,[31] in which the Federal Supreme Court found that, in a contract for the provision of manpower (*Dienstverschaffungsvertrag*), dependence on the instructions of the general employer would only be severed if the employees were completely separated from the general employer. Retention of the right to recall the personnel at any time and assign them elsewhere was deemed sufficient to prevent the link being severed:

> Where the employees are integrated into the receiving organisation, they can be regarded as *Verrichtungsgehilfen* of the temporary employer. If the separation from the general employer is incomplete, claims could be entertained against both employers as *Geschäftsherrn* within the meaning of § 831 BGB.[32]

Professors Viney and Jourdain, in favouring a test based on the overall economic relationship of the party, have argued that the general employer should usually be found liable, unless the employee may be said to be genuinely integrated into the hirer's organisation for a

---

surgeon in the operating theatre, described in Chapter 2, where the nurse may be considered subordinate to the surgeon or the hospital, depending on the duties he or she is undertaking at the time: Civ 2, 15 March 1976 Bull civ II N° 100, D 1977.27.

[28] Gaudu, 'La responsabilité civile', N° 27.
[29] See also Viney and Jourdain, *Traité de droit civil*, N° 793.
[30] See, for example, the Canadian case of *McKee v Dumas* (1976) 70 DLR (3d) 70 (Ont CA), decided on very similar facts to *Suteau*, where the driver of a tractor-trailer failed to see a red flashing signal and was hit by a train. See also Lord Macmillan in *Mersey Docks* [1947] AC 1 at 14.
[31] BGH 26 January 1995 NJW-RR 1995, 659: workers sent to assist the claimant in the demolition of a stadium roof had disobeyed the instructions of the claimant's foreman and damaged the roof pillars, with the result that three days later, the roof collapsed and damaged the stadium. See also MünchKommBGB/Wagner, 5th edn (Munich: C.H. Beck, 2009), §831, Rn 22; OLG Düsseldorf NJW-RR 1995, 1430.
[32] Translation taken from W. van Gerven, J. Lever and P. Larouche, *Tort law (Common Law of Europe Casebooks)* (Oxford: Hart, 2001), 5.G.9.

definite period of time, on the basis that this is most likely to reflect the availability of insurance.[33] As Trindade, Cane and Lunney have commented, the traditional rule of the common law has the benefit of avoiding uncertainty not only as to who the claimant should sue, but which employer is responsible for obtaining insurance against the risk. Liability should therefore only be transferred where the temporary employer has complete control (as in the Australian case of *McDonald v Commonwealth* where the lender lent a vehicle and its driver for a purpose of which the lender was completely unaware and the employee was acting wholly under the instructions of the temporary employer's foreman).[34] In such circumstances, the general employer is in no position to assess the risk inherent in the employee's performance and should therefore not be liable.[35]

We end 4.2 by examining an alternative approach to the 'borrowed employee' question, which seeks to divide responsibility between general and temporary employer, either equally or according to the level of control exercised.

4.2.1 Dual liability?

Although the approach so far has been to identify whether the general or temporary employer will be liable, a further option is to render both parties jointly liable for the errant employee. Atiyah in his 1967 monograph commented that:

> It is perhaps strange that the [common law] courts have never countenanced what might be thought the obvious solution to the problem, namely to hold *both* employers liable to the plaintiff, and leave them to dispute amongst themselves as to whether the one is entitled to an indemnity or contribution from the other.[36]

In Atiyah's view, it was unjust to leave the claimant with the difficult task of deciding whether to sue the general or temporary employer:

---

[33] Viney and Jourdain, *Traité de droit civil*, N° 793. See also Atiyah, *Vicarious liability*, pp. 163–4, and Vertes J in *Hardisty v 851791 NWT Ltd* (2004) 26 CCLT (3d) 305 (NWTSC), aff'd (2005) 35 CCLT (3d) 100 (NWTCA). Jourdain argues that the notion of who profits from the employee's action should be taken into account: see Civ 2, 6 February 2003 Bull civ 2003 II N° 33, D 2004.som 1341 obs P. Jourdain.

[34] (1946) 46 SR (NSW) 129.

[35] F. Trindade, P. Cane and M. Lunney, *The law of torts in Australia*, 4th edn (Australia: OUP, 2007), 16.3.2.3.

[36] Atiyah, *Vicarious liability*, p. 156 (emphasis original).

'He ought to be able to sue both and leave them to dispute among themselves who should bear the burden.'[37]

In 2005, the English Court of Appeal in *Viasystems (Tyneside) Ltd v Thermal Transfer (Northern) Ltd* overturned the long-standing rule that dual vicarious liability did not exist at common law. In accepting dual liability as a possible solution to the question of liability, the Court of Appeal agreed with Professor Atiyah that, although it had been assumed since the early nineteenth century that liability must rest on one employer or the other, but not both,[38] such an assumption was based on slender authority and the basis for the contrary had never been properly argued.[39] In *Viasystems*, ducting work in a factory had been subcontracted to the second defendant, which had contracted with the third defendant for the supply of fitters and their mates on a labour-only basis. Strang, a fitter's mate, had negligently caused a flood in the factory. At the time of the accident, Strang had been acting on the instructions of the fitter (employed by the third defendant), but both had been under the supervision of the second defendant's employee, Horsley. On the facts, it was unclear whether the general or temporary employer should be liable in circumstances where both parties exercised control over the negligent fitter. The Court of Appeal held that both would be liable.

In so doing, the Court clearly divorced the issue of the nature and incidence of the employee's employment from the question of vicarious liability. Rix LJ gave general guidance.[40] Liability will normally rest on the general employer where the employee is used for a limited time in the general employer's own sphere of operations, operating the general employer's equipment. In contrast, where the employee is seconded for a substantial period of time to the temporary employer to perform a role embedded in that employer's organisation, the temporary employer will be solely liable. Joint vicarious liability is most likely to be found with contracted-out labour, selected and possibly trained by the general employer, but employed at the temporary employer's site, using the temporary employer's equipment and subject to the latter's instructions. May LJ nevertheless indicated that dual liability would occur

---

[37] Ibid., p. 163.
[38] See, for example, *Laugher v Pointer* (1826) 5 B & C 547, 108 ER 204 and *Jones v Scullard* [1898] 2 QB 565.
[39] [2005] EWCA Civ 1151, [2006] QB 510 at para. 20 per May LJ.
[40] Ibid., at para. 80.

rarely and that, in most cases, the general rule that liability would normally remain with the general employer would apply.[41]

On this basis, where there is shared control between employers, dual vicarious liability appears to be the logical response. Such liability, found the court, would be joint and several and, despite the discretion under the Civil Liability (Contribution) Act 1978, a 50/50 division would be close to a logical necessity.[42] In a situation where neither employer is personally liable and vicarious liability is acting as a policy device to redistribute the incidence of loss from a supposedly impecunious employee to solvent and insured employers, 'dual and shared' liability would generally (subject to questions of personal fault and any contractual agreements as to contribution) result in equal responsibility.

A number of other legal systems continue to resist the application of dual liability in this context. In France, the Cour de cassation rarely imposes liability on both employers,[43] although the courts are more willing to contemplate joint liability where it is unclear to the victim who the employer may be, for example due to a sham which shields the real *commettant*. Gaudu argues that it is a question of balancing competing policies: the policy interest in accident prevention suggests that the body with principal authority over the employee should be liable, but this must give way if a strict application appears likely to jeopardise the ability of the victim to gain compensation.[44] Equally, the Australian courts have yet to overturn their traditional view stated in *Oceanic Crest Shipping Co v Pilbara Harbour Services Pty Ltd*[45] that an employee cannot serve two masters at a time. Luntz defends the Australian position.[46] Although the notion of dual vicarious liability has received some obiter support from industrial tribunals,[47] such a radical change would be at

---

[41] Ibid., at para. 46.   [42] See ibid., at para. 52 per May LJ, and at para. 85 per Rix LJ.
[43] Viney and Jourdain, *Traité de droit civil*, N° 793.
[44] Gaudu, 'La responsabilité civile', N° 23. The courts have also accepted that more than one *commettant* might be liable in circumstances where the *préposé* is working for more than one *commettant* at the same time, e.g. a shepherd herding sheep for more than one farmer: Civ 2, 9 February 1967 Gaz Pal 1967.1.224.
[45] [1986] HCA 34, (1986) 160 CLR 626, although May LJ in *Viasystems* [2005] EWCA Civ 1151, [2006] QB 510 at para. 40, focused on the dissenting judgment of Brennan J which does not rule out the possibility of joint liability and also finds some US support: *Gordon v SM Byers Motor Car Co.* (1932) 309 Pa 453; *Siidekum v Animal Rescue League of Pittsburg* (1946) 353 Pa 408; and *Morgan v ABC Manufacturer* 710 SO 2d 1077.
[46] H. Luntz et al., *Torts: cases and commentary*, 6th edn (Australia: LexisNexis, 2009), 17.2.14.
[47] For example, *Morgan v Kittochside Nominees Pty Ltd* (2002) 117 IR 152; and see comment by R. Cullen, 'A servant and two masters? The doctrine of joint employment in Australia', *Australian Journal of Labour Law*, 16 (2003), 359.

odds with a large number of statutory and other obligations which assume the existence of one employer.

In contrast, the Supreme Court of Canada in *Blackwater v Plint*[48] has recently accepted dual vicarious liability, albeit in three paragraphs without any discussion of prior contrary authority, relying solely on Professor Atiyah's monograph. In *Blackwater*, former students of an aboriginal residential school claimed damages for sexual abuse by a dormitory supervisor (Plint), which had occurred whilst they were resident at a school operated by the Government of Canada and the United Church. In facing an extremely high profile case on a matter of considerable controversy in Canada, the Supreme Court concluded that both the Church and Canada were vicariously liable for the wrongful acts of Plint, focusing on the policy objectives underlying vicarious liability, as stated in the earlier case of *Bazley v Curry*.[49] Dual liability was thus permissible on the basis that 'if an employer with *de facto* control over an employee is not liable because of an arbitrary rule requiring only one employer for vicarious liability, this would undermine the principles of fair compensation and deterrence'.[50]

In contrast to *Viasystems* above, the Supreme Court of Canada in *Blackwater* approved the trial judge's division of liability on the basis of 75/25.[51] It was held that an unequal apportionment of responsibility would be appropriate where one party was more senior and exercised more control, which placed it in a better position to supervise the situation and prevent loss. Neyers has questioned whether the application of the ordinary principles of joint liability between *tortfeasors* is appropriate where the parties are held strictly liable without fault.[52] There is also a clear distinction between the Court of Appeal's notion of '*shared* and dual liability'[53] where liability is shared between both parties in circumstances where it is difficult to identify who has principal control of the employee (thereby logically giving a 50/50 division of liability) and

---

[48] (2005) 258 DLR (4th) 275. Note also the position in German law (stated above at text to n. 32): BGH 26 January 1995 NJW-RR 1995, 659, 660.
[49] [1999] 2 SCR 534.   [50] (2005) 258 DLR (4th) 275 at para. 38 per McLachlin CJ
[51] Note also the position in German law: BGH 26 January 1995 NJW-RR 1995, 659.
[52] J.W. Neyers, 'Joint vicarious liability in the Supreme Court of Canada', *Law Quarterly Review*, 122 (2006), 195.
[53] Brodie thus comments that 'the decision [in *Viasystems*] is actually a remarkably conservative one ... [and] as a consequence the decision constitutes a modest refinement of *Mersey Docks*': D. Brodie, 'The enterprise and the borrowed worker', *Industrial Law Journal*, 35 (2006), 87 at 88.

Atiyah's broader notion of dual liability, adopted by the Supreme Court of Canada. The former provides a residual test where it is impossible to determine whether the general or temporary employer has control. The latter provides, as intended by Atiyah, an alternative test to that currently used.

Nevertheless, what one sees in both *Viasystems* and *Blackwater* is recognition that the question of dual liability cannot be addressed without recognition of the distinct policy concerns which justify the imposition of vicarious liability. Dual vicarious liability frees the victim from the risk of suing the wrong employer and provides a useful tool in the courts' compensatory toolbox. Although the English courts adopt a strict interpretation which, they accept, signifies that it will be rarely used, it provides a powerful argument for recognising the need to move away from a rigid view of the employment contract.

4.3 Temporary workers: vicarious liability for casual or agency staff?

A further difficulty arises from the insecure nature of many modern employment relationships. Workers may be employed as casual staff, filling in when permanent staff are on holiday or unavailable, or at busy times of year such as Christmas. Alternatively, a person may be working for different employers via an agency, which itself enters a contract with each employer for the supply of staff. Fitting these relationships into the traditional contract of employment model has proven difficult. In each case, the employee resembles an independent contractor, providing his labour on demand. And yet the number of workers employed as temporaries, casuals, home-workers, freelancers or self-employed subcontractors continues to grow, signifying a shift towards vertical disintegration of production and a steady growth in subcontracting and self-employment as firms outsource their labour requirements. For example, in *Carmichael v National Power plc*,[54] the House of Lords found that part-time guides at a power station, employed on a 'casual as required basis' were independent contractors. The claimants were not obliged to accept work and were not guaranteed that casual work would be available. The defendants were under no obligation to provide or accept work; a moral obligation of loyalty would not suffice.

This second category of claims raises particular problems for vicarious liability. The question here is not *which* employer will be vicariously

[54] [1999] 1 WLR 2042.

liable, but will *anyone* be vicariously liable for the wrongful acts of the worker in question?

The agency model is particularly problematic in this respect. The employee (Y) joins an employment agency and signs a contract with the agency (A). The agency will attempt to find him work and, if successful, the agency will enter a contract with the employer (B) to supply the services of Y. There is no contract linking Y and B. Y's remuneration will be received from A. However, Y clearly does not work for A: the whole basis of the contract is that Y will work for another. In terms of the basic test for identifying a contract of employment – does the defendant pay the claimant a wage or some other remuneration for which he is obliged to provide his own work and skill for the defendant?[55] – the answer is clearly, 'No'.

This triangular relationship is illustrated in Diagram 2.

For the victim of the tort, therefore, it is difficult to establish vicarious liability for Y. Although undertaking work for B, he has no contract with B and is not paid directly by him. Alternatively, although paid by A and contracting with A, Y does not commit the tort in the course of any duties owed to A. On this basis, vicarious liability would not appear to operate. As Phegan J has commented, 'In tort law, it creates the prospect of a decreasing number of cases in which the injured plaintiff can assume that an employer, in the traditional master–servant sense, will be available to be held liable for the negligence of the employee in the

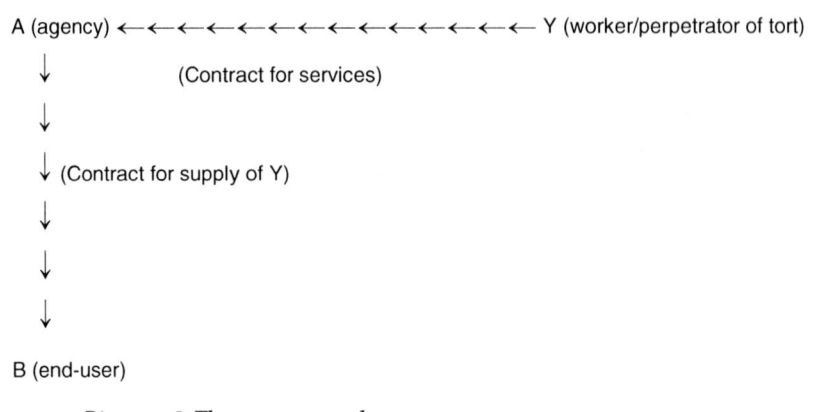

```
A (agency) ←—←—←—←—←—←—←—←—←—←—←—←— Y (worker/perpetrator of tort)
   ↓                (Contract for services)
   ↓
   ↓  (Contract for supply of Y)
   ↓
   ↓
   ↓
B (end-user)
```

Diagram 2 The agency worker

---

[55] MacKenna J in *Ready Mixed Concrete* [1968] 2 QB 497 at 515.

course of employment. As more work is contracted out by employers, the typical employment relationship becomes one of employer–independent contractor rather than employer–employee.'[56]

This may appear harsh when one considers that many casual workers are used on a regular basis and may regard this work as their main source of income. Further, due to contracting-out policies undertaken by many public bodies and large organisations, matters such as cleaning and security are commonly undertaken by agency staff, who are considered to be more cost effective than permanent staff. Agency staff may thus work for one employer for a number of years, although, for reasons of cost, will not be accepted as permanent staff. Should vicarious liability thus depend on the employment practices of the employer? More pertinently, should the victim's ability to rely on the principle of vicarious liability to ensure compensation depend on whether the person wearing the company's uniform is actually permanent or agency staff?

4.3.1 Finding liability

Concern has been raised that a strict application of this test serves to deprive temporary workers of the rights provided to employees. For example, in *O'Kelly v Trusthouse Forte*,[57] casual waiting staff at a hotel were held not to be employees, even though they worked on a regular basis exclusively for the hotel. The Court of Appeal held that in the absence of an *obligation* on the claimants to accept work and on the hotel to provide it, no contract of employment would arise. An assurance of priority for any available work created no more than an expectation of work. It was not a contractual promise.[58]

The majority of the Court of Appeal in *Nethermere (St Neots) Ltd v Taverna and Gardiner*[59] adopted a more flexible approach when faced with a similar situation. Here, the court was prepared to accept that homeworkers, operating on a piecework basis for more than two years, were in reality employees under a contract of employment implied by conduct. Well-founded expectations of continuing homework over a year or more could thus harden into an enforceable contract of service.[60] By implying an 'overall' or 'umbrella' contract obliging the company to continue to

---

[56] 'Employers' liability for independent contractors in tort law' *Judicial Review*, 4 (2000), 395.
[57] [1984] 1 QB 90.   [58] See ibid., at 116 per Ackner LJ.
[59] [1984] ICR 612 (Kerr LJ dissenting), relying on *Airfix Footwear Ltd v Cope* [1978] ICR 1210.
[60] See [1984] ICR 612 at 627 per Stephenson LJ.

provide and pay for work and the workers to continue to accept and perform the work provided, the applicants were able to bring claims for unfair dismissal.

The more recent English case of *Brook Street Bureau (UK) Ltd v Dacas*[61] demonstrates that a more generous approach may also be developed for agency staff. Mrs Dacas had worked for Wandsworth Council as a contract cleaner for over four years, although throughout that time had been supplied to the local authority through the Brook Street agency. She had been paid by the agency on the basis of time sheets supplied by the council. When dismissed, the question arose against whom any claim for unfair dismissal should be brought? Was she employed by the council, or the agency, or was she an independent contractor? The majority of the Court of Appeal held that, depending on the evidence, it could be argued that Mrs Dacas was employed by the council by means of an implied contract of employment. In view of her long service and the fact that she could be said to be paid indirectly by the council, mutual obligations could be found.[62]

The courts have, as yet, been reluctant, however, to find a contract of employment between the worker and the end-user, save where it satisfies the test of necessity and does not conflict with any express terms of the contracts between the parties.[63] Such an approach has led commentators to suggest that there has been 'a reversal of the "employee protective" and policy-oriented approach developed in *Franks*, *Dacas* and *Muscat* . . . returning to the classic orthodoxy of common law principles'.[64]

---

[61] [2004] EWCA Civ 217, [2004] ICR 1437. See also *Frank v Reuters Ltd* [2003] EWCA Civ 417, [2003] ICR 1166. Although technically obiter, the reasoning was approved by the Court of Appeal in the later case of *Cable & Wireless plc v Muscat* [2006] EWCA Civ 220, [2006] ICR 975 (contract of employment found with end-user where Muscat had initially been an employee of the end-user, but had been persuaded by the company to provide his services via an agency, without any change in function).

[62] Contrast the view of Munby J dissenting that such a conclusion was impossible unless the end-user paid the worker. Note also the earlier case of *McMeechan v Secretary of State for Employment* [1997] ICR 549: agency could be 'employer' in respect of individual assignments, but subsequent case law has re-emphasised the need to find mutual obligations on employer/employee: see *Montgomery v Johnson Underwood Ltd* [2001] EWCA Civ 318, [2001] ICR 819.

[63] See *Cable & Wireless plc v Muscat* [2006] EWCA Civ 220 at paras. 38–9 per Smith LJ; and *James v Greenwich LBC* [2008] EWCA Civ 35, [2008] ICR 545.

[64] M. Wynn and P. Leighton, 'Agency workers, employment rights and the ebb and flow of freedom of contract', *Modern Law Review*, 72 (2009), 91 at 92.

4.3.2 A less technical approach?

A number of difficulties arise here. The formalism of common law contract law – the requirement of consideration moving from promisor to promisee, privity of contract, restrictions on terms implied in fact – all obstruct a more general application of the principle of vicarious liability based on the 'totality of the relationship', including who controls the work of the employee. The analysis of the courts runs the risk of finding no one strictly liable for the worker, classifying him an independent contractor. In a situation where casual or agency staff are most unlikely to obtain insurance, subject to any specific contractual requirements, there is an obvious risk of failing to meet the policy objectives of vicarious liability, be they compensation to the victim, accident prevention or loss distribution. It is noticeable that civil systems, possessing no doctrine of consideration,[65] have been more ready to find an employer liable for the torts of such temporary staff. Applying the general tests of subordination (French law) or the right to give instructions (German law), one sees a greater readiness in agency situations to render the end-user liable, subject to express contractual conditions. In Germany, for example, if the worker is found to be fully integrated into the work of the end-user (and it is for the end-user to terminate the relationship), then the end-user will be the *Geschäftsherr* for the sake of § 831 BGB.[66] In France, the so-called *intérimaires* (temporary workers) problem is dealt with under the ordinary 'subordination' test – again, it being most likely that the end-user will be found to be the *commettant* under Article 1384(5) as the body exercising direction and control over the worker.[67] Again, the express terms of the contract between the agency and the end-user will be relevant. For example, in 1985, the Criminal chamber of the Cour de cassation held that a clause stating without any ambiguity that, during the course of the detachment, the end-user is the worker's employer/*commettant*, signified that the end-user would be liable under

---

[65] K. Zweigert and H. Kötz, *An Introduction to Comparative law*, 3rd edn (Oxford: Clarendon Press, 1998), ch. 29.
[66] See OLG Dusseldorf, 23 December 1994 NJW-RR 1995, 1430, upheld by BGH on appeal; and see van Gerven et al., *Tort law*, 5.G.9.
[67] See Gaudu, 'La responsabilité civile' Nos 24–5. This also deals with the problem of '*stagiaires*', undertaking placements under government schemes. Although there was some initial doubt whether the agency or the end-user should be liable (see, for example, Civ 29 November 1973 D 1974.194 note B. Dauvergne; RTD civ. 1974.419 obs G. Durry), modern case law favours rendering the end-user liable: see Crim 10 May 1976 D 1976 IR 175, RTD civ. 1976.785 obs G. Durry; Paris 25 February 1977 D 1977 IR 329 obs C. Larroumet.

Article 1384(5).[68] Neither claim prevents a contractual remedy by the end-user against the agency for supplying incompetent staff, which may allow it to recoup damages paid to the victim as consequential loss.[69]

4.4 Conclusion

In the two examples of borrowed employees and temporary workers, the common law approach of attempting to find a genuine contract of employment may be seen to obstruct the aims and objectives of vicarious liability. In requiring a contract supported by consideration and meeting the requirements of certainty and completeness, the courts limit their ability to intervene.

It is noticeable that, in the context of borrowed employees, the courts have refused to adopt a strict contractual line, most obviously in *Viasystems*.[70] Indeed, the possibility of dual vicarious liability makes little sense if a genuine contract of employment is required. It is a basic principle of law that a worker cannot be transferred from the service of one employer to another without the worker's consent. As Atiyah noted in 1967, the loan of an employee rarely involves the employee entering into a new contract of employment with the temporary employer: 'If a genuine transfer of the servant was necessary before the temporary employer could be held liable there would be no "doctrine of master and servant *pro hac vice*" at all.'[71] As Denning LJ explained in *Denham v Midland Employers' Mutual Assurance Ltd*,[72] the whole notion of borrowed employees is premised on the fiction that the employee is transferred, without, in reality, any change of his contractual arrangements with his employer: 'The supposed transfer, when it takes place, is nothing more than a device – a very convenient and just device, mark you – to put liability on to the temporary employer.' The courts here recognise the peculiar context of the borrowed employee and, in so doing, focus more openly on the key elements determining the imposition of vicarious liability.

In relation to casual or agency staff, the examples from civil law jurisdictions again suggest the need for a less technical approach. Without the need to invent consideration, implied terms or overcome the

---

[68] Crim 15 January 1985 Bull crim N° 24, p. 59.
[69] See Gaudu, 'La responsabilité civile', N° 36 imposing at least an obligation to take reasonable care (*obligation de moyens*).
[70] *Viasystems (Tyneside) Ltd v Thermal Transfer (Northern) Ltd* [2005] EWCA Civ 1151.
[71] Atiyah, *Vicarious liability*, 155.   [72] [1955] 2 QB 437 at 443.

doctrine of privity of contract, the courts focus on who has control over the tortfeasor and one sees increasing use in French law (by academics at least) of reference to the economic framework and loss distribution concerns. Cases such as *Dacas*[73] and *Nethermere*[74] demonstrate that the ingenuity of the common law may be able to imply a contract, but such a solution will have limited impact if the courts continue to adhere to the orthodox approach of requiring a genuine contract of employment. It is submitted that the real issue is whether the common law should continue to apply the same test for the employment contract regardless of context. Although *Dacas* did not in fact involve the question of vicarious liability, Mummery and Sedley LJJ both expressly recognised the doctrine would raise distinct concerns in determining when claimants injured by agency workers would be able to obtain compensation.[75]

The practice of contracting-out of core tasks creates, therefore, a potential gap in the protection offered by vicarious liability to victims injured by workers. Whilst civil law jurisdictions have sought to close that gap by rendering the end-user liable, the common law still lags behind. This leads potentially to arbitrary results: if you are injured by the tortious conduct of a waitress or cleaner, anonymous but for their uniform, although you may assume that this person works for the restaurant or offices in which you are injured, the availability of vicarious liability will depend on whether the worker is employed on a permanent or casual basis. Of course, there must be limits. If I hire a person for a few hours only, I am unlikely to invest in accident prevention or assume that I must insure against any risks arising from this person's conduct. However, where temporary staff are treated as *de facto* permanent staff, or, if one prefers, integrated into the end-user's business, this argument becomes far weaker. In the cases, therefore, of casual or agency staff employed on a long-term basis as a cheaper alternative to permanent staff, it is difficult to justify treating them as independent contractors for which their *de facto* employer is not liable and change is clearly needed.

Power and control may, however, exist in other relationships than that of employer and employee. You might exercise control over fellow partners in a law firm, over your agents or even over friends assisting you with a specific task. This raises the interesting question of the extent to which vicarious liability can be said to be limited to the employment

---

[73] *Brook Street Bureau (UK) Ltd v Dacas* [2004] EWCA Civ 217.
[74] *Nethermere (St Neots) Ltd v Taverna and Gardiner* [1984] ICR 612.
[75] [2004] EWCA Civ 217 at para. 2 per Mummery LJ, and para. 72 per Sedley LJ.

context. Chapter 5 will examine relationships outside the employment context in which one party has been found strictly liable for the tortious acts of others. Such relationships include those arising in agency law and by statute itself. In determining *who* will be liable for the harmful acts of others, Chapter 5 will consider how far modern legal systems are prepared to extend liability outside the central employer/employee relationship.

5 Other relationships giving rise to liability

5.1 Introduction

The employer/employee relationship represents the most common example of a relationship giving rise to vicarious liability in tort. Nevertheless, the key characteristics of one person acting ostensibly in the interests of another with the latter being held responsible for the former's tortious actions may be identified in other relationships. As will be seen, there is case law authority in both common and civil law jurisdictions that vicarious liability extends beyond the employer/employee relationship. Legislation may additionally, for specific policy reasons, designate a relationship as giving rise to vicarious liability.

This chapter will seek to define the boundaries of the relationships giving rise to vicarious liability in tort. In civilian systems, extending liability beyond the employer/employee relationship raises no great conceptual difficulties. Use of the broader terms of '*commettant/préposé*' and '*Geschäftsherr/Verrichtungsgehilfe*' under Article 1384(5) of the French Civil Code or § 831 of the German Civil Code, signifies that the courts, if it is considered appropriate, may apply the codal provisions to any relationships capable of meeting the tests of subordination or the right to give instructions. In contrast, the common law requirement of a contract of employment (or contract of service) has rendered extensions of the doctrine to other analogous relationships problematic. This has not, however, prevented an extension of strict liability beyond the employment relationship. As we will see, a variety of techniques are utilised. In common with civil law, specific legislation has served to include relationships where the application of the principle of vicarious liability is considered desirable. More controversially, the common law has also resorted to parallel doctrines, namely agency[1] and non-delegable duties, to extend liability to non-employees. These doctrines bear a considerable resemblance to the doctrine of vicarious liability and this, in a sense, is the problem. In all three, one person (the employer/principal/employer) is rendered liable for the torts of another (employee/agent/independent contractor) unless that other is acting outside the course of his employment/outside the scope of his authority/engaged in collateral negligence. However, liability for agency and non-delegable duties is *primary*, not vicarious. The principal/employer is held to account on the basis of personal fault. As will be seen, this fundamental conceptual difference has not prevented statements by the courts that the principal will be held vicariously liable for the torts of his agent or resort to the concept of non-delegable duty to circumvent the limitations of vicarious liability.[2]

In examining the various means utilised to extend the relationships to which 'vicarious liability' applies and the conceptual problems which may arise, this chapter will address three main issues. First, it will consider the extent to which statute is relied upon to pursue distinct policy needs. Secondly, it will examine case law intervention and the lack of any overall rationalisation. Finally, in view of the attempt by all systems examined to apply vicarious liability principles beyond the employer/employee relationship, it will analyse whether it is possible to find a new test reflecting the changing face of employment relations, identified in Chapters 3 and 4. Two alternatives arising in recent case law will be considered: the suggestion by the courts of Australia and New Zealand of an intermediate category of 'agent' to mitigate the strict divide between employee and independent contractor, and the development in France of liability based on the power to direct, control and manage the activities of another. If there is a general desire to extend vicarious liability principles beyond the employment relationship, is it possible to find a more socially responsive test which avoids the conceptual complexity of, in particular, the common law?

---

[1] In French law, although the concepts of *commettant/préposé* and *mandat* (French concept of agency) may overlap, the liability of a contractual agent will usually be dealt with by the law of contract: see Crim 24 February 1934 Gaz Pal 1934.1.654 (only liability under Article 1384(5) if *mandataire* is also *préposé* of *mandant*).

[2] See 5.3.2.1 and 5.3.2.2.

5.2 Relationships giving rise to vicarious liability beyond the contract of employment: statute

In codified systems, legislation will usually be the starting point for legal analysis, be it the civil code or other legislative instruments. As seen in earlier chapters, the French Civil Code imposes vicarious liability in two provisions: Article 1384(5) (*commettant/préposé*) and Article 1384(1) (liability of those with the power to direct, control and manage another). Such liability is supplemented by statute, for example, Article L511-III of the Insurance Code which provides that the insurer is civilly liable under Article 1384 for harm caused to its clientele by those it has entrusted to sell insurance, regardless of their legal status.[3]

In contrast, the German Code adheres to fault based liability in all but one provision: § 833 (liability of animal keeper/*Haftung des Tierhalters*):

If a human being is killed by an animal or if the body or the health of a human being is injured by an animal or a thing is damaged by an animal, then the person who keeps the animal is liable to compensate the injured person for the damage arising from this. Liability in damages does not apply if the damage is caused by a domestic animal intended to serve the occupation, economic activity or subsistence of the keeper of the animal and either the keeper of the animal in supervising the animal has exercised reasonable care or the damage would also have occurred even if this care had been exercised.[4]

As will be seen, even this provision reverts to a presumption of fault in relation to working animals, although Brüggemeier notes that there is now support for the differentiation between working and non-working animals to be removed and strict liability to be applied generally.[5]

In contrast, in common law, codification or legislation is the exception. Statutes, in general, intervene to clarify the common law. One common difficulty is the status of police officers, who, as public servants, are technically neither employees of the Crown nor of the police

---

[3] Modified by the *loi* N°2005-1564 du 15 December 2005 – Art. 1 (*JORF* 16 December 2005). On this basis, all such persons are *préposés* whether they are salaried employees or agents ('*Pour cette activité d'intermédiation, l'employeur ou mandant est civilement responsable, dans les termes de l'article 1384 du code civil, du dommage causé par la faute, l'imprudence ou la négligence de ses employés ou mandataires agissant en cette qualité, lesquels sont considérés, pour l'application du présent article, comme des préposés, nonobstant toute convention contraire.*'). Note also the provisions of the Consumer Code, Article L121-9.

[4] For the background to this provision and the choice of risk and fault-based liability, see G. Brüggemeier, *Haftungsrecht: Struktur, Prinzipien, Schutzbereich* (Heidelburg: Springer, 2006), pp. 108–12. In contrast, the liability of a person contracted to supervise the animal for the keeper is again based on presumed fault as under § 831: see § 834.

[5] Brüggemeier, *Haftungsrecht*, p. 109.

authority.[6] In England and Wales, section 88 of the Police Act 1996[7] now provides that the chief officer of police for a police area shall be liable in respect of any unlawful conduct of constables under his direction and control in the performance or purported performance of their duties in the same manner as an employer.[8] Legislation has also intervened to render the cab driver, with respect to members of the general public, the employee of the cab owner, generally not the position at common law.[9]

Equally, the liability of partners in a firm is dealt with by statute, rather than case law. Vicarious liability of partners was recognised by the mid nineteenth century,[10] and formed part of the codification of partnership law in the Partnership Act 1890. Section 10 provides that:

Where, by any wrongful act or omission of any partner acting in the ordinary course of the business of the firm, or with the authority of his co-partners, loss or injury is caused to any person not being a partner in the firm, or any

---

[6] *Fisher v Oldham Corp.* [1930] 2 KB 364. For Canadian law, see LN Klar, *Tort law*, 4th edn (Toronto: Carswell, 2008), p. 666, who notes that apart from statute, there is no vicarious liability for the torts of the police.

[7] Replacing section 48 of the Police Act 1964 (discussed in K. Williams, 'Suing policemen', *New Law Journal*, 139 (1989), 1664). Section 88(1) reads: '(1) The chief officer of police for a police area shall be liable in respect of any unlawful conduct of constables under his direction and control in the performance or purported performance of their functions in like manner as a master is liable in respect of torts committed by his servants in the course of their employment, and accordingly shall, in the case of a tort, be treated for all purposes as a joint tortfeasor.' Similarly other Commonwealth jurisdictions have used legislation to impose vicarious liability for the torts of police officers, see for example, Police Act, RSBC 1996, c. 367, sections 11 and 21 (British Columbia); Australian Federal Police Act 1979 section 64B (Cwth.); Employees Liability Act 1991, section 2A (NSW).

[8] Note, however, that the Police Act 1996 does not create a relationship of employer and employee between the parties: *Farah v MPC* [1998] QB 65.

[9] See London Hackney Carriage Act 1843 (London) (see *Keen v Henry* [1894] 1 QB 292; *Gates v Bill* [1902] 2 KB 38) and the Town Police Clauses Act 1847 (outside London) (see *Bygraves v Dicker* [1923] 2 KB 585). For private hire cabs, see *Rogers v Night Riders* [1983] RTR 324, CA (non-delegable duty to take reasonable steps to ensure that the vehicle so provided was properly maintained and reasonably fit for that purpose). See also the Pilotage Act 1987, section 16, re-enacting the Pilotage Act 1913, section 15, which renders shipowners liable for any loss or damage caused by faulty navigation of a vessel by a ship's pilot, who is otherwise regarded as an independent professional: *Rossano v Swan Hunter & Wigham Richardson Ltd (The Arum)* [1921] P 12 and *Oceangas (Gibraltar) Ltd v Port of London Authority (The Cavendish)* [1993] 2 Lloyd's Rep 292.

[10] *Ashworth v Stanwix* (1860) 3 E & E 701, 121 ER 701, although Atiyah notes that such vicarious liability entered English law relatively late and that, as late as 1849, its validity had been questioned: see P. S. Atiyah, *Vicarious liability in the law of torts* (London: Butterworths, 1967), p. 116.

penalty is incurred, the firm is liable therefor to the same extent as the partner so acting or omitting to act.[11]

In the leading case of *Dubai Aluminium Co. Ltd v Salaam*,[12] the House of Lords examined the relationship between partnership and vicarious liability.[13] Whilst admitting that the relationship between partners was essentially one of agency, their Lordships applied the ordinary principles of vicarious liability to the relationship. Lord Millett justified this on the basis that it would be absurd to distinguish between a firm's vicarious liability for the torts committed by its employees[14] and its partners.[15]

Such examples are far from revolutionary. There is no reason, however, why statute cannot be used more proactively to extend the scope of vicarious liability. In the Canadian provinces, for example, legislation has introduced liability for the owners of motor vehicles for the torts committed by persons driving the vehicles with their consent.[16] The policy objective is straightforward:

'The provision reflects a longstanding public concern that persons who engage in an inherently dangerous activity, such as the operation of a motor vehicle, should be financially responsible for damage they may cause to themselves or others . . . By allowing recourse against two persons, both the owner and the driver, instead of one, the legislation placed the injured party in a more favourable position . . . [S]ince the advent of compulsory automobile insurance . . . the concept remains significant in two respects: for indemnification and for recovery outside the scope of insurance coverage.'[17]

Such statutory intervention may be contrasted with the position in English law, outlined in 5.3.2.1 below. In Australia, there is legislation in all States and Territories (apart from Queensland) providing that

---

[11] The same legislation applies in the common law provinces of Canada: see, for example, Partnership Act, RSBC 1996, c. 348. For Australia, see, for example, sections 14, 14A and 16 of the Partnership Act 1963 (ACT) and section 10 of the Partnership Act 1891 (South Australia).
[12] [2002] UKHL 48, [2003] 2 AC 366.
[13] R. C. I'Anson Banks, *Lindley & Banks on partnership*, 18th edn (London: Sweet & Maxwell, 2002), pp. 12–93 to 12–110.
[14] For example, *Lloyd v Grace, Smith & Co.* [1912] AC 716.
[15] See [2002] UKHL 48 at para. 106, citing the remark by Winn LJ in *Meekins v Henson* [1964] 1 QB 472 at 477 of the 'necessary equation of a partnership firm with employers for this purpose'.
[16] See Klar, *Tort law*, pp. 596–7.
[17] Law Reform Commission of British Columbia, *Report on vicarious liability under the Motor Vehicle Act* (Vancouver: author, 1989), 10.

community organisations will be liable for the wrongs of volunteers carrying out community work for the organisation.[18] Such legislation is context-specific and varies in content, but demonstrates that the legislator may extend the scope of vicarious liability by increasing the relationships to which it applies where necessary.

Legislation, therefore, does provide a means whereby the legislator may extend vicarious liability to non-employee relationships. The Australian and Canadian examples demonstrate the potential for the legislator to intervene to deal with specific social situations where it is considered socially desirable to render one party liable for the wrongful (and harmful) acts of another. However, such intervention is limited in scope and subject to the principles of statutory interpretation. More significant is the ability of the courts themselves to extend liability and therefore reshape the operation of the doctrine of vicarious liability.

5.3 Relationships giving rise to vicarious liability beyond the contract of employment: case law

5.3.1 Civil law systems

As stated earlier, in civilian systems, the use of more general terminology, such as *commettant/préposé* and *Geschäftsherr/Verrichtungsgehilfe*, has rendered the extension of liability outside the contract of employment a straightforward exercise. Utilising the tests of subordination or the right to give instructions (detailed in Chapter 3), these systems have demonstrated a willingness to extend liability beyond the employer/employee context. French law has indeed embraced the opportunity to impose vicarious liability for relatives and even casual acquaintances given a designated task. In a case of 1971,[19] for example, a nurse, running a first aid station, asked a volunteer helper, whom she knew did not have a driving licence, to use her vehicle for an errand. The criminal chamber of the Cour de cassation found that she had given the volunteer orders or instructions on the manner of fulfilling this task, albeit without payment and on a temporary basis. As the note to the decision comments, liability under Article 1384(5) arose due to the right of the nurse to give the helper orders. Similarly, an electoral candidate was held liable when one of his supporters got into a fight with a supporter of the other

---

[18] F. Trindade, P. Cane and M. Lunney, *The law of torts in Australia*, 4th edn (Australia: Oxford University Press, 2007), pp. 796–8.
[19] Crim 25 May 1971 D 1971 somm 168.

candidate, which led to that other's death.[20] Liability may thus arise between husband and wife,[21] or even friends.[22]

Liability will not arise, however, where one person cannot be said to be subordinate to another. Where, therefore, an assistant retains his freedom to manoeuvre or acts on his own initiative, liability will not arise.[23] On this basis, independent contractors who are truly independent will not fall under Article 1384(5): the court distinguishing a *contrat d'entreprise* from a *contrat de travail*. However, the line in practice is not so clear-cut. The court may, as a matter of fact, find that the independent contractor is subordinate to the employer. In a case of 1988,[24] for example, an independent contractor used by the department store, Galeries Lafayette, to install goods purchased at the store was found to be acting as a *préposé* when negligently installing the equipment. Although working on his own account (having previously been employed by the store), on the facts, he was routinely given a work list of clients and could thus be said to be under the control and supervision of the store after-sales service division.[25]

Such flexibility is thereby used to fulfil the perceived aims of vicarious liability: protect innocent victims and spread the cost of liability. Nevertheless, it does run the obvious risk of targeting uninsured defendants, who may not anticipate liability arising in a domestic or casual context (or be insured for such occasions), and has been criticised for causing uncertainty.[26] The courts have clearly made some policy-based choices, for example, case law excluding a union from being held liable as the *commettant* of its strikers.[27] Writers such as Viney and Jourdain, who

---

[20] Crim 20 May 1976 Gaz Pal 1976.2.545 note YM; RTD civ. 1976.786 obs G. Durry.
[21] See Req 12 July 1887 S 1887.1.384, Civ 8 November 1937 Gaz Pal 1938.1.43, Crim 27 December 1961 Bull crim N° 563, p. 1074; D 1962 somm 75; JCP 1962 II 12652, Civ 1, 17 July 1979 D 1980 IR 114. See also Civ 2, 28 April 1955 Bull civ II N° 219, p. 132 (son-in-law *préposé* of father-in-law) and Civ 20 July 1970 Gaz Pal 1970 2 somm 57 (father and son).
[22] Req 1 May 1930 DP 1930.1.137 note R. Savatier.
[23] See, for example, Soc 21 July 1986 Bull civ 1986 V N° 421 p. 320: employee, who had been instructed by his employer to take a lorry to a garage for its service and who chose to assist the garage employees dealing with another lorry, found to be acting on his own initiative and not temporary *préposé* of garage. See also Civ 21 February 1979 D 1979 IR 350: lorry-driver trying to assist another driver.
[24] Crim 22 March 1988 Bull crim N° 142, p. 369; RTD civ. 1988.774 obs P. Jourdain.
[25] See also Civ 2, 11 December 1996 Resp civ et assur 1997 comm N° 84.
[26] See N. Molfessis, 'La jurisprudence relative à la responsabilité des commettants du fait de leurs préposés ou l'irrésistible enlisement de la Cour de cassation' in D. Mazeand (ed.), *Mélanges Gobert* (Paris: Economica, 2004), pp. 495 at 509–12.
[27] Soc 9 November 1982 D 1982.621 and D 1983.531 note H. Sinay and Soc 17 July 1990 Bull civ V N° 375, p. 324. cf. *Fullowka v Pinkerton's of Canada Ltd* [2010] SCC 5 at paras. 147–50.

generally favour risk-based liability, have also sought to emphasise that 'this fringe of questionable case law remains, all the same, relatively narrow',[28] and that the majority of case law relates to employment contracts. More fundamentally, Viney and Jourdain question whether, with the expansion of liability under Article 1384(1) – discussed at 5.4.2 below – there remains any need to adopt a broad interpretative power under Article 1384(5) when it risks distorting the very notion of the *commettant/préposé* relationship.

The French experience demonstrates, however, the ability of the courts to utilise Article 1384(5) to extend vicarious liability beyond the employment context when it is deemed socially desirable. For the common law, however, this ability is strictly confined. In the absence of an employer/employee relationship or statutory intervention, the courts' power to intervene is limited.

The next section will examine the two tools used by the common law to extend the benefits of vicarious liability to innocent victims: agency and non-delegable duties. Neither may be accurately described as vicarious liability. Both, in fact, give rise to *primary* liability.[29] The use of primary liability to render one person liable for the torts of another will be examined below.

5.3.2 Common law 'relationships': using agency and non-delegable duties to extend strict liability for the torts of others

5.3.2.1 Agency

The concept of agency indeed has a number of similarities with vicarious liability,[30] in that it also renders one person liable for the tortious acts of

---

[28] G. Viney and P. Jourdain, *Traité de droit civil: les conditions de la responsabilité*, 3rd edn (Paris: LGDJ, 2006), N° 796 (my translation). Note also in German law that, despite the loose terminology, there are few instances of the application of § 831 to casual relationships: see W. van Gerven, J. Lever and P. Larouche, *Tort law: ius commune casebooks for the common law of Europe* (Oxford: Hart Publishing, 2000), p. 499; MünchKommBGB/Wagner, 5th edn (Munich: C.H. Beck, 2009), § 831, para 15; but see BGH VersR 1992, 844, 845 (daughter employee of her mother).

[29] See respectively F. M. B. Reynolds, *Bowstead & Reynolds on agency*, 18th edn (London: Sweet and Maxwell, 2006) pp. 8–177; and J. Swanton, 'Non-delegable duties: liability for the negligence of independent contractors (pt I)', *Journal of Contract Law*, 4 (1991), 183 at 188.

[30] See US Restatement of the Law (3d) of Agency (2006), § 7.01 Agent's Liability to Third Party: 'An agent is subject to liability to a third party harmed by the agent's tortious conduct. Unless an applicable statute provides otherwise, an actor remains subject to liability although the actor acts as an agent or an employee, with actual or apparent authority, or within the scope of employment.' Section 7.07(2) defines when an agent who is an employee acts within the scope of employment. Note the influence of

another within the scope of his authority. Although there is no agreed definition of agency,[31] it has been described by one leading text as 'the fiduciary relationship which exists between two persons, one of whom expressly or impliedly manifests assent that the other should act on his behalf so as to affect his relations with third parties, and the other of whom similarly manifests assent so to act or so acts pursuant to that manifestation'.[32] Such a technical definition is at odds with the tendency of courts (and ordinary individuals) to use the term 'agent' in a less technical sense of simply one person acting at another's behest. The Oxford English Dictionary, for example, defines an agent as 'One who does the *actual work* of anything, as distinguished from the instigator or employer; hence, one who acts for another, a deputy, steward, factor, substitute, representative, or emissary.'[33] The courts equally have used the terms 'agent' and 'servant' interchangeably.[34] As Gleeson CJ remarked in the Australian case of *Scott v Davis*, 'the protean nature of the concept of agency ... bedevils this area of discourse'.[35] In reality, as has been rightly observed, the word 'agent' is being used in this context to extend the tort doctrine of vicarious liability beyond employees to those working gratuitously for the defendant.[36]

On this basis, the courts have found the master/employer to be 'vicariously liable' for the torts of his agents. As stated above, this is conceptually problematic. Agency renders the principal primarily liable for the

---

O.W. Holmes, 'Agency', *Harvard Law Review*, 4 (1891), 345, *Harvard Law Review*, 5 (1892), 1, and W. A. Seavey, 'The rationale of agency', *Yale Law Journal*, 29 (1920), 859.

[31] See G. McMeel, 'Philosophical foundations of the law of agency', *Law Quarterly Review*, 116 (2000), 387, who notes that there are different accounts of the basis of the law of agency. See also Reynolds, *Bowstead & Reynolds on agency*, pp. 1–003.

[32] Ibid., at 1–001. The authors concede that it is partly based on the US Restatement of Agency (3d) § 1.01: 'Agency is the fiduciary relationship that arises when one person (a "principal") manifests assent to another person (an "agent") that the agent shall act on the principal's behalf and subject to the principal's control, and the agent manifests assent or otherwise consents so to act.'

[33] http://dictionary.oed.com (emphasis in original).

[34] Notably in the context of fraud (see *Houldsworth v City of Glasgow Bank* (1880) 5 App Cas 317 at 326–7 per Lord Selbourne; *Lloyd v Grace, Smith & Co* [1912] AC 716 at 734–5 per Lord Macnaghten; *Uxbridge Permanent Benefit Building Society v Pickard* [1939] 2 KB 248 at 254 per Greene MR; but see also Willes J in *Barwick v English Joint Stock Banking Co.* (1866–67) LR 2 Exch 259 at 265–6: 'with respect to the question, whether a principal is answerable for the act of his agent in the course of his master's business, and for his master's benefit, no sensible distinction can be drawn between the case of fraud and the case of any other wrong. The general rule is, that the master is answerable for every such wrong of the servant or agent as is committed in the course of the service".

[35] (2000) 204 CLR 333 at 338.

[36] S. J. Stoljar, *The law of agency* (London: Sweet and Maxwell, 1961), p. 9.

actions of his agent within the scope of his authority. It determines the ability of the agent to enter legal transactions on the principal's behalf. The commission of torts will be incidental to this.[37] Liability is limited by the scope of the agent's authority, be it actual or apparent, and the general principle of ratification.[38] As such, agency as a concept is distinct from that of vicarious liability.

Nevertheless, two categories of claims persist, which merge vicarious liability with ideas of agency: liability arising from the loan of a motor vehicle to a negligent driver, and liability for the tort of deceit or fraud. The second example will be examined in Chapter 6 as the notion of agency arises in the context of determining the scope of the employer's liability for the fraudulent misstatements of his staff. The first, however, directly affects the relationship of the parties: lending your car to your husband, friend or acquaintance may give rise to strict liability for their torts whilst driving.

Vicarious liability, agency and motor vehicles
Whilst there is no conceptual difficulty with a principal *employing* an agent to drive his car and being held vicariously liable for his torts qua employee, it is quite a different matter to hold one person strictly liable for the negligent driving of another purely because he lent him his car. In the absence of consideration (and contractual intent), such parties are not employees, but mere volunteers to whom the principles of vicarious liability would not normally apply. Nevertheless a body of law exists which imposes liability on the basis of agency.

The origins of this principle derive from case law concerning horse and buggy accidents in the early nineteenth century, where the question of control was deemed to justify rendering the master liable, regardless of who actually had hold of the reins at the time.[39] These cases were used in *Samson v Aitchison* in 1912 in relation to the negligent driving of a motor

---

[37] See B. S. Markesinis and R. J. C. Munday, *An outline of the law of agency* (London: Butterworths, 1998), p. 7; and G. H. L. Fridman, *The law of agency*, 7th edn (London: Butterworths, 1996), p. 303.

[38] Reynolds, *Bowstead & Reynolds on agency*, pp. 3–001 and 2–047.

[39] See *Chandler v Broughton* (1832) 1 C & M 29, 149 ER 301; *Booth v Mister* (1835) 7 C & P 66, 173 ER 30; and *Wheatley v Patrick* (1837) 2 M & W 650, 150 ER 917. Atiyah also notes the influence of the belief, before modern notions of vicarious liability became established, that mere ownership of a vehicle was sufficient to fix liability for any damage it caused to third parties: Atiyah, *Vicarious liability*, p. 125. As Atiyah notes, however, the focus on these cases was the correct form of action (trespass or case) and not vicarious liability at all: ibid., p. 126.

VICARIOUS LIABILITY BEYOND CONTRACT OF EMPLOYMENT   111

car by a son, test-driving the vehicle for his mother who intended to purchase it.[40] Here, the Privy Council held that where the owner was in the car and had allowed the son to take over the wheel, in the interests of selling the car, he had not abandoned the control which prima facie belonged to him; it being a 'matter of indifference' whether the son was termed 'agent' or 'employee' in performing this particular task.[41]

From such early beginnings, the case law has identified two conditions: that the vehicle owner has a right to control the use of the vehicle,[42] and an interest in the purpose for which the vehicle is used. The first condition – right of control[43] – has an obvious similarity with the test (discussed in Chapter 3) for finding the contract of employment and has raised a number of difficult questions: can you be in control if not in the vehicle?[44] Can you avoid being in control if in the vehicle? The leading case of *Chowdhary v Gillot*[45] deals with the latter point where the vehicle owner, taking his car to the garage for repairs, was given a lift to the nearest railway station in the car by one of the garage employees. The court held that by bailing the car to the garage, he had abandoned his right of control and therefore could not be held liable when the employee caused an accident.[46] The Australian case of *Soblusky v Egan*[47] indicates that one can remain in direction and control of one's agents, even if asleep.

It is not enough, however, that the person retains control – the driver must be acting, at least partly, for the defendant's purposes or interests.[48] Two key decisions here demonstrate how this works in practice. In *Hewitt v Bonvin*,[49] a son had borrowed his father's car (with permission) to

---

[40] [1912] AC 844 (PC). Considered by *Gramak v O'Connor* (1974) 41 DLR (3d) 14 (Ont CA): owner of car vicariously liable for negligence of volunteer mechanic due to power of control over mechanic.

[41] [1912] AC at 850 per Lord Atkinson.

[42] Note that the focus on *actual* control in the nineteenth century becomes a *right* or *power* to control in the twentieth century, although in *Samson* the car-owner could still be said to be actively directing the driver on the test drive.

[43] The test is one of control over, not ownership, of the vehicle, although it will usually be easier to prove control if the person in question owns the vehicle: see *Candler v Thomas (t/a London Leisure Lines)* [1998] RTR 214 at 218; *Nottingham v Aldridge* [1971] 2 QB 739; and *Rambarran v Gurrucharran* [1970] 1 WLR 556, PC.

[44] *Parker v Miller* (1926) 42 TLR 408: yes.   [45] [1947] 2 All ER 541.

[46] Such reasoning has been criticised as unsatisfactory, involving a manipulation of the control test: Atiyah, *Vicarious liability*, p. 128.

[47] (1960) 103 CLR 215, HCA.

[48] See also *Vandyke v Fender* [1970] 2 QB 292; and *Candler v Thomas (t/a London Leisure Lines)* [1998] RTR 214 (only partly for owner's benefit and partly for own); but not in *Klein v Caluori* [1971] 2 All ER 701 nor *Nottingham v Aldridge* [1971] 2 QB 739.

[49] [1940] 1 KB 188.

drive some friends home. Due to his negligence, there was an accident and one of his passengers was killed. The claim against the father failed. The son did not have express or implied authority to drive on his father's behalf and his father had no interest in his son's actions.[50] In the later case of *Ormrod v Crosville Motor Services Ltd*,[51] however, a vehicle owner, who had expressly requested that his friend drive his car to Monte Carlo where he would join him prior to going on holiday together, was liable for a collision caused due to the driver's negligence. Devlin J, whose judgment was upheld by the Court of Appeal, held that while the mere granting of permission to drive would not suffice, where the owner requests another to drive his car, he who complies with the request is his agent since he who makes the request has an interest in it being fulfilled.[52]

It is difficult to discern a principled approach to liability from the cases discussed above. As the High Court of Australia commented in 1960, 'it is easier to see the direction in which the branch grows than to understand the support it obtains from the main trunk of traditional doctrine governing vicarious responsibility'.[53] Clerk and Lindsell comment that, at best, it may be regarded as a special category of case *sui generis* to agency.[54] Bowstead and Reynolds go further: 'the cases do not link to agency, at least in the central sense of that word. Further details should therefore be sought in works on tort.'[55]

Why, then, is the imposition of vicarious liability for agents driving motor vehicles still considered good law? The answer may be stated in two words: motor insurance. Trindade, Cane and Lunney note that almost all the cases invoking agency in this context represent an attempt to find an insured defendant.[56] Where, therefore, the insured driver lends the vehicle to a member of his family or friend, who is not insured and causes an accident, the victim will not wish to sue the

---

[50] The reasoning here is problematic. MacKinnon LJ relied on the fact that the son was not an employee, whilst Du Parcq LJ treated the case as based on agency.
[51] [1953] 1 WLR 409. Confirmed by the Court of Appeal: [1953] 1 WLR 1120. See also authority extending the doctrine to boats – see *'Thelma' (owners) v University College School* [1953] 2 Lloyd's Rep 613 and *Pawlak v Doucette* [1985] 2 WWR 588 – and possibly even a negligently managed teapot: *Moynihan v Moynihan* [1975] 1 IR 192 (Irish Supreme Court, although criticised in *O'Keeffe v Hickey* [2008] IESC 72).
[52] [1953] 1 WLR at 410–11.
[53] *Soblusky v Egan* (1960) 103 CLR 215 at 229 (judgment of Dixon CJ, Kitto and Windeyer JJ).
[54] T. Dugdale (gen. ed.), *Clerk and Lindsell on torts*, 19th edn (London: Sweet and Maxwell, 2008), pp. 6–70.
[55] Reynolds, *Bowstead & Reynolds on agency*, p. 8–187.
[56] Trindade, Cane and Lunney, *The law of torts*, p. 783.

tortfeasor, but find some way to render the insured owner of the vehicle liable. This is ably illustrated by the leading English case of *Morgans v Launchbury*.[57] In this case, the motor car was owned and insured by the wife, but used by the husband to drive to work. The husband had promised his wife that, if he was ever too drunk to drive, he would ask a sober friend to drive him home or ring for her to come and fetch him. On the day in question, the husband went out drinking with friends and, realising himself unfit to drive, asked a friend, Cawfield, to drive. After continued drinking, Cawfield drove himself, the husband and three more friends for a meal (the husband by this stage being in a soporific condition) and, due to his negligent driving, caused an accident in which he and the husband were killed and the other passengers injured. The passengers brought an action against the wife. As Viscount Dilhorne observed, 'Presumably she was sued personally in the hope that claims against her by passengers were covered by a policy of insurance, whereas the claims against the other defendants were unlikely to be.'[58]

Lord Denning MR in the Court of Appeal sought to rationalise the law on the basis of loss distribution, arguing that '[s]ocial policy demanded that the victims of careless driving should be compensated'.[59] On this basis, the theoretical bases for vicarious liability – loss distribution; victim compensation, for example, – could be said to justify an extension of liability to all those using the family car wholly or partly on the owner's business. His Lordship readily conceded that the words 'principal' and 'agent' had no link with their meaning in contract law but were used as 'shorthand to denote the circumstances in which vicarious liability is imposed'.[60]

This argument, influenced by the US doctrine of the 'family car', which imposes liability on the owner of a vehicle for its negligent operation when the owner gives express or implied consent for its general use by members of the family in the same household provided it is used for authorised purposes,[61] was regarded as 'naked legislation'

---

[57] [1973] AC 127 (HL).   [58] Ibid., at 137–8.
[59] *Launchbury v Morgans* [1971] 2 QB 245 at 254. See also *Ormrod v Crosville Motor Services Ltd* [1953] 1 WLR 1120 at 1123.
[60] [1971] 2 QB at 255.
[61] This agency doctrine is said to be at least as old as *Lashbrook v Patten* 1 Duv 316 (Ky, 1864): see W. L. Prosser et al. (eds.), *Prosser and Keeton on the law of torts*, 5th edn (St Paul, MN: West Group Publishing, 1984), p. 524. See G. H. L. Fridman, 'The doctrine of the "family car": a study in contrasts', *Texas Technical Law Review*, 8 (1976), 323; and D. B. Dobbs, *The law of torts* (St Paul, MN: West Group Publishing, 2000), p. 935: 'the doctrine represents a social policy generated in response to the problem presented by massive use of the automobile'. The courts of approximately twenty States follow this doctrine.

by the House of Lords.[62] Adopting a more conservative approach, their Lordships stressed the need for the driver to be acting for the owner's purposes under a delegation of a task or duty, which was not the case here.[63] The vague assurance given by the husband to the wife that he would not drive if intoxicated did not meet this requirement: it demonstrated nothing more than that, like most wives, she was concerned for her husband's safety.

A number of comments may be made. First, their Lordships do not attempt to address the conceptual difficulties arising from using 'agency' to impose vicarious liability on a defendant, but recognise that agency in this context reflects a value judgement that the car-owner should pay.[64] Secondly, any extension of liability was found to raise difficult questions of policy, including the impact on the existing insurance framework, more suited to consideration by the government and Parliament than the courts;[65] their Lordships expressly refusing to allow speculation as to insurance cover to influence the scope of the liability rule.[66]

Post-1972, this doctrine has continued to be used,[67] but has been subject to notable criticism from the High Court of Australia in 2000,[68] where the doctrine was confined by the majority to motor vehicles and its very foundation questioned. In *Scott v Davis*,[69] Gummow J commented that 'On closer reading it becomes apparent that any general principle

---

[62] [1973] AC 127 at 151 per Lord Salmon.
[63] See, for example, Lord Wilberforce ibid., at 135: 'in order to fix vicarious liability upon the owner of a car in such a case as the present it must be shown that the driver was using it for the owner's purposes, under delegation of a task or duty.'
[64] See Lord Wilberforce ibid.
[65] See, for example, Lord Wilberforce ibid., at 137; Lord Pearson ibid., at 142–3; Lord Salmon ibid., at 151.
[66] See Lord Salmon ibid., at 147: 'the question as to whether she is liable to the plaintiffs cannot in any way be affected by whether or not her liability would be covered by insurance.'
[67] See, for example, *John Laing Construction v Ince* [2001] CLY 4543 (Southend county court), but note the more restrictive approach in *Norwood v Navan* [1981] RTR 457 (owner of a car not vicariously liable for his wife's negligent driving even though one of the purposes of her trip was to do the general 'family shopping', thereby avoiding a legal principle dependent on what she bought).
[68] And by a number of Australian commentators: see J. Keeler, 'Driving agents: to vicarious liability for (some) family and friendly assistance?', *Torts Law Journal*, 8 (2000), 41; and L. McCarthy, 'Vicarious liability in the agency context', *Queensland University of Technology Law and Justice Journal*, 4(2) (2004), 68.
[69] (2000) 204 CLR 333 (McHugh J dissenting), noted by F. M. B. Reynolds, 'Casual delegation', *Law Quarterly Review*, 117 (2001), 180. Applied in *Gutman v McFall* [2004] NSWCA 378 (principle does not extend to hire and operation of dinghy).

respecting "agency" and "vicarious liability" derived from those cases cannot have a sound foundation ... There has been entanglement in it of the relationships of master and servant, and principal and agent, with the law relating to negligent driving, further confused by the tendency of the common law to embrace fictions and by the technicalities of the common law system of pleading as it operated before the introduction of the Judicature system.'[70] Callinan J noted also that the presence in the background of an insurer had led to a distortion of legal principle in an area characterised by its artificial and unconvincing reasoning.[71]

More fundamentally, in practice, the introduction of compulsory motor vehicle insurance, extending often to third parties, has diminished the need for judicial intervention in this area of law. As previously stated, in the Canadian provinces, legislation has been introduced imposing liability on owners of motor vehicles for the torts committed by persons driving the vehicles with their consent. Further, the decision of most Australian jurisdictions to require car-owners to take out a policy of insurance covering the liability of the owner and any driver (driving with the authority of owner or not) for personal injury and death caused by or arising out of the use of the motor vehicle, has removed the need to resort to this area of law, save in the case of property damage. In England and Wales, compulsory insurance is governed by section 143 of the Road Traffic Act 1988 (as amended), but a number of EC Directives[72] have extended the scope of compulsory cover in relation to property damage, accidents occurring in public places other than roads, and accidents caused by any person driving the assured's vehicle whether or not the assured had consented (including thieves).

Section 143(1) now reads:

(1) Subject to the provisions of this Part of this Act—
    (a) a person must not use a motor vehicle on a road or other public place unless there is in force in relation to the use of the vehicle by that person such a

---

[70] (2000) 204 CLR 333 at paras. 159–61.   [71] Ibid., at para. 346.
[72] Since 1972 the Community legislature has adopted Directives to approximate the laws of the Member States relating to insurance against civil liability in respect of the use of motor vehicles. See, for example, Directive 84/5/EEC, concerning the extent of compulsory insurance cover, which specifies in Art. 1(1) that 'The insurance referred to in Art. 3(1) of Directive 72/166/EEC shall cover compulsorily both damage to property and personal injuries': Second Council Directive 84/5/EEC of 30 December 1983 on the approximation of the laws of the Member States relating to insurance against civil liability in respect of the use of motor vehicles, OJ 1984 No. L008, p. 17.

policy of insurance or such a security in respect of third party risks as complies with the requirements of this Part of this Act, and
(b) a person must not cause or permit any other person to use a motor vehicle on a road or other public place unless there is in force in relation to the use of the vehicle by that other person such a policy of insurance or such a security in respect of third party risks as complies with the requirements of this Part of this Act.

On this basis, the policy justification for using agency to extend vicarious liability to the loan of motor vehicles has virtually disappeared. It remains an odd remnant of the common law, originating in horse and buggy cases and developing, in the twentieth century, to respond to the needs of victims of motor vehicle accidents. As such, it adds little to our understanding of the principles of vicarious liability, save the willingness of the common law courts to extend the benefits of vicarious liability regardless of principle (and legal coherence) to achieve the aims of social justice.

5.3.2.2 Non-delegable duties

As previously stated, the common law draws a fundamental distinction between employees and independent contractors for whom employers will *not* be held vicariously liable. This distinction may be traced back to *Quarman v Burnett*[73] in 1840 where Baron Parke stated that defendants would not be liable for the negligence of a hired driver 'on the simple ground, that the servant is the servant of *another*, and his act the act of another'.[74] Naturally, circumstances may arise where the employer authorises or ratifies the tort of the independent contractor or is personally at fault, becoming jointly liable to the victim,[75] but such liability arises under the ordinary principles of fault liability.

This section will examine circumstances where the employer is held strictly liable for the torts of another using the mechanism of non-delegable duties. Such duties render the employer personally liable for the negligence of *any* person to whom he has entrusted or delegated the performance of a particular task. As described by Lord Blackburn in 1882:

If such a duty was cast upon the defendant he could not get rid of responsibility by delegating the performance of it to a third person. He was at liberty to employ such a third person to fulfil the duty which the law cast on himself . . . but

---

[73] (1840) 6 M & W 499, 151 ER 509. Followed by *Reedie v London and North Western Ry* (1849) 4 Ex 244, 154 ER 1201.
[74] 151 ER 509 at 514 (my emphasis).
[75] *Ellis v Sheffield Gas Consumers Co.* (1853) 2 El & Bl 767, 118 ER 955 (if act itself wrongful, employer will be held responsible jointly for the wrong committed by contractor).

the defendant still remained subject to that duty, and liable for the consequences if it was not fulfilled.[76]

The operation of this doctrine greatly resembles that of vicarious liability. Indeed, in Australia, the Ipp Report of 2002[77] expressed the view that liability for breach of a non-delegable duty was in essence equivalent to an extension of the principles of vicarious liability and recommended that liability for breach of a non-delegable duty should be treated as equivalent in all respects to vicarious liability.[78] The orthodox view, however, is that it represents a variety of *personal* duty imposed on employers for which responsibility cannot be shifted by entrusting performance of the duty to another. As will be seen, while it is difficult to find one overall explanation for non-delegable duties,[79] they may be loosely grouped as occasions where, for policy reasons such as public safety, protection of property rights, and the protection of vulnerable

---

[76] *Hughes v Percival* (1882–83) LR 8 App Cas 443 at 446 (non-delegable duty to maintain party wall).
[77] *Review of the Law of Negligence Report* (Commonwealth of Australia, 2002).
[78] See now Civil Liability Act 2002 (NSW): '5Q Liability based on non-delegable duty: (1) The extent of liability in tort of a person (*the defendant*) for breach of a non-delegable duty to ensure that reasonable care is taken by a person in the carrying out of any work or task delegated or otherwise entrusted to the person by the defendant is to be determined as if the liability were the vicarious liability of the defendant for the negligence of the person in connection with the performance of the work or task. (2) This section applies to an action in tort whether or not it is an action in negligence, despite anything to the contrary in section 5A.' Alternatively Barak has suggested that they represent an intermediate category of 'mixed liability': A. Barak, 'Mixed and vicarious liability – a suggested distinction', *Modern Law Review*, 29 (1966), 160.
[79] Although this has not prevented academic attempts to do exactly that: see, for example, the early formulation of a general principle by S. Chapman, 'Liability for the negligence of independent contractors', *Law Quarterly Review*, 50 (1934), 71; J.A. Jolowicz, 'Liability for independent contractors in the English common law – a suggestion', *Stanford Law Review*, 9 (1957), 690, who argues that the particular interest affected and the character and magnitude of risk, serve to explain the imposition of a non-delegable duty; and J. Murphy, 'Juridical foundations of common law non-delegable duties' in J. Neyers, E. Chamberlain and S. G. A. Pitel (eds.), *Emerging issues in tort law* (Oxford: Hart, 2007), who states that two characteristics may be identified: assumption of responsibility and the presence of an affirmative duty. Witting has argued that, in fact, non-delegable duties should be analysed as an independent tort with its own distinctive elements: C. Witting, 'Breach of the non-delegable duty: defending limited strict liability in tort', *University of New South Wales Law Journal*, 29 (2006), 33. This view was rejected by the High Court of Australia in *Leichhardt Municipal Council v Montgomery* (2007) 230 CLR 22 at 51 (Kirby J) and received criticism from Murphy: J. Murphy, 'The liability bases of common law non-delegable duties – a reply to Christian Witting', *University of New South Wales Law Journal*, 30 (2007), 86.

parties, the courts impose positive duties on the employer regardless of the status of the person undertaking the work on his behalf.

Three categories of duties will be examined below: those which circumvent the limits of the doctrine of vicarious liability, those which focus on issues of public safety and risk, and a final residual category of other duties. As will be seen, primary liability can be used to overcome the limitations of vicarious liability or simply render an employer liable for high risk activities, regardless of the status of the worker involved. It remains difficult to find any overall theoretical justification explaining all three categories. In view of their disparate historical origins, any ex post facto attempt to identify a unified explanation for all instances of non-delegable duties is likely to be artificial and, in some instances, forced.[80]

Overcoming barriers to vicarious liability: hospitals and employers

As discussed in Chapter 3, the courts in all jurisdictions have experienced doubts in applying the doctrine of vicarious liability to physicians due to their professional independence and the limited control possible over their actions.[81] For example, in *Hillyer v Governors of St Bartholomew's Hospital*,[82] the hospital was not held liable for the negligence of members of the hospital staff exercising professional skill, where the governors of the hospital could not properly interfere either by rule or by supervision.[83] Denning LJ in *Cassidy v Ministry of Health*[84] was critical of the refusal to accept that physicians working full-time for the hospital were employees, but suggested that, in any event, the hospital owed a primary duty of care to patients that reasonable care would be taken in their treatment.[85] In such circumstances, liability would no longer depend on the distinction between a contract for services and a contract of service; a distinction which meant nothing to patients, who would also be relieved from identifying a particular doctor or nurse as negligent.[86]

---

[80] Indeed, Stevens argues that it is a mistake to search for a single factor grouping all such duties together: R. Stevens, 'Non-delegable duties and vicarious liability' in Neyers et al. (eds.), *Emerging issues*, p. 367.
[81] See 3.3.1.   [82] [1909] 2 KB 820. See also *Evans v Liverpool Corpn* [1906] 1 KB 160.
[83] [1909] 2 KB at 829 per Kennedy LJ.
[84] [1951] 2 KB 343 (is a consultant surgeon an employee of the hospital?). Note also his judgment in *Roe v Minister of Health* [1954] 2 QB 66 at 82.
[85] [1951] 2 KB at 362–6. See also *Albrighton v Royal Prince Alfred Hospital* [1980] 2 NSWLR 542; *Ellis v Wallsend District Hospital* (1989) 17 NSWLR 553.
[86] [1951] 2 KB at 365.

On this basis, regardless of the status of the physician, the hospital would be held to owe a non-delegable duty that reasonable care is provided for patients.[87] As Lord Phillips MR acknowledged in *A v Ministry of Defence*,[88] there are 'strong arguments of policy for holding that a hospital, which offers treatment to a patient, accepts responsibility for the care with which that treatment is administered, regardless of the status of the person employed or engaged to deliver the treatment'.[89]

Perhaps the most well-known non-delegable duty in common law systems is that of the employer to ensure that reasonable care is taken towards its employees.[90] This duty is multi-faceted: to provide competent staff, adequate material and equipment, a proper system and effective supervision and a safe place of work.[91] Again, its historical origins may be traced back to an obstacle to vicarious liability: the doctrine of common employment.[92] This stated that an employee could not sue a fellow employee for negligence. In such circumstances, the employer could not be held vicariously liable for workplace accidents caused by the negligence of fellow employees. The employer's personal liability was, however, a different matter. By imposing a non-delegable, i.e. personal duty on the employer, the courts were able to circumvent the perceived injustice of the common employment rule.[93]

Although the doctrine of common employment was abolished in 1948,[94] the non-delegable duty remains, forming part of the protection

---

[87] See also the comments of Sir Nicholas Browne-Wilkinson in *Wilsher v Essex Area Health Authority* [1987] QB 730 at 778 (CA, reversed by the House of Lords on other grounds [1988] AC 1074); and Lord Phillips MR in *A v Ministry of Defence* [2004] EWCA Civ 641, who recognised an 'organisational' duty to use reasonable care to ensure that the hospital staff, facilities and organisation provided are those appropriate to provide a safe and satisfactory medical service for the patient.

[88] [2004] EWCA Civ 641, [2005] QB 183. See M. Brazier and J. Beswick, 'Who's caring for me?', *Medical Law International*, 7 (2006), 183.

[89] [2004] EWCA Civ 641 at para. 63.

[90] *Wilsons & Clyde Coal Co. Ltd v English* [1938] AC 57; *Stevens v Brodribb Sawmilling Co. Pty Ltd* (1986) 160 CLR 16 at 44. In *W v Commissioner of Police of the Metropolis* [2000] 1 WLR 1607, the House of Lords accepted that the duty would extend to protecting a claimant from victimisation and intimidation by her fellow employees, when this caused physical or mental harm.

[91] *Wilsons & Clyde Coal Co. Ltd v English* [1938] AC 57 at 78 per Lord Wright.

[92] See G. Williams, 'Liability for independent contractors', *Cambridge Law Journal* [1956], 180 at 190.

[93] See [1938] AC at 79–80 per Lord Wright; Bowen LJ in *Thomas v Quartermaine* (1887) 18 QBD 685 at 692; and, memorably, MacKinnon LJ in *Speed v Thomas Swift & Co.* [1943] KB 557 at 569: 'a doctrine which lawyers who are gentlemen have long disliked'.

[94] Law Reform (Personal Injuries) Act 1948, s. 1.

afforded to employees in modern law. An example of its modern application may be found in *McDermid v Nash Dredging & Reclamation Co. Ltd*,[95] where the House of Lords permitted an employee, seconded to a tug owned by the defendants' Dutch parent company, to bring a claim against his English employer for breach of the non-delegable duty it owed to him in failing to devise and operate a safe system of work for him. As McKendrick noted, by rendering the employer primarily liable for the *operation* of the system of work, that is, as implemented negligently by the parent company's staff, the liability in *McDermid* very much resembles that of vicarious liability.[96] Mason J in the High Court of Australia sought to rationalise the continued existence of such a non-delegable duty despite the abolition of the doctrine of common employment. By drawing an analogy between the non-delegable duties of hospitals and employers, he found a number of common factors: the hospital or employer either has care, supervision or control of the victim, or has assumed a particular responsibility for the safety of that person or their property.[97] It is the relationship between employer and employee, by which the employer has exclusive responsibility for the safety of the appliances, premises and the system of work to which the employee is subjected (and for which the employee has no choice but to accept and rely on the employer's actions) which justifies the imposition of liability: 'there is no unfairness in imposing on [the employer] a non-delegable duty; it is reasonable that he should bear liability for the negligence of his independent contractors in devising a safe system of work'.[98] Although this rationalisation has been criticised,[99] it highlights the reluctance of the courts to remove a provision which safeguards the

---

[95] [1987] AC 906.

[96] E. McKendrick, 'Vicarious liability and independent contractors – a re-examination', *Modern Law Review*, 53 (1990), 770 at 773–4.

[97] See *Kondis v State Transport Authority* (1984) 154 CLR 672 at 687. Also see *The Commonwealth v Introvigne* (1982) 150 CLR 258 at 271 (Mason CJ); and *Burnie Port Authority v General Jones Pty Ltd* (1994) 179 CLR 520 at 551 (Mason CJ, Deane, Dawson, Toohey and Gaudron JJ).

[98] *Kondis* (1984) 154 CLR 672 at para. 35. Brennan J added that the non-delegable duty remained useful in ensuring workplace safety regardless of the status (employee/independent contractor) of the actual tortfeasor: ibid., at para. 2.

[99] Doubts, for example, were expressed that this could provide a general explanation of the non-delegable duty cases, which seem to be more about correcting perceived injustices and other shortcomings in related areas of law, although Mason J had never claimed that his explanation covered all non-delegable duties: see Gummow J in *Scott v Davis* (2000) 204 CLR 333 at para. 248 and *New South Wales v Lepore* (2003) 212 CLR 511 at para. 246.

safety of employees or patients, regardless of the technical status of the tortfeasor in question.

Broader policy concerns: public safety and risk
Alternatively strict liability for the wrongful acts of others may be extended for broader policy reasons,[100] beyond what might be termed 'technical' problems with the operation of the doctrine of vicarious liability. Industrial legislation may, for example, impose absolute non-delegable duties to protect employees regardless of who is responsible for the accident in question.[101] Such statutory intervention will be subject to the rules of statutory interpretation, determining the level of duty involved and its scope. Equally, non-delegable duties have been developed to deal with inherently hazardous activities,[102] and the escape of fire.[103] The safety of the public using the public highway has also given rise to a non-delegable duty on those engaged in work on[104] or adjoining the public highway.[105]

Other duties
In addition to these two broad categories is a third category of miscellaneous instances where the common law courts, in their ingenuity,

---

[100] See, for example, the examination of policy in relation to maintenance of public roads in the leading Canadian case of *Lewis (Guardian ad litem of) v British Columbia* [1997] 3 SCR 1145, (1997) 153 DLR (4th) 594 (statute imposed non-delegable duty on Crown in relation to construction and maintenance of the provincial highways).

[101] See, for example, *Gray v Pullen* (1864) 5 B & S 970, 122 ER 1091; *Groves v Lord Wimborne* [1898] 2 QB 402; *Hosking v De Havilland Aircraft Co. Ltd* [1949] 1 All ER 540; *Smith v Cammell Laird and Co. Ltd* [1940] AC 242.

[102] *Honeywill and Stein Ltd v Larkin Bros Ltd* [1934] KB 191: early photography. Klar notes that this principle has been applied in several Canadian cases: Klar, *Tort law*, p. 665.

[103] *Black v Christchurch Finance Co.* [1894] AC 48. See also Fire Prevention (Metropolis) Act 1774 (UK). Escape of fire may also fall under the rule in *Rylands v Fletcher* if a non-natural use of the land is involved: *Hobbs (Farms) Ltd v Baxenden Chemical Co. Ltd* [1992] 1 Lloyd's Rep 54.

[104] See, for example, *Holliday v National Telephone Co.* [1899] 2 QB 392. See also *Hardaker v Idle District Council* [1896] 1 QB 335 (council owed duty to the public so to construct a sewer as not to damage a gas main) and *Pickard v Smith* (1861) 10 CB (NS) 470, 142 ER 535 (occupier liable for failure of independent contractors to secure opening to coal cellar on railway platform). Glanville Williams comments, however, that it is fundamentally incomprehensible how a policy to protect the public could ignore the greatest danger on a public highway: the motor car (Williams, 'Liability', 185).

[105] *Tarry v Ashton* (1876) 1 QBD 314: occupier of property adjacent to highway held to owe a positive, continuing and non-delegable duty to keep the premises in repair so as not to prejudice the public. But no application to work carried out near to a highway which might cause injury to persons on the highway: *Salsbury v Woodland* [1970] 1 QB 324.

122 OTHER RELATIONSHIPS GIVING RISE TO LIABILITY

have introduced non-delegable duties. One of the earliest common law non-delegable duties was that of providing lateral support to your neighbour's adjacent land.[106] Other duties include those of bailees for reward for goods in their care,[107] and possibly not to commit a private nuisance.[108]

Confining the modern doctrine of non-delegable duty: collateral negligence and the need for caution

Such examples demonstrate the utility of non-delegable duties as a means of extending strict liability for the wrongful acts of others, regardless of the status of the actual culprit. The rigidity of the common law vicarious liability framework has arguably rendered resort to such duties necessary.[109] Fleming famously termed them 'a disguised form of vicarious liability',[110] and it is difficult to deny that, in practical terms, non-delegable duties blur the distinction between the employer's relationship with employee and independent contractor, which is said to lie at the heart of the common law concept of vicarious liability. The main difficulty lies with the apparently ad hoc nature of such duties – the employer is not liable for all wrongful acts of independent contractors, but only *some*. From the very beginning, liability has also excluded 'casual or collateral acts' for which the employer will not be liable. Denning LJ explained this restriction in *Cassidy*: '[The employer] cannot escape the consequences of a breach of his own duty, but he can escape responsibility for collateral or casual acts'.[111] Yet, despite repeated statements to this effect,[112] there are few instances of claims failing on this account. One of the few successful cases is the leading (yet poorly reported) case of *Padbury v Holliday and Greenwood Ltd*,[113] where an iron

---

[106] *Bower v Peate* (1876) 1 QBD 321; *Dalton v Henry Angus & Co.* (1881) 6 App Cas 740.
[107] *Morris v CW Martin & Co.* [1966] 1 QB 716.
[108] *Matania v National Provincial Bank* [1936] 2 All ER 633.
[109] See D. J. Ibbetson, *A historical introduction to the law of obligations* (Oxford University Press, 1999), p. 183: 'the judges were able to avoid the structures of the newly developed rules of vicarious liability, but in doing so they added to the fragmentary and atomized nature of the law of tort(s) by setting in place a further set of near-arbitrary rules'.
[110] J. G. Fleming, *The law of torts*, 9th edn (North Ryde: LBC Information Services, 1998), p. 434. See also Williams, 'Liability', p. 193, who labels them a 'logical fraud'.
[111] See *Cassidy v Ministry of Health* [1951] 2 KB 343 at 364.
[112] From *Pickard v Smith* (1861) 10 CB (NS) 470 at 480, 142 ER 535 at 539 per Williams J (not liable for casual act of wrong or negligence) and *Dalton v Angus* (1881) 6 App Cas 740 at 829 per Lord Blackburn, to *McDermid v Nash Dredging & Reclamation Co. Ltd* [1987] AC 906 at 911–12 per Lord Hailsham and 919–22 per Lord Brandon.
[113] (1912) 28 TLR 494. Contrast *Holliday v National Telephone Co.* [1899] 2 QB 392.

tool placed carelessly on a window ledge by a sub-contractor's employee was deemed collateral to his duties. It will not, however, always be easy to determine what is 'collateral' to the task for which the independent contractor is hired. Sachs LJ commented in *Salsbury v Woodland* that 'I derived no assistance at all from any distinction between "collateral and casual" negligence and other negligence. Such a distinction provides too many difficulties for me to accept without question, unless it simply means that one must ascertain exactly what was the occupier's duty and then treat any act that is not part of that duty as giving rise to no liability on his part.'[114]

In view of the unsatisfactory nature of the collateral negligence doctrine, other courts have sought to restrict non-delegable duties by targeting specific duties. The Court of Appeal in *Salsbury v Woodland*,[115] for example, refused to extend *Tarry v Ashton* to work undertaken *near* the highway in circumstances where, if care was not taken, injury to passers-by might be caused. The High Court of Australia has gone further. In *Stevens v Brodribb Sawmilling Co. Pty*,[116] the High Court rejected the inherently hazardous activities duty, despite its application in the United States and Canada, as having no place in Australian law. Although its later decision in *Burnie Port Authority v General Jones Pty Ltd*,[117] which replaced the rule in *Rylands v Fletcher* with a non-delegable duty owed by those in control of premises who introduce dangerous substances or activities onto the premises, has thrown doubt on this,[118] a recent decision has sought to confine *Burnie* to its specific context and to reassert the principle decided in *Stevens v Brodribb*.[119] In *Leichhardt Municipal Council v Montgomery*,[120] the High Court also refused to follow English authority that a road authority was liable for the

---

[114] [1970] 1 QB 324 at 348.
[115] [1970] 1 QB 324. See also *Rowe v Herman* [1997] 1 WLR 1390, rationalising the highway cases on the basis that they involve obstruction to the highway as a result of work being carried out under statutory powers.
[116] (1986) 160 CLR 16.   [117] (1994) 179 CLR 520.
[118] Swanton, for example, notes that the majority judgment in *Burnie*, without even discussing *Brodribb*, appears to reintroduce the notion of extra-hazardous activities, though in an apparently narrower form: J. Swanton, 'Another conquest in the imperial expansion of the law of negligence: Burnie Port Authority v General Jones Pty Ltd', *Torts Law Journal*, 2 (1994), 101 at 112–13.
[119] *Transfield Services (Australia) v Hall; Hall v QBE Insurance (Australia)* [2008] NSWCA 294.
[120] (2007) 230 CLR 22. Noted by C. Witting, 'Leichhardt Municipal Council v Montgomery: non-delegable duties and roads authorities', *Melbourne University Law Review*, 32 (2008), 333 and A. Corkhill, 'Vicarious liability in sheep's clothing? Non-delegable duties of care in Leichhardt Municipal Council v Montgomery', *Torts Law Journal*, 15 (2007), 111.

negligence of independent contractors who repaired the public highway. Non-delegable duties were thus treated as exceptional, confined to well-established categories. These reservations towards the *Honeywill* extra-hazardous duty have also been shared recently by the English Court of Appeal, which, in a number of decisions, has sought to impose liability under the ordinary principles of negligence rather than rely on an ill-defined non-delegable duty.[121]

The High Court of Australia ruling in *New South Wales v Lepore; Samin v Queensland; Rich v Queensland*,[122] in relation to the non-delegable duty owed by school authorities to pupils,[123] is also revealing. In confining the non-delegable duty of the school to ensuring that *reasonable* care is taken of pupils in State schools, the majority held that an extension of the duty to protection against intentional wrongdoing would be 'too broad and ... too demanding'.[124] Gummow and Hayne JJ warned that in view of the lack of any general principle unifying non-delegable duties, 'considerable caution' should be exercised before developing any new species of non-delegable duty.[125] Vines has commented that *Lepore* gives a strong indication that the non-delegable duty, as it is conceived in Australia, is a concept on the wane.[126]

One is left to consider the future role of non-delegable duties in relation to vicarious liability. Practically, they provide a means by which the vicarious liability can be extended to non-employees without requiring a revision of the traditional vicarious liability

---

[121] See the judgments of Brooke LJ in *Bottomley v Todmorden Cricket Club* [2003] EWCA Civ 1575, [2004] PIQR P18 and Stanley Burnton LJ in *Biffa Waste Services Ltd v Maschinenfabrik Ernst Hese GmbH* [2008] EWCA Civ 1257, [2009] QB 725, which both question the continued existence of the *Honeywill* exception. Note also *Gwilliam v West Hertfordshire Hospitals NHS Trust* [2002] EWCA Civ 1041, [2003] QB 443 where the Court of Appeal preferred to impose a duty of care on the person engaging an independent contractor to perform a risky operation than resort to a non-delegable duty of care.

[122] (2003) 212 CLR 511 (sexual abuse by schoolteachers).

[123] The leading case is *The Commonwealth v Introvigne* (1982) 150 CLR 258.

[124] (2003) 212 CLR 511 at para. 34 per Gleeson CJ. Contrast McHugh J, dissenting, who argued that the non-delegable duty of the State to use reasonable care would encompass intentional conduct. Note that the Supreme Court of Canada had also rejected the non-delegable duty argument in relation to sexual abuse in the school context: see *EDG v Hammer* (2003) 230 DLR (4th) 554 (sexual abuse by night janitor in public elementary school) and *Blackwater v Plint* (2005) 258 DLR (4th) 275 (dormitory supervisor in a residential school).

[125] See (2003) 212 CLR 511 at para. 247.

[126] P. Vines, 'New South Wales v Lepore; Samin v Queensland; Rich v Queensland: schools' responsibility for teachers' sexual assault: non-delegable duty and vicarious liability', *Melbourne University Law Review*, 27 (2003), 612, 623–5.

framework.[127] However, one might question whether such a 'fiction' is in reality desirable. If one wishes to extend vicarious liability, is the answer to develop new notions of 'agency' or 'non-delegable' duties,[128] or to re-examine the relationship giving rise to vicarious liability in the first place? Atiyah in 1967 suggested that the opposition towards vicarious liability for independent contractors required re-examination: 'there is much to be said for imposing liability on the employer except perhaps in certain cases e.g. where the work contracted for is of a trivial nature (such as hiring a taxi) or is extremely unlikely to cause injury to anyone.'[129] Employers tend to be better placed to prevent accidents and ultimately seek to benefit from the work of both employee and independent contractor. In contrast, Glanville Williams famously condemned such an extension as based on the assumption that all employers are large businesses and all independent contractors small concerns, which is clearly not always the case. In certain circumstances, it may be the contractor, rather than the employer, who is best placed to prevent accidents.[130] Williams concluded, 'it may be questioned whether the social evil of the occasional insolvent tortfeasor contractor is of sufficient gravity to justify the somewhat complicated rules and the imposition of vicarious liability.'[131]

Despite Atiyah's arguments, few systems would contemplate rendering an employer strictly liable for all torts of independent contractors. The civilian systems examined above do not accept this. Atiyah himself accepted that it would not appropriate to render an employer strictly liable for *all* independent contractors and, indeed, I would not expect to be liable for the window cleaner who occasionally cleans my windows or the taxi-driver who drives me to the station. The justifications underlying vicarious liability are far weaker in relation to independent contractors. Their very independence – economically and in terms of risk control – makes such

---

[127] See, for example, Hayne J in *Leichhardt* (2007) 230 CLR 22 at para. 142: 'it is apparent that the postulated duty is both a form of strict liability and a form of vicarious liability'. See also Gleeson CJ ibid., at para. 24.

[128] For arguments in favour of using the concept of non-delegability to reduce the rigidity of the employee/independent contractor distinction: see J. Swanton, 'Non-delegable duties: liability for the negligence of independent contractors' (Pt I), *Journal of Contract Law*, 4 (1991), 183 and (Pt II), *Journal of Contract Law*, 5 (1992), 26.

[129] Atiyah, *Vicarious liability*, p. 334. See also McHugh J in *Northern Sandblasting Pty Ltd v Harris* (1997) 188 CLR 313 at 366–7. For loss distribution arguments in favour of employer liability for independent contractors, see W. O. Douglas, 'Vicarious liability and administration of risk' *Yale Law Journal*, 38 (1928–29), 584 at 594ff.

[130] Williams, 'Liability', pp. 193–8.   [131] Ibid., at 198.

a vast extension of liability difficult to support. Independent contractors are likely to take out their own insurance and may, as Williams stated, be large concerns, for example, contractors working on large construction sites. Flannigan argues that the rationales supporting the imposition of vicarious liability do not operate where the employer only has nominal control and that, in such circumstances, the independent contractor should be viewed as an independent risk-taker, operating on his own account.[132]

There is, however, greater consensus that while it would be an overreaction to extend the doctrine of vicarious liability to all independent contractors, there is a stronger argument in favour of extending its principles to cover *some* workers currently classified as independent contractors. The changes in modern employment practices, discussed in Chapters 3 and 4, suggest that an extension of vicarious liability may be necessary. As previously stated, employers will now 'out-source' work formerly undertaken by employees to independent contractors. Although this may be for tax or other reasons, the net result is that employees, who previously would have been employed as permanent staff, are being treated as self-employed.[133] Such independent contractors are unlikely to obtain insurance (unless it is required by contract or statute) and are often undistinguishable from other employees, for example, they may be required to wear the company uniform or logo. McKendrick validly questions why vicarious liability should not extend to this new large class of so-called 'independent contractors'.[134]

The next section will therefore take this argument a step further. Can an alternative be found which extends employer liability for the torts of *some* independent contractors without resort to the much-criticised concepts of agency or non-delegable duties? Two options will be examined arising from common and civil law which attempt to overcome undue formalism in the legal system by the provision of more wide-ranging concepts: the 'representative agent' and the 'power to direct, manage and control the activities of another'. Both attempt to respond to economic and policy changes in the employment relationship and provide more socially responsive instruments.

---

[132] R. Flannigan, 'Enterprise control: the servant-independent contractor distinction', *University of Toronto Law Journal* (1987), 25.

[133] See H. Collins, 'Independent contractors and the challenge of vertical disintegration to employment protection laws', *Oxford Journal of Legal Studies*, 10 (1990), 353 and A. Stewart, 'Redefining employment? Meeting the challenge of contract and agency labour', *Australian Journal of Labour Law*, 15 (2002), 235.

[134] McKendrick, 'Vicarious liability', 780–1.

5.4 A new model to meet contemporary needs: representative agents or liability arising out of the ability to direct, control and manage the activities of another?

5.4.1 The 'representative agent'

Our analysis in the preceding chapters has illustrated the difficulties of determining the employment relationship and increasing pressure to extend vicarious liability to protect victims injured by workers who are not technically employees, but bear all the hallmarks of a traditional employee: in other words, the 'non-independent' independent contractor or, to use a better phrase, the 'dependent contractor'. The dependent contractor is often indistinguishable from true employees, being economically dependent on the employer and working, usually exclusively or near-exclusively, for the same employer for a long period of time, often in uniform, with few of the indicia which mark out the true entrepreneur.[135]

The Australian case of *Hollis v Vabu*,[136] discussed in Chapter 3, illustrates many of these problems. Mr Hollis was injured due to the negligence of a bicycle courier, unidentifiable save for his uniform, who was making a delivery for the defendant courier business. He was paid at a fixed rate and used his own bicycle, but was allocated jobs by radio and subject to strict instructions regarding dress, delivery procedures and client care. The High Court recognised the difficulties of applying the traditional concept of vicarious liability, derived from mediaeval notions of headship of a household, to modern employment practices, particularly when the same key terms – 'employer', 'employee', 'principal', and 'independent contractor' – had been utilised over a long period of time and adapted to very different social conditions.[137] In a system which is prepared to accept a trapeze artist as a circus employee,[138]

---

[135] See G. Davidov, 'The three axes of employment relationships: a characterization of workers in need of protection', *University of Toronto Law Journal*, 52 (2002), 357, who notes use of the term 'dependent contractor' in most Canadian jurisdictions to designate a worker in a position of economic dependence upon, and under an obligation to perform duties for, an employer/client, that person more closely resembling an employee than an independent contractor, e.g. the Ontario Labour Relations Act SO 1995 Sched. A, s. 1 (although the actual provision deals with the ability of such individuals to participate in collective bargaining) and, recently, *McKee v Reid's Heritage Homes Ltd* [2009] ONCA 916.
[136] (2001) 207 CLR 21.
[137] Ibid., at paras. 33–4 per Gleeson CJ, Gaudron, Gummow, Kirby and Hayne JJ.
[138] See *Zuijs v Wirth Brothers* (1955) 93 CLR 561 (High Court of Australia).

the nature of the 'true' contract of employment becomes increasingly difficult to determine.

The response of the majority, discussed in Chapter 3, was to adopt a more flexible interpretation of the employment relationship which included reference to policy factors such as deterrence. McHugh J, however, went further and asserted the need to recognise a third category of relationship in this context: the representative agent.[139] The 'representative agent' is not an independent contractor, but a party working for and on behalf of the employer. Liability will arise where the agent is performing a task which the principal has agreed to perform (or a duty which the principal is obliged to perform) and the principal has delegated that task or duty to the agent. Two conditions thus exist:[140]

1. Where a duty has been delegated, it must be owed to a third person and where a task has been delegated, it must be one which the principal has undertaken to a third person to perform.[141]
2. The agent must be under the general control of the principal and not an independent functionary.

When these two conditions exist, the delegate stands in the shoes of the principal.

Control is thus relevant, but, consistent with the developments noted in Chapter 3, only the power to control, rather than its actual exercise, must be shown. In the words of McHugh J: 'The right of the principal to exercise general control is what distinguishes an "agent" from an independent contractor.'[142]

In *Hollis* itself, finding the courier not to be an employee (in contrast to the majority),[143] McHugh J held that vicarious liability should nevertheless arise where Vabu had delegated to the courier a task which it had agreed to perform and the courier was not acting as an independent functionary, but was carrying out the task as Vabu's representative. The courier being subject to Vabu's general direction and control and acting

---

[139] See also his judgment in *Scott v Davis* (2000) 175 ALR 217 at 224, para. 34. Justice McHugh draws on the agency cases considered above and, in particular, the extension of the motor vehicle cases by Dixon J in *Colonial Mutual Life Assurance Society Ltd v Producers and Citizens Co-operative Assurance Co. of Australia Ltd* [1931] HCA 53, (1931) 46 CLR 41 (liability of principal for agent's defamatory statements), see, in particular, Gavan Duffy CJ and Starke J at 46, and Dixon J at 49–50.

[140] *Scott v Davis* (2000) 175 ALR 217 at para. 110.

[141] It is not a necessary condition of liability that the duty or undertaking is legally enforceable.

[142] (2001) 207 CLR 21 at para. 110.   [143] Ibid., at paras. 69–73.

within the scope of the authority conferred on him by Vabu, it would only be just that Vabu should be liable for any injury caused.[144] The policy justifications relied upon are interesting:[145] the victim obtains compensation where the individual perpetrator could not be identified/lacked means (effective compensation), the perpetrator was acting for the economic benefit of Vabu (fairness), and Vabu had known of the risk the couriers posed to other users of the highway (deterrence). Justice McHugh concludes:

> It is true that the couriers employed by Vabu are neither employees nor independent contractors in the strict sense. But there is no reason in policy for upholding the strict classification of employees and non-employees in the law of vicarious liability and depriving Mr Hollis of compensation. Rather than expanding the definition of employee or accepting the employee/independent contractor dichotomy, the preferable course is to hold that employers can be vicariously liable for the tortious conduct of agents who are neither employees nor independent contractors ... To hold that an employer is vicariously liable for the conduct of a worker who is not an employee or independent contractor does not affect their relationship in other areas of the law or their freedom to contract between themselves or to arrange their business affairs. And it has the great advantage of ensuring that the doctrine of vicarious liability remains relevant in a world of rapidly changing work practices.[146]

Kirby J, dissenting in *Sweeney v Boylan Nominees Pty Ltd*,[147] adopted a similar, if more restrictive view, that agency principles could be applied more generally to render the employer strictly liable for the actions of some independent contractors where they acted as 'representative agents' performing the functions and advancing the economic interests of the employer, effectively as part of its enterprise.[148]

The New Zealand Court of Appeal in *S v Attorney-General*[149] also utilised agency reasoning to extend the scope of vicarious liability. The question raised by this case was whether the Department of Social Welfare could be held liable for intentional torts committed by foster parents against children placed by the Department in their care. Foster parents are not State employees, but nevertheless the majority,[150] in contrast to the

---

[144] Ibid., at para. 73.
[145] Primarily based on the judgment of McLachlin J in *Bazley v Curry* [1999] 2 SCR 534, see in particular at para. 36.
[146] (2001) 207 CLR 21 at para. 93.   [147] (2006) 226 CLR 161.   [148] Ibid., at para. 38.
[149] [2003] 3 NZLR 450. For comment, see S. Varnham, 'Vicarious liability for sexual abuse', *New Zealand Law Journal* [2004], 60 and S. Todd, 'Tort action by victims of sexual abuse', *Tort Law Review*, 12 (2004), 40.
[150] Blanchard, McGrath, Anderson and Glazebrook JJ.

position in England and Wales and Canada,[151] imposed liability on the basis of agency, finding the abuse to be sufficiently connected with the purpose of parenting for which the foster placements were made:

> It seems to us that the more appropriate characterisation ... is of an agency. For, while there was certainly no employer/employee relationship, the position of the foster parents was not established by means of any formal contract and they were not undertaking a business venture for profit (or loss). The Superintendent had a duty imposed upon him by statute to take care of the children. He was obliged to fulfil that duty by placing them in suitable private homes where there was supposed to be adherence to practices in accordance with a Departmental manual and continued Departmental monitoring. The Department had a right of inspection and a right to remove any child at any time ... We think that in this setting it would be quite inappropriate to regard such an arrangement as constituting the foster parents as independent contractors. Because of the continuing statutory duty of the Superintendent to provide for the special protection of each child, the foster parents should be regarded as having been made agents of the State, albeit that their agency was of an unusual, indeed unique, nature.[152]

Tipping J, in the minority, agreed with the result, but preferred to describe the relationship giving rise to vicarious liability as '*sui generis* i.e. of its own special kind', to be determined in novel situations by analogy to other cases and by reaching a balance between the competing policy factors.[153] The reasoning of the majority in *S v Attorney-General* was applied in the later decision of *Dollars & Sense Finance Ltd v Nathan*[154] where a borrower, entrusted to obtain his parents' signatures to guarantee his loan, was deemed to act as the finance company's agent when he obtained his mother's signature fraudulently. Policy was clearly important in both cases. In the first, the majority hoped that this result would provide an incentive for the State to take even greater precautions in the future for the protection of children in its care by way of vetting and monitoring of foster parents.[155] In the second, by imposing liability on financial institutions for the fraudulent acts of borrowers, the court sought to warn financiers to discontinue the unsound practice of

---

[151] See *S v Walsall MBC* [1985] 1 WLR 1150 (CA) and the majority in *KLB v British Columbia* (2003) 230 DLR (4th) 513 (inherent in the nature of family-based care for children that foster parents are in important respects independent, and that the government cannot exercise sufficient control over their activities for them to be seen as acting 'on account' of the government).
[152] [2003] 3NZLR 450 at para. 68.   [153] Ibid., at paras. 101–2.
[154] [2008] NZSC 20, [2008] 2 NZLR 557, noted S. Watson and C. Noonan, 'The widening gyre of vicarious liability', *Torts Law Journal*, 17 (2009), 144.
[155] *S v Attorney-General* [2003] 3 NZLR 450 at para. 71.

leaving it to borrowers to organise the signatures of guarantors or risk finding the resultant guarantee worthless.[156] In both cases, despite the absence of an employment relationship, agency was used to render an innocent defendant liable where this would satisfy the policy goals of the courts.

These judgments propose the existence of an intermediate category of 'workers' for whom, by analogy with agency principles, the employer should be held liable. If we take the idea of an 'intermediate' category of representative agents, then, a number of clear advantages may be observed. The first is much needed flexibility in an area of law still tied to strict notions of the employer/employee relationship. By divorcing vicarious liability from other areas of law, one focuses on the policy issues and need not consider any implications outside this attribution of responsibility, for example, change of taxation status, availability of remedies confined to 'employees', etc. Secondly, it recognises that it will not always be clear in modern conditions whether the culprit is an employee or independent contractor – consider the temporary employee/agency cases examined in Chapter 4 – and the unpredictability of the composite test (outlined in Chapter 3). Thirdly, this intermediate category may be compared with the position in civil law, whereby the broader notions of *commettant/préposé* and *Geschäftsherr/Verrichtungsgehilfe* have already been accepted and play a significant role in rendering civil law systems responsive to social changes.

Nevertheless, it should be noted that the views of McHugh J and Kirby J in *Hollis* and *Sweeney* respectively, were contained in minority dissenting judgments and strongly opposed by the majority. Equally, the New Zealand decisions focus on particular fact situations – the Supreme Court in *Dollars & Sense Finance Ltd* remarking that it will be very much a question of factual assessment and judgment whether an agency relationship exists in each case[157] – and the notion of 'agency' used appears far looser than the McHugh/Kirby JJ formulation.[158] In the High Court of Australia decision of *Sweeney*, the majority criticised the idea of 'representative agents' as too general, going well beyond the bounds set by previous tests.[159] To use the term 'agent' was to begin the enquiry,

---

[156] *Dollars & Sense Finance v Nathan* [2008] NZSC 20, [2008] 2 NZLR 557 at para 25.
[157] Ibid.   [158] See Watson and Noonan, 'The widening gyre'.
[159] See (2006) 226 CLR 161 at paras. 26–33. See also the majority in *Scott v Davis* (2000) 204 CLR 333, which rejected the contention that the owner of an aircraft was vicariously liable for the negligence of the pilot of that aircraft if the pilot operated the aircraft with the owner's consent and for a purpose in which the owner had some concern.

not end it.[160] It concluded that the employee/independent contractor distinction was 'too deeply rooted to be pulled out'.[161] The tests have also been subject to academic criticism. In the fourth edition of their textbook, Trindade, Cane and Lunney find the notion problematic: apart from contractual agency, the circumstances in which the agency can arise appear open-ended, and run the risk of confusing contractual agency principles with that of the new doctrine.[162] McCarthy adds that 'At the outset, it is worth noting that this area of the law is beset not only by inherent terminological ambiguities, but also by undisciplined use of that terminology . . . It is commonly recognised that a precise definition of the term "agent" is elusive, if not impossible.'[163] In his view, McHugh J failed to undertake a sufficiently detailed examination of the fundamental principles involved and arguably, as a result, causes greater confusion in this area of law.

There is much to be said for these reservations. As we have seen, the term 'agency' is already used far too readily in the vicarious liability context, despite the fact that a true agency relationship imposes *primary*, not vicarious, liability on the principal for the actions of his agent within the scope of the authority conferred by the principal. Consider, for example, the House of Lords decision of *Lloyd v Grace, Smith & Co.*,[164] described by Lord Steyn in *Lister v Hesley Hall Ltd*[165] as a breakthrough case which finally establishes that vicarious liability is not necessarily defeated if the employee acted for his own benefit, in which Sandles, the managing clerk, is referred to as an agent throughout.[166] To use a concept – agency – which already gives rise to confusion in this context may thus be seen as ill-advised. A no-man's land of loosely defined 'representative agents' presents a clear danger of ending with the worst

---

[160] See majority in *Sweeney* (2006) 226 CLR 161 at para. 29 and Gummow J in *Scott v Davis* (2000) 204 CLR 333 at para. 268.
[161] (2006) 226 CLR 161 at para. 33.
[162] Trindade, Cane and Lunney, *The law of torts*, p. 782. See also G. Dal Pont, 'Agency: definitional challenges through the law of tort', *Torts Law Journal*, 11 (2003), 68, who argues that the approach, although ingenious, risks negatively affecting the nature and scope of the accepted law of agency. In his view (at 94), 'agency should have little or no interplay with the law of tort – its focus should remain in contract – and instead tort liability . . . ought to be sourced through the progressive development of the law of vicarious liability'.
[163] McCarthy, 'Vicarious liability' 1. [164] [1912] AC 716.
[165] [2001] UKHL 22, [2002] 1 AC 215 at para. 17.
[166] See, for example, Lord Shaw [1912] AC at 742 and Earl Loreburn ibid., 725, to which may be added the classic statement by Willes J in *Barwick v English Joint Stock Bank* (1867) LR 2 Ex 259 at 266.

of all possible options.[167] To be blunt, if the 'representative agent' is incapable of providing greater clarity than the composite test, then it is not capable of resolving the difficulties raised by this test in terms of uncertainty and unpredictability. Indeed, the factors relied upon by McHugh J in *Hollis* in justifying the imposition of liability – the degree of direction and control exercised by Vabu,[168] manifesting itself in detailed instructions and the provision of uniforms – do not appear sufficiently distinct from those influencing the majority to justify taking such a step.

5.4.2 *The power to organise, direct and control the activities of another: the development of Blieck and Article 1384(1) of the French Civil Code*[169]

French civil law offers an alternative means of extending liability. Despite the already broad notion of *commettant/préposé* under Article 1384(5), the courts have extended Article 1384(1) of the Civil Code to render one party (usually an institution or association) strictly liable for the torts of persons under its control or whose activities it controls. In so doing, the French courts, in a blatant example of judicial creativity, have laid the foundations for a general head of liability based on authority over others, potentially encompassing all relationships where a disparity of economic power may lead to the imposition of vicarious liability.

The starting point is Article 1384(1) which provides that 'A person is liable not only for the damage he causes by his own act, but also for that which is caused by the acts of persons for whom he is responsible, or by things which are in his custody.' This was originally treated as a general introduction to the provisions which followed, but in 1896, the French Supreme Court recognised a strict liability principle for 'things' in one's custody.[170] After some debate,[171] in 1991, it was finally accepted that

---

[167] Burnett comments that '[*Sweeney*] is more noteworthy for its failure to consider the broader question of whether an employer should be vicariously liable for the acts of independent contractors': J. Burnett, 'Avoiding difficult questions: vicarious liability and independent contractors in *Sweeney v Boylan Nominees*', *Sydney Law Review*, 29 (2007), 163 at 174.
[168] (2001) 207 CLR 21 at paras. 101–2.
[169] See L. Perdrix, 'La garde d'autrui', thesis, Université Paris I (2006).
[170] See, notably, *l'arrêt* Teffaine (Cass civ 16 June 1896, S 1897.1.17 note A. Esmein, D 1897.1.433 concl L. Sarrut, note R. Saleilles) and *l'arrêt* Jand'heur (Ch réun 13 February 1930 DP 1930.1.57 concl P. Matter, rapport A. Le Marc'hadour, note G. Ripert, S 1930.1.121 note P. Esmein).
[171] A parallel doctrine of liability for 'persons' had been proposed by Procureur général Matter in his conclusion to the *Jand'heur* case and the celebrated jurist, Saleilles, as early as the 1930s (R. Savatier, 'La responsabilité générale du fait des choses que l'on a

there was a corresponding strict liability principle imposing liability for the 'acts of persons for whom one is responsible'.

In the 1991 leading case (*l'arrêt de principe*) of *Blieck*,[172] the French Supreme Court found an association, caring for mentally handicapped adults, strictly liable under Article 1384(1) for the acts of one of their charges, who had set fire to a forest in which he had been working.[173] This case is notable for a number of reasons. First, the French Supreme Court accepted that a relationship, which did not fit under the Article 1384 list of relationships (parents; employers/*commettants*; teachers; apprentice-masters) could still give rise to liability for the acts of others. Liability was based on the fact that 'the association had accepted the responsibility to organise and to control, permanently, the way of life of this handicapped person'.[174] Secondly, the Supreme Court did not disagree with the view of the Court of Appeal[175] that such liability arose due to the increased risk of harm to innocent members of the public resulting from more liberal means of rehabilitation or re-education of individuals capable of endangering the public, such as offenders and the mentally handicapped.[176] Thirdly, this decision follows the lead of the administrative courts whereby State organisations have been held liable for harm caused by delinquent minors, the mentally handicapped and other potentially dangerous parties in their care.[177] It was considered undesirable that victims should be subject to two different

---

sous sa garde a-t-elle pour pendant une responsabilité générale du fait des personnes dont on doit répondre?', DH 1933 chron 81), but was rejected by the courts and the majority of legal commentators, notably Mazeaud.

[172] (*Association des centres éducatifs du Limousin et autre c/ Consorts Blieck*) Ass plén 29 March 1991 D 1991.324 note C. Larroumet, chr G. Viney p. 157, somm 324 obs J.L. Aubert; JCP 1991 II 21673, concl D.-H. Dontenwille, note J. Ghestin, Def 1991.1.729 art 35062 N° 44 obs J.-L. Aubert; RTD civ. 1991.541 obs P. Jourdain.

[173] For the historical background to the 1991 development, see F. Terré, P. Simler and Y. Lequette, *Droit civil: les obligations*, 10th edn (Paris: Dalloz, 2009), N°s 848–9 and the conclusions of Dontenwille to the *Blieck* case (n. 172 above).

[174] My translation.

[175] CA Limoges 1, 23 March 1989 Resp civ ass Nov 1989 comm N° 361.

[176] The decision, in fact, refers to the fact that the culprit had total freedom of movement during the day. Radé notes that the Court of Appeal was also careful to check that the association was covered by insurance: Ch. Radé, *Jurisclasseur responsabilité civile et assurances, Fasc 140: droit à reparation — responsabilité du fait d'autrui: principe général* (Paris: Lexis Nexis 2005), para. 19.

[177] For offenders, see CE 3 February 1956 (*Thouzellier*) D 1956.596 note J. M. Auby, JCP 1956 II 9608 note D. Lévy; 29 April 1987 (*Ministère de la Justice*) JCP 1988 II 20920 note B. Pacteau. See also CE 13 July 1967 (*Département de la Moselle*) Rec p. 341, D 1967.675 note F. Moderne (mentally ill patients on a trial outing).

regimes dependent on whether the body in question was subject to the provisions of public or private law.[178]

The *Blieck* principle has since been applied to other analogous relationships, characterised by the ability of (usually) an institution to organise and control the way of life of individuals capable of endangering the public. On this basis, educational services dealing with juvenile offenders[179] and even organisations protecting minors[180] have been found liable under Article 1384(1) for harm caused by those under their control. It has even been extended to guardians,[181] although the courts have drawn the line at grandparents gratuitously looking after their grandchildren on a temporary basis.[182] Such liability is strict and cannot be rebutted by proof of absence of fault.[183]

In a sense, such liability amounts to an extension of parental liability under Article 1384(4), discussed in Chapter 7. In modern society, parents are not the only persons who assume responsibility for children, the handicapped or vulnerable adults. The breakdown of the nuclear family and the rise of the welfare state means that other bodies, in addition to parents, will have a role to play, be they social services, the prison service or other bodies, and these roles will grant them powers to supervise and control such persons. It has been submitted that the extension of the

---

[178] See Larroumet's note to *Blieck* (n. 172 above). Radé, *Jurisclasseur responsabilité*, para. 21 adds that it also brings tort and contract law closer together. Terré, Simler and Lequette, *Droit civil*, N° 855, ask, however, whether such difference is necessarily a bad thing.

[179] Civ 2, 7 May 2003 D 2003.2256 note M. Huyette cf CE sec 11 February 2005 AJDA 2005.663; D 2005.1762 note F. Lemaire; JCP 2005 II 10070 concl C. Devys and note M. C. Rouault; RFD admin 2005.595 concl C. Devys and note P. Bon; LPA 1 June 2005, p. 8 and note E. Matutano.

[180] Crim 10 October 1996 Bull crim N° 357; JCP 1997 II 22833 note F. Chabas; D 1997.309 note M. Huyette, Civ 2, 20 January 2000 Bull civ II N° 15; D 2000.571 note M. Huyette; RTD civ. 2000.588 obs P. Jourdain (damage caused to other children placed in establishment) and Civ 2, 7 May 2003 Bull civ II N° 129; D 2003.2256 note M. Huyette; JCP 2004 I 101 N° 19 obs G. Viney. Even when resident with parents: Civ 2, 6 June 2002 D 2002.2750 note M. Huyette; JCP 2003 II 10068 note A. Gouttenoire-Cornut et N. Roget, RTD civ. 2002.825 obs P. Jourdain: JCP 2003 I 154 N° 37 obs G. Viney.

[181] Crim 28 March 2000 Bull crim N° 140; JCP 2001 II 10457 note C. Robaczewski; JCP 2000 I 241 N° 9/10 obs G. Viney; D 2000 somm 466 obs D. Mazeaud, RTD civ. 2000.586 obs P. Jourdain. Contra Civ 2, 25 February 1998 D 1998.315 concl R. Kessous; JCP 1998 II 10149 note G. Viney, RTD civ. 1998.388 obs P. Jourdain.

[182] Civ 2, 18 Sept 1996 Bull civ II N° 217; D 1998.118 note J. Rebourg; RTD civ. 1997.436 obs P. Jourdain, 5 Feb 2004 Petites Affiches 24 June 2005 p. 14 note D. Bertol.

[183] Only *cause étrangère* (force majeure or fault of the victim) will suffice: see Crim 26 March 1997 JCP 1997 II 22868 rapp F. Desportes; D 1997.496 note P. Jourdain; JCP 1997 I 4070 N° 19 obs G. Viney.

strict liability of parents to any harmful acts of their children[184] should also apply to this form of liability, thereby creating a social fund of compensation for any innocent parties injured by persons under the organisation and control of others, although this view is not universally shared.

Such a view is contentious for a number of reasons – the absence of compulsory insurance, existing criticism of the extension of parental liability,[185] the conflict with corrective justice and ideas of individual responsibility being the most obvious – but it is a further development of the *Blieck* principle which is interesting here. Parallel to the liability of *commettants*, this principle has been extended beyond associations dealing with potentially dangerous persons to associations whose members engage in risk-producing activities. The second chamber of the French Supreme Court in two cases in 1995[186] found that a rugby club would be liable under Article 1384(1) where a player had been injured (in one case fatally) by one of its players during a match:

> Sporting associations, having the object to organise, manage and control the activities of their members when they participate in sporting competitions, are liable for the harm they cause in the course of such activities.[187]

This principle has been extended to injuries caused during training sessions[188] and friendly matches.[189] In one notorious case, it was

---

[184] See the *Fullenwarth* decision of 1984 (Ass plén 9 May 1984 (2nd case) D 1984.525 concl J. Cabannes, note F. Chabas, (1st case) JCP 1984 II 20255 note N. Dejean de la Bâtie), the *Bertrand* decision of 1997 (Civ 2, 19 February 1997 Bull civ II N° 56 p. 32) and the decision of the Assemblée Plénière in 2002 (Cass Ass Plén 13 December 2002 Bull Ass plén N° 4, p. 7), discussed in Chapter 7.

[185] See, for example, H. Groutel, 'L'enfant mineur ravalé au rang de simple chose?' Resp civ et assur 2001 chron 18 and Ph. Brun, 'Le nouveau visage de la responsabilité du fait d'autrui (vers l'irresponsabilité des petits?)' in *Etudes à la mémoire de Ch Lapoyade-Deschamps* (Pessac: PUB, 2003), p. 105.

[186] Civ 2, 22 May 1995 Bull civ II N° 155; JCP 1995 II 22550 note J. Mouly, I 3893 N° 5 obs G. Viney; D 1996 somm 29 note F. Alaphilippe, RTD civ. 1995.899 obs P. Jourdain. Followed by Civ 2, 3 February 2000 JCP 2000 II 10316 note J. Mouly, I 241 N° 5 obs G. Viney; D 2000.862 note S. Denoix de Saint Marc; D 2000 somm 465 obs P. Jourdain; Def 2000.724, art 37188 N° 44 obs D. Mazeaud.

[187] My translation. Contrast English law where primary liability is imposed on the association when it assumes responsibility to individual players: *Vowles v Evans & Welsh Rugby Union* [2003] EWCA Civ 318 (referee); *Watson v BBBC* [2001] QB 1134 (boxing association); *Wattleworth v Goodwood Road Racing Co. Ltd* [2004] EWHC 140, [2004] PIQR P25 (motor racing organiser).

[188] Civ 2, 21 October 2004 Bull civ II N° 477, D 2005.40 note J. B. Laydu, RTD civ. 2005.412 obs P. Jourdain.

[189] Even, in one case, finding a scout association liable for the harm caused by the scouts: CA Paris 14, 9 June 2000 Resp civ et assur 2000, comm. 74 obs L. Grynbaum.

extended to a drum majorette who injured another with her baton.[190] Such a 'sport' is not obviously risky, but nevertheless was found to fall within Article 1384(1). Jourdain comments that such case law indicates that liability is not in reality based on risk, but on the authority and powers of the institution over the author of the damage.[191]

This line of case law marks a distinct change of direction to the *Blieck* decision. Here, liability is based not on the risks caused to society by certain individuals, but the *activity* the individuals are engaged upon. Such activities are not dangerous per se, but may cause risks to others. The control exercised by the associations here is, however, not comparable to that seen in Blieck. It is temporary and limited in nature. At best, rugby club members must agree to follow club rules and are subject to some disciplinary procedures, but it is hardly equivalent to an institution undertaking responsibility for the care of a mentally handicapped child or juvenile offender. It is important, however, to see the 1995 decisions in context, namely that it was assumed that an amateur sportsman could not be held to be a *préposé* under Article 1384(5) and that Article 1384(1) was needed to fill the gap. In the absence of proof of the classic relationship of subordination, an alternative test of the ability to organise, manage and control the activities of another would suffice. Fault would still be a requirement.[192] The plenary assembly of the Supreme Court removed any doubts in 2007 that liability would depend on a finding of fault – in the sporting context, requiring a violation of the rules of the sport.[193]

Professor Viney has suggested that this line of authority may be taken a step further to include relationships of economic dependence which do not fit precisely within Article 1384(5).[194] In the proposals for the

---

[190] Liability imposed on association of drum majorettes: Civ 2, 12 December 2002 Bull civ II N° 289, JCP 2003 IV 1220, JCP 2003 I 154 N° 49, obs G. Viney; D 2003 somm 2541 obs F. Lagarde. See also CA Aix-en-Provence 9 October 2003 Resp civ et assur April 2004. comm 89 note C. Radé (liability of football supporters' club). For a discussion of the conceptual problems arising from this area of law, see J. Mouly, 'Les paradoxes du droit de la responsabilité civile dans le domaine des activités sportives', JCP 2005 I 134 p. 833.
[191] RTD civ. 2003.305 at 307.
[192] This is contested in relation to the *Blieck* line of decisions on the basis that it is not necessary for parental liability.
[193] Ass plén 29 June 2007 D 2007.2455 note J. François and chron 2408 obs P. Brun, JCP 2007 II 10150 note J.-M. Marmayou, RTD civ. 2007.782 obs P. Jourdain. See F. Millet, 'L'acceptation des risqué rehabilitee? Une application aux responsabilités du fait d'autrui' D 2005.2830 (who explains the decision on the basis of voluntary assumption of risk in sport).
[194] Viney and Jourdain, *Traité de droit civil*, N° 788-11 and N° 789-25.

138   OTHER RELATIONSHIPS GIVING RISE TO LIABILITY

reform of the French Civil Code, the Tort Working Group (chaired by Professor Viney) suggested two categories of claims should exist: one founded on the control over the way of life of minors or adults whose condition or situation requires special supervision, and the other relating to persons who organise and profit from the activities of another person.[195] This second category goes beyond liability currently existing under Article 1384(5) to include 'the liability of physical or legal persons who organise and have an interest in the activity of professionals or businesses (not being their employees)'.[196] Article 1360 therefore extends liability for others to non-employment relationships including some 'independent' workers, franchisors/franchisees and parent companies/subsidiaries.[197] In this way, the Working Group sought to 'adjust the law of liability so as to reflect the radical changes which have occurred in the way in which economic relations are structured, as regards both production and distribution'.[198]

The idea of a general principle of liability based not on the *commettant/ préposé* relationship, but on the basis of a relationship where one controls and organises the activities of another or, to use the wording of the French reform proposals, 'organise and profit from the activity of other persons' is still at an early stage in French law. The general view is that there is, at present, no general principle which unites all the case law under Article 1384(1).[199] There has been a reluctance by some courts to extend liability

---

[195] For comment, see Ph. Le Tourneau, 'Les responsabilités du fait d'autrui dans l'avant-projet de réforme', *Revue des contrats* [2007], 109.

[196] P. Catala, *Avant-projet de réforme du droit des obligations et de la prescription* (Paris: La Documentation française, 2006); translation by S. Whittaker and J. Cartwright: www.justice.gouv.fr/art_pix/rapportcatatla0905-anglais.pdf at 190.

[197] Article 1360: 'Apart from cases involving a relationship of employment, a person is liable for harm caused by another person whose professional or business activity he regulates or organises and from which he derives an economic advantage where this occurs in the course of this activity. This includes notably the liability of healthcare establishments for harm caused by the doctors to whom they have recourse. The claimant must show that the harmful action results from the activity in question. Similarly, a person who controls the economic or financial activity of a business or professional person who is factually dependent on that person even though acting on his own account, is liable for harm caused by this dependant where the victim shows that the harmful action relates to the first person's exercise of control. This is the case in particular as regards parent companies in relation to harm caused by their subsidiaries or as regards those granting a concession in relation to harm caused by a person to whom the concession is granted.'

[198] Whittaker and Cartwright, above n. 196, at 180.

[199] Viney and Jourdain, for example, highlight the distinction between strict liability provisions based on the control of the activities of another (based on the idea of risk/ profit) and strict liability based on control over the person herself which derives

beyond the sporting context, for example liability has not been extended to unions on the (not wholly convincing) ground that it is neither their object nor mission to organise, manage and control the activities of their members.[200] The proposals of the reformers have further met a cool reception from some academics and the business community generally.[201]

In any event, a number of difficulties may be identified with the French proposed extension of liability. First, the *commettant/préposé* categorisation is already broad and rather than creating a separate category for amateur rugby players, they might as easily be reinterpreted as *préposés* in the first place.[202] Secondly, if the aim is to circumvent the limits of Article 1384(5), that is, the requirement of a wrongful act and that the act must take place in the course of the *préposé's* functions, then, this is to suggest a new form of liability, creating inconsistencies with Article 1384(5) itself. Finally, in recommending the need to retain the requirement of wrongful act in relation to the liability of sporting associations, the *avocat général* Duplat highlighted the insurance framework within which such claims take place. Whilst sporting associations are required by a 1984 statute to obtain civil liability insurance,[203] Duplat warned that extending liability would threaten access to sport and discourage the practice of any risky activities, to the detriment of French society and the international reputation of sport in France.[204] There is also concern that Article 1384(1) lacks a clear framework for liability. As Fabre-Magnan remarks, it merely states that a person is liable for damage caused by the acts of persons for whom he is responsible: a tautology which gives no clear rules as to its application.[205] If the

from the protective duty imposed on those caring for persons of limited physical or mental capacity: Viney and Jourdain, *Traité de droit civil*, N° 789–30. See also P. Jourdain, 'Existe-t-il un principe général de responsabilité du fait d'autrui?', Resp civ et assur Nov 2000.

[200] Civ 2, 26 October 2006 Bull civ II N° 299; JCP 2007 II 10004 note J. Mouly; D 2007.204 note J. B. Laydu; LPA 3 Jan 2007.15 note M. Brusorio; JCP 2007 I 115 N° 5 obs P. Stoffel-Munck.

[201] See B. Fagès, 'Réforme de la responsabilité du fait d'autrui et sort réservé aux sociétés mères', *Revue des contrats* [2007], 115 and the report of the Paris Chamber of Commerce which expresses particular concern at the impact of such liability on insurance premiums: *Pour une réforme du droit des contrats et de la prescription conforme aux besoins de la vie des affaires* (2006) at 33; see www.etudes.ccip.fr/archrap/pdf06/reforme-droit-des-contrats-kli0610.pdf.

[202] See P. Jourdain D 2000 somm 465. See also J. Mouly in JCP 1995 II 22550 N° 5 and P. Jourdain RTD civ. 1995.900.

[203] Now codified: Articles L321–1 ff, Sporting Code.

[204] Avis de M. Duplat to Ass plén 29 June 2007 [2007] BICC 668.

[205] M. Fabre-Magnan, *Droit des obligations, 2 Responsabilité civile et quasi-contrats* (Paris: PUF, 2007), N° 122.

French courts have outgrown the categories of Article 1384 and the modern welfare state requires a new category for potentially dangerous persons whose lives are controlled and organised by others, then it is quite a different step to create another category resting loosely on the power of a body to exercise some control over the activities of another. Although the 2007 decision to limit liability to wrongful actions outside the risks of the game is a step forward, doubts must be expressed at the coherency of this extension of liability to non-employees.

5.5 An appraisal: a new model to meet contemporary needs?

As may be seen, both the Australian and French models possess problems. Whilst both may be seen as organic developments from existing case law, the notion of a 'representative agent' or person with 'power' to control the activities of another are vague and do not provide a clear framework for future legal development. Further, they have received little support from their judicial or academic communities, primarily due to their threat of destabilising existing legal principles. Nevertheless, this chapter has identified a line of authority in each legal system which supports the application of vicarious liability principles *beyond* that of the employer/employee relationship. Identifying the contract of employment will not suffice. The question remains: if there is consensus that some non-employment relations should attract the principles of vicarious liability, how should this be conceptualised?

The easiest option would be to include all workers within the doctrine of vicarious liability. Atiyah raised this suggestion in his 1967 monograph and McHugh J in *Northern Sandblasting Pty Ltd v Harris*[206] accepted his arguments as convincing. However, as already discussed in this chapter, such a move has received damning criticism from commentators such as Glanville Williams and would amount to a considerable extension of strict liability, in the absence of any overwhelming policy rationale for such an extension. Removing the employer/independent contractor distinction may be neat, but is not advocated by even the more generous legal systems, such as the French, and threatens to overwhelm the existing insurance and other financial arrangements which fund the vicarious liability framework.

---

[206] (1997) 188 CLR 313 at 366–7. However, as the court had not been invited to re-examine the basis of the liability of an employer for the acts of an independent contractor, Justice McHugh left this question to be determined at a later date.

Logic suggests that a preferable model would be one that encompasses existing extensions of liability, but in a more coherent framework. As shown already in this chapter, use of agency is conceptually confusing and the rather odd common law motor vehicle example may be dismissed as a particular response to motor accident compensation claims rather than any valid extension of liability. Few would today seek to justify the use of agency in this context. Equally, non-delegable duties may in part be explained by the frustrations of the courts with the limitations of the doctrine of vicarious liability, resorting to primary liability to achieve the required goal of rendering the employer liable for the worker's torts. French reliance on Article 1384(1) represents a similar example of judicial frustration at the limits of liability under Article 1384(5), despite its broader notion of *commettant/préposé*. If an amateur rugby player cannot be classified as a *préposé* and yet is capable of causing serious injury in a rugby match to a fellow employee in circumstances where the exact culprit cannot be identified (and therefore be held personally responsible), then the courts will not leave the victim uncompensated, particularly when, since 1984, the rugby club will be subject to compulsory insurance. The policy rationale to this development is clear to all, even if it leaves the interpretation of Article 1384(1) in some disarray. Yet the response to the French sporting cases may offer some assistance. A number of commentators argue that in the 1995 cases the French Supreme Court should have supported the Court of Appeal, that is, extended Article 1384(5) to amateur sportsmen, thereby avoiding, as stated by Mouly, the rather odd division between professional sportsmen (subject to Article 1384(5)) and amateurs (subject to Article 1384(1)).[207] In other words, a broader notion is needed of the employer/employee relationship which is capable, in the specific context of vicarious liability, of extending to non-traditional employer/worker relationships, but does not extend so far as to encompass all independent contractors.

McKendrick has proposed a new contextual approach which treats all workers integrated into the employer's organisation as 'employees' for the sake of vicarious liability, regardless of their status in other areas of law.[208] Although one might question his use of the 'integration' test,

---

[207] See J. Mouly, 'Les paradoxes du droit de la responsabilité civile dans le domaine des activités sportives', JCP 2005 I 134 p. 833.

[208] E. McKendrick, 'Vicarious liability and independent contractors – a re-examination', *Modern Law Review*, 53 (1990), 770 at 780–1. See also N. Foster, 'Vicarious liability for independent contractors revisited: *Sweeney v Boylan Nominees Pty Ltd*', *Torts Law Journal*,

which, as discussed in Chapter 3, is difficult to apply in practice, McKendrick highlights an important issue: the key policy dilemmas in this area of law are no longer motor vehicle accidents or the status of medical personnel, but who, if anyone, takes responsibility for accidents caused by temporary or agency workers whose status, described in Chapter 4, remains unclear. As discussed in previous chapters, workplace patterns have changed. Permanent employment contracts are frequently replaced by reliance on agency staff, who may even be former employees who have changed status due to the financial advantages to both employer and employee. The labour market's shift towards the increased use of contractors in both the public and private sectors has, as noted by Sedley LJ in *Brook Street Bureau (UK) Ltd v Dacas*,[209] exposed the limits of vicarious liability whereby victims injured by workers, not technically classified as employees, will be left to a personal claim against the culprit. Cases such as *O'Kelly v Trusthouse Forte*[210] demonstrate the risks which arise. Here, casual waiting staff at a hotel were held not to be employees, even though they worked on a regular basis exclusively for the hotel. Any guest injured by the negligence of a person working for the hotel is therefore left with a dilemma: is this person casual or permanent staff? A guest's ability to obtain compensation would seem to rest on this legal distinction.

It is submitted that vicarious liability has for far too long lagged behind changes in employment practices and two key steps must be taken. First, the common law should look to its civilian counterparts and abandon the idea of a legal definition of the contract of employment applicable to *all* contexts. As demonstrated in Chapter 4, the strict rules of contract law have been abandoned in relation to the law relating to borrowed employees, and impose an unjustifiable restriction on what is, in reality, a principle of responsibility based on the policy justifications. To superimpose the contractual requirements of mutuality of obligations is to misunderstand what vicarious liability is trying to achieve. Vicarious liability is a rule of responsibility. It should be treated as distinct from other areas of law and therefore possess its own definition

---

14 (2006), 219, and R. Flannigan, 'Enterprise control: the servant-independent contractor distinction', *University of Toronto Law Journal* (1987), 25, who advocates a broader notion of employee based on the concept of enterprise control, whereby unless the control by the employer is nominal, the policies underlying vicarious liability dictate that the worker should not be viewed as an independent risk-taker, i.e. independent contractor, working on his own account.

[209] [2004] EWCA Civ 217, [2004] ICR 1437 at para. 72.   [210] [1984] 1 QB 90.

of the relationship necessary to give rise to vicarious liability. On this basis, it should not be considered inconsistent to develop its own line of authority, ignoring the rules defining employment contracts in other areas of law.

Secondly, the common law clearly needs a broader definition of the 'employer/employee' relationship than currently exists. It should be extended to include temporary or agency workers with some degree of permanency: in effect, those who would be viewed as employees but for the legal arrangements adopted to avoid tax or employment protection. If revenue and labour law are irrelevant to the characterisation of the relationship, then the composite test may be used to extend liability to encompass these relationships and protect victims from the indeterminate nature of modern employment relations. This, in fact, is what was achieved by the High Court of Australia in *Hollis v Vabu*.[211] Whilst I would agree with McHugh J that '[i]f the law of vicarious liability is to remain relevant in the contemporary world, it needs to be developed and applied in a way that will accommodate the changing nature of employment relationships',[212] it is suggested that the answer is not to invent another concept which must be interpreted by the courts, but to adopt a more flexible interpretation of the employer/employee relationship specific to the needs of vicarious liability. What is needed is a test which examines the substance of the relationship between employer and worker. Where the worker is acting on behalf of the employer on a regular basis, either exclusively or near-exclusively, and manifests the basic characteristics of the employee, notably economic dependency, then, for the sake of vicarious liability, they should be treated as an employee. On this basis, Mrs Dacas, working for over four years exclusively as a cleaner for Wandsworth Council would be treated in any vicarious liability claim as an 'employee'. In this way, this category of 'dependent contractors' would be included within the doctrine of vicarious liability, utilising existing case law tests and providing a more focused application of the law.

5.6 Conclusion

The Australian judge Kirby J commented recently that 'The great expansion in recent years of the use by public authorities of contractors, and the "out-sourcing" to agents in the place of employees, suggests

---

[211] (2001) 207 CLR 21.   [212] Ibid., at para. 85.

the possible need to reconceptualise the foundations of vicarious liability.'[213] This chapter builds on previous chapters to submit that this is indeed necessary. In this chapter, I have highlighted the weaknesses of existing law. Common law resort to the notions of agency and non-delegable duties, it is suggested, derives from frustration at the limits of vicarious liability rather than any considered conceptual development of these doctrines. As seen in French law, even with a codified system of vicarious liability and a broader notion of the relationship required to found liability, courts may seek to extend liability further, but run the risk of creating incoherence and indeterminate liability. It is submitted that the Blieck extension of liability for the activities of others under Article 1384(1) is unnecessary and that such liability should continue to be dealt with under the flexible provisions of Article 1384(5).

What is needed is a more focused approach. A more flexible interpretation of the employment relationship at common law, specific to vicarious liability claims, would resolve the 'dependent contractor' problem by including it within the vicarious liability employer/employee relationship, and eliminate the need for resort to primary liability to bypass the limitations of the current law. Such an interpretation would simplify considerably the law described in the last three chapters. By removing the need for reliance on notions such as agency or non-delegable duties, a clearer and more conceptually coherent basis for the relationship needed to found vicarious liability may be found.

Understanding vicarious liability requires, however, more than a clearer understanding of the relationship needed. Liability in all systems will only arise where the 'employee', 'préposé' or 'Verrichtungsgehilfe' are acting in the course of their employment/ in the functions for which they have been employed[214]/when carrying out their assigned task.[215] Liability is therefore limited to circumstances where a connection exists between the relationship and the wrongful act committed by the tortfeasor. The nature of this connection will be examined in the next chapter.

---

[213] *Leichhardt Municipal Council v Montgomery* [2007] HCA 6, (2007) 233 ALR 200 at para. 50.
[214] Article 1384(5), Code Civil: *dans les fonctions auxquelles ils les ont employés.*
[215] § 831 BGB: *in Ausführung der Verrichtung.*

6 Acting in the course of one's employment/functions/assigned tasks: determining the scope of vicarious liability

6.1 Introduction

This chapter will examine the scope of vicarious liability, that is, assuming that the requisite relationship exists between the person who harms the victim (for the sake of clarity, we will call him the 'employee'),[1] and the defendant (the 'employer'), *the extent to which* the employer will be adjudged civilly responsible for the employee's wrongful actions and thereby required to compensate the person injured. In all systems surveyed, the employer will not be held strictly liable for *all* torts committed by the employee. Liability will be limited by the requirement that a connection must exist between the tortious act or omission and the parties' relationship. In the common law, this takes the form of a rule that the tort in question must take place in the course (or scope) of employment.[2] Article 1384(5) of the French Civil Code provides that 'Masters and employers [are liable] for the damage caused by their servants and employees *in the functions for which they have been employed*'.[3]

---

[1] The use of the terms 'employer' and 'employee' here is simply one of convenience, being the most common relationship in which vicarious liability arises, and in no way signifies that the law in this chapter only applies to employer/employee relationships (see earlier chapters for the relationships giving rise to vicarious liability).

[2] We will use the term 'course of employment', which is often used interchangeably with that of 'scope of employment'. Lord Clyde warned, however, in *Lister v Hesley Hall Ltd* [2002] 1 AC 215 at para. 40 that care should be taken to distinguish use of the term in vicarious liability from the various statutory occasions where the phrase 'in the course of his employment' or similar words have often been used (see, for example, *Jones v Tower Boot Co. Ltd* [1997] ICR 254: distinct interpretation of 'course of employment' under Race Relations Act 1976 s. 32(1)). The term 'scope of employment' is used in US law to delimit the scope of liability: § 7.07 Restatement (3d) of Law of Agency.

[3] 'Les maîtres et les commettants, du dommage causé par leurs domestiques et préposés dans les fonctions auxquelles ils les ont employés.'

145

German law, despite adhering to fault-based liability in § 831 BGB, similarly confines liability to harm caused 'in the accomplishment of the tasks set'.[4] These tests are intended to ensure that a proportionate burden is placed on defendants held liable for the wrongful acts of others.

In examining the development and operation of these tests, a number of observations may be made. First, in recent years, the courts have shown a willingness to extend the boundaries of the scope of liability to include both negligent and intentional (often criminal) misconduct. This has threatened the conceptual clarity of the tests used in each system. If, for example, it is deemed to be 'within the course of employment' to commit crimes such as child abuse (as accepted by the common law courts), or 'within the employee's functions' to commit acts of fraud whilst selling insurance policies (as recognised by French law), then the courts are adopting an approach which focuses more on the interests of the victim than a strict interpretation of the duties expected of an employee under his contract of employment. Secondly, this development has been justified in terms of ensuring compensation for victims and demonstrates a movement in modern legal systems towards increased reliance on the doctrine of vicarious liability to meet the social goals of compensation and a corresponding willingness to increase the compensatory burden on innocent defendants. In all the systems surveyed, the courts have struggled to provide a response which is able to balance society's concern for the victims of torts against providing a clear and workable test for litigants which does not impose an unjustifiable burden on innocent defendants. The extent to which the courts have been successful in this goal will be examined below.

This chapter will thus set out and critically analyse the tests used by the courts to determine the connection needed between the tort committed and the relationship linking tortfeasor and defendant. It will start, however, with a brief outline of the derivation of these tests, before examining their operation in practice.

---

[4] 'Wer einen anderen zu einer Verrichtung bestellt, ist zum Ersatz des Schadens verpflichtet, den der andere in Ausführung der Verrichtung *einem Dritten widerrechtlich zufügt*.' Although § 831 BGB includes a similar test to that of the common and French law, this will not be examined in detail in this chapter on the basis that, not being a vicarious liability provision, its case law is of limited guidance in this context.

6.2 Limiting the scope of liability: acting in the course of employment/one's functions/assigned tasks

The origins of the requirement of a limit on employers' liability may be traced back to Roman law. David Johnston[5] has argued that the idea of a functional limit was developed by Roman jurists in the case of contractual agency and was introduced into delict by subsequent commentators such as Pothier in his *Traité des obligations*.[6] Whilst Roman law rendered the *paterfamilias* liable for the delicts of children and slaves in his power, liability could only be said to be limited in the sense that, instead of paying damages for the delict, the *paterfamilias* could choose to surrender the offending family member or slave (noxal surrender).[7] No functional limit as such appears to have existed in the law of delict. As Zimmermann explains, 'The *paterfamilias*, in other words, was "vicariously" liable for the wrongful acts of persons in his power, but his liability was of a "noxal" character . . . The Roman lawyers had, indeed, dealt with a whole variety of instances of liability for others . . . but they did not develop any general and clear-cut rules in this regard.'[8]

Nevertheless, later commentators on the Digest, notably Johannes Voet,[9] used various passages of the Digest to assert that masters were only liable for the delicts of their servants committed in an office to which they were appointed. Pothier, equally inspired by certain Roman texts, laid down the foundations for Article 1384 of the French Civil Code in his *Traité des obligations*, stating that 'It is not only in contracting that employees bind their employers. A person who has entrusted another with a certain function is responsible for the delicts and quasi-delicts which his employee has committed in the exercise of the functions for which he has been employed.'[10] Whilst Johnston is critical of the

---

[5] 'The development of law in classical and early medieval Europe: limiting liability: Roman and the civil law tradition', *Chicago-Kent Law Review*, 70 (1995), 1515.
[6] Paris: Chez Debure, 1768.
[7] J. A. C. Thomas, *Textbook of Roman law* (Amsterdam: North-Holland, 1976), ch. XXXIII. The practice of surrendering daughters had become obsolete in the Republic and was abolished for sons by Justinian: A. Borkowski and P. du Plessis, *Textbook on Roman law*, 3rd edn (Oxford University Press, 2005), 5.1.2.1.
[8] R. Zimmermann, *The law of obligations: Roman foundations of the civilian tradition* (Oxford: Clarendon, 1996), pp. 1118–20.
[9] See *Commentarius ad Pandectas* (1827/1829), lib. IX, tit. IV, 10, whose influence is noted by Johnston, 'The development of law', 1527–9; R. Zimmermann, *Roman law, contemporary law, European law* (Oxford University Press, 2001), pp. 123–4.
[10] Pothier, *Traité*, p. 453. Translation by Johnston, 'The development of law', 1529, who notes that both Pothier and Voet rely on Digest 14.3.5.8.

manipulation of these texts, he acknowledges that this is undertaken to achieve ends thought to be socially and legally desirable.[11] This may be contrasted with the more faithful exposition of Roman law adopted by nineteenth-century German legal writers, whose focus on fault-based liability matches different social and political goals.[12] Nevertheless, § 831, in common with the liability of companies for their organs under § 31 BGB,[13] does contain a limitation to acts 'in the accomplishment of the task set' and a similar restriction has been read into the regime of contractual liability for the acts of others under § 278 BGB.[14]

At common law the notion of a functional limit on liability seems to have developed from the late seventeenth century onwards.[15] Despite the imposition of liability for all wrongs committed by a person's servants in early medieval law,[16] by the sixteenth century the common law of England had relieved an employer of liability for his servant's wrong unless he had specifically commanded, or consented to, the act causing the wrong.[17] From the late seventeenth century, the master could be held liable for acts he did not expressly command, provided that they were for his benefit[18] and the servant was about his master's business.[19] Zimmermann argues that Chief Justice Holt in the two important

---

[11] See Johnston, 'The development of law', 1532.

[12] It is therefore unsurprising that in contrast to Voet and Pothier, Zimmermann has noted a tendency of German legal writers to read Roman texts in a way as to conform to the axiom of no liability without fault: *The law of obligations*, p. 1125. He cites Digest 19. 2. 25. 7 as one of the key sources upon which nineteenth-century German legal writers sought to reject the notion of strict liability for the acts of another. For the reasons for the German rejection of strict liability, see 1.2.

[13] 'The association is liable for the damage to a third party that the board, a member of the board or another constitutionally appointed representative causes through an act committed by it or him *in carrying out the business with which it or he is entrusted*, where the act gives rise to a liability in damages.' (emphasis added).

[14] Note the discussion of §§ 31 and 278 BGB in 2.3.

[15] J. H. Baker, *An introduction to English legal history*, 4th edn (London: Butterworths, 2002), p. 410; J. G. Fleming, *The law of torts*, 9th edn (Sydney: LBC Information Services, 1998), p. 409.

[16] J. H. Wigmore, 'Responsibility for tortious acts: its history – I', *Harvard Law Review*, 7 (1894), 315 at 330–7.

[17] J. H. Wigmore, 'Responsibility for tortious acts: its history – II', *Harvard Law Review*, 7 (1894), 383 at 391.

[18] *Turberville v Stampe* (1698) 1 Ld Raym 264, 91 ER 1072. This requirement was overturned by *Lloyd v Grace Smith and Co.* [1912] AC 716, overturning *Barwick v English Joint Stock Bank* (1867) LR 2 Ex 259 on this point.

[19] W. S. Holdsworth, *A history of English law* (London: Methuen, 1966 reprint), vol. VIII, pp. 474–5.

decisions of *Boson v Sandford* (1691)[20] and *Turberville v Stampe* (1698)[21] drew his inspiration from some Roman law precedents.[22] Certainly, English law had reached a position similar to that stated in the French Civil Code by 1804. Lord Kenyon CJ, for example in *Ellis v Turner* in 1800, stated that 'The defendants are responsible for the acts of their servant in those things that respect his duty under them, though they are not answerable for his misconduct in those things that do not respect his duty to them'.[23] From the 1800s onwards, in a number of cases, the courts determined when employees would be deemed to be 'on a frolic of their own' – where the employer would not be liable – or within the course of their employment. In the 1834 case of *Joel v Morison*,[24] for example, Baron Parke stated that 'The master is only liable where the servant is acting in the course of his employment. If he was going out of his way, against his master's implied commands, when driving on his master's business, he will make his master liable; but if he was going on a frolic of his own, without being at all on his master's business, the master will not be liable.' In *Limpus v London General Omnibus Co.*,[25] the Exchequer Chamber found a negligent bus driver was acting in the course of his service when he pulled across in front of the plaintiff's bus to prevent it passing him, despite the fact that he had been given instructions by his employer not to obstruct any bus. In the view of the majority,[26] he had been acting in his employers' interests (interfering with the trade of a rival bus company) and could not be said to be acting on his own behalf. Nevertheless, the distinction between acting on a frolic of one's own or remaining within the course of one's employment remains problematic to this day.[27]

---

[20] 2 Salk 440, 91 ER 382.   [21] 1 Ld Raym 264, 91 ER 1072.
[22] See Zimmerman, *Roman law, contemporary law*, p. 125. Holmes equally makes this observation: O. W. Holmes, 'Agency', *Harvard Law Review*, 4 (1891), 345 at 363. Holdsworth, *A history of English law*, p. 475 notes two main influences: a Roman influence which filtered through the Court of Admiralty and mercantile custom (*Boson v Sandford* being, for example, a shipping case) and an English influence derived from the medieval modifications of the general common law principle governing the master's liability.
[23] (1800) 8 TR 531 at 533, 101 ER 1529 at 1531. See also *Laugher v Pointer* (1826) 5 B & C 547, 108 ER 204.
[24] (1834) 6 Car & P 501 at 503 per Parke B (172 ER 1338 at 1339). For an account of the historical background, see Y. B. Smith, 'Frolic and detour', *Columbia Law Review*, 23 (1923), 444.
[25] (1862) 1 H & C 526, 158 ER 993. See also *Croft v Alison* (1821) 4 B & Ald 590, 106 ER 1052; *Huzzey v Field* (1835) 2 CM & R 432, 150 ER 186; *Mitchell v Crassweller* (1853) 13 CB 237, 138 ER 1189; and *Bayley v Manchester, Sheffield and Lincolnshire Ry Co.* (1873) LR 8 CP 148.
[26] Wightman J dissenting.   [27] See below in this chapter, *passim*.

6.3 Determining the test for 'course of employment', 'les fonctions auxquelles ils les ont employés', 'in Ausführung der Verrichtung'

The analysis in 6.2 demonstrates that whether imposing liability on the basis of strict or fault-based liability, all systems accept the need for some limitation on the defendant's liability. Each system requires evidence of some connection between the actions of the tortfeasor and his relationship with the defendant who is rendered liable for the former's actions. This is a fundamental aspect of liability. Before examining in detail judicial attempts to provide tests capable of determining this requirement, two initial comments must be made. First, in determining the scope of the employer's liability, the courts have been influenced by policy concerns. Secondly, in all systems, mere prohibition of misconduct will not exclude vicarious liability. The question thus remains: whether, despite instructions to the contrary, the employee is still acting in a way connected to his employment. The impact of these two factors will be examined below, to be followed by an examination of the common and civil law tests as developed by the courts.

6.3.1 The significance of policy

In determining the scope of liability, much will rest on how the courts interpret the tasks assigned to the employee. A restrictive interpretation will reduce the incentives for the employer to undertake preventative measures and diminish the ability of the victim to seek compensation from a (usually) wealthier defendant. In contrast, too generous an interpretation will impose an undue burden on defendants, who may not be able to spread the entire loss through insurance cover, and will also ignore the impact of alternative means of compensation. In balancing these concerns, the courts will be influenced by policy arguments. As Fleming stated, '"the course of employment" is an expansive concept which provides ample scope for policy decisions'.[28] In this light, it is perhaps unsurprising that, in practice, all systems have found it difficult to provide a test capable both of providing conceptual clarity and of reaching the correct balance between the needs and burdens of the three members of the vicarious liability triangle: victim – employee – employer.

The impact of policy concerns may be seen in the four cases below, examples taken from common and civil law systems.

[28] Fleming, *The law of torts*, p. 421.

6.3.1.1 Case law examples

In the English case of *Century Insurance Co. Ltd v Northern Ireland RTB*,[29] a driver of a petrol lorry was held to be acting in the course of his employment when he negligently discarded a lighted match, which he had used to light a cigarette, while delivering petrol. This led to an explosion which damaged the tanker, a car and several nearby houses. Lighting a cigarette was held to be an act of comfort and convenience[30] which would not be treated as outside the course of his employment. It was irrelevant that the act in question was not for the employer's benefit.[31]

The second English example (*Smith v Stages*[32]) involves two employees, Machin and Stages, sent to work away from their normal place of employment for which they were paid for the time spent travelling in addition to a travel allowance. Both were injured in a car crash due to the negligent driving of Stages, having worked all night without sleep before driving home. The House of Lords accepted that generally a man travelling to or from his place of work would not be acting in the course of his employment, but distinguished the facts of this case. Here, the employees had received payment for the time spent travelling to and from the site, for which a normal working day had been allocated. Lord Lowry advised that where the employee is obliged to use the employer's transport,[33] or is travelling in the employer's time between workplaces or to a workplace other than his regular workplace or in the course of a peripatetic occupation, in the absence of an express condition to the contrary, travel would be in the course of the employment.[34] Receipt of wages[35] (as here) would indicate that the employee is travelling in the employer's time and for his benefit and in the course of his employment.

---

[29] [1942] AC 509.   [30] Ibid., at 519 per Lord Wright.
[31] *Lloyd v Grace Smith & Co.* [1912] AC 716.
[32] [1989] AC 928. See comment by C. A. Hopkins, 'Vicarious liability – negligence on the way to work', *Cambridge Law Journal* [1989], 368, and B. Barrett, 'Vicarious liability and defective systems of work', *Industrial Law Journal*, 18 (1989), 159, who contends that the case could have been argued on the basis of the employers' personal liability for the safety of the system of work.
[33] Not the case here. The employees had been given the equivalent of the return rail fare, but were not required to use public transport.
[34] [1989] AC 928 at 955–6 where Lord Lowry lists six 'prima facie propositions'. However, any deviation or interruption of the journey (unless incidental) would take the employee out of the course of his employment.
[35] But not receipt of a travelling allowance.

Therefore, despite the fact that the employees had received payment for eight hours sleeping time after their shift, but chose to drive home immediately, their Lordships found the employer vicariously liable. Whilst driving home, they were still going about the employer's business.

In both the common law cases, the imposition of vicarious liability appears to be linked to related policy concerns. In *Century Insurance*, the claim itself, as the name suggests, was made by the employer's insurance company which was trying to evade responsibility for the loss caused. In contrast, in *Smith v Stages*, Mr Stages was uninsured and the possibility of intervention by the Motor Insurers' Bureau had been lost.[36] In the absence of vicarious liability, the victim's injuries would go uncompensated.

A similarly generous interpretation was adopted by the criminal chamber of the French Supreme Court in 1988,[37] in relation to thefts by the defendants' manager of a large number of boxes of clothes belonging to the claimant which had been stored in the defendants' warehouse. The manager's tasks included drawing up collection slips for merchandise stored in the warehouse and in fraudulently drawing up slips to suggest that the goods in question had already been collected, he was deemed to be acting within the functions for which he was employed, even though he acted without authorisation and for purposes alien to the tasks entrusted to him.

The German courts have also demonstrated some flexibility in their interpretation of course of employment (*in Ausführung der Verrichtung*) under §831 BGB.[38] In a 1966 decision,[39] the German Supreme Court found that an employee, an excavator driver who had been instructed to bring an excavator from the yard to the repair workshop for a check-up using a low-loading trailer, was acting in the course of employment

---

[36] Lord Lowry [1989] AC 928 at 939, commented that the case arose because the driver was uninsured and the time limits under the Motor Insurers' Bureau agreement had not been complied with.

[37] Crim 23 June 1988 Bull crim 1988 N° 289 p. 4. Compare *Frans Maas (UK) Ltd v Samsung Electronics (UK) Ltd* [2004] EWHC 1502 (Comm) (employer vicariously liable for theft of mobile telephones, belonging to the defendant, from claimants' warehouse facility) and *Morris v C W Martin & Sons Ltd* [1966] 1 QB 716 (theft by employee of fur entrusted to drycleaner).

[38] See MünchKommBGB/Wagner, 5th edn (Munich: CH Beck, 2009), §831, paras. 24–7 and J. von Standinger, D. W. Belling and C. Eberl-Borges, *Kommentar zum Bürgerlichen Gesetzbuch* (Berlin: De Gruyter, 2008), §831, paras. 79–92. Liability under §§ 31 and 278 BGB is discussed at 2.3.

[39] BGH 20 September 1966 VersR 1966, 1074.

when he decided to drive it instead along the highway and collided with the claimant. An act will fall within the course of employment where there is 'a substantive connection between the conduct leading to injury and the entrusted task'.[40] The key test here is one of 'substantive connection'/*innerer, sachlicher Zusammenhang* which is distinct from an extraneous connection (*äußerer Zusammenhang*) such as coincidence of time and space.[41] In this case, the Supreme Court found that the employee's driving was substantively connected with his employment. He had been instructed to take the excavator to the workshop and although he had disobeyed his employer's instructions to use the trailer, this only amounted to a deviation as to how the task would be accomplished.

In all these cases, the courts focus on the facts of the case and what connects the wrongful act of the employee with the employment relationship. Such emphasis on the particular circumstances of each case diminishes the precedent value of such authority – would *Century Insurance*, for example, be decided the same way today when smoking is far less common (and indeed often banned in the workplace)? What is clear is that the common law and French courts, in particular, adopt a flexible approach to the test: smoking whilst delivering a flammable substance, driving home immediately after completing an all-night shift and stealing goods he was employed to store, do not naturally fall within activities an employee is employed to undertake in the course of his employment; in fact one might suggest quite the opposite. Such generous interpretations of the relevant tests suggest the influence, notably, of the policy ground of ensuring victim compensation and a focus on reaching a just decision based on the subjective facts of each case.

6.3.2 *Prohibited conduct*

It is equally clear that disobedience of instructions will not automatically remove any connection between the employee's actions and his employment. If, as seen in the 1966 German case in 6.3.1.1, the actions amount only to a 'deviation' in how the task is accomplished or, to use

---

[40] Translation by A. Hoffmann and Y. P. Salmon in W. van Gerven, J. Lever and P. Larouche, *Tort law: ius commune casebooks for the common law of Europe* (Oxford: Hart, 2001), p. 511. The court relied upon the earlier authority of BGH 2 February 1955 VI ZR 225/53 – VersR 1955, 205, BGH 23 February 1955 VI ZR 14/54 – VersR 1955, 214 and BGH 30 October 1959 – VI ZR 156/58 – NJW 1960, 355 = VersR 1960, 134.

[41] See, for example, BGH 4 November 1953 BGHZ 11, 151 = NJW 1954, 505 (no substantive connection where employee of a building contractor used opportunity to steal from the building site) which also gives the example (at para. 4) of an electrician stealing an object from a room in which he is dismantling the chandelier.

common law terminology, the instructions merely regulate how the job is performed rather than limiting the sphere of employment,[42] then liability may still arise. The reasons for this are clear: employers should not be able merely to give instructions not to commit tortious acts to avoid liability. 'The law is not so futile as to allow a master, by giving secret instructions to his servant, to discharge himself from liability.'[43]

Further, there is an obvious risk that employees may disobey instructions at certain times. The courts are particularly reluctant to exclude actions by employees representing a misguided attempt to further their employer's interests. A number of cases illustrate these points. In *Bayley v Manchester, Sheffield and Lincolnshire Rly Co.*,[44] the plaintiff had been injured after being violently pulled out of a railway carriage by a porter, just after the train had started. The porter had been acting under the mistaken belief that the passenger was on the wrong train. The court held that it was part of the general duties of a porter to prevent passengers travelling in the wrong carriages and to act in their discretion in the best interests of passengers and the railway company. The porter was therefore acting in the course of his employment when he ejected the plaintiff, since he was carrying out these duties, albeit in a 'stupid, blundering manner'.[45] In *Limpus v London General Omnibus Co.*,[46] as mentioned in 6.2, the fact that the driver had deliberately acted contrary to his employer's instructions did not prevent the court finding the employer vicariously liable for his negligence. In contrast, in *Beard v London General Omnibus Co.*,[47] a bus conductor, who decided at the end of a journey to turn the bus around for the next journey, was not found to be acting in the course of his employment: 'it is not the duty of the conductor to drive any more than it is the duty of the driver to take fares'.[48]

---

[42] See Lord Dunedin in *Plumb v Cobden Flour Mills Co. Ltd* [1914] AC 62 at 67: 'there are prohibitions which limit the sphere of employment, and prohibitions which only deal with conduct within the sphere of employment'.

[43] *Limpus v London General Omnibus Co.* (1862) 1 H & C 526 at 539 per Willes J; cf. BGH 15 December 1959 BGHZ 31, 358, 366 = NJW 1960, 669.

[44] (1873) LR 8 CP 148.   [45] Ibid., at 155 per Blackburn J.

[46] (1862) 1 H & C 526, 158 ER 993.   [47] [1900] 2 QB 530.

[48] Ibid., at 532 per A.L. Smith LJ, although it was noted in *Kay v ITW Ltd* [1968] 1 QB 140 that here the conductor did not merely turn the vehicle around for the next journey but drove the horses at considerable speed around the neighbouring streets on what might be regarded as a wholly unauthorised jaunt. Followed, nevertheless, by the Court of Appeal in *Iqbal v London Transport Executive* (1973) 16 KIR 329, although this decision seems out-of-tune with current case law. To what extent was it influential that the conductor, acting contrary to instructions, negligently managed to crush the actual bus driver? Would the decision be different if he had crushed an innocent third party?

Tensions between a broad and narrow interpretation of the employees' tasks may be seen in a number of motor vehicle cases. In the Privy Council case of *Canadian Pacific Railway Company v Lockhart*,[49] an employee, who disregarded written notices prohibiting employees from using their own cars for company business without adequate insurance, was found to be acting in the execution of his duties when he negligently caused an accident while on company business in an uninsured vehicle. Here what was prohibited was merely the non-insurance of the motor-car;[50] the Privy Council indicating that it would have been different if the employee had been absolutely forbidden to drive his own car in the course of his employment. In *Twine v Bean's Express Ltd*,[51] however, Lord Greene MR refused to impose vicarious liability where a hitchhiker had been given a lift contrary to express instructions and was fatally injured by the employee's negligence.[52] This may be contrasted with the later view of the majority of the Court of Appeal in *Rose v Plenty*.[53] Here, a milkman, contrary to express instructions, had employed a 13-year-old assistant to assist him with his milk deliveries. Whilst riding on the milk float, the boy was injured by the milkman's negligent driving. In finding vicarious liability, the majority noted, in particular, that the boy had been injured in the course of delivering milk for the employer. Australian authority also supports a more generous approach to prohibited conduct which purports to serve the interests of the employer, rather than amounting to a personal whim.[54] As predicted by Lord Denning MR in *Rose*, however, the advent of compulsory third party insurance has served to reduce the need for the courts to intervene in driving cases.[55]

---

[49] [1942] AC 591.

[50] In effect, it merely determined who should take out the insurance policy to cover liability. Contrast, however, *R v Crown Diamond Paint Co. Ltd* [1983] 1 FC 837 (CA) and *Bickman v Smith Motors Ltd* [1955] 5 DLR 256 (Alta CA).

[51] (1946) 62 TLR 458 affg [1946] 1 All ER 202. Followed by *Conway v George Wimpey & Co. Ltd* [1951] 2 KB 266. See comment by F. H. Newark, 'Twine v Bean's Express, Ltd', Modern Law Review, 17 (1954), 102 at 114 and P. S. Atiyah, *Vicarious liability in the law of torts* (London: Butterworths, 1967), pp. 246–51.

[52] Arguably influenced by the fact that trespassers were owed a minimal duty of care by occupiers in 1946.

[53] [1976] 1 WLR 141. See J. Finch, 'Express prohibitions and scope of employment', Modern Law Review, 39 (1976), 575. See also *London County Council v Cattermoles (Garages) Ltd* [1953] 1 WLR 997.

[54] See *Bugge v Brown* (1919) 26 CLR 110 (employee ignoring employer's express instructions where to light a fire to cook mid-day meal) and *Colonial Mutual Life Assurance Society Ltd v Producers & Citizens Co-operative Assurance Co.* (1931) 46 CLR 41 (principal liable for deliberate slander of rival company by commission agent despite express prohibition).

[55] See [1976] 1 WLR 141 at 145 (1972 in the United Kingdom).

Civil law systems have equally sought to distinguish between disobedient acts which fall within the scope of the employee's functions or tasks and those which fall outside the scope of liability. Again, much will depend on the interpretation of the facts and to what extent the courts are prepared to find wrongful acts connected to the employer's purposes. The practice of the French criminal courts, adopted by the civil courts post-1988, has been generous. In the classic case of 1946,[56] a driver, instructed to take a lorry for repairs and then return it to the garage, was still deemed to be acting within his functions when he chose to hire out the lorry to take a group of people to a local dance.[57] The 1989 decision of the German Supreme Court[58] demonstrates a more cautious approach. Here, a private pilot had been employed by the defendant, the manager of a small airline company, to bring an aircraft to the airport which the defendant would fly himself. On arrival, the pilot was instructed to inform the guests that the defendant would be late and wait with them. Instead the pilot took off with the guests for a demonstration flight and caused an accident. The German Supreme Court found that the pilot had been assigned a clear-cut task which had nothing to do with the undertaking of demonstration flights. In such circumstances, there was no substantive connection between the tasks assigned to him – delivering the plane and notifying the passengers – and his unauthorised flight.[59]

---

[56] Cass crim 18 October 1946 S 1947.1.39.

[57] There is authority, however, which suggests a more restrictive approach may be adopted where the victim is aware of the prohibition. A case of 1979, on facts similar to *Twine v Bean's Express*, goes so far as to suggest that it will be for the unauthorised vehicle passenger to demonstrate that he could not have known that the lorry-driver was not allowed to give lifts: Civ 2, 11 July 1979 JCP 1979 IV 317; D 1980 IR 36 obs C. Larroumet. Larroumet notes, however, that the court's approach derives from the position of the Second Civil Chamber in 1979, which, as shown in 6.3.6, changed dramatically in 1988.

[58] BGH, 14 February 1989 NJW-RR 1989, 723; MünchKommBGB/Wagner, §831, para. 26

[59] '... zwischen der H. aufgetragenen Verrichtung und seiner schadenstiftenden Tätigkeit besteht deshalb zwar ein kausaler und zeitlicher, **nicht aber ein innerer, sachlicher Zusammenhang**' (Therefore, the connection between the task assigned to H and his course of conduct might be causal and temporal, but it is not substantive: translation by A. Hoffmann and Y. P. Salmon (emphasis added).) The courts use the term '*Schwarzflug*' or '*Schwarzfahrt*' to signify the unauthorised use of vehicles outside the tasks assigned to the employee: RG DR 1942, 1280; Staudinger-Belling, §831 paras. 88–92. Note, however, the provisions of the Road Traffic Act of 19 December 1952 (BGBl I., 837) (as amended) (Strassenverkehrsgesetz, StVG) § 7 which imposes strict liability on the keeper of a vehicle, regardless of the codal provisions, subsection (3) providing: 'If somebody uses the vehicle without the knowledge and consent of the keeper of the vehicle that person is liable to pay compensation for the damage in the place of the keeper; in addition the keeper himself remains liable to pay compensation if the use of the motor vehicle was

The fact that an employee may disobey instructions may be regarded as such a common occurrence in business and industry that it may be fairly regarded as a necessary incident to any enterprise employing others to perform its services.[60] In this sense, it seems correct that such actions should be regarded as within the scope of liability. Nevertheless, all systems accept that not all prohibited acts will be covered and that at times the express prohibition will take such actions outside the scope of the employment relationship. Again in determining where this line is drawn, the courts may adopt a narrow or broad approach. Much appears to depend again on the facts of the case, but some relevant factors may be identified: who is injured (there appears to be a greater willingness to protect innocent third parties), who possesses insurance cover, and the reason why the employee undertook the prohibited act (to benefit the employer or solely the employee)?

6.3.3 The common law test: 'course of employment'[61]

In determining the test for course of employment at common law, the starting point has traditionally been the definition given by the textbook writers, Salmond and Heuston (the so-called Salmond test):

A master is not responsible for a wrongful act done by his servant unless it is done in the course of his employment. It is deemed to be so done if it is either (1) a wrongful act authorised by his master, or (2) a wrongful and unauthorised mode of doing some act authorised by the master.[62]

---

facilitated by his negligence. *The first sentence of this paragraph does not apply if the person using the vehicle was employed by the keeper for the purpose of operating the vehicle or if he was entrusted with the vehicle by the keeper.*' (emphasis added)

[60] Smith, 'Frolic and detour', 721.

[61] Note also the US Restatement on Agency (3d) (2006–2009) which provides at § 7.07: '(1) An employer is subject to vicarious liability for a tort committed by its employee acting within the scope of employment, (2) An employee acts within the scope of employment when performing work assigned by the employer or engaging in a course of conduct subject to the employer's control. An employee's act is not within the scope of employment when it occurs within an independent course of conduct not intended by the employee to serve any purpose of the employer.' This would appear to be narrower than the systems examined in this chapter in that liability will not arise where the tortfeasor does not serve some purpose of the employer: see *Monty v Orlandi* 337 P 2d 861 (Cal App 1959) (bar owner not liable when bartender assaults patron outside bar in course of personal dispute); *Mahar v Stone Wood Transp* 823 A 2d 540 (Me 2003); and *Los Ranchitos v Tierra Grande Inc* 861 P 2d 263 (NM App 1993).

[62] J. W. Salmond, *The law of torts* (London: Stevens and Haynes, 1907), p. 83 (now found in the latest edition of *Salmond & Heuston on the law of torts*, 21st edn (London: Sweet and Maxwell, 1996), p. 443). This test was adopted by Canada: see *Lockhart v Canadian Pacific*

Thus, the employee is held to be acting in the course of employment if his conduct is authorised by the employer, or is considered to be an unauthorised means of performing the job for which he is employed. There is also clear authority that, to be actionable, all necessary features of the tort must be committed in the course of employment.[63]

6.3.3.1 A wrongful act authorised by the employer

Although this category can be traced to early cases dealing with commands (express or implied) by the employer, rendering the employer liable for the torts of the employee, it arguably makes little sense in modern law. An act which is authorised or ratified by the employer under the principles of agency becomes the action of the employer himself. Lord Millett in the leading English case of *Lister v Hesley Hall Ltd*[64] remarked that:

> This passage [from Salmond & Heuston] has stood the test of time. It has survived unchanged for 21 editions, and has probably been cited more often than any other single passage in a legal textbook. Yet it is not without blemish. As has often been observed, the first of the two alternatives is not an example of vicarious liability at all. Its presence (and the word 'deemed') may be an echo of the discredited theory of implied authority.[65]

This first category thus risks once again confusing primary/agency liability with that of vicarious liability and is best discarded as unhelpful. It will not be considered further in 6.3.

6.3.3.2 A wrongful and unauthorised mode of doing some act authorised by the employer

It is this second category which states a principle of vicarious liability: the employer is held liable for the torts of the employee which occur in the course of his employment, that is, which amount to an unauthorised means of doing acts authorised by the employer. As with many tests, it is easier to state than explain. The distinction between an unauthorised mode of doing something authorised and doing something so unconnected with the employment that it should be regarded as an independent act is not necessarily straightforward.

Railway Co. [1942] AC 591 at 599 and *WW Sales Ltd v City of Edmonton* [1942] SCR 467. For Australia, see *Deatons Pty Ltd v Flew* (1949) 79 CLR 370 at 385.
[63] See *Credit Lyonnais NV v Export Credits Guarantee Department* [2000] 1 AC 486, HL.
[64] [2002] 1 AC 215.
[65] Ibid., at para. 67. See also Auld LJ in *Majrowski v Guy's and St Thomas's NHS Trust* [2005] EWCA Civ 251, [2005] QB 848 at para. 29.

DETERMINING TEST FOR 'COURSE OF EMPLOYMENT', ETC.   159

This test nevertheless dominated the application of the 'course of employment' test in the twentieth century. Where the employee has performed his duties negligently, for example driving a delivery van too fast, then it is not difficult to perceive this as an 'unauthorised' way of driving. The modern approach, as Diplock LJ stated in *Ilkiw v Samuels*, is to look at the matter 'broadly, not dissecting the servant's tasks into its component activities – such as driving, loading, sheeting and the like – by asking: what was the job on which he was engaged for his employer?'.[66] Problems arise, however, in determining whether incidental acts may fit within this test. In *Century Insurance* in 6.3.1.1 above, for example, smoking whilst delivering a flammable substance was regarded as incidental to the employee's performance. In *Staton v National Coal Board*,[67] Finnemore J was prepared to accept that an employee, who had finished work for the day but was cycling across the colliery forecourt to collect his wages, was still acting in the course of employment when he negligently injured the plaintiff's husband. In advocating a common-sense approach, the judge distinguished collecting wages from the employer at the end of the working day from going off on a frolic of one's own,[68] but such a distinction is not necessarily straightforward. Compare, for example, *Whatman v Pearson*[69] – employee in the course of employment when, contrary to instructions, driving home for dinner – with *Storey v Ashton*[70] – employee not in the course of employment when driving to a friend's house after business hours.[71] Atiyah has commented that it is hard to disagree that the distinction drawn between the two cases is meaningless and arbitrary and argues that 'the only rational ground for exempting the master from liability for the servant who is deviating from the prescribed route, would be that that possibility of the servant's doing so, is so remote and unforeseeable that the risk cannot be regarded as reasonably incidental to the conduct of the defendant's business'.[72]

Despite such concerns, it is only in recent years that common law systems have come to question the continuing validity of the Salmond test. To quote Lord Millett in *Lister* again, 'More pertinently, the second [category of the Salmond test] is not happily expressed if it is to serve as

---

[66] [1963] 1 WLR 991 at 1004.   [67] [1957] 1 WLR 893.   [68] Ibid., at 896.
[69] (1868) LR 3 CP 422.   [70] (1869) LR 4 QB 476.
[71] The court distinguished between going a roundabout way home and starting an entirely new journey on his own account which could not be said to be within the course of his employment.
[72] Atiyah, *Vicarious liability*, p. 254.

a test of vicarious liability for intentional wrongdoing.'[73] Whilst it is possible to conceive of negligence as an 'unauthorised' means of doing one's job, it becomes extremely difficult to apply this test to include deliberate wrongdoing. Although cases such as *Poland v John Parr and Sons*[74] had been able to apply the concept of 'implied authority' to justify imposing vicarious liability for employee assaults (here on the basis that the employee struck the plaintiff in the misguided attempt to protect the employer's property from theft), the decision of the common law courts to include serious intentional torts such as sexual abuse within the scope of vicarious liability has rendered the continued use of the Salmond test problematic. To deem serious criminal offences an 'unauthorised mode' of performing one's tasks requires a distortion of the test to include acts which no reasonable employer would ever consider authorising.

Lister provides a very useful illustration of this problem and a starting point for a discussion of the modern common law approach to the 'course of employment' test.

6.3.4 Deliberate wrongdoing and the search for a new 'course of employment' test in the common law world

Lister v Hesley Hall Ltd[75] concerned allegations of sexual abuse against the warden of an institution, operated by the defendants, which provided a school and boarding annexe for children who, in the main, had emotional and behavioural difficulties. Between 1979 and 1982, a number of boys had been systematically sexually abused by the warden.[76] To render the defendants vicariously liable under the Salmond test, the claimants were required to establish that the acts of sexual abuse were a 'wrongful and unauthorised mode of doing some act authorised by the master' in circumstances where the employer would clearly never have authorised such serious criminal misconduct. The Court of Appeal in the earlier case of *Trotman v North Yorkshire County Council*[77] had refused to accept that similar misconduct could be deemed to be in the course of his

---

[73] [2002] 1 AC 215.   [74] [1927] 1 KB 236.
[75] [2002] 1 AC 215 (hereafter *Lister*). See comment by C. A. Hopkins, 'What is the course of employment?', *Cambridge Law Journal* [2001], 458 and P. Giliker, 'Rough justice in an unjust world', *Modern Law Review*, 65 (2002), 269.
[76] In the early 1990s, a police investigation led to the warden (Grain) being sentenced to seven years' imprisonment for multiple offences involving sexual abuse.
[77] [1999] LGR 584 (deputy headmaster sexually assaulting a teenager on a foreign holiday).

employment: '[This] seems to me to be far removed from an unauthorised mode of carrying out a teacher's duties on behalf of his employer. Rather it is a negation of the duty of the council to look after children for whom it was responsible.'[78] If vicarious liability were to extend to cover intentional misconduct, contrary to the employers' interest, then a new test would be needed.

Three years earlier, the same question had come before the Supreme Court of Canada in *Bazley v Curry*[79] and *Jacobi v Griffiths*.[80] Both cases involved the sexual abuse of minors. In *Bazley*, an employee of a non-profit organisation, which operated two residential care facilities for the treatment of emotionally troubled children, had been convicted of 19 counts of sexual abuse, two of which related to the plaintiff. *Jacobi*, decided concurrently with *Bazley*, related to another non-profit organisation, here a boys' and girls' club, which had employed Griffiths as its programme director. Griffiths was subsequently found guilty of sexual assaults involving members of the club. The High Court of Australia also faced this question in the 2003 conjoined cases of *New South Wales v Lepore; Samin v Queensland; Rich v Queensland*[81] which involved claims against the State for sexual assaults which had occurred while the plaintiffs were at State-run schools.[82] All three systems had adopted tests based on the Salmond test to determine *when* the employee's conduct would be deemed to be in the course of his employment.

These cases respond to the weakness of the Salmond test in different ways. The majority of judgments consider that intentional torts *may* occur in the course of employment. The rationale behind this extension of liability will be examined in Chapter 8 which considers the policy reasons *why* legal systems utilise the doctrine of vicarious liability. Once this decision is taken, it is difficult to continue relying upon the Salmond test as a general test for course of employment for the reasons stated in *Trotman* above. Equally, it appears undesirable that a *different* test would apply for intentional and negligent conduct, leading to unnecessary complications.

---

[78] Ibid., at 591 per Butler-Sloss LJ. *Trotman* was overruled by the House of Lords in *Lister*.
[79] (1999) 174 DLR (4th) 45 (hereafter *Bazley*).
[80] (1999) 174 DLR (4th) 71 (hereafter *Jacobi*). Both *Bazley* and *Jacobi* are noted by P. Cane, 'Vicarious liability for sexual abuse', Law Quarterly Review, 116 (2000), 21.
[81] (2003) 212 CLR 511 (hereafter *Lepore*).
[82] Note also the New Zealand case of *S v Attorney-General* [2003] 3 NZLR 450 (Crown vicariously liable for sexual abuse by foster parents). The law in New Zealand has less impact due to the fact that sexual assaults after 1 April 1974 are covered by the no-fault system of compensation.

The different formulae adopted by the courts in these cases will be examined below. As will be noted, the first three tests focus on finding a *close connection* between the tort committed and the tortfeasor's employment.

6.3.4.1 The tests for course of employment

(i) McLachlin J in *Bazley*: is there a significant connection between the creation or enhancement of a risk and the wrong which results? Where this is so, vicarious liability serves the policy considerations of provision of an adequate and just remedy and deterrence.[83]

(ii) Lord Steyn in *Lister*: were the employee's torts so closely connected with his employment that it would be fair and just to hold the employers vicariously liable?[84]

(iii) *Lepore*: an Australian 'close connection' test?

(iv) Lord Hobhouse in *Lister*: has the employer assumed a relationship to the claimant which imposed specific duties in tort upon the employer which he entrusted to his employee?[85]

These four tests will be examined below.

(i) McLachlin J in Bazley: *a significant/strong connection between the creation or enhancement of a risk and the wrong which results*

The approach of the Supreme Court of Canada was to recognise explicitly the role played by policy in determining the scope of vicarious liability. Giving the leading judgment in *Bazley*, McLachlin J rejected the Salmond test in favour of a two-fold approach which examined, first, whether there are any precedents which unambiguously determine on which side of the line the case falls and, secondly, if this fails, whether vicarious liability should be imposed in the light of the broader policy rationales which underlie strict liability.[86] Liability will thus arise where the employment relationship not only provides the opportunity for harm, but materially increases the risk of the tort occurring.[87]

---

[83] See (1999) 174 DLR (4th) 45 at para. 41.   [84] See [2002] 1 AC 215 at para. 28.
[85] Ibid., at para. 54.
[86] See (1999) 174 DLR (4th) 45 at para. 15. See comment by M. Hall, 'Responsibility without fault: *Bazley v Curry*', *Canadian Bar Review*, 79 (2000), 474, who, at 487, describes it as 'a manifestly coherent and fair approach to apportioning liability for the abuse of children in institutional "care" settings'.
[87] '[P]laintiffs must demonstrate that the tort is sufficiently connected to the tortfeasor's assigned tasks that the tort can be regarded as a materialization of the risks created by the enterprise': McLachlin CJ in *KLB v British Columbia* [2003] 2 SCR 403, 230 DLR (4th) 513 at para. 19.

A test of 'close connection' is thus interpreted with reference to the policy rationales underlying vicarious liability, here identified to be the provision of a just and practical remedy for the damage suffered and the deterrence of future harm. It is fair and just to place liability on the employer when the employer puts into the community an enterprise which carries with it certain risks.[88] Deterrence is equally deemed relevant – encouraging employers to take steps to reduce accidents by efficient organisation and supervision.[89] In the words of McLachlin J, 'The question in each case is whether there is a connection or nexus between the employment enterprise and that wrong that justifies imposition of vicarious liability on the employer for the wrong, in terms of fair allocation of the consequences of the risk and/or deterrence.'[90]

This test – which may be characterised as one of enterprise risk[91] – has a number of advantages. It focuses on the rationale for applying vicarious liability and extending it to cover intentional misconduct. Courts are asked to consider not only precedent, but the policy objectives of the doctrine and its wider impact on the community as a whole. It is flexible – adapting to each factual situation – and permits an extension of liability outside the confines of the Salmond test. Nevertheless, such advantages may, in a different light, be deemed disadvantages. Flexibility may also be termed uncertainty in application. The weight of policy objectives may be viewed differently by each judge, who has limited access to the economic and sociological data required to assess the impact of enterprise risk reasoning fully. There is also a divergence of views between judges as to the utility of past case law in relation to questions of vicarious liability in which each case will, to a certain extent, be factually different.[92] In *Jacobi*, decided concurrently

---

[88] (1999) 174 DLR (4th) 45 at para. 31 per McLachlin J. [89] Ibid., at para. 32.
[90] Ibid., at para. 37. McLachlin J (at para. 41) also suggested that in relation to intentional torts a number of subsidiary principles may be relevant: the opportunity that the enterprise afforded the employee to abuse his power; the extent to which the wrongful act may have furthered the employer's aims (and hence be more likely to have been committed by the employee); the extent to which the wrongful act was related to friction, confrontation or intimacy inherent in the employer's enterprise; the extent of power conferred on employees over potential victims by, and the level of vulnerability of potential victims to that power.
[91] McLachlin J (at ibid., para. 38) cited Sykes (A. O. Sykes, 'The boundaries of vicarious liability: an economic analysis of the scope of employment and related legal doctrines', *Harvard Law Review*, 101 (1988), 563) in which 'enterprise causation' is suggested as the key to vicarious liability, imposing strict liability where the employment relation increases the probability of each wrong.
[92] Contrast, for example, the approaches of McLachlin CJ in *Bazley* and Binnie J in *Jacobi*.

with *Bazley*, McLachlin J found herself in the minority where the majority held that the operators of a recreational club for children were not vicariously liable for sexual assaults by its employee. The majority held that whilst the job had presented the employee with the *opportunity* to meet the children, the abuse had taken place outside club facilities and outside club hours, in circumstances in which the employee had not been placed in an intimate relationship with the children.[93] The club was set up to offer group activities in the presence of volunteers and the defendants would not be responsible for the employee abusing his position to isolate his victims from the group. Nevertheless, the facts of *Jacobi* do resemble those of *Bazley*. In both cases, children had been sexually abused by employees, whom the employer had entrusted to deal with children and gain their trust. In *Bazley*, the employee had been placed in a position of great intimacy with the child, acting effectively as a substitute parent, whilst in *Jacobi*, the employee had merely been encouraged to develop a positive rapport with the children. The scope of vicarious liability would therefore seem to be a matter of degree, depending on the factual circumstances of employment (and how they are characterised by the court).

In view of the tension between *Bazley* and *Jacobi*, it is unsurprising that, in practice, the strong connection test has not been easy for the courts to apply and the case law exhibits a divergence of judicial opinions on its application to fairly similar situations.[94] The decisions following *Bazley* may thus be characterised as 'cautious'. Vicarious liability claims relating to sexual abuse against provincial governments for abuse by foster parents[95] and a probation officer,[96] against a residential school for abuse by the school baker,[97] and against school boards for abuse by a physical

---

[93] The minority (McLachlin, L'Heureux-Dubé and Bastarache JJ) argued that the nature of Griffiths' employment involved mentoring and moral guidance, which would suggest a greater level of intimacy, increasing the risk of abuse, which would justify the imposition of vicarious liability.

[94] L. Klar, *Tort law*, 4th edn (Toronto: Carswell, 2008), pp. 660–1.

[95] *KLB v British Columbia* (2003) 230 DLR (4th) 513 (connection too weak due to the highly independent manner in which foster parents discharge their duties). See also *MB v British Columbia* (2003) 230 DLR (4th) 567. Contrast the New Zealand approach where the majority proceeded on the basis of agency, finding abuse to be sufficiently connected with the purpose of parenting for which the foster placements were made: *S v Attorney-General* [2003] 3 NZLR 450.

[96] *G (BM) v Nova Scotia (Attorney-General)* 2007 NSCA 120.

[97] *EB v Order of the Oblates of Mary Immaculate (British Columbia)* (2005) 258 DLR (4th) 385 (hereafter *EB*). See B. Feldthusen, 'Civil liability for sexual assault in Aboriginal residential schools: the baker did it', *Canadian Journal of Law and Society*, 22 (2007), 61.

education teacher[98] and a janitor[99] have all been rejected. The courts, in rejecting vicarious liability, have emphasised that the possibility of direct liability should not be overlooked.[100] Only where there is a strong or significant connection[101] between the acts of abuse and the duties given to the employee in question have the courts imposed liability. In *John Doe v Bennett*,[102] for example, the court did find a strong and direct connection between the wrongs done to the victims and the conduct of the diocesan enterprise where a Roman Catholic priest had been entrusted with an enormous degree of power by the bishop over the isolated parishes in which he worked.[103]

The 'close connection' test thus becomes a test of 'strong or significant connection', as demonstrated by the employer materially increasing the risk of a wrongful act. This gives greater emphasis to the *closeness* of the connection, but not necessarily clearer guidance as to *when* the connection will reach the required level. Equally, a number of commentators have questioned the use of 'enterprise risk' in relation to non-profit organisations.[104] This point was raised in *Bazley* itself where McLachlin J rejected the argument that charitable 'enterprises' should be treated differently, asserting that, while such institutions are not acting to advance their economic interests, it would still be just and fair for them to shoulder the burden of compensating for wrongs arising from risks they have created and that liability would still have a deterrent effect.[105] Binnie J in *Jacobi v Griffiths*[106] was less convinced, questioning whether the policies of compensation

---

[98] *H (SG) v Gorsline* [2005] 2 WWR 716.
[99] *EDG v Hammer* (2003) 230 DLR (4th) 554 (sexual abuse by night janitor in public elementary school).
[100] See, for example, the majority in *Jacobi* and *EB*.
[101] Both terms are used by McLachlin J in *Bazley* at paras. 41 and 42.
[102] (2004) 236 DLR (4th) 577.
[103] See ibid., paras. 27–32 per McLachlin CJC. The court also stressed that the bishop had provided the priest with the opportunity to abuse his power, and that the priest's wrongful acts were strongly related to the psychological intimacy inherent in his role as priest. Note also the imposition of liability in *Blackwater v Plint* (2005) 258 DLR (4th) 275 (dormitory supervisor in a residential school) and *3464920 Canada Inc v Strother* (2007) 281 DLR (4th) 640 (breach of fiduciary duty by solicitor).
[104] See, for example, C. R. Tremper, 'Compensation for harm from charitable activity', *Cornell Law Review*, 76 (1991), 401 at 426–8. Contrast K. E. Davis, 'Vicarious liability, judgment proofing, and non-profits', *University of Toronto Law Journal*, 50 (2000), 407, who argues that the deterrent effect operates equally in relation to non-profit organisations.
[105] (1999) 174 DLR (4th) 45 at paras. 47–56.   [106] (1999) 174 DLR (4th) 71 at para. 68.

166   DETERMINING SCOPE OF VICARIOUS LIABILITY

and deterrence operate as successfully with non-profit organisations as with commercial enterprises.[107]

The ambitious Canadian test thus raises a number of questions. To what extent may law courts integrate economic reasoning into their analysis and, at the same time, achieve the consistency needed for the common law system of precedent? Can it be assumed that the only policy motivations underlying vicarious liability are indeed the need to provide a just and practical remedy for the harm and the deterrence of future harm,[108] and do these arguments apply indiscriminately to all types of defendants, be they small businesses, large enterprises, religious or other charitable organisations? How do the courts balance consistency with individual justice?[109]

(ii) *Lord Steyn in* Lister: *were the employee's torts so closely connected with his employment that it would be fair and just to hold the employers vicariously liable?*[110]

The English House of Lords in *Lister* found the *Bazley* test 'luminous and illuminating . . . Wherever such problems are considered in future in the common law world, these judgments will be the starting point. On the other hand, it is unnecessary to express views on the full range of policy considerations examined in those decisions.'[111] In adopting a test of close connection, their Lordships did not, therefore, favour the Supreme Court of Canada's focus on policy. Lord Hobhouse distinguished clearly between a test establishing the criteria for its application and 'an exposition of the policy reasons for a rule . . . simply explaining the reasons for the existence of the rule and the social need for it, instructive though that may be'.[112] It is unfortunate that in advocating a more 'practical' approach to the close connection test, a number of different approaches may be identified in the House of Lords. In addition to the approach of

---

[107] 'If the objectives of effective compensation and deterrence are not advanced to the same extent or in the same way, these differences in function or performance undercut the argument for expansion and may indeed call for a measure of judicial restraint': ibid.

[108] This will be discussed in Chapter 8.

[109] Contrast the approach of McLachlin J in *Bazley* ('the best route to enduring principle may well lie through policy' (1999) 174 DLR (4th) 45 at para. 27) with that of the majority in *Jacobi* ('at the end of the day, judicial policy must yield to legal principle' at (1999) 174 DLR (4th) 71 at para. 37).

[110] [2002] 1 AC 215 at para. 28.   [111] Ibid., at para. 27 per Lord Steyn.

[112] Ibid., at para. 60. See also Lord Clyde, ibid., at para. 35: 'I am not persuaded that there is any reason of principle or policy which can be of substantial guidance in the resolution of the problem of applying the rule [of vicarious liability] in any particular case.'

Lord Steyn,[113] differences may be identified between the opinions of Lords Millett and Clyde and, notably, that of Lord Hobhouse, which is considered in more detail at test (iv) below. Whilst Lord Clyde looked at the matter in the round, giving general guidelines,[114] Lord Millett emphasised the role of vicarious liability as a loss-distribution device and accepted that the employer should be liable for the risks which experience shows are inherent in the nature of the defendants' business.[115] It is difficult, therefore, to discern one overall approach.

It was thus left to subsequent case law to identify a general test for 'close connection' and the courts have, in the main, favoured the approach of Lord Steyn, with some reference to that of Lord Clyde and Lord Millett. In *Dubai Aluminium Co. Ltd v Salaam*,[116] Lord Nicholls stated the test as follows:

> Perhaps the best general answer is that the wrongful conduct must be so closely connected with acts the partner or employee was authorised to do that, for the purpose of the liability of the firm or the employer to third parties, the wrongful conduct *may fairly and properly be regarded* as done by the partner while acting in the ordinary course of the firm's business or the employee's employment.[117]

In the House of Lords decision of *Majrowski v Guy's and St Thomas's NHS Trust*[118] Lord Nicholls reiterated this test in extending vicarious liability to cover the statutory tort of harassment taking place in the workplace.[119] His Lordship openly acknowledged that fairness required that those responsible for risk-creating activities should bear the cost of any

---

[113] With whom Lord Hutton agreed.
[114] See paras. 41–5, indicating that courts should examine the purpose and nature of the act, together with its context and the circumstances in which it occurred.
[115] Ibid., at para. 65.
[116] [2002] UKHL 48, [2003] 2 AC 366 at para. 23 with whom Lords Slynn and Hutton agreed.
[117] Ibid., italics in original. This has been followed by the Court of Appeal in *Mattis v Pollock* [2003] EWCA Civ 887, [2003] 1 WLR 2158 at 2164; by the Privy Council in *Attorney-General of the British Virgin Islands v Hartwell* [2004] UKPC 12, [2004] 1 WLR 1273 at para. 16; *Bernard v Attorney-General of Jamaica* [2005] IRLR 398 at [18]–[19] and *Brown v Robinson* [2004] UKPC 56 at para. 11.
[118] [2006] UKHL 34, [2007] 1 AC 224 (hereafter *Majrowski*).
[119] Ibid., at para. 10. Section 3 of the Protection from Harassment Act 1997 imposes civil liability for harassment. This case is controversial in that it imposes vicarious liability for *personal* acts of harassment: see P. Giliker, 'The ongoing march of vicarious liability', *Cambridge Law Journal* [2006], 489. The House of Lords took the view that unless a statute expressly or impliedly indicated otherwise, the principle of vicarious liability would apply.

resulting injury.[120] Lord Steyn in *Bernard v Attorney-General of Jamaica*,[121] equally recognised the need for a composite approach, including questions of risks arising from the defendants' business and, more generally, matters of practical justice:[122]

> The correct approach is to concentrate on the relative closeness of the connection between the nature of the employment and the particular tort, and to ask whether looking at the matter in the round it is just and reasonable to hold the employers vicariously liable. In deciding this question a relevant factor is the risks to others created by an employer who entrusts duties, tasks and functions to an employee.[123]

A number of comments may be made.

First, their Lordships accepted that the scope of vicarious liability should extend to intentional torts. This is not new. Although in the early years of vicarious liability, the courts had taken the view that there could never be liability for wilful acts,[124] this was not maintained and the common law courts acknowledged that, in certain circumstances, an employer might be held vicariously liable for actions of employees amounting to fraud,[125] assault,[126] and theft.[127] A line had been drawn, however, where the employee acted for personal motives such as revenge or spite, for example, a bus conductor striking a bus passenger

---

[120] [2006] UKHL 34 at para. 9. It is interesting to note certain similarities between his judgment and that of La Forest J in *London Drugs Ltd v Kuehne & Nagel International Ltd* (1992) 97 DLR (4th) 261 (both influenced by the policy concerns identified by Fleming, *Law of Torts*, pp. 409–11.

[121] [2004] UKPC 47, [2005] IRLR 398.

[122] Which does not signify, his Lordship stressed, a vague notion of justice between man and man: ibid., at para. 23.

[123] Ibid., at para. 18. Followed by Clarke MR in *Gravil v Carroll* [2008] EWCA Civ 689, [2008] ICR 1222 at para. 21.

[124] See *Croft v Alison* (1821) 4 B & Ald 590, 106 ER 1052 (employer's coachman deliberately striking plaintiff's horses with the result that they bolted and the carriage was overturned); *The Druid* (1842) 1 Wm Rob 391, 166 ER 619 (captain of steam tug deliberately running into other vessel); and *Chester v Bailey* [1905] 1 KB 237 (coachman involved in theft).

[125] *Lloyd v Grace, Smith & Co.* [1912] AC 716 (see, further, at 6.3.5).

[126] *Dyer v Munday* [1895] 1 QB 742; *Poland v John Parr and Sons* [1927] 1 KB 236; *Ryan v Fildes* [1938] 3 All ER 517; *Pettersson v Royal Oak Hotel Ltd* [1948] NZLR 136; *Daniels v Whetstone Entertainments Ltd* [1962] 2 Lloyd's Rep 1 (first assault only); *Vasey v Surrey Free Inns plc* [1996] PIQR 373.

[127] *Morris v Martin* [1966] 1 QB 716. See also F. D. Rose 'Liability for an employee's assault', *Modern Law Review*, 40 (1977), 420 and J. Swanton, 'Master's liability for the wilful tortious conduct of his servant' *University of Western Australia Law Review*, 16 (1985), 1, who advocate wider acceptance of vicarious liability for intentional torts.

with his ticket punch when criticised.[128] Secondly, it was recognised that such an extension of liability would require an alternative test to the traditional Salmond test. This was supplied by the 'close connection' test.[129] Finally, rather than adopting the 'enterprise risk' test of the Canadian Supreme Court, their Lordships applied a more 'practical' test, which examined the factual circumstances of each case and whether vicarious liability would be 'fair and just' in the circumstances. Weekes has commented on the resemblance of these terms to the 'fair, just and reasonableness' element of the duty of care test adopted in English law,[130] and indeed these terms would appear to grant the English courts a discretion in interpreting the test in each case. It is noticeable that this will include consideration of the risks arising from carrying on a business enterprise.[131] In *Lister* itself, the warden (Grain) had been employed to provide a home for the boys and supervise them on a day-to-day basis in circumstances where he and his disabled wife were often the only members of staff on the premises. Such close contact was sufficient to satisfy the court that there was a close connection between what he had been employed to do and the acts of abuse committed. These facts could be distinguished, however, from the case where the acts of abuse had been committed by a groundsman, where, due to the nature of his duties, there would have been no close connection between his job and the torts in question.[132]

---

[128] *Keppel Bus Co v Sa'ad bin Ahmad* [1974] 1 WLR 1082 (PC). See also *Warren v Henlys Ltd* [1948] 2 All ER 935 (garage attendant assaulting customer who threatened to report him to his employer), but criticised in *Mattis v Pollock* [2003] EWCA Civ 887, below in this section.

[129] Their Lordships focused on a subsequent comment in Salmond (*Law of Torts*, pp. 83–4) that 'a master . . . is liable even for acts which he has not authorised, provided they are so *connected* with acts which he has authorised, that they may rightly be regarded as modes – although improper modes – of doing them': see Lord Steyn [2006] UKHL 34, [2007] 1 AC 224 at para. 15 who adds that 'Salmond's explanation is the germ of the close connection test adumbrated by the Canadian Supreme Court in *Bazley*'.

[130] See R. Weekes, 'Vicarious liability for violent employees', *Cambridge Law Journal* [2004], 53, referring to the test stated in *Caparo Industries plc v Dickman* [1990] 2 AC 605. Note, however, the policy objectives attributed to these terms in *Bazley*.

[131] D. Brodie ('Enterprise liability: justifying vicarious liability', *Oxford Journal of Legal Studies*, 27 (2007), 493) has suggested that enterprise liability is the most weighty policy factor supporting the existence of vicarious liability, but the practice of the English courts is far from consistent, despite reference to risk by senior judges, and bears little relation to the structured application of the *Bazley* material increase in risk test seen in the Canadian case law examined at 6.3.4.1 and test (i).

[132] Example given by Lord Hobhouse in *Lister* [2002] 1 AC 215 at para. 62. For a more borderline case, see *Maga v Birmingham Roman Catholic Archdiocese Trustees* [2010] EWCA Civ 256 (church vicariously liable for priest's abuse of non-Catholic).

In practice, however, this interpretation of the 'close connection' test has also led to uncertainty. In the well-known decision of *Mattis v Pollock (t/a Flamingo's Nightclub)*,[133] Judge LJ described the question to be answered as 'deceptively simple'.[134] Mattis had been attacked leaving a nightclub by its bouncer (Cranston), who bore a grudge against him and his group of friends. Cranston was subsequently convicted for the assault, and evidence was given that the nightclub owner had been aware of his violent character. Despite previous authority excluding vicarious liability for acts of personal revenge,[135] the Court of Appeal found the employer to be liable for Cranston's actions. Bearing in mind that the incident in question took place *outside* the nightclub and was an act of retaliation for earlier humiliation, this must be considered a generous decision. The Court of Appeal approached the matter 'broadly' and determined that, on balance, the nightclub owner retained responsibility for the actions of his errant bouncer. The Court of Appeal also conceded that, if it had been necessary to decide the point, it would have held the employer personally liable for employing a bouncer who had a history of violence and whose aggressiveness the employer had encouraged. This, it is suggested, would have been the more logical basis for liability in *Mattis*, avoiding an unnecessary extension of the 'course of employment' requirement.[136] Nelson J in *N v Chief Constable of Merseyside Police*[137] equally struggled to resolve whether an off-duty policeman, who raped the claimant after offering to give her a lift to a police station when she had been carried out of a nightclub while severely intoxicated, was acting in the course of his employment. In finding that, despite the fact that he was still in uniform and had shown her, and the club first-aider, his warrant card, he was not acting in the course of his employment, the judge confessed that '(t)he test may sometimes be easier to state than it is to apply'.[138] *N* may be contrasted with the rather more

---

[133] [2003] EWCA Civ 887, [2003] 1 WLR 2158 (hereafter *Mattis*). [134] Ibid., at para. 19.
[135] See *Warren v Henlys Ltd* [1948] 2 All ER 935 and *Daniels v Whetstone Entertainments Ltd* [1962] 2 Lloyd's Rep 1, which received disapproval from the Court of Appeal.
[136] Compare the Privy Council decision in *Attorney-General of the British Virgin Islands v Hartwell* [2004] UKPC 12, [2004] 1 WLR 1273 where vicarious liability was rejected in favour of imposing primary liability on the police authorities who had entrusted a police officer with a gun in circumstances where they should have realised him to be volatile and unstable following a number of incidents.
[137] [2006] EWHC 3041 (QB), [2006] Po LR 160 (hereafter *N*).
[138] Ibid., at para. 13. The court's decision may also have been influenced by the fact that the off-duty officer was sitting in his own private vehicle and not in the area where he would have worked if he had been on duty when the offence took place.

generous view of the course of a police officer's employment adopted by the Privy Council in *Bernard v Attorney-General of Jamaica*,[139] where a police officer, who had shot the plaintiff whilst off-duty, in a dispute over a public telephone, was found to be acting in the course of employment.[140] The key factors here appear to be the officer's assertion that he was a policeman (implying that he was on police business),[141] his subsequent arrest of Bernard and the risk created by the police authorities in giving the officer a revolver for use at home.[142]

This is not to state that some cases will not be clear-cut,[143] but that in some cases, notably those involving serious criminal offences, application of the close connection test will not necessarily be a straightforward exercise. As textbook writers have commented, it is not even clear from the cases whether the test should be confined to intentional torts or applied to all tortious conduct, a matter still awaiting authoritative resolution.[144] Lord Nicholls acknowledged in *Dubai Aluminium Co. Ltd v Salaam*[145] that, realistically, uncertainty is inevitable and the onus is therefore on the court to make an evaluative judgment in each case, having regard to the particular factual circumstances and previous court decisions.[146] It is hard to disagree with Lord Nicholls' own assessment in *Dubai* that:

---

[139] [2004] UKPC 47, [2005] IRLR 398.
[140] See also *Weir v Bettison* [2003] EWCA Civ 111, [2003] ICR 708 (off-duty police constable assaulting suspected criminal whilst apparently acting in his capacity as a constable) and *Brown v Robinson* [2004] UKPC 56, where the Privy Council emphasised that the criminal acts of the security guard were part of his attempts to restrain an unruly crowd.
[141] Nelson J in *N* [2006] EWHC 3041, distinguished *Bernard* and *Weir v Bettison* on the basis that the tortfeasor was purporting to perform a police function such as arrest, or enforcing police authority.
[142] [2004] UKPC 47 at paras. 25-8.
[143] Consider, for example, *JJ Coughlan Ltd v Ruparelia* [2003] EWCA Civ 1057, [2004] PNLR 4 where the Court of Appeal found no close connection between promotion of 'preposterous' fraudulent scheme promising risk-free investment with return of 6,000% per annum and ordinary course of solicitor's business; and *Gravil v Carroll* [2008] EWCA Civ 689 where a punch thrown in post-scrum 'melée' during a rugby match was found to have a very close connection to the first defendant's employment as a rugby player.
[144] See W. V. H. Rogers, *Winfield & Jolowicz on tort*, 18th edn (Sweet and Maxwell, 2010), 20-09, but contrast R. Glofcheski, 'A frolic in the law of tort: expanding the scope of employers' vicarious liability', *Tort Law Review*, 12 (2004), 1.
[145] [2002] UKHL 48, [2003] 2 AC 366.
[146] Ibid., at para. 26. His Lordship argued that, in this field, the assistance provided by previous court decisions may be particularly valuable, whilst noting the infinite range of circumstances in which the question of vicarious liability arises. It is noticeable that

This 'close connection' test focuses attention in the right direction. But it affords no guidance on the type or degree of connection which will normally be regarded as sufficiently close to prompt the legal conclusion that the risk of the wrongful act occurring, and any loss flowing from the wrongful act, should fall on the firm or employer rather than the third party who was wronged.[147]

(iii)   An Australian 'close connection' test?

The Australian courts have equally utilised the Salmond test.[148] In the classic case of *Deatons Pty Ltd v Flew*,[149] a hotel barmaid, who had thrown a glass of beer at a customer, was found not to be acting in the course of employment. It was not incidental to what she was employed to do, but 'a spontaneous act of retributive justice'.[150] However, post-*Bazley* and *Lister*, the High Court of Australia has also faced the question as to whether an employer should be held vicariously liable for acts of sexual abuse which are the very antithesis of what the employee, be he carer or teacher, was employed to do. The judgments in the leading case of *New South Wales v Lepore*[151] highlight many of the difficulties facing the common law. In a system of precedent, how important is previous case law as opposed to the actual facts of the case? Should arguments of loss distribution and deterrence justify an extension of the scope of vicarious liability, despite concerns that charitable or smaller enterprises may have a limited ability to spread losses and that there may be little deterrent value in holding the employer of the offender liable when the criminal law itself has not deterred the culprit from engaging in such practices?[152] Should certainty be sacrificed to achieving a fair and just result in the circumstances? In reaching differing conclusions to these very pertinent questions, the High Court highlights the difficulty of finding a working definition for 'course of employment'. Whilst this is

---

in England and Wales, as in Canada, the courts have expressed mixed views of how useful such earlier authority will be.

[147] Ibid., at para. 25.

[148] See, for example, Williams J in *Deatons Pty Ltd v Flew* (1949) 79 CLR 370 at 385: 'we cannot do better, I think, than rely ... on the statement of the law in the passage from *Salmond on Torts*, 9th ed. (1936), p. 495 cited with approval in the judgment of the Privy Council in *Canadian Pacific Railway Co. v Lockhart* [1942] A.C. 591, at p. 599.'

[149] (1949) 79 CLR 370. Cf. *Pettersson v Royal Oak Hotel Ltd* [1948] NZLR 136 (barman who threw a broken piece of glass at an intoxicated customer found to be acting within the course of employment).

[150] (1949) 79 CLR 370 at 382 per Dixon J.

[151] (2003) 212 CLR 511, noted by N. McBride, 'Vicarious liability in England and Australia', *Cambridge Law Journal* [2003], 255.

[152] (2003) 212 CLR 511 at para. 219 per Gummow and Hayne JJ.

helpful on a theoretical level, it has left Australian law in a state of some uncertainty; White and Orr commenting that it is 'not so much a work in progress, as a work of the oracular'.[153]

Lepore consisted of three conjoined cases,[154] all involving claims of sexual abuse by schoolteachers. As discussed in Chapter 5, the plaintiffs' arguments, based on a non-delegable duty owed by the State to pupils to protect them from intentional torts, were rejected by all except McHugh J.[155] The remaining justices considered the alternative claim based on vicarious liability. For Callinan J, the answer was straightforward: deliberate criminal conduct is not properly to be regarded as within the course of employment.[156] For the remaining five justices, the answer was not so clear-cut. Three justices referred to the need for a 'close connection', varying from that of Kirby J who drew on *Bazley* and *Lister* to that of Gaudron J who linked it to ideas of estoppel.[157] In contrast, Gummow and Hayne JJ were critical of the test which, in their view, merely restated the problem presented by the concept of 'course of employment'.[158] Going back to *Deatons*, a narrower test would be required which confined the scope of liability to wrongful acts performed in the intended (or ostensible) pursuit of the employer's interests or in the apparent execution of authority which the employer held out the employee as having.[159] Risk-based reasoning was firmly rejected as a 'radical departure' from previous law.

---

[153] S. White and G. Orr, 'Precarious liability: the High Court in *Lepore, Samin* and *Rich* on school responsibility for assaults by teachers', *Torts Law Journal*, 11 (2003), 101 at 112. See also P. Vines, 'Schools' responsibility for teachers' sexual assault: non-delegable duty and vicarious liability', *Melbourne University Law Review*, 27 (2003), 612, who comments on the lack of clear guidance to education authorities and other employers leading, inevitably, to further litigation.

[154] *New South Wales v Lepore; Samin v Queensland; Rich v Queensland*.

[155] McHugh J, dissenting, was prepared to impose a non-delegable duty on the State to take reasonable care to prevent harm, be it intentional or negligent, to pupils. In view of his finding, he considered it unnecessary to determine whether the actions were in the course of employment.

[156] (2003) 212 CLR 511 at para. 342: 'In my opinion, deliberate criminal misconduct lies outside, and indeed usually will lie far outside the scope or course of an employed teacher's duty.'

[157] Ibid., at para. 131 ('Ordinarily, a person will not be estopped from denying that a person was acting as his or her servant, agent or representative unless there is a close connection between what was done and what that person was engaged to do'). Gleeson CJ, in contrast, favoured a version of the 'close connection' test which, in the context of sexual abuse, assessed whether the employee had been placed in a position of such power and intimacy that his conduct could fairly be regarded as so closely connected with his responsibilities as to be in the course of his employment: para. 85.

[158] Ibid., at para. 213.   [159] Ibid., at para. 231.

In view of these differences, it is difficult to determine a clear ratio. Whilst the majority favoured imposing some form of strict liability for intentional torts, the 'close connection' test was favoured by a minority and there was still support for the Salmond test, notably from Gummow and Hayne JJ. Concerns were expressed that the 'close connection' test would be unable to keep the doctrine of vicarious liability within limits. Callinan J, for example, commented that:

> In practice there would be few situations in which a 'connexion' between the duties and the conduct would not be able to be demonstrated. Distinguishing between 'opportunity' which would almost always be available to any teacher, and a 'connexion' of the kind referred to by their Lordships [in *Lister*] would be very difficult. Cases would, as a practical matter, be decided according to whether the judge or jury thought it 'fair and just' to hold the employer liable. Perceptions of fairness vary greatly. The law in consequence would be thrown into a state of uncertainty.[160]

It is of little surprise that the Australian courts have found it problematic to apply *Lepore*. Whilst it is clear that Australia has not adopted the *Bazley* test,[161] subsequent case law has referred to the need for a 'connection' with reference made to judgments in *Lepore*, but also the Salmond test and *Deatons*.[162] As Vines observes, 'what is clear from all the judgments is an insistence on scrutiny of the detail of the employment as a way of deciding on whether the employee acted in the course of employment',[163] but it is difficult to see how this differs from the ordinary application of the Salmond test. In *Sprod v Public Relations Orientated Security Pty Ltd*,[164] Ipp JA in the New South Wales Court of Appeal advised that the safest course is to apply the Gleeson/Gaudron/Gummow and Hayne/Kirby formulations to the facts of each case: 'The answers that this course produces will assist in resolving the issue, particularly if the answers, or a substantial majority of them, are the same.'[165] It is legitimate to question whether this gives sufficient guidance: Ipp JA concluding that 'In the end, the only explanation that is satisfactory is that of policy, and judicial policy at that.'[166]

---

[160] Ibid., at para. 345.
[161] Note criticism by Gaudron J ibid., at para. 126 and Gummow and Hayne JJ at para. 223.
[162] See, for example, *Starks v RSM Security Ltd* [2004] NSWCA 351; *Zorom Enterprises Pty Ltd v Zabow* [2007] NSWCA 106; and *Nationwide News Pty Ltd v Naidu* [2007] NSWCA 377.
[163] See Vines, 'Schools' responsibility', 625.   [164] [2007] NSWCA 319.
[165] Ibid., at para. 54. See also *Ryan v Ann St Holdings* [2006] QCA 217 at para. 18 per Williams JA and *Sandstone DMC Pty Ltd v Trajkovski* [2006] NSWCA 205 at paras. 14–18 per Ipp JA.
[166] [2007] NSWCA 319 at para. 53.

(iv) Lord Hobhouse in Lister: *has the employer assumed a relationship to the claimant which imposed specific duties in tort upon the employer which he entrusted to his employee?*[167]

This test differs from the other tests outlined above in that it examines the connection between the employer and victim. Lord Hobhouse asserted in *Lister* that 'where the defendant has assumed a relationship to the plaintiff which carries with it a specific duty towards the plaintiff, the defendant is vicariously liable in tort if his servant, to whom the performance of that duty has been entrusted, breaches that duty'.[168] This version of the test is problematic.[169] By focusing on the relationship between employer and victim to whom the employer assumes responsibility, his Lordship is setting out a relationship of *primary*, not vicarious, liability. It is certainly arguable that primary, that is fault-based, liability provides a more acceptable basis for an extension of liability to encompass serious criminal offences, being consistent with the principles of corrective justice, but, as will be noted, Lord Hobhouse does not go this far and liability is still described as 'vicarious'. A failure to distinguish clearly between primary and vicarious liability is, as seen in Chapter 5, a problem not unknown to the common law. Indeed, the Court of Appeal judgment relied upon in *Lister* of *Morris v Martin*[170] provides a good example of such confusion: liability being alternatively described as based on vicarious liability or primary liability in bailment. As stated in Chapter 5, it is important to distinguish between primary fault-based liability and that of vicarious liability in tort if one is to avoid legal fiction. If the House of Lords in *Lister* wished to extend the scope of *vicarious* liability, then reference to non-delegable duties or agency (explicit or implicit) should be avoided. It is therefore unsurprising that subsequent English courts have preferred to adopt the Steyn test outlined in test (ii) above.

6.3.5 *A different test for fraud?*

In addition to the conceptual difficulties outlined above, there is ongoing authority that a more restrictive test applies to one particular tort: that of fraud or deceit. Traditionally, the courts had been reluctant to impose vicarious liability for fraud. The common law courts finally admitted claims in the middle of the nineteenth century, but only where

---

[167] See [2002] 1 AC 215 at para. 54.   [168] Ibid., at para. 57.
[169] Although it was initially followed by Laddie J in *Balfron Trustees Ltd v Petersen* [2001] IRLR 758.
[170] [1966] 1 QB 716.

the fraud also benefited the employer.[171] This limitation was removed by the key common law case of *Lloyd v Grace, Smith & Co.*,[172] where a firm of solicitors was held to be vicariously liable for the fraudulent activities of its managing clerk. The clerk had been permitted to conduct the conveyancing business of the firm without supervision and, acting as its representative, had induced Mrs Lloyd to give him instructions to sell the two cottages she owned, which he dishonestly disposed of for his own benefit. The House of Lords held the firm liable for his activities, but on the basis that the clerk had been given ostensible authority by the firm to transact on its account: 'If the agent commits the fraud purporting to act in the course of business such as he was authorised, or held out as authorised, to transact on account of his principal, then the latter may be held liable for it.'[173]

Liability would therefore appear to arise not where the employee is acting in the course of employment, but within the scope of his actual or ostensible[174] authority. This invokes expressly the language of agency. This may be interpreted in two ways: either the deceit cases should actually be viewed as contractual agency cases,[175] or there is a special 'course of employment' test for deceit. In *Armagas Ltd v Mundogas SA (The Ocean Frost)*[176] the latter option was chosen. Here, as part of a fraudulent

---

[171] *Barwick v English Joint Stock Bank* (1867) LR 2 Ex 259.

[172] [1912] AC 716 (hereafter *Lloyd*). See also *Uxbridge Permanent Benefit Building Society v Pickard* [1939] 2 KB 248 and *The Queen v Levy Bros* (1961) 26 DLR (2d) 760 (a case of mail theft by custom officers authorised to deal with dutiable mail).

[173] [1912] AC 716 at 725 per Earl Loreburn.

[174] Ostensible authority has been defined as arising 'when the principal, by words or conduct, has represented that the agent has the requisite actual authority, and the party dealing with the agent has entered into a contract with him in reliance on that representation. The principal in these circumstances is estopped from denying that actual authority existed': *The Ocean Frost* [1986] AC 717 at 777 per Lord Keith. His Lordship also draws a distinction between ostensible general authority, i.e. the agent may deal with third parties in relation to transactions of the kind in question, and the very rare and unusual case of ostensible specific authority where the agent is known to have no general authority, but the principal indicates that he may be prepared to grant specific approval to the transaction.

[175] See, for example, F. Pollock's note on *Lloyd* which emphasised the personal liability of the solicitor for failing to supervise the work of the fraudulent clerk: (1913) 29 LQR 10. See also S. J. Stoljar, 'The servant's course of employment', *Modern Law Review*, 12 (1949), 44 at 58 and notably the judgments of Gummow and Hayne JJ in *New South Wales v Lepore* (2003) 212 CLR 511 at paras. 235–8 which suggest that *Lloyd* may be more simply analysed as a breach of contract case (see also Gaudron and Callinan JJ). Consider also the dicta of Dixon J in *CML v Producers and Citizens' Co-operative Co.* (1931) 46 CLR 41 in relation to liability of the principal for defamatory statements by agents.

[176] [1986] AC 717 (hereafter *The Ocean Frost*).

scheme, the defendants' chartering manager (M) had informed the claimants that he had authority to agree the sale of the ship to them with a three-year charter-back to the defendants. He did not have authority to do so. The House of Lords found that the defendants were not vicariously liable. The claimants had known that M did not have any general authority to enter into a three-year charterparty and, in the absence of any representation by the defendants as to his authority, the claimants could not have reasonably believed him to possess specific authority to do this.

The need for a special 'course of employment' test is said to derive from the nature of the tort itself. Deceit (or fraudulent misrepresentation)[177] requires that the employee makes a false representation, knowing it to be untrue, or at least being reckless as to its truth, with the intention to mislead the victim, and which causes the victim to rely upon it to his or her detriment.[178] In determining which statements are in the 'course of employment', the courts will also consider the requirement of reliance by the victim[179] and have established that only statements which can be said to be within the authority the employee possesses (actual) or may reasonably be said to possess (ostensible) may be said to be 'closely connected' to what the defendant was employed to do. This extra condition derives from a particular characteristic of the tort: victim participation. Thus, where the victim relies on statements which he knows or believes to be made by an employee acting outside the scope of his actual or apparent authority, then the courts will refuse to impose vicarious liability.[180] In the words of Lord Keith:

> the essential feature for creating liability in the employer is that the party contracting with the fraudulent servant should have altered his position to his detriment in reliance on the belief that the servant's activities were within his authority, or, to put it another way, were part of his job . . . the

---

[177] The modern development of this tort dates from *Pasley v Freeman* (1789) 3 Term Rep 51, 100 ER 450.

[178] See *Clerk & Lindsell on torts*, 19th edn (London: Sweet and Maxwell, 2006), 18-01; *Derry v Peek* (1889) LR 14 App Cas 337.

[179] See *Smith v Chadwick* (1881–82) LR 20 Ch D 27; *Edgington v Fitzmaurice* (1885) LR 29 Ch D 459. If the misrepresentation is of such a nature that it would be likely to play a part in the decision of a reasonable person to enter into a transaction, it will be presumed that it did so unless the representor satisfies the court to the contrary: *Dadourian Group International Inc v Simms* [2009] EWCA Civ 169, [2009] 1 Lloyd's Rep 601.

[180] See, for example, *JJ Coughlan Ltd v Ruparelia* [2003] EWCA Civ 1057 (preposterous investment scheme sold by solicitor in which claimant was party to a number of false statements himself).

essence of the employer's liability is reliance by the injured party on actual or ostensible authority.[181]

Such a test may also be justified on policy grounds:

> At the end of the day the question is whether the circumstances under which a servant has made fraudulent misrepresentation which has caused loss to an innocent party contracting with him are such as to make it just for the employer to bear the loss. Such circumstances exist where the employer by words or conduct has induced the injured party to believe that the servant was acting in the lawful course of the employer's business.[182]

Liability will thus be determined according to what *authority* the employee has been given to make statements, be it actual or ostensible. Although the term 'authority' has echoes of agency – a fact not assisted by the contractual context of many of these cases – the term is used here to determine the scope of vicarious liability, not attribute primary liability to the principal. With this in mind, two conclusions may be drawn. First, torts which do not require proof of reliance by the victim should *not* raise the question of actual or ostensible authority.[183] Reference to ostensible authority in early assault cases must therefore be attributed to the lingering influence of the command theory of vicarious liability.[184] Secondly, on this basis, the House of Lords' decision to use the ordinary 'close connection' test in *Dubai Aluminium Co. Ltd v Salaam*,[185] rather than that of ostensible authority, is explicable due to its finding that the equitable wrong of dishonestly assisting a breach of fiduciary duty does not require proof of reliance by the victim.[186] It does not, therefore, signify that the 'close connection' test will replace the question of authority in fraud cases.[187]

---

[181] *The Ocean Frost* [1986] AC 717 at 781–2 (emphasis added). See also *Man Nutzfahrzeuge AG v Freightliner Ltd* [2005] EWHC 2347 (Comm).

[182] [1986] AC 717 at 782 per Lord Keith. See also Robert Goff LJ ibid., at 739 (CA) and Lord Shaw in *Lloyd* [1912] AC 716 at 740.

[183] [1986] AC 717 at 739–40 per Robert Goff LJ.

[184] See *Poland v John Parr and Sons* [1927] 1 KB 236.   [185] [2002] UKHL 48, [2003] 2 AC 366.

[186] See ibid., at paras. 28–9 per Lord Nicholls: 'I also leave aside cases where the wronged party is defrauded by an employee acting within the scope of his apparent authority.'

[187] Although Mitchell notes that Lord Nicholls avoided addressing the issue of the relationship between deceit and the close connection test in his speech and judicial clarification of this point is needed 'as a matter of some urgency': C. Mitchell, 'Partners in wrongdoing?', *Law Quarterly Review*, 119 (2003), 364 at 368. See also R. Stevens, 'Why do agents "drop out"?', *Lloyd's Maritime and Commercial Law Quarterly* [2005], 101 at 106, who argues that the actual and ostensible authority tests do not fit with the approach of the House of Lords in *Lister*.

The Ocean Frost does, however, raise two difficult questions. The tort of negligent misrepresentation also has a requirement of reliance,[188] and so logically the courts should also utilise the notion of 'authority' to determine the scope of liability.[189] This draws, however, an uncomfortable line between ordinary cases of negligence to which the 'course of employment' test is applicable and where the employee's negligence consists of misrepresentations. The Court of Appeal decision of *HSBC Bank plc v 5th Avenue Partners Ltd*[190] rejected an argument that the 'actual or ostensible' authority test should apply outside the tort of deceit. The House of Lords in *The Ocean Frost* and *Dubai Aluminium* had not ruled on the position of negligent misrepresentation and thus the Court of Appeal, in the absence of any reported authority,[191] sought to unite the principles applicable to tortious wrongdoing.[192] Clearly this is the most straightforward approach and the courts will be expected to take a common-sense approach to the 'reasonableness' of the claimant's reliance.

A second question deals with the actual context of *The Ocean Frost*: how to deal with a situation where the employee's fraud relates to his authority to act. The House of Lords resolved that vicarious liability would only arise where there was an independent reason for the victim to believe that the employee possessed the authority he claimed to have.[193] This rule imposes a stricter rule than that stated in *Lloyd* and has received criticism. Trindade, Cane and Lunney comment that 'it is not clear why the law should not adopt the attitude that a person is entitled to believe such an assertion of authority by a servant unless there is some good reason to be suspicious of the truth'.[194] The Court of

---

[188] *Hedley Byrne v Heller and Partners* [1964] AC 465.
[189] See *Kooragang Investments Pty v Richardson & Wrench* [1982] AC 462 (PC) (no vicarious liability where aware that employee has no authority to act), but for criticism, see A. Tetternborn, 'Authority, vicarious liability and negligent misstatement', *Cambridge Law Journal* [1982], 36 and note that Lord Wilberforce at [1982] AC 475 also commented that the employee's valuation was without any connection to the defendants' business.
[190] Also known as *So v HSBC Bank plc* [2009] EWCA Civ 296, [2009] 1 CLC 503.
[191] *Kooragang Investments Pty v Richardson & Wrench* [1982] AC 462 is notably not cited and presumably was not raised by Counsel.
[192] (n 190 above) [2009] EWCA Civ 296 at para. 62 per Etherton LJ.
[193] Lord Keith in *The Ocean Frost* [1986] AC 717 commented, at 783, that vicarious liability will not arise when the claimants' belief 'has been brought about through misguided reliance on the servant himself, when the servant is not authorised to do what he is purporting to do, when what he is purporting to do is not within the class of acts that an employee in his position is usually authorised to do, and when the employer has done nothing to represent that he is authorised to do it.'
[194] F. Trindade, P. Cane and M. Lunney, *The law of torts in Australia*, 4th edn (Australia: OUP, 2007), 19.9.1.2.3.

Appeal in *First Energy (UK) Ltd v Hungarian International Bank Ltd*,[195] although decided on the basis of contractual agency, was sceptical that claimants would query an assertion of authority by someone of considerable importance in a small organisation by seeking confirmation from head office. To expect such behaviour was to ignore commercial reality and common sense.[196] A comparison may be made here with French law. Under the doctrine of *apparence*,[197] the courts will be willing to impose vicarious liability where the fraud gives the victim the impression that the employee is acting for his employer,[198] and it is only where it is (or should be) apparent to the victim that the employee is acting outside his functions that the courts draw the line.[199] The courts thus seek a balance, 'ensur[ing] reasonable protection for the victims whilst encouraging them to be vigilant and making it possible to thwart possible collusions with the dishonest employee'.[200] The English approach appears questionable in imposing a burden on the victim to verify an assertion of authority in these particular circumstances, and contrary to the basic principle underlying the tort of deceit that 'Seeing somebody must be a loser, by this deceit, it is more reason that he that employs and puts a trust and confidence in the deceiver should be a loser, than a stranger.'[201]

One fundamental issue remains: should deceit continue to apply its own version of the 'course of employment' test? *The Ocean Frost* was decided in 1986, over a decade before the adoption of the 'close connection' test in *Lister*. Recent case law has either avoided this issue or sought, at least, to apply the 'close connection' test to the related tort of negligent misrepresentation and the equitable wrong of dishonestly assisting a breach of fiduciary duty. It is submitted, however, that there are three reasons to maintain the *Armagas* position. First, there is a real concern in the deceit cases that the claimant should in no way be party to the fraud, either by being aware of the fraud or at least turning a blind eye to suspicious activities. A second related point is that the courts are not

---

[195] [1993] 2 Lloyd's Rep 194. See comment by F. M. B. Reynolds, 'The ultimate apparent authority', *Law Quarterly Review*, 110 (1994), 21.
[196] [1993] 2 Lloyd's Rep 194 at 208 per Nourse LJ.
[197] G. Viney and P. Jourdain, *Traité de droit civil: les conditions de la responsabilité*, 3rd edn (Paris: LGDJ, 2006), N° 805.
[198] See, for example, the leading French case of Ass plén 19 May 1988 D 1988.513 note C. Larroumet.
[199] Cass civ 2, 7 July 1993 Bull civ II N° 249, p. 137, JCP 1993 IV 2325.
[200] G. Viney JCP 1993 I 3727 N° 24 (my translation).
[201] *Hern v Nichols* (1708) 1 Salk 289, 91 ER 256 per Holt CJ.

prepared to protect all reliance, and victims are expected to take some steps to protect themselves from fraud. By requiring that the fraudster is clothed with at least ostensible authority, the balance between victim protection and encouraging vigilance is arguably achieved. Finally, simplicity is not everything and a stronger argument for homogeneity would exist if the operation of the 'close connection' test was clearer. In view of the uncertainties which appear inherent in its current operation, abandoning a tried-and-tested position must be considered with caution.

6.3.6 The civil law test: the French example of 'les fonctions auxquelles ils les ont employés'

In civil law, liability is equally confined to wrongful acts taking place in the course of the 'functions' or 'tasks' for which the person is employed or asked to work. Bearing in mind the difficulties experienced by the common law courts, it is perhaps unsurprising that civil law courts have found it equally problematic to provide a clear definition of what acts or omissions will fall within the scope of vicarious liability. This section will focus on the struggles of the French courts which provide an excellent illustration of the relevant debates in this field. For thirty years, the French Supreme Court sought to establish a clear test defining when *préposés*, committing a tort, would be deemed to be acting within *les fonctions auxquelles ils les ont employés* (within the functions for which they have been employed).[202] With obvious parallels to the common law Salmond test, the question is characterised in France as one of *abus de fonctions* (abuse of one's functions); the wrongful conduct of the *préposé*/ employee being classified either as a *'détournement'* (diversion) from his tasks, or a *'dépassement'* (exceeding) of his tasks.[203] As in common law, the application of this test may in many cases be self-evident, for example, the *commettant*/employer will be liable where his truck driver drives negligently whilst delivering goods. The question becomes more difficult if the driver takes a different route from that recommended by his employer or uses the truck during the weekend to take his friends to a football match. Does it make a difference if the driver deliberately runs over a pedestrian in a fit of pique rather than accidently hitting another vehicle whilst delivering goods? These questions,

---

[202] Article 1384(5): 'Les maîtres et les commettants, du dommage causé par leurs domestiques et préposés dans les fonctions auxquelles ils les ont employés.'
[203] D. Veaux, 'L'abus de pouvoirs ou de fonctions en droit civil français' in *Trav Assoc H. Capitant* (Paris: LGDJ. 1977) p. 77 at 79.

which have troubled the common law courts, have equally raised concerns in the civil law courts.

Although the wording of Article 1384(5) is potentially restrictive, requiring conduct connected to the functions of the *préposé*, the courts initially came to adopt a generous approach. In a case of 1946,[204] for example, Favreau was employed by Alexis as an '*aide-chauffeur*' for his garage. On the day in question, Favreau had been instructed to take a lorry for repairs and then return it to the garage. For this purpose, he was given the key to the garage. Favreau, however, decided to hire out the lorry for a sum of money to take a group of people to a local dance. An accident occurred in which one of the passengers was killed and Favreau was convicted of manslaughter. The Criminal Chamber of the Cour de cassation found the employer liable. Although it was an '*abus de fonction*', the victim had believed that the driver was acting for the employer at the time and was acting within his general driving function. This approach is victim-centred – the *commettant* is seen as the '*garant*'/ 'guarantor' of the *préposé*, providing the victim with a solvent defendant from whom to recover compensation – and requires evidence of a mere connection between the tort and the workplace, for example that the tort took place during working hours at the place of work or using tools or materials provided by the employer. As a '*garant*', the guarantor may seek an indemnity from the debtor (the employee), but the primary goal is to ensure that the victim's needs are met. These early cases illustrate a very broad interpretation of the requirement that the tort must be committed 'in the functions for which they have been employed', extending to serious criminal misconduct.[205]

From the 1950s until 1988, however, a division developed between the approach of the civil and criminal chambers of the Cour de cassation.[206] Whilst the criminal chamber continued the liberal approach of the past, the civil chambers, notably the second chamber, favoured a more restrictive approach which excluded liability where the employee was acting for his own ends. On four occasions, attempts were made by the *Chambres réunies*, and *Assemblée plénière* of the Supreme Court to reconcile these approaches with, as will be seen, limited success.

---

[204] Cass crim 18 October 1946 S 1947.1.39. See also Crim 25 February 1907 DP 1907.1.413; 20 July 1931 DH 1931.493.
[205] Crim 5 November 1953 JCP 1953 II 7818 bis (rape and murder).
[206] Compare the approach of Civ 2, 1 July 1954 (two cases) D 1954.628 and Crim 20 March 1958 Bull crim N° 280, p. 484.

6.3.6.1 1960–1985: narrowing the scope of liability

The first two cases of the *Chambres réunies* in 1960[207] and the *Assemblée plénière* in 1977[208] concerned the misuse of vehicles provided by the employer. In the 1960 decision, an agricultural worker, who did not have a driving licence, had 'borrowed' his employer's van in his absence and later crashed it through a shop window. The court found this act to be 'for his own ends (*à des fins personnelles*), in defiance of the orders and without the knowledge of his employer'.[209] It was independent of the job he was employed to do, which only gave him the opportunity to take the van. In the 1977 decision, the driver had been employed to drive the delivery van in which his friends were injured (and one killed) as a result of his negligent driving on a Saturday night. He was told to garage the van at home, but forbidden to use the van outside work. Nevertheless, the court found that using the van '*sans autorisation, à des fins personnelles*' took him outside the course of his employment; a clear contrast to the 1946 decision in 6.3.6.

Both decisions supported the more restrictive approach of the civil chamber, circumscribing the *commettant's* liability. Nevertheless, the divergence between the civil and criminal chambers of the Supreme Court continued; the criminal chamber confining the 1977 decision to the wrongful use of the employer's vehicle.[210] Whilst the *loi Badinter* of 1985[211] effectively took over the question of wrongful use of motor vehicles by providing for strict liability for motor vehicle accidents,[212] this did little to resolve the issue in other contexts.

---

[207] *Ch réun* 9 March 1960 D 1960.329 note R. Savatier, JCP 1960 II 11559 note R. Rodière, Gaz Pal 1960.1.313.
[208] *Ass plén* 10 June 1977 D 1977.465 note C. Larroumet, JCP 1977 II 18730 concl P. Gulphe, Def 1977.1517 note J. L. Aubert, RTD civ. 1977.74 obs G. Durry.
[209] My translation.
[210] The 1960 decision was considered not to provide sufficient clarity to change the practice of the criminal courts. See comments of C. Larroumet D 1977.466 and Crim 18 July 1978 Bull crim N° 237, p. 627, but in other contexts: Crim 18 June 1979 Bull crim N° 212; D 1980 IR 36 obs C. Larroumet. Comment T. Hassler, 'La responsabilité des commettants, la jurisprudence de la Chambre criminelle depuis l'arrêt de l'Assemblée plénière du 10 juin 1977', D 1980 chron 125.
[211] *Loi* 5 July 1985, no. 85-677: Loi tendant à l'amélioration de la situation des victimes d'accidents de la circulation et à l'accélération des procédures d'indemnisation. See also Article L211-1, Insurance Code, requiring third party vehicle insurance, extending to situations where the driver has not been authorised to drive the vehicle and Y. Lambert-Faivre, 'L'abus de fonction', D 1986 chron 143.
[212] Viney and Jourdain, *Traité de droit civil*, N° 1024.

A 1983 decision of the *Assemblée plénière*[213] presented a slightly different situation: a lorry-driver legitimately driving his lorry, but trying to steal a cargo of oil destined for a client. Suspecting that he was being followed, the driver panicked and dumped the fuel in a quarry which led to environmental pollution. At the time in question, he was supposed to be working for the employer. In response to a claim for compensation from the local municipalities, the court again adopted a strict line:

> Article 1384(5) of the Civil Code does not apply to the employer in cases of injury caused by an employee, who, acting without authorisation for ends foreign to his tasks, has placed himself outside the scope of his employment.[214]

This formula is repeated in a later decision of 1985[215] where an employee had deliberately set fire to the factory he was employed to protect, supposedly to highlight insufficient security measures. These decisions were intended to send a clear message to the lower courts that merely giving an employee the opportunity to commit a tort should not give rise to liability under Article 1384(5).

One may observe that at this stage the approach of the French civil courts was more restrictive than that of the common law, despite the fact that both systems focus on whether the employee is 'on a frolic of his own'[216] or acting 'à des fins personnelles'. The 1985 decision may be contrasted with the 1980 House of Lords' decision in *Photo Production v Securicor*[217] which found in favour of vicarious liability where a security guard had deliberately started a small fire in a factory he was employed to protect.[218]

---

[213] *Ass. plén* 17 June 1983 JCP 1983 II 20120 concl P. A. Sadon, note F. Chabas, D 1984.134 note D. Denis, RTD civ. 1983.749 obs G. Durry.

[214] My translation.

[215] *Ass plén* 15 November 1985 D 1986.81 note J.-L. Aubert, JCP 1986 II 20568 note G. Viney, RTD civ. 1986.128 obs J. Huet.

[216] Parke B in *Joel v Morison* (1834) 6 C & P 501 at 503.

[217] *Photo Production Ltd v Securicor Transport Ltd* [1980] AC 827. Cf. BGH VersR 1967, 353, 354.

[218] Although it was alternatively decided on the basis of breach of contract by Securicor itself: see Lord Wilberforce [1980] AC 827 at 846. Lords Keith and Scarman expressed agreement with Lord Wilberforce. Vicarious liability was not found to arise in Canada where a security guard committed arson for his own amusement: *Plains Engineering Ltd v Barnes Securities Services Ltd* (1987) 43 CCLT 129 (Alta QB), but see *British Columbia Ferry Corp. v Invicta Security Service Corp.* [1998] 4 WWR 536 (BCCA). Some French commentators have equally argued that the 1985 case should have been decided on the basis of breach of contract, where the employer would have been held liable: Viney and Jourdain, *Traité de droit civil*, N° 804.

6.3.6.2   1988: A new test

By 1988, despite the four decisions described in 6.3.6.1, dissent still existed as to the appropriate test for *abus de fonctions*. In its decision of 19 May 1988,[219] the *Assemblée plénière* for the first time approved liability where the employee had acted in an unauthorised manner in his own interests. An insurance company was thus held responsible for its employee, M Héro, who had defrauded Mme Guyot while advising her at her home; Mme Guyot believing that M Héro was acting on behalf of the company, which had authorised M Héro to accept funds. This decision marked a turning point in French law. Although M Héro had acted for his own ends, the court found him to be acting within his duties giving rise to liability under Article 1384(5). In so doing, the court provided a modified formula for determining the scope of liability. Liability for the acts of others will now exist *unless* the act of the employee is:

(i)   without authorisation/*sans authorisation*;
(ii) for his own ends/*à des fins étrangères à ses attributions*; and
(iii) outside the normal duties of his job/*hors de ses fonctions*.

This test is cumulative. Unless the employer can demonstrate all three factors, he will be liable. The key issue is therefore whether the job provides '*l'occasion et les moyens de sa faute*' (the opportunity and means for his tort). The employee will thus still be acting within his functions, regardless of his motives, if his job provides the occasion or time and place of the tort (for example, it takes place during the working day),[220] and the means by which the tort is committed (for example, the victim is knocked over by a car that the employee is told to drive). As Terré notes, by focusing on whether the job gave the opportunity and means for the tort, the court adopted the traditional position of the criminal chamber and its primary concern for the welfare of victims.[221] Such a development, at first glance surprising in view of the gradual movement of the criminal chamber towards acceptance of the 1985 decision of the

---

[219] D 1988.513 note C. Larroumet, Gaz Pal 1988.2.640 concl M. Dorwling-Carter, Def 1988.1097 note J.-L. Aubert, RTD civ. 1989.89 obs P. Jourdain. Followed by Crim 4 January 1996 JCP 1996 IV 1028.

[220] Here there is a rebuttable presumption that it is in the course of employment. The classic example of a tort outside the course of employment is that of a murder outside working hours for personal reasons: see F. Terré, P. Simler and Y. Lequette, *Droit civil: les obligations*, 10th edn (Paris: Dalloz, 2009), N° 834; Crim 15 February 1977 D 1977 IR 330 obs C. Larroumet.

[221] Terré, Simler and Lequette, *Droit civil*, N° 835.

Assemblée plénière,[222] reflects a recognition of the increased role of no fault liability in French law.[223] As seen in Chapter 5, the courts have recently shown themselves willing not simply to impose liability on defined groups of people – employers and parents – but, under Article 1384(1), on anyone who has the power to organise, manage and control another in the absence of *force majeure*, act of a third party or fault of the victim.[224] The 1988 decision represents not simply a new formula, but an acceptance of the principle of vicarious liability as a means of responding to the risks arising from misconduct of employees.[225] Acts taking place during the working day using means supplied by the employer will thus be treated as sufficiently connected to the employee's duties to justify the imposition of liability. Some limits do, however, exist. In a 2004 case, the Civil Chamber accepted that where an employee had simply entered a parked car and started it out of curiosity, the employer would not be liable under Article 1384(5) for what was '*une initiative personnelle sans rapport avec sa mission*' (a personal initiative unrelated to his job).[226] Subsequent courts have refused liability where, for example, the victim has reason to believe that the employee is acting outside the scope of his employment,[227] although, as Viney points out, this will only arise where the parties have a pre-existing, usually contractual, relationship.[228] Uncertainty, however, remains. The 1988 formula still leaves the courts a margin of appreciation which has permitted the criminal courts to adopt a generous interpretation of the test,[229] arguably rendering it

---

[222] See Cass crim 15 May 1986 Gaz Pal 1986.2.682; 22 January 1987 Bull crim N° 37, p. 91; 10 November 1987 D 1988 IR 23.

[223] It may also owe something to its context: the fraudster had acted without authorisation on a frolic of his own and, without more, the employer could escape liability.

[224] See *l'arrêt Blieck* (Ass plén 29 March 1991 D 1991.324 note C. Larroumet, chr G. Viney p. 157, JCP 1991 II 21673, concl H. Dontenwille, note J. Ghestin). Note also the courts' willingness to increase the burden on parents under Art. 1384(4) for damage resulting from their children's acts: see Chapter 7.

[225] Consider, for example, Civ 2 16 June 2005 Bull civ II N° 158, p. 141; D 2005 IR 1806 (extortion of funds from elderly resident by warden of residential home); cf *Lister v Hesley Hall* [2002] 1 AC 215.

[226] Civ 2, 3 June 2004 Bull civ 2004 II N° 275, p. 233; JCP 2005 I 132 N° 5; Gaz Pal 2004.2.3857 note F. Gréau, RTD civ 2004.742 obs P. Jourdain (who welcomes the decision for imposing reasonable limits on the scope of liability).

[227] See Civ 2, 22 May 2003 Bull civ 2003 II N° 156 p. 132, Banque et droit 2003.76 N 91. For criticism, see N. Molfessis, 'La jurisprudence relative à la responsabilité des commettants du fait de leurs préposés ou l'irrésistible enlisement de la Cour de cassation' in *Mélanges Gobert* (Paris: Economica, 2004), N° 29.

[228] Viney and Jourdain, *Traité de droit civil*, N° 802.

[229] P. Malinvaud, *Droit des obligations*, 10th edn (Paris: Litec, 2007), N° 602.

impossible to state that a clear and certain overall test exists.[230] Nor has it discouraged academic writers from suggesting new means for determining the notion of *abus de fonctions*.[231] Tensions continue to exist between writers who favour a test based on risk, whereby the employer should be held liable for all torts causally linked to the employment,[232] and those who prefer the notion of employer as guarantor,[233] providing victims with compensation in situations where the innocent victim is unaware that the employee is acting against orders.[234]

What is important is that the French Supreme Court has adopted a more liberal approach, leading one commentator to remark that 'the slightest objective link between the *abus de fonctions* and the employee's functions will amount to a connection between them and impose liability on the *commettant*'.[235] Certainly a number of cases would appear to verify this. Compare, for example, the common law case of Heasmans v Clarity Cleaning Co. Ltd[236] with a May 1995 decision of the French Supreme Court.[237] In the former, a cleaning company, contracted to clean Heasmans' offices, was held not to be vicariously liable when one of its employees made telephone calls in the offices costing £1,400. The Court of Appeal held that such acts were wholly outside the course of employment. It was not sufficient that the employment gave the employee the opportunity to commit the act: 'before the master can be held to be vicariously liable for the acts of the servant there must be established some nexus other than mere opportunity between the tortious or criminal act of the servant and the circumstances of his employment'.[238] In the 1995 case, however, the company, hired to clean

---

[230] See Molfessis, La jurisprudence, and G. Viney JCP 2005 I 132 N° 5.
[231] See N. Molfessis, 'Vie professionnelle, vie personnelle et responsabilité des commettants du fait de leurs préposés' Dr Soc 2004.31; J. Julien, *La responsabilité civile du fait d'autrui: ruptures et continuités* (Presses universitaires d'Aix Marseille, 2001).
[232] Even a test based on causation gives rise to division between the two competing theories of causation in French law: equivalence of conditions (the 'but for' test) and the more restrictive 'adequate cause' test.
[233] For example, H. L. and J. Mazeaud, *Traité théorique et pratique de la responsabilité civile*, 6th edn (Paris: Montchrestien, 1965), vol. I, N° 915; C. Larroumet sous Ass plén 19 May 1988 D 1988.514: 'l'obligation de réparation du commettant devrait être conçue comme la mise en œuvre par la victime, d'une obligation de garantie fondée sur la confiance nécessairement placée par le commettant dans son préposé, peu important qu'elle ait été bien ou mal placée.'
[234] See, generally, Viney and Jourdain, *Traité de droit civil*, N° 800.
[235] D. Rebut, *Jurisclasseur responsabilité civile et assurances*, Fasc 143: droit à réparation– responsabilité du fait d'autrui – domaine: responsabilité des commettants (Paris: Editions du Juris-Classeur, 1998), para. 56 (my translation).
[236] [1987] ICR 949. [237] Civ 2, 22 May 1995 Bull civ II N° 154, p. 87.
[238] [1987] ICR 949 at 955 per Purchas LJ.

the offices of a jeweller, was held liable under Article 1384(5) when one of its employees stole some jewellery. The employee had committed the theft in his workplace, to which he had been sent by the employer, during working hours and thus was not acting '*hors de ses fonctions*'. The *commettant* would only avoid liability where (i) the employee in question is clearly acting in a manner unconnected with this work,[239] or (ii) the victim knows (or may be inferred to know) that the employee is acting in his personal capacity.[240]

6.4 Appraisal: what does 'close connection' or 'dans les fonctions' mean? Can a workable definition be found?

What conclusions may we draw from the foregoing analysis? One obvious comment is that the tests of 'course of employment' or '*dans les fonctions*' do not exist in a legal vacuum where an abstract definition may serve to delineate their meaning. These tests play a vital role in limiting the scope of vicarious liability and their interpretation will inevitably indicate the extent to which each legal system deems strict liability to be an appropriate response in the circumstances. French case law adopts the most generous interpretation, reflecting the current dominance of risk-based reasoning as the primary justification for imposing strict liability under Article 1384(5).[241] Strict liability is seen as a means of ensuring compensation for victims, justified by the theory of risk/profit (*théorie du risque/profit*), that is, if you profit from another's actions, you must accept the risks associated with these actions. This theory is acknowledged to be reliant on a background of liability insurance and legislation which requires insurers to meet claims for damages caused by both negligent and intentional misconduct for which the employer is held liable under Article 1384.[242] The parallel extension of liability in public law, together with broad interpretation of Articles

---

[239] See, for example, Civ 2, 6 February 2003 JCP 2003 II 10120 note C. Castets-Renard (swindle by religious minister arising from professional activities in construction company; outside and unconnected with his spiritual duties as minister).

[240] See, for example, Civ 2, 21 May 1997 Bull civ II N° 154, p. 89; Resp civ et assur 1997 comm 252; 14 January 1998 JCP 1998 IV 1479.

[241] See Chapter 8.

[242] Article L 121-2, Insurance Code: 'The insurer shall cover the losses and damage caused by persons for whom the insured is legally liable pursuant to Article 1384 of the Civil Code, regardless of the nature and seriousness of such persons' faults.' This is treated as having the status of '*d'ordre public*' and so cannot be modified by agreement.

APPRAISAL: CAN A WORKABLE DEFINITION BE FOUND? 189

1384(1) and 1384(4) of the Civil Code, has led to a dramatic extension of liability in French law.

French law presents us, therefore, with one example of how vicarious liability should operate. Where the workplace provides the opportunity for misconduct, then the employer must accept responsibility for risks arising from workplace conduct, unless, for example, the employee knows (or should know) that the employee is working for his own purposes.[243] Such a test is dependent on widespread insurance cover and a willingness to accept that employers should be subject to widespread liability.

There is clear common law authority, however, that this is considered a step too far. In *Bazley v Curry*, McLachlin J rejected a test based solely on the opportunities presented by the workplace to commit torts:

> Incidental connections to the employment enterprise, like time and place (without more), will not suffice ... For example, an incidental or random attack by an employee that merely happens to take place on the employer's premises during working hours will scarcely justify holding the employer liable. Such an attack is unlikely to be related to the business the employer is conducting or what the employee was asked to do and, hence, to any risk that was created. Nor is the imposition of liability likely to have a significant deterrent effect; short of closing the premises or discharging all employees, little can be done to avoid the random wrong.[244]

The view is thus taken that liability should only arise where there is more than an incidental connection between the risks created by the workplace and the tort which occurs. To do otherwise, it is suggested, would effectively make the employer an involuntary insurer and Binnie J in *EB* held that such general liability could only be created by the legislature.[245] Such a view is also accepted by the English and Australian courts. Lord Clyde in *Lister* reiterates the view stated in *Heasmans v Clarity Cleaning Co Ltd* at 6.3.6.2: 'there must be some greater connection between the tortious act of the employee and the circumstances

---

[243] André Tunc, the great French advocate of risk-based liability, has gone so far as to suggest that the simplest rule would be to render the employer strictly liable for all torts taking place during working hours, avoiding harmful litigation and legal uncertainty: 'Les problèmes contemporains de la responsabilité civile délictuelle', *Revue International de Droit Comparé*, 19 (1967), 757 at 775.
[244] [1999] 2 SCR 534 at paras. 41–2 and see Binnie J in *Jacobi v Griffiths* [1999] 2 SCR 570 at para. 45. See also *KLB v British Columbia* [2003] 2 SCR 403 at para. 94.
[245] *EB v Order of the Oblates of Mary Immaculate in the Province of British Columbia* [2005] 3 SCR 45, at para. 3.

of his employment than the mere opportunity to commit the act which has been provided by the access to the premises which the employment has afforded'.[246]

The challenge, therefore, is to define a connection which goes beyond mere opportunity and reflects the extent to which vicarious liability is considered desirable. Certain judges have expressed concern that too generous a test of liability will render employers liable for all tortious acts of employees, no matter how remote the wrongdoing from the tasks assigned to them.[247] Asking simply what the employee is employed to do will not suffice. As already seen, employers may be held liable for prohibited and criminal acts by employees, going beyond mere misguided performance of one's duties. In suggesting tests of 'close or significant' connection or 'an unauthorised mode of performing authorised acts', the courts indicate that more than mere opportunity is required, but, as previously seen, give insufficient guidance on how to deal with grey areas where the employee's misconduct is linked in some way to his employment. Consider, for example, the 1988 Privy Council case of *General Engineering Services Ltd v Kingston and Saint Andrew Corp (Jamaica)*.[248] The plaintiffs' building had been destroyed when, due to an industrial dispute, the members of the local fire brigade had adopted a 'go slow' policy in order to bring pressure upon their employers to satisfy their grievances.[249] The Privy Council had 'no hesitation' in finding that such actions were not in the course of employment. Lord Ackner took the view that '[t]heir mode and manner of driving – the slow progression of stopping and starting – was not so connected with the authorised act, that is driving to the scene of the fire as expeditiously as reasonably possible, as to be a mode of performing that act'.[250] This is clearly contentious – is slow driving so different from negligent driving? – and defines the nature of the employees' duties narrowly. A stronger reason appears to be the view that the firemen were acting in furtherance of an industrial dispute, rather than in furtherance of their

---

[246] [2001] UKHL 22 at para. 45. See also *New South Wales v Lepore* (2003) 212 CLR 51, notably Gleeson CJ at para. 74 and Callinan J at para. 345.
[247] See, notably, Binnie J in *EB* [2005] 3 SCR 45 at para. 4, Callinan J in *Lepore* (2003) 212 CLR 51 at para. 345 and Scott Baker LJ in *Majrowski v Guy's and St Thomas's NHS Trust* [2005] EWCA Civ 251.
[248] [1989] 1 WLR 69.
[249] Thereby taking seventeen minutes to cover a distance usually taking three-and-a-half minutes.
[250] Ibid., at 72.

employers' business,[251] but again, this, as Lunney and Oliphant indicate,[252] focuses more on the employees' motives than any application of the connection/unauthorised mode test.

It is worthwhile considering whether this case would be decided differently today and, if so, what distinguishes the 'close connection' test from that utilised by their Lordships in this case? Adopting the Canadian approach – is there a strong or significant connection between the employment enterprise and the wrongful acts such that vicarious liability would be justifiable in terms of the fair allocation of the consequences of risk and deterrence? – at first glance, such a risk would not appear especially linked to that of the particular employment enterprise. Any employers may be subject to industrial action: it is an inherent risk of unionisation. Nevertheless, it might be argued that the consequences of industrial action in the emergency services may give rise to far more serious consequences than, for example, a 'go slow' by university lecturers. Fundamentally, however, this does not answer the larger social question as to who should bear the risks of the consequences of industrial action, often a matter regulated by the legislature itself.[253] The alternate Lord Steyn test – was the wrongful act so closely connected that it would be fair and just to hold the employers vicariously liable? – throws no clearer light on the question, seeming to rest on the issue of whether it would be 'fair and just' to impose liability here; there being an obvious connection between fire-fighting and the speed with which the fire engine is driven. The many and varied views of the High Court of Australia would appear equally inconclusive.

It is more constructive, therefore, to step back and highlight three key factors which appear significant in the court decisions previously examined in this chapter. They are: the facts of the case, the employee's purpose and the policy interest in ensuring victim compensation. In every system, commentators have found it difficult to discern distinct precedents in this field, despite encouragement from judges, such as McLachlin J in *Bazley* and Lord Nicholls in *Dubai*, to follow existing lines

---

[251] To the extent that their conduct amounted to wrongful repudiation of their contracts of employment: ibid.
[252] M. Lunney and K. Oliphant, *Tort law: text and materials*, 4th edn (Oxford University Press, 2010), p. 836. This case has been described as the 'high-water mark' of reasoning that the purpose underlying the employee's conduct must in some way benefit the employer: *British Columbia Ferry Corp. v Invicta Security Service Corp.* [1998] 4 WWR 536 at para. 48 per Rowles J.
[253] See E. McKendrick, 'Vicarious liability and industrial action', *Industrial Law Journal*, 18 (1989), 161.

of authority. Much will depend on the facts of the case and the impact of liability in relation to the vicarious liability triangle of employer – employee – victim. Equally, in all systems, well-meaning, but misguided, employees are more likely to be found to be acting in the course of employment, although even in these cases there will come a point where conduct amounts to a 'frolic of one's own'.[254] In recent years, the courts have also been more open in articulating the goal of victim compensation. According to the vicarious liability triangle, it is the innocent victim who is deserving of greatest protection. The tortfeasor has committed a wrong. The employer has set the wrong in motion, by creating the risk of injury to innocent parties either for its own profit or, in the case of charities, for its own particular social goals. These three factors – the facts of the case; employee purpose; victim compensation – lie at the heart of our modern understanding of the scope of vicarious liability.

Identification of these factors helps us to explain and understand modern law. If the courts are seeking to adapt the test to the peculiar facts of each case and retain sufficient flexibility to reach a just result, then, any test will by its very nature be vague and imprecise. As noted in a leading English textbook, the decisions on course of employment seem to be 'ultimately impressionistic'.[255] Case law in each system will equally produce examples of cases where the courts protect misguided employees. A well-meaning employee, who harms another in the ostensible pursuit of his employers' interests,[256] even when it results in intentional harm to another, will tend to be treated more generously than a selfish employee acting solely on his own behalf. Logically, this might suggest that such self-serving employees would fall outside the scope of vicarious liability, but the final factor, that of victim compensation, in recent years has overcome such concerns. Although contentious – why should an employer be liable when the employee acts against his interests? – vulnerable parties, who have reasonably placed their trust in the employee (deceit) or simply have been injured by employees engaged

---

[254] Note, in particular, the US Restatement on Agency (3d) (2006–2009) § 7.07(2): 'An employee's act is not within the scope of employment when it occurs within an independent course of conduct not intended by the employee to serve any purpose of the employer.'

[255] S. Deakin, A. Johnston, and B. S. Markesinis, *Markesinis and Deakin's tort law*, 6th edn (Oxford University Press, 2007), p. 682.

[256] See, for example, *Dyer v Munday* [1895] 1 QB 742 (vicarious liability for criminal assault by an employee who was seeking repossession of the defendants' goods for non-payment) and *Poland v John Parr and Sons* [1927] 1 KB 236 (vicarious liability for assault against person believed to be stealing the employer's property).

to protect them, are perceived as deserving of our sympathy. As I have suggested elsewhere,[257] the common law extensions of 'course of employment' to intentional acts often occur in circumstances where the employee has been entrusted with the task of protecting the interests of a vulnerable party under the employers' overall protection. The victim is entrusted into the care of an employee, who is instructed to care for him or her. The tort occurs when the employee wrongfully harms the very person he is engaged to protect.[258] Consider, for example, *Bazley* and *Lister*. Here, quasi-public organisations had entrusted the care of vulnerable children to the employee in question and both the Supreme Court of Canada and House of Lords found it in the interests of society that such employers should be held vicariously liable. In contrast, assault by a groundsman[259] or baker,[260] to whom no protective duty had been entrusted, should not give rise to liability. Nor should vicarious liability be imposed where the employee commits a deliberate wrong solely in his own interests and where his duties include no protective or fiduciary elements. Here, it is submitted, liability should only be imposed on the basis of primary liability, that is, the employer was personally at fault either in entrusting this individual with the means to harm the victim or in placing him in a position where he was able to do so.[261]

Increased judicial willingness to intervene in favour of innocent victims also suggests growing acceptance of risk reasoning. The employer, by utilising the employee for his own devices may be said to create the risk of damage to innocent third parties. His ability to act and implement greater accident-prevention measures and to distribute loss via the mechanism of liability insurance, justifies the imposition of

---

[257] P. Giliker, 'Making the right connection: vicarious liability and institutional responsibility', *Torts Law Journal*, 17 (2009), 35.

[258] See Lord Millett in *Lister*: the employee 'abused the special position in which the school had placed him to enable it to discharge its own responsibilities, with the result that the assaults were committed by the very employee to whom the school had entrusted the care of the boys' ([2002] 1 AC 215 at para. 82). Consider also *Morris v Martin* [1966] 1 QB 716. Here, a mink stole had been stolen by the employee entrusted with its care and security. The same key elements justify employer liability: the employee harming the very thing he was employed to protect.

[259] This is the example given in *Lister* where vicarious liability would not arise: see [2002] 1 AC 215 at para. 62 per Lord Hobhouse and ibid., at para. 82 per Lord Millett.

[260] *EB v Order of the Oblates of Mary Immaculate (British Columbia)* (2005) 258 DLR (4th) 385.

[261] See *Attorney-General of the British Virgin Islands v Hartwell* [2004] UKPC 12. Query whether liability in *Mattis v Pollock* [2003] EWCA Civ 887 and *Bernard v Attorney-General of Jamaica* [2004] UKPC 47 should have been primary, not vicarious.

liability. Such arguments have been raised in all the legal systems surveyed. It is more contentious, however, to what extent the notion of risk should be permitted to determine the scope of liability. Atiyah in his 1967 monograph suggested that the employer should be liable where his activities gave rise to a *substantial* risk of his employees committing the kinds of wrongs in question.[262] The Canadian courts have preferred the term 'material risk'. The English courts have been somewhat vaguer; as Lord Steyn commented in *Bernard*, a number of judgments have emphasised the proposition (also taken from Atiyah)[263] that an employer ought to be liable for a tort which can fairly be regarded as 'a reasonably incidental risk' to the type of business he is engaged in.[264] 'Risk', in whichever form is preferred, be it 'substantial risk', 'material increase in risk', 'inherent risk', 'risk/profit', 'risk/enterprise',[265] 'risk/authority',[266] possesses the advantage of providing both a justification for liability and a test for determining the scope of liability. One might question, however, whether it should be the sole response to either question. Its role in justifying the imposition of vicarious liability will be examined in Chapter 8, but here it is noted that many systems have rejected use of 'risk' as the sole determinant of the scope of liability, albeit that most accept that it is a relevant factor. As a term, it may be criticised as inherently uncertain – we may agree that employment gives rise to a risk of employee misconduct, but what level of risk triggers employer liability? How do we assess whether such risks are 'substantial' or 'material' or 'inherent'? We must also bear in mind the limitations of the litigation process in which economic reasoning and empirical evidence play a limited role. Consider, for example, the operation of the material risk test in the Canadian cases of *Bazley* and *Jacobi* discussed earlier where the great advocate of the 'material risk' test, McLachlin CJ, found herself in the minority in *Jacobi*. The French comparison is also relevant. Greater resort to risk in France has resulted in a vast extension of liability, whose desirability may be questioned and has led some commentators to question why, if liability is based on the risk arising

---

[262] *Vicarious liability*, p. 172.
[263] 'The master ought to be liable for all those torts which can fairly be regarded as reasonably incidental risks to the type of business he carries on': ibid., p. 171.
[264] See [2004] UKPC 47 at para. 19. See also Lord Millett in *Lister* [2002] 1 AC 215 at para. 65 and in *Dubai Aluminium* [2002] UKHL 48 at para. 107, and Lord Nicholls in *Dubai Aluminium* [2002] UKHL 48 at para. 23.
[265] Liability arising because the employee's activities represent one of the risks of the enterprise.
[266] Liability arising because the employer exercises authority over the employee.

from the employer's operations, it is still a requirement that the employee commits a wrongful act when logically liability should arise due to the commission of any harmful act connected to the risks arising in the workplace.[267] Risk, it is submitted, is best seen as a relevant, but not determinant, factor influencing the courts' decisions.

A more useful analysis is to focus on the key influential factors – facts of the case, employee purpose and victim compensation. These factors overlap in practice. In examining the facts of the case, the courts will be mindful of the relative position of the parties and the goal of victim compensation and will consider the employee's purposes and motivation. Such analysis does not lend itself to a definitive test. There is much truth in the statement that '[t]he rules governing vicarious liability exhibit the difficulty they do because they have been extended and applied as a matter of policy rather than principle',[268] but the very nature of vicarious liability renders the influence of policy inevitable. Matters such as risk, the vulnerability of potential victims, and the duties placed on public or quasi-public bodies to protect the interests of others, will all influence the essential question: was the employee acting in the course of his employment or functions? This is to recognise the very nature of the doctrine of vicarious liability.

The policy arguments underlying this doctrine will be examined and assessed in Chapter 8. The next chapter, however, will examine an area where the common law has yet to impose vicarious liability. Most European legal systems have extended the concept of liability for the acts of others to include parental liability for the harm caused by their children. The logic is clear. Children are under the control of their parents and, due to their immaturity, there is a clear risk that they may cause injury to innocent third parties. Chapter 7 will consider whether, in view of the expansion of the common law notion of vicarious liability, noted in the first six chapters of this book, there is any prospect of the common law developing a new form of vicarious liability, imposing liability not on employers, but on parents for the tortious acts of their children.

---

[267] M. Billiau JCP 2000.II.10295: discussed in Terré, Simler and Lequette, *Droit civil*, N° 833.
[268] Gummow and Hayne JJ in *Lepore* (2003) 212 CLR 51 at para. 242.

7 Parental liability for the torts of their children: a new form of vicarious liability?

7.1 Introduction

In previous chapters, we have examined the operation of vicarious liability across legal systems, focusing, in particular, on its application to the employer/employee context (its most common use). All legal systems have shown an increasing willingness to hold employers strictly liable for the torts of their employees, thereby ensuring that compensation will be paid to third parties, being innocent victims of employee misconduct connected to the workplace.

In most European States, a further head of special liability exists parallel to that discussed above: liability of parents for the harm caused by their children. As Galand-Carval commented, '[Parental liability] is sufficiently well established in a majority of European countries for it to appear as a "common European rule"'.[1] The notion of a specific category of parental liability is, however, unknown to the common law which adopts the basic proposition that parents, in common with all defendants, should be subject to the ordinary principles of tort law. Nevertheless, clear analogies may be drawn between the parent/child relationship and the employment context. Employers are expected to exercise a degree of control over their employees. They may give them orders, instruct them how to behave and monitor their performance. Likewise, parents are expected to care for and control their children and are best placed to prevent them from harming others. Further, children are a known risk. They are, by virtue of their age, immature and incapable of fully appreciating the risks of their actions and often irresponsible. They

---

[1] S. Galand-Carval, 'Comparative report on liability for damage caused by others: Part I' in J. Spier (ed.), *Unification of tort law: liability for damage caused by others* (Alphen aan den Rijn: Kluwer Law International, 2003), paras. 17–18.

are, additionally, unlikely to possess the means to compensate victims in their own right. From a policy perspective, there is a clear argument that holding parents responsible for the tortious actions of their children would plug a compensatory gap, whilst encouraging parents to take greater responsibility for their children's actions.

This chapter will examine the case for imposing vicarious liability on parents for the actions of their children at common law. This would, as will be seen, bring it more in line with the majority of other European legal systems which impose either strict liability on parents or, at least, a presumption of negligence, which is, in practice, difficult to rebut. It would also reflect a tendency in criminal law to hold parents responsible for the offences committed by their children. In particular, this chapter will consider the French approach towards liability which, in recent years, has moved to a position of strict liability, supported by almost universal insurance. In so doing, it will consider whether, in the light of the more generous tests recently adopted by the common law courts in the employment context,[2] the common law is likely to go so far as to impose vicarious liability on parents. It is submitted that the common law courts are capable of extending vicarious liability to the parent/child relationship.[3] Whether this would be a desirable development will be examined below.

7.2 Parental responsibility at common law

In examining the scope of parental liability for the acts of their children, it is helpful to start with an explanation of the position at common law.[4] This has traditionally favoured a model based on proof of fault in which the parent/child relationship is capable of giving rise to two main heads of parental liability. In the first, the parent may be liable for failing to take reasonable steps to protect his or her child. As we shall see, the courts are reluctant to encourage litigation amongst family members and the little case law which exists suggests a general unwillingness

---

[2] See *Lister v Hesley Hall Ltd* [2002] 1 AC 215 and *Bazley v Curry* (1999) 174 DLR (4th) 45, discussed in Chapter 6.

[3] As Rogers comments 'In a common law system where the higher court is not bound by its own precedents, it is always in theory open to the court to create a new head of vicarious liability': WVH Rogers, 'Liability for damage caused by others under English law' in Spier (ed.), *Unification of tort law*, para. 3.

[4] For a general discussion, see R. Bagshaw, 'Children through tort' in J. Fionda (ed.), *Legal concepts of childhood* (Oxford: Hart, 2001), pp. 127–50.

for tort law to intervene in the parent–child relationship. A different question arises, however, under the second head where the parent is claimed to be liable for failing to take reasonable steps to prevent the child causing injury to another. If the child is in the care of a parent at the time, any failure to take reasonable steps cannot be classified as a 'mere omission' and it is difficult to see why the victim should not sue the parent for negligently failing to prevent the accident. Consideration of the courts' treatment of these claims will provide a basis for a more detailed examination of the policy arguments for and against the imposition of vicarious liability on parents.

7.2.1 Parental liability to their child

The most immediate duty of the parent is to the child. By virtue of the parent–child relationship, the parent-carer will be deemed to assume responsibility for the health and safety of the child.[5] Liability is based on a finding of fault. A parent will be liable if he or she does not take reasonable steps to protect the child against physical injury.[6] In practice, the courts will examine whether the parent's conduct in the circumstances may be characterised as something a 'prudent or reasonable' parent would do. In assessing this standard, the courts have shown a willingness to recognise the pressures of family life and have been wary of requiring too high a standard of care from parents. As Lord Reid states in *Carmarthenshire CC v Lewis*,[7] 'There is no absolute duty; there is only a duty not to be negligent, and a mother is not negligent unless she fails to do something which a prudent or reasonable mother in her position would have been able to do and would have done.' Young children, for example, are recognised as liable to cause mischief in a variety of ways

---

[5] See Children Act 1989, s. 2(1),(2): '(1) Where a child's father and mother were married to each other at the time of his birth, they shall each have parental responsibility for the child. (2) Where a child's father and mother were not married to each other at the time of his birth, the mother shall have parental responsibility for the child.' 'Child' in English law signifies a person below the age of eighteen: see Family Law Reform Act 1969, s.1. Eighteen is also the age of majority in Germany (§ 2 BGB, as amended by the Law of 31 July 1974) and France (Art. 388, Civil Code, as amended by the Law N° 74-631 of 5 July 1974).

[6] *Jauffur v Akhbar* The Times 10 February 1984 (a parent is negligent if, knowing that there are candles in his house, he fails adequately to instruct and supervise his children about them with a view to preventing danger arising from their use). See also *Eastham v Eastham and Eastham* [1982] CLY 2141 (parents not liable for failing to supervise nine-and-a-half-year-old who slipped and fell into a swimming pool on holiday). See also *McCallion v Dodd* [1966] NZLR 710.

[7] [1955] AC 549 at 566.

which are often hard to predict.[8] Kathleen Surtees was only two when she scalded her foot in a wash basin filled with hot water. Left alone for a few minutes, she succeeded in placing her left foot in the basin and accidentally turning on the hot water tap. The majority of the Court of Appeal[9] found that her foster mother was not liable for the severe injuries which resulted.[10] Reasonable care had to be judged in the light of the 'rough-and-tumble of home life'[11] and the courts would be slow to characterise as negligent the ordinary conduct of parents coping with the myriad of duties which fall upon a parent–carer. To find the parent liable in such circumstances would, in the majority's view, impose an impossible standard of care on mothers.[12]

Such a sympathetic approach is perhaps surprising in view of the clear duty of care owed by parents to their children. Although claims are often brought against teachers[13] or foster parents,[14] it is rare for a civil case to be brought against a blood parent.[15] Judges have expressed concern as to the desirability of litigation which raises questions of relative fault amongst family members,[16] and questioned what purpose is served by requiring a parent to pay damages to the child from a fund already used in part for the child's benefit.[17] Perhaps more importantly, the courts

---

[8] See Lord Hoffmann in *Jolley v Sutton LBC* [2000] 1 WLR 1082 at 1093: 'it has been repeatedly said in cases about children that their ingenuity in finding unexpected ways of doing mischief to themselves and others should never be underestimated.' This is, however, a double-edged sword. In this case, this was used to *increase* the standard of care expected of the occupier.

[9] *Surtees v Kingston upon Thames RBC* [1992] PIQR P101, [1991] 2 FLR 559, Beldam LJ dissenting.

[10] Namely virtually the complete destruction of the skin and tissues of the sole of her left foot.

[11] [1992] PIQR P101 at 124 per Lord Browne-Wilkinson VC.

[12] No distinction was drawn in the case between the duties on mothers or the foster mother in the case.

[13] See, for example, *Phelps v Hillingdon LBC* [2001] 2 AC 619 and *Carty v Croydon LBC* [2005] EWCA Civ 19, [2005] 1 WLR 2312.

[14] See *Surtees* [1992] PIQR P101; *S v Walsall MBC* [1985] 1 WLR 1150. In reality the cases against teachers or foster parents are directed at local authorities on the basis either that they are vicariously liable or have authorised the acts in question or are themselves primarily at fault with respect to the victim. Claims against local authorities have received particular impetus in recent years: see *Barrett v Enfield LBC* [1999] UKHL 25, [2001] 2 AC 550 (HL) and *JD v East Berkshire Community Health NHS Trust* [2005] UKHL 23, [2005] 2 AC 373.

[15] Clearly criminal law is a different matter and, in any event, the prosecution is brought by the State.

[16] *Greatorex v Greatorex* [2000] 1 WLR 1970 at 1985 per Cazalet J; *Surtees* [1992] PIQR P101 at 121 and 123 per Beldam LJ and Lord Browne-Wilkinson VC respectively.

[17] See ibid., at 121 per Beldam LJ.

stress the challenges of parenting, which they confess to finding difficult to appreciate: 'The studied calm of the Royal Courts of Justice, concentrating on one point at a time, is light years away from the circumstances prevailing in the average home.'[18] It has also been suggested that it would be wholly inappropriate for a child to sue his or her parents for decisions made by them in respect of the child's upbringing which, with hindsight, may be shown to have been wrong.[19] The main exception is section 2 of the Congenital Disabilities (Civil Liability) Act 1976 (liability of woman driving when pregnant.)[20] Here, the moral objections against children suing their mothers are overcome because the mother, as a driver of a motor vehicle, is, by law, obliged to be insured.[21] In such cases, the insurance company will meet the child's claim.

Such policy objections do not apply where the parent intentionally harms the child, committing the tort of trespass to the person. Parental responsibility here mirrors that of criminal law. One particular limitation should be noted. Parents may discipline their children, provided that it is reasonable and moderate.[22] Section 58(3) of the Children Act 2004 provides that chastisement amounts to reasonable punishment if it causes a temporary and minor injury, but not if it amounts to actual bodily harm.[23]

7.2.2 Parental liability to third parties injured by their child

It is in this second category that the question of vicarious liability arises. The common law has accepted that parents should be liable where they have failed to use reasonable care to prevent their child harming another individual. In the Australian case of *Smith v Leurs*,[24] for example, the High Court of Australia was asked to determine whether the parents had been negligent in failing to confiscate the

---

[18] Ibid., at 124 per Lord Browne-Wilkinson VC.
[19] See *Barrett v Enfield LBC* [2001] 2 AC 550 at 587 per Lord Hutton, but see M. Freeman, 'The end of the century of the child?', *Current Legal Problems*, 53 (2000), 505.
[20] 'A woman driving a motor vehicle when she knows (or ought reasonably to know) herself to be pregnant is to be regarded as being under the same duty to take care for the safety of her unborn child as the law imposes on her with respect to the safety of other people; and if in consequence of her breach of that duty her child is born with disabilities which would not otherwise have been present, those disabilities are to be regarded as damage resulting from her wrongful act and actionable accordingly at the suit of the child.'
[21] Road Traffic Act 1988, s. 143.
[22] *R v H (Assault of Child: Reasonable Chastisement)* [2001] EWCA Crim 1024, [2002] 1 Cr App R 7.
[23] See S. Parsons, 'Human rights and the defence of chastisement', *Journal of Criminal Law*, 71 (2007), 308.
[24] [1945] ALR 392, HCA.

catapult of their adopted son, Brian, aged 13. They had warned Brian of the associated dangers and told him not to use it away from home. Whilst recognising that Brian was under his parents' control at the time, the court took the view that the parents had taken all the precautions which could reasonably be expected in the circumstances. They would not be liable for the injury suffered by a young boy when Brian fired a stone from his catapult and hit him in the eye.

Smith v Leurs is useful in setting out the standard expected of the reasonable parent. The courts will not exact an obligation which is 'almost impossible of performance' or which exceeds that which is practicable and to be expected according to all the circumstances, including the practices of the community.[25]

In applying an objective test of fault, much will depend, in practice, on the facts of the case, as seen in a number of cases involving teenagers with firearms. Whilst in *Newton v Edgerley*[26] a parent was found liable for allowing his twelve-year-old son to use a shotgun, despite strict instructions not to take the gun away from the home, an earlier Court of Appeal did not find a parent negligent in allowing his thirteen-year-old son to play with an air rifle, having put his son on his honour never to use the rifle except in the cellar of the house.[27] There is recognition that less will be expected as the child nears the age of majority.[28] Latitude has also been shown in the case of infants straying out of the family home into the path of oncoming traffic causing injury to others. Lord Reid in *Carmarthenshire CC v Lewis*[29] remarked that parental carers cannot be in two places at once and that it would be wrong to suggest that a young child should never be allowed out to play. The question was whether they had failed to take reasonable and practicable precautions. In *Palmer v Lawley*,[30] for example, the court did not find a mother negligent when her two-year-old child escaped from the back garden by unlatching a side door, walking up an alleyway and then onto the adjoining road. To do so would, according to the judge, place too high a burden on mothers

---

[25] See [1945] ALR 392 and the judgments of Latham CJ, Starke J and Dixon J.

[26] [1959] 1 WLR 1031, stressing the lethal nature of the shotgun.

[27] *Donaldson v McNiven* [1952] 2 All ER 691. See also *Gorely v Codd* [1967] 1 WLR 19 (father gave son sufficient instructions on the use of air rifles) and *Rogers v Wilkinson* The Times 19 January 1963 (father adequately instructed twelve-year-old son in use of gun), but *Bebee v Sales* (1916) 32 TLR 413 (father liable for airgun fired by fifteen-year-old son when he failed to confiscate it after a previous incident).

[28] *North v Wood* [1914] 1 KB 629: father not liable for his seventeen-year-old daughter's failure to control her dog.

[29] [1955] AC 549 at 566.   [30] [2003] CLY 2976, CC (Birmingham).

and signify that every child would have to be locked into the space in which he was playing.

By requiring proof of fault, the common law has maintained its adherence to the view that parents should not be vicariously liable for their children. As Willes J famously stated in *Moon v Towers*:

> I am not aware of any such relation between a father and son, though the son be living with his father as a member of his family, as will make the acts of the son more binding upon the father than the acts of anybody else. [31]

This lenient approach has unfortunate consequences for victims. The primary tortfeasor, that is the child, will rarely be found liable in his own right. Such is the dearth of litigation against minors that it was only in 1997 that the English Court of Appeal formally stated that the standard of care expected of a minor is that of the ordinary prudent and reasonable child of his age in his situation.[32] It is unsurprising that so few cases arise in English law.

This position is to be contrasted with that of parents in criminal law. In recent years, the UK government has placed more emphasis on encouraging parents to take responsibility for the criminal acts of their children and to force parents to recognise their duty to care and control their own offspring.[33] A parent or guardian may thus be required to pay the fine, costs or compensation imposed by the court,[34] or may even be bound over if this is considered desirable in the interests of preventing

---

[31] (1860) 8 CB (NS) 611, 144 ER 1306 per Willes J at 615. See J. G. Fleming, *The law of torts*, 9th edn (Sydney: LBC Information Services, 1998), pp. 748–9.

[32] *Mullin v Richards* [1998] 1 WLR 1304, relying on the Australian case of *McHale v Watson* (1966) 115 CLR 199 and case law on contributory negligence and children (see *Gough v Thorne* [1966] 1 WLR 1387). The decision itself appears lenient – fifteen-year-old girl not able to foresee injury due to plastic ruler breaking during a play fight. See also *Etheridge v K (a minor)* [1999] Ed CR 550 and *Orchard v Lee* [2009] EWCA Civ 295, [2009] PIQR P16.

[33] For a critical study, see K. Hollingsworth, 'Responsibility and rights: children and their parents in the youth justice system', *International Journal of Law, Policy and the Family*, 21 (2007), 190 and R. Leng, 'Parental responsibility for juvenile offending in English law' in R. Probert, S. Gilmore and J. Herring (eds.), *Responsible parents and parental responsibility* (Oxford: Hart, 2009). See, generally, A. Bainham, *Children: the modern law*, 3rd edn (Bristol: Jordan, 2005), ch. 14.

[34] Powers of Criminal Courts (Sentencing) Act 2000, s. 137 (power to order parent or guardian to pay fine, costs, compensation or surcharge). See *R v JJB* [2004] EWCA Civ 14, [2004] 2 Cr App Rev (S) 41 on the application of s. 137 of the 2000 Act. Note also the introduction of parental compensation orders on the application of local authorities: see Crime and Disorder Act 1998, ss. 13A-13E (as inserted by Serious Organised Crime and Police Act 2005).

the commission by the minor of further offences.[35] Parenting orders,[36] which require parents to attend a counselling or guidance programme and, when necessary, comply with certain specified requirements, and parenting contracts[37] form part of the current armoury of criminal courts to involve parents in the punishment of their children. Thus, by imposing financial burdens on parents or prescribing particular courses of action, criminal law, at least, is prepared to hold parents answerable to a certain extent for the criminal activities of their children. Nevertheless, such measures are seen as controversial. Some commentators have suggested that parenting orders may be seen 'as fundamentally authoritarian, an attack on civil liberties and an extraordinary invasion by the State into family autonomy'.[38] It is also unclear to what extent the courts are prepared to ignore the absence of fault by the parent.[39]

7.3 Finding a framework for parental responsibility in tort law

The common law's response to parental liability is therefore limited, at least in tort law. In relation to third party victims, the courts will seek evidence of fault and, in setting the standard of care, will take account

---

[35] Powers of Criminal Courts (Sentencing) Act 2000, s. 150: duty to consider binding over of parent or guardian where offender is aged under 16. See s. 150(2): 'The powers conferred by this section are as follows – (a) with the consent of the offender's parent or guardian, to order the parent or guardian to enter into a recognizance to take proper care of him and exercise proper control over him; and (b) if the parent or guardian refuses consent and the court considers the refusal unreasonable, to order the parent or guardian to pay a fine not exceeding £1,000; and where the court has passed on the offender a sentence which consists of or includes a youth rehabilitation order, it may include in the recognizance a provision that the offender's parent or guardian ensure that the offender complies with the requirements of that sentence.'

[36] Crime and Disorder Act 1998, ss. 8 and 9. There is a duty to consider making such an order if the child is less than 16 and convicted of an offence and give reasons if this option is not chosen: s. 9(1). Such orders are consistent with Article 8, European Convention on Human Rights: *R (on the application of M) v Inner London Crown Court* [2003] EWHC 301, [2003] 1 FLR 994.

[37] These involve agreements between parents and the local education authority or the governing body of a relevant school in case of exclusion or truancy or youth offending teams in case of criminal conduct or anti-social behaviour by which the parent states his agreement to comply with such requirements as may be specified in the contract. See Anti-Social Behaviour Act 2003 in case of exclusion from school or truancy (s. 19) or arising out of criminal conduct or anti-social behaviour (s. 25). Sections 20 and 26 deal with parenting orders in such circumstances.

[38] Bainham, *Children: the modern law*, p. 640.

[39] See *R v JJB* [2004] EWCA Civ 14, [2004] 2 Cr App Rev (S) 41 on the application of s. 137 of the 2000 Act. See also *TA v DPP* [1997] 1 Cr App R (S) 1.

of the difficulties of bringing up children whilst running a house and, presumably in more recent times, with both parents working. Although the cases depict a somewhat stereotypical picture of childcare – a harassed mother plus screaming child – it is, in practice, difficult to bring a successful case against a parent. It is hardly surprising that the majority of claims are, in reality, brought against schools, as either primarily or vicariously liable for the negligence of their teachers, or other professional bodies taking responsibility for childcare.[40] Although the same lenient standard of care is often applied to the actual carer, it is far easier to identify systemic negligence as a basis for imposing liability. In *Carmarthenshire CC v Lewis*,[41] for example, although the teacher was not liable for leaving a four-year-old boy alone, the House of Lords viewed the school's failure to secure a gate which gave onto the public highway as negligent, thus entitling the widow of the lorry driver, who had swerved to avoid the child and was tragically killed as a result, to recover damages.

The remainder of this chapter will question *why* the common law has generally refrained from imposing vicarious liability on parents. One reason has already been raised – the judiciary seems to feel inadequate to judge the difficulties of parenting and has adopted a generous approach towards liability. Yet, one might question whether parents should be let off so lightly. Parenting brings with it responsibilities, together with an awareness that young children, in particular, do not appreciate the risks and dangers of life and need to be both protected against these dangers and prevented from causing injury to others. In view of the increased expectations of parents in criminal law through parenting orders and parenting contracts, is it not the time for the common law to recognise that a greater burden should lie on parents? As will be shown below, the majority of other European legal systems do not favour the approach of the common law courts. It cannot therefore simply be assumed that parents should

---

[40] Case law also indicates that other bodies may be found liable, for example, a shopkeeper in *Burfitt v Kille* [1939] 2 KB 743 who sold a twelve-year-old a safety-pistol and 100 blank cartridges was found liable for the injury the boy caused to his friend when firing the pistol into the air. Much will depend on the potential danger presented by the item sold: *Ricketts v Erith BC* [1943] 2 All ER 629 (shopkeeper not liable for selling ten-year-old boy makeshift bow and arrow).

[41] [1955] AC 549. See also *J (a child) v North Lincolnshire CC* [2000] PIQR P84, using *res ipsa loquitur* to assist the claimant. Also *Ward v Hertfordshire CC* [1969] 1 WLR 790 and *Barnes v Hampshire CC* [1969] 1 WLR 1563. See, generally, *Clerk & Lindsell on Torts*, 19th edn (London: Sweet and Maxwell, 2006), 8-174 to 8-178.

not be vicariously liable for the torts of their children. The question will be approached in two parts. First, the different models for parental responsibility in tort will be examined. Two models may be identified by which parental liability for the wrongful acts of their children is recognised.[42] Secondly, the justifications for these models will be considered. When and why do we impose liability on parents and, most importantly, what are the consequences of the imposition of such liability? Does such liability amount to an attack on parental autonomy or a sensible recognition of the need to provide a satisfactory compensatory framework for the harm children may cause to innocent bystanders?

In the models outlined below, the key distinction is between systems which require fault on the part of the parent (and/or child) and those which are prepared to impose a form of strict liability on the parent. The choice between these options is inevitably based on policy and the difficult balance between parental autonomy and victim protection. The question of liability must therefore be approached with the full recognition that children not only are often incapable of appreciating risks to themselves, but are equally capable of causing injury to others. How a legal system deals with this question thus casts light on its views of corrective and distributive justice.

Model One imposes liability on the parent on the basis of fault. This produces two variants: (a) where the burden is on the claimant to establish fault in the parent's supervision of the child; and (b) where the court presumes fault and the burden is on the parent to demonstrate that he or she has taken reasonable care to supervise the child.

Model Two imposes vicarious or strict liability on the parent. Again two variants may be identified: (a) in which the parent is held strictly liable for the torts of his or her child; and (b) in which the parent is liable for *any* acts of the child which harm another, subject to very limited defences such as *force majeure*.

Whilst it is possible to identify more subcategories of liability, those stated above represent the main approaches currently adopted in common and civil law and will be examined below in more detail, with reference to representative legal systems.

---

[42] These models may be contrasted with the slightly different formulation adopted by J.-P. Le Gall, 'Liability for the acts of minors' in A. Tunc (chief ed.), *International encyclopedia of comparative law* (Tübingen: Mohr, 1983), vol. XI, Torts, ch. 3.

7.3.1 Model One: fault-based liability – English and German law

The first variant of this model has been outlined above. Liability is based on proof of fault. Responsibility thus rests on the parent's assumption of control over the child and a failure to exercise reasonable care in the circumstances will justify the imposition of liability.

Yet, as seen in relation to the common law, much depends on what the courts require in terms of reasonable care. The approach of the common law courts is generally quite generous. Parents are not expected to meet the standard and vigilance of a trained childcare expert and allowances are made for the challenges of the inexperienced and untrained in caring for children. Whilst it is difficult to establish clear standards due to the lack of case law and the tendency of courts to concentrate on the actual facts of the case, the judiciary does appear willing to make allowances, particularly in relation to small children and recognises that less supervision is required of older children who are expected to take greater responsibility for their own actions.

German law provides a useful contrast to the common law.[43] Liability is based on fault, but with a reversed burden of proof. Parents will thus be liable unless they can prove that they were not at fault. § 832 of the German Civil Code (BGB) provides that:

(Liability arising from the duty to supervise/*Haftung des Aufsichtspflichtigen*)

(1) A person who is bound by law to exercise supervision over a person who needs supervision by reason of minority, or by reason of his mental or physical condition, is bound to make compensation for any damage which the latter unlawfully[44] causes to a third party. The duty to make compensation does not arise if he fulfils his duty of supervision, or if

---

[43] See, generally, G. Brüggemeier, *Haftungsrecht: Struktur, Prinzipien, Schutzbereich* (Heidelburg: Springer, 2006), pp. 527–30; M. J. Schmid, 'Die Aufsichtspflicht nach § 832, BGB', VersR 1982, 822; and D Haberstroh, 'Haftungsrisiko Kind – Eigenhaftung des Kindes und elterliche Aufsichtspflicht', VersR 2000, 806.

[44] Liability is thus conditional on an objectively 'unlawful' act by the minor infringing one of the interests protected by § 823, but the child need not be personally charged with fault. Liability will be excluded in cases where the injury was caused by behaviour by the child which would not amount to wrongful if performed by an adult: G. Wagner, 'Children as tortfeasors under German law' in M. Martin-Casals (ed.), *Children in tort law Part I: children as tortfeasors* (Vienna: SpringerWienNewYork, 2006), para. 68.

the damage would have occurred notwithstanding the exercise of proper supervision.[45]

(2) The same responsibility attaches to a person who undertakes the supervision by contract.[46]

Two conditions must be satisfied. First, the person in question must be bound by law to exercise supervision over the child. §§ 1626(1)[47] and 1631 (1) of the BGB establish the parental right to custody which will suffice. In particular, § 1631(1) specifies that parental care (*elterliche Sorge*) includes the duty to supervise the child. Liability thus arises from this right, and residence with the parent is not a requirement. Secondly, the child must have caused harm to a third party. If these conditions are satisfied, the burden then falls on the parent(s) to satisfy the court that either reasonable care has been taken and the duty of supervision fulfilled or that the damage would have occurred in any event. The burden of proof is therefore placed on the parent to exonerate himself or herself from a claim for negligence.

It is interesting to note that, in practice, commentators do not feel that much hinges on this reversal of the burden of proof. Gerhard Wagner comments that:

... the reversal of the burden of proof provided by §832 subs.1 BGB does not really change much. Its main effect is that once the court has fixed the scope of the duty to supervise it is for the parents to prove that they did in fact take all the safety measures required. In this respect, the allocation of the burden of proof to the parents comes naturally as the victim has no access to the sphere of family life and thus lacks the relevant information. In practice, cases rarely turn on the burden of proof.[48]

---

[45] '(1) Wer kraft Gesetzes zur Führung der Aufsicht über eine Person verpflichtet ist, die wegen Minderjährigkeit oder wegen ihres geistigen oder körperlichen Zustands der Beaufsichtigung bedarf, ist zum Ersatz des Schadens verpflichtet, den diese Person einem Dritten widerrechtlich zufügt. Die Ersatzpflicht tritt nicht ein, wenn er seiner Aufsichtspflicht genügt oder wenn der Schaden auch bei gehöriger Aufsichtsführung entstanden sein würde.' Note the similarities with § 831 (discussed in previous chapters).

[46] Those paid to care for children are thus expressly dealt with under the Code, although the courts have been anxious to exclude neighbours helping temporarily with childcare from such provisions: see Landsgericht Karlsruhe in [1981] VersR, 142 (143). Liability, it will be noted, is not confined to parents.

[47] Parental care of custody includes both care of the child (*Personensorge*) and care of the child's property (*Vermögenssorge*): '(1) Die Eltern haben die Pflicht und das Recht, für das minderjährige Kind zu sorgen (elterliche Sorge). Die elterliche Sorge umfasst die Sorge für die Person des Kindes (Personensorge) und das Vermögen des Kindes (Vermögenssorge).' See also § 1672 (living apart where the mother has parental custody). For guardians and carers, see §§ 1793, 1797, 1800, 1909ff, 1915.

[48] See Wagner, 'Children as tortfeasors', para. 51.

The examples arising in the case law are similar to those arising in English law. Both systems adopt an objective standard of care, which takes account of the particular circumstances of the case and the age of the minor. The standard is that of the reasonably prudent parent in the particular situation.[49] The German courts place particular emphasis on the facts of each case, examining 'the age, disposition, characteristics, development, education and all other individual features of the minor'.[50] Markesinis notes that the phraseology used is deliberately vague to permit flexibility, but that 'it should not conceal a discernible trend in recent cases to raise the standard of care expected of modern parents'.[51] A number of cases have focused on the question of the parental duty of supervision in relation to matches, due to the known attraction of children to fire (and the severe damage which can result). Case law indicates that parents should inform children of the dangers associated with playing with fire and ensure that matches are stored out of reach of the child.[52] One case even suggests that a search of the child's body may be necessary if it is believed that the child has taken the matches and has a tendency to play with them.[53] In contrast, explicit orders to a child who is generally obedient and law-abiding may serve to rebut the presumption of fault.[54] This suggests the existence of a more stringent approach than that which is adopted in England, giving priority to the prevention of harm rather than parental discretion to deal with problems as they deem fit.

This assumption appears to be vindicated in the ECTIL[55] study of liability for damage caused by others.[56] National reporters were asked, inter alia, to consider how the courts would deal with a parent who gives his thirteen-year-old child an air rifle with proper instructions on safety. On the basis of the English firearm cases examined in 7.2.2, it is

---

[49] BGH (29 May 1990) BGHZ 11, 282; BGH (26 January 1960) [1960] VersR, 355, 356; BGH (27 October 1965) [1965] VersR 48. BGHZ 111, 282, 285 = NJW 1990, 2553: 'was verständige Eltern nach vernünftigen Anforderungen im konkreten Fall unternehmen müssen, um die Schädigung Dritter durch ihr Kind zu verhindern.'
[50] See RGZ 52, 73 and BGH MDR 1997, 643.
[51] See B. S. Markesinis, *The German law of obligations*, 3rd edn (Oxford: Clarendon Press, 1997), vol. II, The law of torts, p. 899.
[52] BGH Vers R 1983, 734 (parents of seven-year-old liable for fire child caused using easily accessible matches), BGH (28 February 1969) [1969] MDR 564; BGH (17 May 1983) [1983] NJW 2821; BGH (1 July 1986) [1987] NJW-RR 13, 14.
[53] BGH (1 July 1986) [1987] NJW-RR 13, 14.
[54] See OLG Frankfurt (28 March 2001) [2001] MDR, 752.
[55] European Centre of Tort and Insurance Law, based in Vienna.
[56] Spier (ed.), *Unification of tort law*.

unsurprising that the English reporter found that where the parent has given clear instructions and told the teenager not to use the weapon in the open, the parent will generally not be found liable.[57] Fedke and Magnus, however, giving the German response, opine that the parent would be held liable under § 832 due to the high standard of care required for dangerous objects such as bows and arrows, catapults and air rifles.[58] They note that 'some academics go as far as to claim that dangerous objects of this kind simply do not belong in the hands of minors'.[59] The English courts have refused to go this far. Different perceptions therefore exist as to what is acceptable parental behaviour. This will vary according to the social practices of each particular jurisdiction.

The main difference between English and German law lies, in fact, in the greater ability of victims to seek compensation from the child, despite the protection given in § 828.[60] Under § 829 (*Ersatzpflicht aus Billigkeitsgründen*),[61] the courts may impose subsidiary liability in equity on the child where the victim is unable to recover from the third party supervising the child and the child is not deprived of sufficient means for his own upkeep. This is despite the fact that he is not liable in law. This provision is interpreted broadly by the courts to include any circumstances where the minor would be liable but for his age, but is confined to the sum which 'equity' requires.

Nevertheless, both systems recognise that while parents assume responsibility for their children and are best placed to supervise and prevent their children causing harm to others, liability may only be justified on the basis of fault. In practice, much will depend on the standard of care expected of parents and the assessment by the court of each particular case. Although English law adopts a more objective approach to that of the German courts, a close reading of the cases indicates that this is not always

---

[57] Rogers, 'Liability for damage'.
[58] J. Fedke and U. Magnus, 'Liability for damage caused by others under German law' in Spier (ed.), *Unification of tort law*, para. 32.
[59] Ibid.
[60] A child will not be liable in tort below the age of seven (rising to ten in traffic accidents): see § 828 BGB. For a comparative study of the imputability of fault to children, see Brüggemeier, *Haftungsrecht*, pp. 33ff.
[61] 'Wer in einem der in den §§ 823 bis 826 bezeichneten Fälle für einen von ihm verursachten Schaden auf Grund der §§ 827, 828 nicht verantwortlich ist, hat gleichwohl, sofem der Ersatz des Schadens nicht von einem aufsichtspflichtigen Dritten erlangt warden kann, den Schaden insoweit zu ersetzen, als die Billigkeit nach den Umständen, insbesondere nach den Verhältnissen der Beteiligten, eine Schadloshaltung erfordert und ihm nicht die Mittel entzogen werden, deren er zum angemessenen Unterhalt sowie zur Erfüllung seiner gesetzlichen Unterhaltspflichten bedarf.'

adhered to in practice.[62] Fault-based liability gives flexibility and discretion to the courts to set a standard of parental care deemed appropriate in modern society.

7.3.2 Model Two: vicarious or strict liability – English, Spanish and French law

This model imposes liability without fault on the parent; the parental relationship justifying the imposition of strict liability for the harm caused by the child. It takes two forms. Liability is imposed either for the *torts* of the child or simply the *acts* of the child. This distinction may appear to be fine, but is significant in practice. Few examples exist of strict parental liability for the torts of their children. Perhaps surprisingly in view of the frequent statements that parental vicarious liability does not exist in English law,[63] some instances may be found in English law. A parent will be liable if he or she authorises or ratifies the torts of the child, although, as stated in previous chapters, such liability is best described as primary, not vicarious, liability, despite the wording used by the courts.[64] Genuine vicarious liability will arise where the parent employs the child and the child commits the tort in the course of his employment. The reason for such liability, however, is not the parent/child relationship, but the employment context. No distinction is made between a child and other employees, save that the law of contract determines that, whilst a minor may enter a contract of service, it will only be binding if found to be beneficial to him.[65] There is no reason why vicarious liability cannot arise on the basis of such a relationship provided, of course, that the minor is capable of committing the tort in question.

In contrast, Spain has enacted a specific provision in Article 61.3 of the Organic Act on Criminal Liability of Minors (*Ley Orgánica 5/2000, Reguladora de responsabilidad penal de los menores*) which renders the parent jointly and severally liable for the torts of a child, who is younger than

---

[62] See, for example, *Ricketts v Erith BC* [1943] 2 All ER 629 and *Gorely v Codd* [1967] 1 WLR 19.
[63] For example, Lord Goddard CJ in *Donaldson v McNiven* [1952] 2 All ER 691 at 692 remarked that 'Some people have thought that parents ought to be responsible for the torts of their children, but they are not'.
[64] *Moon v Towers* (1860) 8 CB (NS) 611, 144 ER 1306; *Gray v Fisher* [1922] SASR 246.
[65] See, for example, *Clements v London & North Western Railway Co.* [1894] 2 QB 482 and *Slade v Metrodent* [1953] 2 QB 112 (QBD). Contrast *De Francesco v Barnum* (1890) 45 Ch D 430: contract placed inordinate power in hands of apprentice-master, which was not for the infant's benefit.

18 but older than 14, which amount to a crime or misdemeanour.[66] Vicarious liability in this context has, however, received criticism. Martin-Casals, Ribot and Feliu comment that 'it seems completely unreasonable to link criminal liability of the child with a strict liability regime, since more maturity of judgment in fact means that the parents have less means to control the conduct of their children'.[67] Such specific provisions are unusual and resemble, to some extent, the criminal law provisions enacted in England. They also raise the same difficulties of practical implementation: can a parent really control a criminally active fifteen-year-old? Liability for other torts does not, however, rest on vicarious liability but proof of fault by the parent,[68] albeit with a reversed burden of proof.[69] Parents may thus avoid liability by proving that they acted with all due care to avoid the harm caused by the child. In practice, however, the application of Article 1903 Código Civil español has come to resemble quasi-strict liability.[70] The courts have been reluctant to accept proof of exculpation, rendering rebuttal of the presumption of fault a 'purely theoretical possibility'.[71]

The few examples of vicarious liability which exist indicate that the traditional model of vicarious liability does not lend itself easily to the parent/child relationship. The parent is usually targeted not simply because he or she has the means to fund compensation, but because it is difficult to establish tortious liability on the part of

---

[66] M. Martin-Casals, J. Ribot and J. S. Feliu, 'Children as tortfeasors in Spanish law' in Martin-Casals (ed.), *Children in tort*, para. 66.
[67] Ibid., para. 66, n. 80.
[68] Art. 1903 II Código Civil español: '*Los padres son responsables de los daños causados por los hijos que se encuentren bajo su guarda.*' (parents are responsible for the damage caused by their children who are under their guard). Parents will be liable for acts which are objectively negligent even if the child has no tortious capacity: see M. Martin Casals and J. S. Feliu, 'Liability for damage caused by others under Spanish law' in Spier (ed.), *Unification of tort law*, para. 25.
[69] Art. 1903 VI, Código Civil español: '*La responsabilidad de que trata este artículo cesará cuando las personas en él mencionadas prueben que emplearon toda la diligencia de un buen padre de familia para prevenir el daño.*' (The liability referred to in this article shall cease when the persons mentioned in it prove that they employed all the care of a reasonable person to prevent the damage).
[70] See TS 17 June 1980, RAJ 1980 (1) No. 2409, p.1874; TS 10 March 1983, RAJ 1983 (1) No. 1469, p. 1128. Liability has been described as based on risk: TS 22 January 1991, RAJ 1991 (1) No. 304, p. 333.
[71] See C. von Bar and E. Clive (eds.), *Principles, definitions and model rules of European private law: Draft Common Frame of Reference (DCFR). Full Edition* (Munich: Sellier, 2009), pp. 3440–1 (hereafter DCFR).

the minor. Here, there is a clear contrast with the employer/employee relationship, where generally no question as to the capacity of the employee to commit a tort will arise. Children, however, are problematic tortfeasors. They often lack the capacity to be sued in their own right either due to legislative restrictions on age,[72] or due to practical difficulties in proving that the child satisfies the conditions of liability. For example, the child may not possess sufficient intention or foresight to establish liability for intentional torts or negligence. More fundamentally, a society might also have moral and social objections to imposing liability on children due to their age and inexperience. The French legislator overcame this obstacle in relation to mentally handicapped persons by applying an objective standard of care, which ignored their individual incapacities.[73] As we will see, in relation to children, the French courts have gone further and removed any requirement of fault on behalf of the child. Such steps are controversial and represent a willingness to favour distributive justice above the demands of corrective justice. Further, they do not diminish other evidential problems, such as determining what actually happened when young witnesses are involved.

While such problems lessen as the child approaches maturity, the reality is that strict liability for the *torts* of children would cover only a limited number of cases and would place the question of the capacity of the child at the centre of legal discourse. Such liability would appear to be of limited utility and cumbersome. Vicarious liability in the sense used in this book would therefore not appear a desirable option for the common law.

However, whilst vicarious liability for children falters on difficulties of proving fault, it is submitted that the true choice lies between retaining fault-based liability or rendering parents strictly liable for harmful acts of their children. Here, strict liability fulfils the same goals as vicarious liability for employees' misconduct. There is a distribution of social risk, an allocation of responsibility encouraging

---

[72] Consider, for example, § 828(1) BGB: 'A person who has not reached the age of seven is not responsible for damage caused to another person.' § 828(2) adds: 'A person who has reached the age of seven but not the age of ten is not responsible for damage that he inflicts on another party in an accident involving a motor vehicle, a railway or a suspension railway. This does not apply if he intentionally caused the injury.'

[73] Art. 489–2, Civil Code: 'A person who has caused damage to another when he was under the influence of a mental disorder is nonetheless liable to compensation.' See G. Viney RTD civ. 1970.263 and J.-J. Burst JCP 1970 I 2307 No 51.

greater preventative measures and the creation of a single source of compensation. This latter situation exists in France. In 1997, the French courts, despite the wording of the Civil Code, chose to impose strict liability on parents for the acts of their children causing harm to others. The impact of this decision will now be examined.

7.3.3 Strict liability – French law after 1997

The example of French law is particularly useful in this context. In contrast to the common law system, the question of parental liability for children has received considerable attention,[74] which cannot simply be explained due to express provision for such liability in the 1804 Code. As amended, Article 1384 of the Code now reads:

(4) The father and mother, in so far as they exercise 'parental authority', are jointly and severally liable for the damage caused by their minor children who live with them.[75]

(7) The above liability exists, unless the father and mother ... prove that they could not prevent the act which gives rise to that liability.[76]

Prior to 1997, this provision was interpreted consistently with the second variant of Model One – fault-based liability with a reversed burden of proof. The burden was on the parents to establish that the harm was not due to a failure to take reasonable steps to look after or educate their child (*faute de surveillance ou d'éducation*).[77] Liability, it was intended, would encourage fathers to take responsibility for their families and, by so doing, bring up good and virtuous French citizens.[78] Until the 1980s, it was accepted that liability would be

---

[74] The literature is voluminous, but see, in particular, P.-D. Ollier, *La responsabilité civile des père et mère. Etude critique de son régime légal* (Paris: LGDJ, 1961); D. Layré, 'La responsabilité du fait du mineur', thèse, Paris I (1983); J. Julien, *La responsabilité civile du fait d'autrui: ruptures et continuités* (Presses universitaires d'Aix-Marseille, 2001); M.-C. Lebreton, 'L'enfant et la responsabilité civile', thèse, Rouen (1996).

[75] '*Le père et la mère, en tant qu'ils exercent l'autorité parentale, sont solidairement responsables du dommage causé par leurs enfants mineurs habitant avec eux.*' As amended by the loi N° 70–459 of 4 June 1970 and loi N° 2002–305 of 4 March 2002.

[76] '*La responsabilité ci-dessus a lieu, à moins que les père et mère et les artisans ne prouvent qu'ils n'ont pu empêcher le fait qui donne lieu à cette responsabilité.*' As amended by the loi of 5 April 1937.

[77] Civ 2, 12 October 1955 JCP 1955 II 9003 note P. Esmein; D 1956.301 note R. Rodière.

[78] '*Puisse cette charge de la responsabilité rendre les chefs de famille plus prudents et plus attentifs ... La vie que nos enfants tiennent de nous, n'est plus un bienfait, si nous ne les formons pas à la vertu, et si nous n'en faisons pas de bons citoyens*': Treilhard, exposé des motifs, séance du Corps Législatif du 9 pluviôse an XII (30 January 1803).

confined to tortious acts of the child, consistent with the primacy of fault and individual responsibility which lie at the heart of the 1804 Code.[79]

However, over time, the courts have moved from liability based on a presumption of fault to imposing strict liability on parents, without, it must be said, any fundamental change to the wording of the relevant provisions of the Civil Code. From the 1960s, one notes a willingness in the courts to favour the interests of victims over the strict requirements of fault.[80] This goes far beyond the tendency of the German and, especially, the Spanish courts to impose increasingly onerous standards of care of parents to avoid liability. Criticism was, in particular, directed at the application of the *faute de surveillance ou d'éducation* test from which it was extremely difficult to discern any consistent approach.[81]

Three particular cases mark the development of the current strict liability rule: the *Fullenwarth* decision of 1984,[82] the *Bertrand* decision of 1997[83] and the decision of the Assemblée Plénière in 2002.[84] In all three cases, the court chose to adopt an approach which diminished the relevance of fault in favour of comprehensive protection for victims.

In the *Fullenwarth* decision of the Assemblée Plénière, Pascal, a seven-year-old boy, injured his friend whilst playing with a bow and arrow. The court found his parents liable under Article 1384(4), despite the fact that it had not been shown that Pascal had appreciated that his act was wrongful. In finding a 'presumption of liability' – a very different phrase from 'presumption of fault' which the courts had previously used – the court stated:

---

[79] See Article 1382: 'Any act which causes harm to another obliges the person whose fault caused the harm to make reparation.'
[80] See G. Viney and P. Jourdain, *Traité de droit civil: les conditions de la responsabilité*, 3rd edn (Paris: LGDJ, 2006), N° 870.
[81] See, for example, A. Tunc, 'L'enfant et la balle', JCP 1966 I 1983.
[82] Ass plén 9 May 1984 (2nd case) D 1984.525 concl J. Cabannes, note F. Chabas, (1st case) JCP 1984 II 20255 note N. Dejean de la Bâtie.
[83] Civ 2, 19 February 1997 Bull civ II N° 56 p. 32; JCP 1997 II 22848 concl R. Kessous, note G. Viney, D 1997.265 note P. Jourdain, chron 297 par Ch. Radé (giving a strong defence of the judgment) and Somm 290 obs D. Mazeaud; [1997] Resp civ et assur, chron 9 par F. Leduc; [1997] Gaz Pal 2 572 note F. Chabas; RTD civ. 1997.648 obs J. Hauser and 668 obs P. Jourdain.
[84] Cass Ass Plén 13 December 2002 Bull Ass plén N° 4, p. 7; JCP 2003 II 10010 note A. Hervio-Lelong; D 2003 Jur 231 note P. Jourdain; Droit et Patrimoine February 2003 obs F. Chabas.

... for the liability of the father and mother of a minor who is living with them to be presumed, on the basis of Article 1384(4) of the *Code civil*, it is sufficient that the latter has committed an act which is the direct cause of the damage suffered by the victim.[85]

No mention is made of fault in this statement. The presumption of liability arises on establishing a direct causal link between the injury suffered by the victim and the act of the child. Subsequent courts exhibited some disquiet at this apparent movement away from fault-based liability. Dejean de la Bâtie, in his note to the case, questioned whether this was in fact the intention of the court. Nevertheless, the Supreme Court in 2001 confirmed the new approach: proof of the capacity of the child to appreciate the wrongful nature of his act would not be required.[86]

The *Bertrand* case of 1997 took a further step away from fault-based liability: liability on the parent would be strict. In the case itself, Sébastien, aged twelve, had collided with a moped whilst cycling onto a main road. The father argued that the Bordeaux Court of Appeal had been wrong in failing to consider whether he could show that the accident was not due to any fault on his behalf. The Supreme Court disagreed. The question of fault was irrelevant. In the absence of *force majeure* or contributory negligence, the parent would be held strictly liable. No other excuse would suffice.

The implications of this decision are profound. Parents will be liable for their children during the age of minority, that is, up to the age of 18.[87] Only if they can show that an external, unforeseeable and unavoidable event occurred (*force majeure*)[88] or that the victim himself

---

[85] The first decision of the Assemblée plénière (*l'affaire Gabillet*) goes even further – a three-year-old child is found to have custody of a stick such that he may be found liable under Article 1384(1), Civil code, when the stick struck his playmate in the eye: see Ass plén 9 May 1984 (1st case) JCP 1984 II 20255 note N. Dejean de la Bâtie. Article 1384(1) provides that 'A person is liable not only for the damages he causes by his own act, but also for that which is caused by the acts of persons for whom he is responsible, or by things which are in his custody.'

[86] See Civ 2, 10 May 2001 (*Levert*) Bull civ II N° 96; D 2001 Jur 2851 rapp P. Guerder, note O. Tournafond; JCP 2001 II 10613 note J. Mouly; D 2002 somm 1315 obs D. Mazeaud; JCP 2002 I 124 N° 20 obs G. Viney; RTD civ. 2001.601 note P. Jourdain.

[87] Parental authority may also be terminated by emancipation of the child: Art. 371-1, Code civil.

[88] Which the courts have interpreted strictly: see the classic case of Sté Aube-Cristal (Civ 2, 2 December 1998) Bull civ II N° 292, p. 176; D 1999 IR 29; JCP 1999 II 10165 note M. Josselin-Gall; RTD civ. 1999.410 obs P. Jourdain (child accompanied by mother

was at fault,[89] will liability be avoided. Evidence of excellent childcare or supervision will be ignored. Liability is strict.

Under the amended Article 1384(4), however, liability will only be imposed on those exercising 'parental authority'[90] – a phrase which signifies recognition of the diversity of modern parenting. On this basis, one of the corollaries of 'parental authority' is strict liability. This applies whenever such authority is being exercised. However, if, on divorce, only one party is given parental authority, the other parent will no longer be liable under Article 1384(4), even if the damage is caused by the child during a trip to visit the other parent.[91] Equally, where the child is placed in a home or with foster parents as a result of a court decision, the parents will no longer be deemed to exercise parental authority.

Parental authority does not end, however, when the child engages in activities outside the home. In the decision of the Assemblée Plénière in 2002, the fact that the child was in school under the supervision of a schoolteacher made no difference: parental authority continued and the father thus remained strictly liable for an accident caused by his son, Grégory, despite the fact that it took place during a physical education lesson.[92] Here, the court took the opportunity to reinforce the test established by the second chamber of the French Supreme Court: only *force majeure* or contributory negligence can exonerate from liability parents exercising parental control over a minor living with them.[93] This has led a number of commentators to question the relevance of the additional condition for parental liability: that the child 'lives' with his parents when the incident takes place.[94] Article 1384(4) states that 'The father and mother . . . are jointly and severally liable for the damage caused by their

---

slipping in shop for no known reason and knocking over a display cabinet did not amount to *force majeure*).

[89] See Civ 2, 29 April 2004 Bull civ 2004 II N° 202 p. 170; D 2004 IR 1429. Note that this does not include third party contributory negligence which is usually a defence to strict liability in French law.

[90] See Art. 372, Code civil (inserted by *loi* N° 2002-305 of 4 March 2002).

[91] See l'arrêt SAMDA (Civ 2, 19 February 1997) Bull civ 1997 II N° 55; Gaz Pal 1997, 2, 575 note F. Chabas; JCP 1997 IV 834; RTD civ. 1997.670 obs P. Jourdain.

[92] See also Civ 2, 3 July 2003 Bull civ 2003 II N° 230 p. 191; JCP 2003 II 10009 note R. Desgorces (schoolboy injuring friend in play-fight organised and supervised by PE teacher). An alternative action can be brought against the schoolteacher, but will require proof of fault.

[93] Note also the second case here: liability for accident which occurred during an improvised game of rugby.

[94] See M. Fabre-Magnan, *Les obligations* (Paris: PUF, 2004), p. 324. Viney argues at N 876 that the condition should be removed, but this would require legislative intervention due to the wording of Article 1384(4): see Viney and Jourdain *Traité de droit civil*.

minor children *who live with them*.[95] This requirement was relevant when liability rested on the question of whether the parent had properly supervised the child, but in view of the modern interpretation of 'parental authority', this appears to have minimal importance. Recent case law has modified the so-called cohabitation condition to signify a situation where the child 'usually' lives with his parents,[96] but in reality little tends to turn on this condition. The 2005 proposals to reform the French Civil Code[97] recommended, in Article 1356, that the cohabitation condition should be removed due to the difficulties in defining its meaning and anomalies in its application.[98] This reform has not, however, been implemented.

The burden on French parents is thus considerable. As Aline Vignon-Barrault has commented, 'the child is henceforth regarded by virtue of his immaturity and lack of solvency as constituting a risk for others, a risk against which his parents are obliged to provide a guarantee against any harmful consequences.'[99]

7.4 Which model should a legal system utilise?

The two models discussed above demonstrate very different views of the parent/child relationship. In the first model, the courts set a standard of care which the parent must attain. Liability is justified

---

[95] Emphasis added.
[96] Termed '*la résidence habituelle*'. Civ 2, 20 January 2000 Bull civ II N° 14; D 2000 somm 469 obs D. Mazeaud; JCP 2000 II 10374 note A. Gouttenoire-Cornut; JCP 2000 I 241 obs G. Viney; D 2000 IR 61; Resp civ et assur 2000 N° 146 note H. Groutel; RTD civ. 2000. 340 note P. Jourdain. Confirmed Cass crim 29 October 2002 Bull crim N° 197; D 2003 Jur 2112. See also Cass crim 8 February 2005 Bull crim N° 44, p. 131; JCP 2005 II 10049 note M.-F. Steinlé-Feuerbach; JCP 2005 I 149 N° 5 obs G. Viney (thirteen-year-old child staying with grandmother from the age of one); Civ 2, 5 February 2004 Bull civ II N° 50, p. 41; RCA 2004 comm 127, Dr et patrimoine Oct 2004. 103 obs F. Chabas.
[97] P. Catala, *Avant-projet de réforme du droit des obligations et de la prescription* (Paris: La Documentation française, 2006): translation by S. Whittaker and J. Cartwright: www.justice.gouv.fr/art_pix/rapportcatatla0905-anglais.pdf.
[98] Ibid., at 179. Article 1356 provides that 'The following are liable for harm caused by their minor children: fathers and mothers to the extent to which they exercise parental authority...' See Ph. Le Tourneau, 'Les responsabilités du fait d'autrui dans l'avant-projet de réforme', *Revue des contrats* [2007], 109.
[99] A. Vignon-Barrault, *Juris Classeur responsabilité civile*: Fasc 141, *droit à réparation – responsabilité du fait d'autrui – domaine: responsabilité des père et mère* (Paris: LexisNexis, 2008), para. 7. See also F. Boulanger, 'Autorité parentale et responsabilité des père et mere des faits dommageables de l'enfant mineur après la réforme du 4 mars 2002. Réflexions critiques', D 2005.2245 and D. Mazeaud, 'Famille et responsabilité (réflexions sur quelques aspects de l'idéologie de reparation)' in *Le droit privé français à la fin du XXe siècle: Etudes offertes à Pierre Catala* (Paris: Litec, 2001), p. 569, who is critical of the reification of the child.

on the basis that the parent fails to meet this standard. A degree of flexibility clearly exists between systems, which is not solely attributable to the choice whether to place the burden of proof on the victim (English law) or the parent to rebut a presumption of fault (German and Spanish law). The second model manifests a very different view of parental liability as one that is depersonalised and victim-orientated. Such a model can only be funded by insurance. The choice, therefore, is practically between two options: either the parent is liable for fault in their care of the child (as we have seen, this imposes a standard of care which can vary according to national perceptions of the parenting role), or the parent is strictly liable for the acts of the child which harm another.

Each variant reflects key policy choices as to the nature of the burden which parents should bear in relation to damage caused by their children. The most significant gap is between the cautious English response and the strict liability imposed by the French courts. There is a striking difference in approach towards the question of what is expected of parents and the deemed role of tort law in setting standards of behaviour. Regardless of the care and precautions taken by parents in France, liability will persist if the child directly causes harm to another whilst living with his parents and subject to 'parental authority'.

Such divergences thus reflect a different perspective of the relationship between tort law and parental liability. Most fundamentally, distinct views clearly exist as to the extent to which family life should be subject to litigation and parents thereby held to account.[100] English law is characterised by the very few reported cases, which predominantly concern serious firearm accidents. A number of explanations may be given for such limited legal intervention. First, the courts are reluctant to become involved in domestic matters, where involvement is generally seen as a matter of family or criminal law. Family autonomy is seen as having particular value. Parents should therefore be permitted to bring up their children as they deem appropriate, subject to regulation by criminal law and the family courts. Tort law has thus a limited role. For parental liability, clear evidence of fault is required; the courts taking a very tolerant approach to the pressures of parenting. To this, one may add

---

[100] See Le Gall, 'Liability for the acts of minors', who notes the relevance of local traditions and the economic and social development of each individual country.

pragmatism. Small claims are unlikely to be pursued due to the uncertainties (and costs) of litigation; minor injuries are covered by free NHS treatment in any event. Even where serious injury or damage has been suffered, children and their parents are generally considered unlikely to possess liability insurance to cover accidents caused by their offspring. Oliphant has commented that this argument is misconceived in that a large proportion of parents and children are covered by liability insurance policies taken out by parents.[101] Even if this is so, this does not correct the general perception that such actions are not worth pursuing. Additionally, such insurance, in contrast to France, will usually exclude deliberate or criminal acts, which diminishes the impact of such cover in any event. In general, English law appears to take the view that liability is inconsistent with respect for parental autonomy, despite the fact that the introduction of parenting contracts and orders in criminal law signifies a move towards greater regulation of the family group.

French law, in contrast, demonstrates a very different attitude towards liability. Commentators such as Professors Viney and Jourdain have berated the justice system for failing to protect victims injured by the acts of minors.[102] The view is taken that children are, by their very nature, irresponsible and, particularly at an early age, lack the awareness and discernment to appreciate the existence of risks and how to avoid them. Parents are in a unique position to control and educate the child by virtue of the authority placed on them by law and to stop the child causing harm. On this basis, fault-based liability is inadequate to control those risks and protects parental autonomy at the expense of innocent citizens. As Jourdain explains in the note to the *Bertrand* case, children are likely to cause damage and rather than expecting the victim to meet the cost of such damage, parents, exercising legal authority over their children, should be held accountable.[103]

---

[101] K. Oliphant, 'England and Wales case note to *Cass Ass Plén* 13 December 2002', *European Review of Private Law*, 12 (2004), 718 at 724. Insurance cover may be obtained as part of the buildings insurance policy (liability as owner of building) or through the household contents policy, either as occupier or for personal liability, and it may extend to losses caused by immediate family. All are subject to caps: see www.abi.org.uk.

[102] Viney and Jourdain, *Traité de droit civil*, N° 887.

[103] See P. Jourdain D 1997.265. See also P. Jourdain D 2003 Jur 231 at para. 7: 'c'est parce que l'activité des mineurs, en raison de leur fragilité et de leur inexpérience, expose les tiers à des risques objectifs de dommage que l'on estime juste d'employer la responsabilité des parents.'

By accepting these arguments, the Supreme Court determined that liability could no longer be justified in terms of corrective justice or familial solidarity.[104] Parents, by virtue of their parental authority, take responsibility for the risks which might be caused by their offspring and therefore may be said to 'guarantee' their child against risks caused by his conduct. On this basis, victims so injured may seek compensation from the guarantor, subject to the doctrines of *force majeure* and contributory negligence. Although technically recourse may be made by the 'guarantor' to the 'original debtor', that is the parent may try to recover the damages paid from the child,[105] this occurs rarely in practice. Children will be unlikely to have sufficient funds and, most importantly, the Insurance Code prevents the insurer from seeking an indemnity from children.[106]

Such a step demonstrates a very different perception of the role of tort law from that seen in England. Civil law is seen as a means of providing a system of loss distribution based on social risk. The decision of the Supreme Court in October 2002 provides a startling example of the extent of parental liability for the criminal acts of one's offspring. Here, the mother had sent her son to a holiday centre which was 1,000 km from the family home. She was found liable for the thefts and violent acts committed by her son in the nearby camping site.[107]

Funding is met by insurance.[108] The avocat général Gouttes, prior to the 2002 decision of the Assemblée Plénière mentioned above, reminded the court that about 97 per cent of French citizens take out multi-risk

---

[104] For criticism, see H. Mazeaud D 1985 chron 13. See also H. Mazeaud et al., *Leçons de droit civil*, 9th edn (Paris: Montchrestien, 1998), tome II, vol. 1, *Obligations: théorie générale*, N° 497; and B. Starck, H. Roland and L. Boyer, *Droit civil: obligations*, 3rd edn (Paris: Litec, 1988), vol. I, *Responsabilité delictuelle*, N° 781.

[105] But see Rouen 7 May 2003 Res civ et assur Oct 2003 comm 54 par Ch. Radé. L. Francoz-Terminal, F. Lafay, O. Moréteau and C. Pellerin-Rugliano, 'Children as tortfeasors under French law' in Martin-Casals (ed.), *Children in tort*, paras. 129–33 stress the exceptional nature of this case, notably that the mother had been found liable for the criminal acts of a mature adolescent and that she was not insured.

[106] Article L121–12, Insurance Code.

[107] Cass crim 29 October 2002 D 2003 Jur 2112 note L. Mauger-Vielpeau; RTD civ. 2003.101 obs P. Jourdain; JCP 2002 IV 3080. See also Civ 2, 28 June 2000 Bull crim N° 256; D 2001 somm 2792 obs L. Dumaine; JCP 2000 I 280 obs G. Viney (divorced father liable for armed robberies of daughter after she had left home to live with her boyfriend with whom she had a child).

[108] Note, however, some concerns as to the possible increase in the level of insurance premiums: P. Jourdain D 2003 Jur 231 at 234: 'Increasing excessively parental liability... risks creating a serious increase in insurance premiums'. The *Commissions d'indemnisation des victimes d'infractions* (CIVI) and *Fonds de garantie des victimes des actes de terrorisme et autres infractions* also offer some supplementary support for victims: Articles 706–3 et ff, Code of Criminal Procedure.

home insurance,[109] which in 90 per cent of cases includes '*responsabilité civile familiale*', that is, liability for all damage caused by minors in their parents' care wherever it takes place.[110] Insurance will also cover intentional misconduct (*faute intentionnelle*).[111] In addition, schools will often insist on the provision of school insurance. The 1997 *Bertrand* decision has led to a significant decrease of litigation in this area and Galand-Carval has noted that the extreme narrowness of the *force majeure* defence is a powerful incentive for insurance companies to settle claims.[112] Gaps, however, will occur for about 10 per cent of citizens, usually the poorest in society, who do not possess insurance. Most commentators regard compulsory insurance as a necessary next step.[113] This, however, has yet to occur.

The French approach – putting the victim before family – does raise some difficult questions. It has been criticised for diminishing the personal responsibility of both the child and the parent and the normative role of civil justice. Parents, however financially precarious, in reality must purchase insurance or risk bankruptcy and liability is left in the hands of the insurance companies with their greater contracting power.[114] It may be questioned whether this, in fact, encourages parents to take greater responsibility for their children,[115] or simply forces them to bear the cost of injury, however vigilant they are. Concern has also been expressed at the so-called '*privatisation du droit*' in which compensation is, in reality, placed in the hands of insurance companies, not the courts.[116] Further criticism has been expressed towards the confinement

---

[109] Which is compulsory for tenants, but not for freeholders.
[110] Using data supplied by the *Centre de documentation et d'information de l'assurance* (www.ffsa.fr/).
[111] Article 121-2, Insurance Code: 'The insurer guarantees the loss and damages caused by the person whom the subscriber is liable for on the ground of Article 1384 of the Civil Code, whatever the nature or the severity of the fault committed by these persons.'
[112] Galand-Carvel 'Comparative report on liability', para. 29.
[113] See, notably, G. Durry RTD civ. 1978.655; F. Terré, P. Simler and Y. Lequette, *Droit civil, les obligations*, 10th edn (Paris: Dalloz, 2009), N° 823; Viney and Jourdain, *Les conditions*, N° 892. Note the comments of the Cour de cassation in its 2002 Report, p. 23 (www.courdecassation.fr/).
[114] See Gouttes' report to the 2002 decision noted in n. 84 above. One particular concern has been the use of exclusion clauses in such policies, to which the Cour de cassation has adopted a very restrictive approach.
[115] As suggested by P. Jourdain D 1997.265 and B. Puill D 1988 chron 185. In contrast, Julien, *La responsabilité civile du fait d'autrui*, N°s 121-35 asserts that it is not a question of responsibility but that liability is the counterpart of choosing to become a parent. This brings with it powers ('*les prérogatives parentales*'), but also duties.
[116] See Desgorces under Civ 2, 3 July 2003 JCP 2003 II 10009 (n. 92 above).

of liability to the person with parental authority with whom the child usually resides. This has the iniquitous consequence that, on separation or divorce, the parent with only a right of contact and visiting rights can avoid strict liability.[117]

Parental liability also raises discrete issues of how far the law should regulate how children are raised, how much independence children should be permitted as they grow older,[118] and the acceptability of characterising children as 'risk-creation devices'[119] for whom someone must take responsibility. Two aspects of the French system are perhaps most striking. First, liability extends beyond the home to include trips to relatives,[120] holiday camps[121] and even while resident at boarding schools.[122] These are situations where the parent cannot practically exert control, albeit that he or she, as a matter of law, retains parental authority. There is clearly also potential for an overlapping claim against the institution. Secondly, the failure to recognise any diminution of control until the eighteenth birthday appears unrealistic. As children grow older, it is inevitable, and indeed desirable, that they are given greater independence and start to make decisions for themselves. Arguably, maturity requires learning from one's mistakes, rather than shielding the child from any sense of responsibility. French law appears to ignore this social reality and creates the remarkable situation that a victim injured by Françoise

---

[117] Francoz-Terminal, Lafay, Moréteau and Pellerin-Rugliano, 'Children as tortfeasors under French law', para. 105. See also Le Tourneau, 'Les responsabilités du fait', 110.

[118] Note, for example, T. Gill, *No fear: growing up in a risk-averse society* (London: Calouste Gulbenkian Foundation, 2007) who argues that children need to build up skills to protect themselves.

[119] Thereby treating children like inanimate objects or even animals, which clearly ignores the intelligence and initiative displayed by children (see O. Tournafond D 2001.2851 at 2856, H. Groutel Resp civ et assur 2001.chron N° 18, J. Mouly JCP 2001 II 10613); an analogy firmly rejected by the English House of Lords in *Carmarthenshire CC v Lewis* [1955] AC 549.

[120] See l'arrêt Schott (Civ 2, 20 January 2000 Bull civ II N° 14; D 2000 somm 469 obs D. Mazeaud; JCP 2000 II 10374 note A. Gouttenoire-Cornut; JCP 2000 I 241 obs G. Viney; D 2000 IR 61; Resp civ et assur 2000 N° 146 note H. Groutel; RTD civ. 2000.340 note P. Jourdain. Cass crim 8 February 2005 D 2005 IR 918; JCP 2005 I 149 obs G. Viney and II 10049 note M.-F. Steinlé-Feuerbach.

[121] Cass crim 29 October 2002 Bull crim 2002 N° 197 p. 733; D 2003 Jur 2112 note L. Mauger-Vielpeau.

[122] Civ 2, 29 March 2001 Bull civ II N° 69; JCP 2002 II 10071 note S. Prigent; Civ 2, 16 November 2000 Bull civ II N° 69; JCP 2001 I 340 obs G. Viney; RTD civ. 2001.603 obs P. Jourdain. See also Cass crim 18 May 2004 Bull crim N° 123, p. 470; D 2004 IR 1937; Petites affiches 3 November 2004, p. 7, note J.-B. Laydu; RTD civ. 2005.140 obs P. Jourdain.

one day before her eighteenth birthday and Alain one day after his eighteenth birthday will find himself dealing with two different legal regimes. In the former case, the parents will be strictly liable save for limited defences. In the latter case, the parents will not be liable and the victim will have to prove fault under the ordinary rules of delictual liability.[123] Such a distinction appears at best arbitrary, particularly as the victim will be unlikely to appreciate the exact age of the culprit at the time of the accident.

7.5 Conclusion: a common law doctrine of strict parental liability?

It is in this light that one readdresses the question raised in this chapter: should common law systems impose strict liability on parents for the harm caused to innocent third parties by their children? The models examined in this chapter indicate that legal systems have a choice between variants of fault-based liability or the strict liability model employed by the French; the vicarious liability model being rejected due to the difficulties in establishing proof of a tort by a minor. Indeed, the French example demonstrates that it is possible both to extend strict liability to the parent–child relationship and provide a working system funded by insurance. The 1997 *Bertrand* decision drew on extensions of vicarious liability elsewhere in French law, notably the *Blieck* case of 1991 discussed at 5.4.2,[124] accepting that the person able to control the risk of injury and possessing authority over the person causing the damage should be treated as a guarantor of any resultant risk. Recognition that social risk should be met by the tort system has thus spread across a number of factual contexts. The French system does, however, have a number of failings. By removing the need for fault by either parent or child, it provides a model incapable of setting normative behavioural standards. Most worryingly, as a system based primarily on risk allocation via the mechanism of insurance, the absence of compulsory insurance raises the problem of gaps in cover. The burden on parents, liable whatever steps they take to control their unruly children, is extremely onerous.

---

[123] See Article 1382.
[124] Ass plén 29 March 1991 D 1991.324 note C. Larroumet, chr G. Viney p. 157, JCP 1991 II 21673, concl H. Dontenwille, note J. Ghestin.

It is unsurprising that leading commentators have remarked recently that 'in France today, the child is seen not as a sign of luck and the promise of a future, but as a source of trouble and risk'.[125]

In contrast, English law continues to adhere to a system based on fault and to prioritise principles of individual responsibility. A parent will be judged by the standard of the reasonable parent and the difficulties of parenting recognised. Although criminal law indicates that attitudes may be changing in relation to parental responsibility for the criminal conduct of minors,[126] tort law continues to treat parents as ordinary tortfeasors. Oliphant is correct to identify that absence of insurance is an easy excuse. Liability would encourage insurance and existing cover could be extended at limited additional cost. What one sees is a resistance to extending parental liability for the acts of their children. The question remains whether this continuing opposition can be justified.

Any reform would be likely to require legislative intervention.[127] In 1985, the Irish Law Reform Commission faced this question and resolved that, on balance, the imposition of strict or vicarious liability on parents would be unjust.[128] The family, unlike a business, does not operate on a commercial basis under which the child can be regarded as an 'expense'. Such liability would be 'too drastic a solution' and one which failed to take account of the difficulties of parenting in an increasingly liberal society. Waller, in one of the few common law articles on this topic, puts the argument more strongly.[129] The parental position is distinct from other commercial bodies. They cannot spread the cost of their premium through the price of their product or services. (Indeed, the only way to spread the cost would be by reducing the child's pocket money.) Further,

---

[125] H. Capitant, F. Terré and Y. Lequette, *Les grands arrêts de la jurisprudence civil*, 12th edn (Paris: Dalloz, 2008), vol. II, p. 459 (my translation). It is noticeable that the Draft Common Frame of Reference, discussed in Chapter 9, in suggesting a set of model rules of European private law, at Book VI – 3:104 (accountability for damage caused by children or supervised persons), favours the German approach, providing that a person is not accountable under this Article for the causation of damage if that person shows that there was no defective supervision of the person causing the damage, limiting it also to parental care of persons under fourteen years of age: DCFR (see n. 71 above).

[126] See Leng, 'Parental responsibility for juvenile', pp. 330–1.

[127] Rogers, 'Liability for damage'. Nevertheless, the Animals Act 1971 provides a precedent for such a reform: Animals Act 1971, s. 6(3) deems the head of the household to be keeper of the animal owned (or possessed) by a member of the household under the age of sixteen.

[128] *Report on the liability in tort of minors and the liability of parents for damage caused by minors* (LRC 17–1985) (see www.lawreform.ie/publications/publications.htm).

[129] P. L. Waller, 'Visiting the sins of the children', *Melbourne University Law Review*, 4 (1963–4), 17 at 38.

parents cannot 'fire' clumsy or deceitful children to terminate any future liability. In Waller's view, 'in a society where it is increasingly expensive and difficult to raise and educate children, it is suggested that there must be a real warrant, which does not so far appear to have been made, for imposing such strict liability.'[130]

The position in the United States is also revealing in this context. Whilst all forty-nine States (excluding New Hampshire) have statutes imposing some form of strict liability on parents for damage arising from the criminal acts of their children,[131] the majority of this legislation was introduced in the 1950s and 1960s to deal with the problem of juvenile delinquency and therefore may be seen as an aspect of crime control. Such legislation represents a distinct penal policy initiative rather than a general move towards parental liability in civil law.[132]

Much therefore seems to depend on the particular social view taken of the parent–child–victim triangle and the desirability of tort intervention. Whilst French law is prepared to utilise the law of tort (or delict) to meet the risks caused by the immaturity of children, the common law courts have been more reluctant to condemn those struggling to bring up children. Respect for family autonomy and individual responsibility, the absence of a culture of parental liability insurance and a focus on criminal frameworks to deal with parental responsibility, signify that there is little support for change in the common law. In contrast, greater support may be found in recent years for holding primarily liable public bodies acting as 'quasi-parents': for example, schools, foster parents, and adoption agencies. Such systemic negligence satisfies the basic requirements of tort law:[133] focusing on fault and setting objective standards capable of improving and guiding future behaviour, whilst being targeted at bodies with the means to provide compensation to victims.

---

[130] Ibid., at 38–9. Waller argues for a reversal of the burden of proof. As seen in Germany, this will not necessarily have a great impact on claims – the real issue is what standard is set for parents by the system in question.

[131] See P. K. Graham, 'Parental responsibility laws: let the punishment fit the crime', *Loyola of Los Angeles Law Review*, 33 (1999), 1719 at 1725–29 and L. Gentile, 'Parental civil liability for the torts of minors', *Journal of Contemporary Legal Issues*, 16 (2007), 125, who lists in the appendix the parental liability provisions of every US State.

[132] Damages are generally limited by statute and the aim of the legislation is clearly juvenile crime control, not restitution: see, for example, the California Civil Code, Art. 1714.1.

[133] See M. Hall, 'Institutional tortfeasors: systemic negligence and the class action', *Torts Law Journal*, 14 (2006), 135.

In essence, what one sees is a clash of philosophies as to the role of tort in familial matters: either using tort law to encourage individual responsibility through the mechanism of fault, or using tort law to provide a framework based on social risk to meet the risks created by children via the mechanism of household insurance. In choosing the former, the common law acknowledges the limitations of tort law as a mechanism for social change – such a role being left to criminal law as seen above. Although, as seen in this chapter, the standards of care set by the common law may seem generous and make too great an allowance for the perils of parenting, in recognising the pressures of parenthood and the limitations of the civil law in correcting anti-social behaviour, an attempt is made to establish realistic standards for caring for children. Whilst more can be done to reach a sensible balance between the rights of victims, parents and children, there is little sign of the fundamental change in approach needed to instigate a move from fault-based to strict liability.

8 Understanding vicarious liability: reconciling policy and principle

8.1 Introduction

This book has examined the operation of vicarious liability[1] across legal systems. As we have seen, one may identify a common general framework and three basic criteria: a particular relationship, the commission of a tort and some connection between the tort and the relationship in question. Beyond these key criteria a number of variables exist. Should the system be based on strict liability or fault? To what extent may an innocent party, forced to pay compensation to the innocent victim, be able to seek an indemnity from the tortfeasor? How broadly should the relationships giving rise to vicarious liability extend in the light of changing employment conditions? What connection is needed to trigger vicarious liability?

Previous chapters have sought to respond to these questions, analysing critically different legislative and judicial responses and assessing the ability of modern legal systems to establish a clear and socially-responsive doctrine of vicarious liability. This chapter has a different aim: to identify the key policy arguments which influence how legal systems apply the doctrine of vicarious liability. The nature of these arguments has altered with time, moving, as we will see, from a basis of fault to that of risk-based liability. The weight given to these rationales serves both to explain the legal responses of each system examined in this book, but also to enable us to critically assess the

---

[1] As explained in Ch. 1, this book uses the term 'vicarious liability' in a neutral sense. Despite its common law origins, it is preferable to the civilian term 'liability for the acts of others' which covers more ground, extending to strict liability in contract and tort, and liability for actions not amounting to torts. 'Vicarious liability' is used here to signify rendering one person/body strictly liable for the torts of another in the law of tort.

effectiveness of modern legal systems in responding to contemporary social and economic conditions.

8.2 Theoretical justifications for vicarious liability in common and civil law

This section will critically examine the many and varied justifications for vicarious liability and assess to what extent they provide credible explanations for this doctrine. Few would now share the strident views of Thomas Baty at the start of the twentieth century that vicarious liability is 'a principle dubious in origin, and unjust in operation – one, moreover ... for which little or no theoretical justification is even to be found advanced'.[2] In contrast, as Patrick Atiyah has commented, 'we are all so familiar with the concept of vicarious liability that we simply take it for granted'.[3] Baty is correct, however, to recognise the lack of attention given to justifying the operation of this doctrine at common law. Although clearly established by the eighteenth century, initially a tendency existed to rely on two Latin maxims by way of explanation: *respondeat superior* (the superior shall answer) and *qui facit per alium facit per se* (who brings something about through another does it himself).[4] The latter invokes the theory of identification – the fault of the servant is attributed to the master – but the former does no more than state the doctrine in Latin. Other views emerge: 'the reason that I am liable is this, that by employing him I set the whole thing in motion; and what he does, being done for my benefit and under my direction, I am responsible for the consequences of doing it' (Lord Brougham);[5] 'there ought to be a remedy against some person capable of paying damages to those injured' (Mr Justice Willes);[6] 'The person employing has the selection of the party employed, and it is reasonable

---

[2] T. Baty, *Vicarious liability* (Oxford: Clarendon Press, 1916), Preface, p. 3, described as 'this ingenious controversial book' by F. Pollock, *Law Quarterly Review*, 32 (1916), 226.

[3] P. S. Atiyah, 'Personal injuries in the twenty-first century' in P. Birks (ed.), *Wrongs and remedies in the twenty-first century* (Oxford: Clarendon Press, 1996), p. 15.

[4] That is, the act of the employee is the act of the employer: see, for example, Parke B in *Sharrod v London and North Western Railway Co.* (1849) 4 Ex 580 at 585, 154 ER 1345 at 1347–8; *Hutchinson v York etc. Railway Co.* (1850) 5 Exch 343 at 350, 155 ER 150 at 153 (Alderson B); and Lord Kenyon CJ in *Mitchell v Tarbutt* (1794) 5 TR 649 at 651, 101 ER 362 at 363: 'it is immaterial whether the tort were committed by the defendant or his servant, because the rule applies *qui facit per alium, facit per se*.'

[5] *Duncan v Findlater* (1839) 6 Cl & Fin 894 at 910, 7 ER 934 at 940.

[6] *Limpus v London General Omnibus Co.* (1862) 1 H & C 526 at 539, 158 ER 993 at 998.

that he who has made choice of an unskilful or careless person to execute his orders, should be responsible for any injury resulting from the want of skill or the want of care of the person employed.' (Baron Rolfe);[7] business is a dangerous enterprise, giving rise to responsibilities (Pollock).[8] Ibbetson concludes that vicarious liability became a rule more or less arbitrary in nature, dependent on public policy and convenience; a factor exacerbated by the presence of juries in civil cases until the early part of the twentieth century.[9]

Civil law systems have equally struggled to find a single rationale to justify strict liability for the acts of others. Bertrand de Greuille, in the preparatory work to the French Civil Code, gives, in fact, three reasons for the strict liability of *commettants*/employers: that the *préposé*/employee acts on the employer's behalf, that the employer may be presumed to be at fault in placing faith in an employee whose misconduct harms others; and that the employer sets in motion the activity leading to harm to others.[10] In both common and French law, one sees, therefore, early references to the theory of identification or agency, notions of fault and even a skeletal notion of enterprise liability. Glanville Williams concludes that no profit is gained from examining the history of the rule, due to the fact that the doctrine was developed by judges who had different ideas of its justification or underlying policy or, as he cynically comments, 'no idea at all'.[11]

It is in the twentieth century and beyond, therefore, that one might most usefully assess the justification for the continued application (and as we have seen expansion) of this doctrine. From the late nineteenth century, commentators have sought to explain the reasoning underlying

---

[7] *Reedie v London and North Western Railway Co.* (1849) 4 Exch 244 at 255, 154 ER 1201 at 1206.
[8] F. Pollock, *Essays in jurisprudence and ethics* (London: Macmillan, 1882), p. 125.
[9] D. J. Ibbetson, *A historical introduction to the law of obligations* (Oxford University Press, 1999), pp. 181–2. It is legitimate to dismiss the suggestion by Holmes that the modern doctrine may be traced back to ancient times and the idea of the liability of the head of the household for family members and servants, albeit based on a fiction that within the scope of the agency, principal and agent are one (O. W. Holmes, 'Agency', *Harvard Law Review*, 4 (1891), 345 and *Harvard Law Review*, 5 (1891), 1). As rightly stated by Wigmore (and discussed in earlier chapters), the ancient law on which Holmes based his argument had completely disappeared in England by the sixteenth century; the modern doctrine of vicarious liability was introduced by Holt C. J. shortly before 1700: J. H. Wigmore, 'Responsibility for tortious acts: its history', *Harvard Law Review*, 7 (1894), 315, 383, 441.
[10] See Bertrand de Greuille, *rapporteur* to the *Tribunat*, also reported in P. A. Fenet, *Recueil complet des travaux préparatoires du Code civil* (1827) (Osnabrück: O. Zeller, 1968) XIII at 476.
[11] G. Williams, 'Vicarious liability and the master's indemnity', *Modern Law Review*, 20 (1957), 220 and 437, at 231. See also G. Williams, 'Vicarious liability: tort of the master or the servant?', *Law Quarterly Review*, 72 (1956), 522 at 545.

the expanding doctrine of vicarious liability and to identify a justification for strict liability in a system dominated by fault-based liability, ideas of individual responsibility, accountability and corrective justice. Baty, in his 1916 work, *Vicarious liability*, identified no fewer than nine different policy bases for the doctrine,[12] concluding that 'In hard fact, the real reason for employers' liability is [that] the damages are taken from a deep pocket.'[13] It is possible, nevertheless, in modern law to identify three dominant rationales which continue to be utilised to support the doctrine of vicarious liability in tort, namely fault, victim compensation and risk.[14] The first is uncontroversial. Taking the most common situation of the employer/employee relationship as our example, if the employer is at fault, for example in choosing a careless employee, then it is just to hold him to account. Victim compensation – the policy identified by Baty above – in contrast, espouses different policy concerns: ensuring the protection of innocent third parties even where it signifies making another innocent party pay on the basis that he has means to do so. The last concept – risk – takes a number of forms. We may envisage it in precise economic terms – an actuary assessing the risk related to a particular form of action – or more loosely as a predicted consequence of one's actions, for example starting a business and employing staff. All three rationales will be examined below.

[12] Baty, *Vicarious liability*, ch. VIII, p. 148, listing nine possible grounds for the doctrine: control, profit, revenge, carefulness and choice, identification, evidence, indulgence, danger and satisfaction.

[13] Ibid., at 154.

[14] Other explanations may be found, but these are the key arguments which cross legal systems. Consider, for example, the alternative explanation put forward by Jason Neyers (J. W. Neyers, 'A theory of vicarious liability', *Alberta Law Review*, 43 (2005), 287) based on breach of contract, namely that the employment contract contains an implied term that the employer must indemnify the employee for any torts committed in the workplace. Liability thus arises on the basis of strict liability for breach of contract – committed by the employer, not the employee. It is submitted that, however ingenious, objections may be raised: this theory can only provide a justification where a contract of employment exists (as we have seen vicarious liability goes beyond this context) and could logically be excluded by express contractual terms (subject to controls on exclusion clauses and unfair terms). A court is equally unlikely to imply a term to indemnify employees from intentional criminal misconduct. As Stevens indicates, it also raises issues in common law systems of privity of contract: the claimant is the third party beneficiary of this agreement and the success of his tort action will depend on the enforceability of this agreement: R. Stevens, 'Non-delegable duties and vicarious liability' in J. Neyers, E. Chamberlain and S. G. A. Pitel (eds.), *Emerging issues in tort law* (Oxford: Hart, 2007), p. 335, n. 23. Other rationales include it being a response to the voluntary acquisition of authority over the other (J. Julien, *La responsabilité civile du fait d'autrui: ruptures et continuités* (Presses universitaires d'Aix Marseille, 2001).

8.2.1 *Fault:* culpa in eligendo/in vigilando *and the theory of identification*

This category encompasses two distinct arguments. The first seeks to find independent fault on the part of the employer: the employee was only able to harm the claimant because the employer was at fault in his choice of employee or failed to supervise him properly. The employer has, in effect, caused the accident by setting the whole incident in motion by employing a careless employee. This philosophy is reflected in the German Civil Code of 1896. §831(1) provides that:

> A person who uses another person to perform a task is liable to make compensation for the damage that the other unlawfully inflicts on a third party when carrying out the task. Liability in damages does not apply if the principal exercises reasonable care when selecting the person deployed and, to the extent that he is to procure devices or equipment or to manage the business activity, in the procurement or management, or if the damage would have occurred even if this care had been exercised.

On this basis, although liability is presumed, the employer may rebut this presumption of fault by demonstrating that he had taken reasonable care in the selection or supervision of employees, or simply that the accident would have occurred in any event. Such a provision, appearing at the height of the industrial revolution, demonstrates adherence to traditional notions of corrective justice, combined, of course, with lobbying from the entrepreneurial classes.[15] Such reasoning has echoes in the French Civil Code of 1804 which, despite imposing strict liability in Article 1384, did so on the basis that fault in the choice or supervision of the relevant employee could be presumed, albeit such presumption being irrebuttable.[16] This serves to explain the presence of a strict liability provision in a section of the Code dominated by the concept of fault. Pothier, whose work influenced the French Civil Code, referred expressly to the necessity of making men careful in the selection of their servants.[17]

Yet, as we have seen in earlier chapters, this no longer represents the view of French law. Equally, whilst § 831(1) survived the amendments to

---

[15] See H. H. Seiler, 'Die deliktische Gehilfenhaftung in historischer Sicht', *Juristenzeitung* (1967), 525 and MünchKommBGB/Wagner, 5th edn (Munich: C. H. Beck, 2009), §831, para. 1.

[16] de Greuille, *Recueil complet*, XIII at 476: 'N'a-t-il pas à se reprocher d'avoir donné sa confiance à des hommes méchans, maladroits ou imprudens?' See also P. Jourdain, 'La responsabilité du fait d'autrui à la recherche de ses fondements' in P. Conte et al. (eds.), *Mélanges Lapoyade-Deschamps* (Presses Universitaires de Bordeaux, 2003), pp. 67 at 68.

[17] R. J. Pothier (1699-1772) *Oeuvres II* (Paris, 1848), N° 121.

the German Civil Code in 2002,[18] the German courts soon came to develop new ways of circumventing the fault requirement of § 831, either directly, by rendering the presumption of fault more and more difficult to rebut, or indirectly, by relying on the law of contract or the company law provisions of the Code.[19] It was always accepted that the legislature might impose strict liability for others. For example, the 1871 Imperial Law of Liability (*Reichhaftpflichtgesetz*) – 29 years before the German Civil Code came into operation – imposed strict liability on railway companies for death or personal injury caused through the operation of the railways. On this basis, even a system which expressly premised liability on fault has come to accept the limitations of fault-based liability in this context.[20]

Nevertheless, fault is still invoked in the modern context, despite recognition of the distinction between actual negligence by the employer, giving rise to a direct claim under the tort of negligence (common law),[21] Article 1382(3) of the French Civil Code and § 823(1) BGB (German Civil Code), and indirect liability via vicarious liability or liability under Article 1384(5) of the French Civil Code. The theory of identification – expressed by the maxim *qui facit per alium facit per se* – provides an alternative means of holding the employer responsible: the fault of the employee attributed to the employer.[22] This idea is also found in France,[23] and is consistent with early ideas of command and control. By the sixteenth century, the common law of England had relieved an employer of liability for a servant's wrongs unless the employer had specifically commanded, or consented to, the act causing the wrong. Logic dictates that if the employer has personally commanded or authorised the tortious act, then he should be held personally liable. However, as seen in Chapter 1, the idea of the 'master's tort', on which the theory of identification depends, has been rejected by the

---

[18] *Gesetz zur Modernisierung des Schuldsrechts* of 26 November 2001. The revised BGB was promulgated on 2 January 2002. See R. Zimmermann, *The new German law of obligations* (Oxford University Press, 2005).

[19] See Chapter 2.

[20] See G. Brüggemeier, *Haftungsrecht: Struktur, Prinzipien, Schutzbereich* (Heidelburg: Springer, 2006), p. 177.

[21] The employers' non-delegable duty, described in Chapter 5, is best viewed as a type of primary liability, although it is argued that it owes its origins to judicial circumvention of the limits to vicarious liability imposed by the doctrine of common employment.

[22] Termed the "master's tort theory" by Glanville Williams: Williams, 'Vicarious liability: tort of the master' 522. See also Holmes, 'Agency', 4 *Harvard Law Review*, 351.

[23] See J. Domat, *Les loix civiles dans leur ordre naturel* (1689) (Paris, 1777), Book 1, tit. XVI, Sect. III, N° 1: '*le fait de ces préposés est de leur propre*'.

House of Lords in *Staveley Iron and Chemical Co. Ltd v Jones*[24] and *Imperial Chemical Industries Ltd v Shatwell*.[25] It is now generally accepted that it is the tort of the servant which is in question. In the words of Lord Reid, 'an employer, though guilty of no fault himself, is liable for the damage done by the fault or negligence of his servant acting in the course of his employment'.[26] Equally while acts authorised by the employer will be attributed to him, it has been argued throughout this book that this is primary liability and should not, in any event, be classified as vicarious liability.

Nevertheless, the theory of identification continues to find modern adherents. Ernest Weinrib in *The idea of private law*[27] used this idea to fit vicarious liability within his theory of corrective justice: '*respondeat superior* fits into corrective justice only if the employer can, in some sense, be regarded as a doer of the harm. Corrective justice requires us to think that the employee at fault is so closely connected with the employer that responsibility for the former's acts can be imputed to the latter.'[28] Robert Stevens equally has asserted that what is attributed is not the liability of the tortfeasor, but his actions, rendering the person to whom the action is attributed personally liable.[29] Such reasoning, he argues, is consistent with a rights-based model of tort law. François Chabas, in France, has maintained the opposition of Mazeaud to risk-based reasoning and continued to favour the traditional French view that the law identifies the employer with the employee's fault: 'fault remains therefore the basis for the *commettant's* liability: the fault of the *préposé* is, from the victim's perspective, the personal fault of the *commettant*'.[30] What one sees is the ongoing appeal of an explanation based, however tangentially, on fault, thereby avoiding the difficulties of justifying strict liability within a primarily fault-based edifice. Indeed, Lord Hobhouse's focus in *Lister v Hesley Hall Ltd*[31] on the relationship between employer and victim (rather than employee and victim) exemplifies the

---

[24] [1956] AC 627.   [25] [1965] AC 656.   [26] [1956] AC 627 at 643.
[27] E. Weinrib, *The idea of private law* (Harvard University Press, 1995).
[28] Ibid., 186.
[29] R. Stevens, *Torts and rights* (Oxford University Press, 2009), ch. 11. See also R. Stevens, 'Vicarious liability or vicarious action', *Law Quarterly Review*, 123 (2007), 30.
[30] H. L. Mazeand, J. Mazeaud and F. Chabas, *Leçons de droit civil*, 9th edn (Paris: Montchrestien, 1998) tome II, vol. 1, *Obligations: théorie générale*, N° 484 (my translation). See also E. Bertrand, 'Les aspects nouveaux de la notion de préposé et l'idée de représentation dans l'article 1384 al 5 nouveau du Code civil, étude critique de jurisprudence', thesis, Université d'Aix-Marseille (1935).
[31] [2002] 1 AC 215 at paras. 54 and 57: see Ch. 6.

ongoing popularity of such ideas, using fault-based liability to provide a more acceptable basis for extending the doctrine to encompass serious criminal offences. It is the view of this book that primary and vicarious liability should be seen as distinct and that, on this basis, primary liability cannot be seen as a justification for vicarious liability. At best, it is a fiction, at worst misleading. An explanation based on the reassurance of a fictional fault is hardly an adequate explanation for this doctrine.

8.2.2 Victim compensation and loss distribution

The second explanation is based on concerns for social justice and pragmatism. The victim is the (most) innocent party in the employer/employee/victim triangle. He has no involvement in the employer/employee relationship, has nothing to gain from this relationship and yet falls victim to a tort by an individual who may not have the means to compensate him. As Holt CJ expressed it in 1708 in relation to a fraud claim: 'for seeing somebody must be a loser by this deceit, it is more reason that he that employs and puts a trust and confidence in the deceiver should be a loser than a stranger'.[32] In French law, it has been termed a simple rule of *équité* or fairness and social justice[33] that the employer in such circumstances should compensate the victim for the loss; acting effectively as a solvent 'guarantor'[34] for the employee's debt (*la théorie de la garantie*).[35] A victim may further find it difficult to identify which employee, of many, was the actual culprit of the tort.[36] Vicarious liability, combined with the doctrine of *res ipsa loquitur*, overcomes this obstacle, thereby facilitating victim compensation.[37] Such arguments rest on the assumption that the employer, unlike the employee, is a person of means. At common law, this is frequently termed the 'deeper pockets' doctrine. Glanville Williams in 1957

---

[32] *Hern v Nichols* (1709) 1 Salk 289, 91 ER 256.
[33] See R. Rodière, *La responsabilité civile*, 2nd edn (Paris: Rousseau et cie, 1952), N° 1472 and 1473.
[34] Logically, on this basis, the guarantor/employer may seek an indemnity from the original debtor/employee.
[35] See B. Starck, H. Roland and L. Boyer, *Obligations* 5th edn (Paris: Litec, 1996), vol. I, *Responsabilité délictuelle*, N°s 893–7, who, rejecting *équité* as too vague, argue that the guarantee arises by virtue of using the services of another in one's activities.
[36] One of the difficulties arising, it may be recalled, in *Hollis v Vabu* (2001) 207 CLR 21; see Ch. 3.
[37] Provided, of course, the activity in question had not been contracted out to independent contractors: see the arguments in earlier chapters of the difficulty of the employee/independent contractor distinction in relation to modern employment practices.

stated cynically: 'However distasteful the theory may be, we have to admit that vicarious liability owes its explanation, if not its justification, to the search for a solvent defendant.'[38]

Yet not all employers will necessarily be men of means. This potential flaw is met by the existence of insurance. It is the development of insurance provision in the latter part of the nineteenth century, combined with workmen's compensation legislation during this period,[39] which arguably rendered vicarious liability both workable and acceptable to employers. Although the passing of such legislation was often controversial, arousing opposition from manufacturing interests and the upper legislative chamber, in rendering employers strictly liable for workplace accidents, the resulting legislation may be seen as an acknowledgement that employers should bear the cost of such accidents as the party best able to bear and spread the costs.[40] More pragmatically, it also led to a widespread practice of obtaining insurance cover against such costs.[41] Smith, writing in 1923, noted that 'A reason which occurs to the writer is that which has been offered in justification of workmen's compensation statutes. In substance it is the belief that it is socially more expedient to spread or distribute among a large group of the community the losses which experience has taught are inevitable in the carrying on of industry, than to cast the loss upon a few.'[42]

---

[38] Williams, 'Vicarious liability and the master's indemnity', 232. For a more positive view, see B. Feldthusen, 'Vicarious liability for sexual torts' in N. J. Mullany and A. M. Linden (eds.), *Torts tomorrow* (North Ryde, NSW: LBC Information Services, 1998), p. 224: 'One of the most important social goals served by vicarious liability is victim compensation. Vicarious liability improves the chances that the victim can recover the judgment from a solvent defendant.'

[39] See Workmen's Compensation Act 1897 (UK); Act of 9 April 1898 (France); Act of 6 July 1884 (Germany: the first of its kind in the world, promoted by Otto von Bismarck to counter socialist demands). In the United States, Canada and Australia, it is deemed a State or provincial matter, but some form of legislation had generally appeared by the first half of the twentieth century.

[40] See J. Witt, 'Speedy Fred Taylor and the ironies of enterprise liability', *Columbia Law Review*, 193 (2003), 1. Accounts of the origins of enterprise liability in the United States have also pointed toward the enactment of workmen's compensation statutes in the 1910s as a foundational moment for the subsequent expansion of enterprise liability: G. L. Priest, 'The invention of enterprise liability: a critical history of the intellectual foundations of modern tort law', *Journal of Legal Studies*, 14 (1985), 461 at 465–7.

[41] Atiyah, for example, reports that 51 new insurance companies were set up following the passing of the Workmen's Compensation Act 1897: P. S. Atiyah, *Vicarious liability in the law of torts* (London: Butterworths, 1967), p. 24. See also E. P. Hennock, *The origin of the welfare state in England and Germany, 1850–1914* (Cambridge University Press, 2007), ch. 5, pp. 101ff.

[42] Y. B. Smith, 'Frolic and detour', *Columbia Law Review*, 23 (1923), 444 at 456–7.

In modern times where employer insurance is usually compulsory,[43] the effect is to distribute losses throughout the relevant sector. In economic theory at least, loss distribution will extend beyond the employers to the public in general; the cost of insurance premiums being passed onto customers in the form of higher prices.[44] It may be argued that even where enterprises do not insure or are unable because of competition to pass on extra costs to consumers, loss distribution will still occur by passing on costs to shareholders via lower dividends or by reducing other fixed costs, for example staff wages.[45] In contrast, the employee is less able to spread costs or negotiate individual insurance premiums. Employee self-insurance is likely to be inefficient: employees, even if willing to obtain insurance, are likely to purchase the cheapest alternative possible, will not have the negotiating power of a large employer and, in reality, this would lead to double insurance against the same risk (employers still obtaining insurance to cover the possibility of vicarious liability and insurance being in any event usually compulsory).

Again we find recognition of the rationale of victim compensation in all legal systems. In Chapter 3, we saw a willingness to extend hospital liability for the torts of doctors as the State overtook maintenance of the health sector in lieu of private charitable arrangements. Equally, our study of French law has shown that the French courts have long been willing to view the employer/*commettant* as guarantor of his employees/ *préposés*, thereby ensuring victims compensation subject to the right of the guarantor to seek an indemnity from the debtor (*préposé*/tortfeasor). Victim compensation thus remains a key element of the continued existence of vicarious liability.

---

[43] For the UK, see the Employers' Liability (Compulsory Insurance) Act 1969 (at present the minimum level of cover required is £5 million, which includes costs, although most insurers automatically provide cover of at least £10 million). However, most public organisations including government departments and agencies, local authorities, police authorities and nationalised industries; health service bodies including National Health Service trusts, health authorities, primary care trusts and Scottish health boards; and some other organisations which are financed through public funds, such as passenger transport executives and magistrates' courts committees are not required to have insurance and many will self-insure. See, generally, P. Cane, *Atiyah's accidents, compensation and the law*, 7th edn (Cambridge University Press, 2006), 9.3.

[44] See MacDonald J in *Hamilton v Farmers Ltd* [1953] 3 DLR 382 at 393 (NSSC): vicarious liability 'probably reflects a conclusion of public policy that the master should be held liable for the incidental results of the conduct of his business by means of his servants as a means of distributing the social loss arising from the conduct of his enterprises.' See also Atiyah, *Vicarious liability*, p. 26.

[45] See Atiyah, *Vicarious liability*, p. 23.

However, as Cane has stated, 'loss-spreading ... is not self-justifying'.[46] It does not tell us amongst whom the losses should be spread and why, indeed, it should be confined to accidents caused by tortious acts and not simply any injury connected with the workplace. Most significantly it does not explain why systems use *this* method to compensate victims. Rebut, commenting on French law, argues that commentators have confused the valuable function of vicarious liability in ensuring victim compensation with a search for its justification.[47] Victims may be compensated by a number of means. Governments may provide assistance centrally via social security or specific compensation funds. Alternatively, victims may be encouraged to take out private insurance cover and take responsibility for their own injuries, subsidised by a centralised insurance fund. Patrick Atiyah famously moved from advocating social insurance in his 1967 work[48] to envisaging first party insurance as the answer in *The damages lottery* in 1997.[49] The importance of victim compensation tells us why some scheme is needed, but it does not dictate *which* scheme should be used.

8.2.3 Risk and deterrence

8.2.3.1 Risk

Employees are hired to work in the interests of the employer. As human beings, they may commit torts, either negligently or intentionally. This is a risk which derives from any business activity, be it for commercial gain or not. Where the employer is acting for profit, the notion of risk/profit arises: an employer who profits from the activities of his employees, should also bear any losses that those activities cause.[50] One of the

---

[46] P. Cane, 'Justice and justifications for tort liability', *Oxford Journal of Legal Studies*, 2 (1982), 30 at 52. See also R. Flannigan, 'Enterprise control: the servant–independent contractor distinction', *University of Toronto Law Journal*, 37 (1987), 25 at 29 and Williams, 'Vicarious liability and the master's indemnity', 440.

[47] D. Rebut, *Juris Classeur responsabilité civile et assurances*, Fasc 143: droit à réparation – responsabilité du fait d'autrui – domaine: responsabilité des commetants (Paris: Editions du Juris-Classeur, 1998), para. 5.

[48] 'If risks of this kind were met out of general taxation the cost would be spread more widely still, and would also be imposed primarily on those more able to pay': Atiyah, *Vicarious liability*, p. 27.

[49] P. S. Atiyah, *The damages lottery*, (Oxford: Hart Publishing, 1997).

[50] Modern French authors have argued that this basic notion may be found even in the *travaux préparatoires* of the French Civil Code; B. de Greuille commenting 'N'est-ce pas en effet le service dont le maître profite qui a produit le mal qu'on le condamne à réparer": see Fenet, *Recueil complet*, XIII at 476. See also M. Rives-Langes, 'Contribution à l'étude de la responsabilité des maitres et commettants', JCP 1970 I 2309, esp N°s 24–5. For an early

'costs' of employing the employee is his or her potential to cause harm. Harold Laski, writing in 1916, saw vicarious liability in this sense as an aspect of social justice: 'The promotion of social solidarity is an end it is peculiarly incumbent upon the law to promote, since its own strength, and even life, depends upon the growth of that sentiment.'[51] On this basis, if industrialisation is to maximise public good, a social distribution of profit and loss indicates that the employer should bear the burden of his employee's torts even when he is personally without fault. The theory of enterprise risk goes further, placing liability on the employer for losses incurred in the course of his enterprise on the basis that it is fair in such situations to require the employer to internalise these risks.[52] As Fleming stated, 'a person who employs others to advance his own economic interest should in fairness be placed under a corresponding liability for losses incurred in the course of the enterprise'.[53]

The idea of risk possesses a number of related benefits. It may be seen to encourage accident prevention and avoidance. If an employer will be held liable to compensate for injuries deriving from risks associated with its enterprise, there is an obvious incentive to prevent such incidents occurring by taking greater measures to instruct staff, implement safety measures and ensure health and safety regulations are enforced. Put bluntly, vicarious liability presents employers with a financial interest in protecting third parties from injury. As seen in Chapter 6, such reasoning was embraced by McLachlin J in *Bazley v Curry*.[54] Viney and Jourdain have strongly argued that, from the 1990s, French law has also moved towards a recognition that an enterprise should bear the risks created by its activities. On this basis, liability under Article 1384(5)

> advocate of risk-based reasoning, see R. Demogue, *Traité des obligations en général. Source des obligations* (Paris: A. Rousseau, 1925), vol. V, N°881: 'toute personne dirigeant un organisme social qui augmente sa puissance, qui l'enrichit, dont elle a le profit, doit répondre des actes délictueux de ses subordonnés qui en sont comme le risque professionnel.'

[51] H. J. Laski, 'The basis of vicarious liability', *Yale Law Journal*, 26 (1916), 105 at 121. See also W. O. Douglas, 'Vicarious liability and administration of risk', *Yale Law Journal*, 38 (1928–1929), 584 and 720, who seeks to provide an economic and social basis for the doctrine of vicarious liability.

[52] See G. C. Keating, 'The theory of enterprise liability and common law strict liability', *Vanderbilt Law Review*, 54 (2001), 1285, 1287 and 'The idea of fairness in the law of enterprise liability', *Michigan Law Review*, 95 (1997), 1266.

[53] J. G. Fleming, *The law of torts*, 9th edn (North Ryde: LBC Information Services, 1998), p. 410.

[54] (1999) 174 DLR (4th) 45 at para. 31.

represented a means by which to attribute to the enterprise the risks created by the activities of the employees in its service (the so-called theory of *risque/activité*).[55] In so doing, it establishes a regime adapted to modern social needs, identifies who should bear the cost of insurance cover and encourages the enterprise to undertake preventative measures. Ideas of loss distribution are equally applicable here. The 'fairness' of risk-based liability is enhanced by the fact that it is more expedient to spread or distribute losses arising from industry over a sector of the community.

Such arguments require a particular view to be taken of the role of tort law in society. Risk requires us to move from a notion of corrective justice, based on an individual being held accountable for his subjective fault, to a view based on distributive justice whereby broader distributive goals replace notions of individual fault.[56] It also requires us to characterise enterprise as a source of risk, rather than a positive source of benefit to the national economy. Such reasoning is supported by the existence of insurance. Compulsory insurance provides the means by which the costs of liability may be absorbed within the industrial sector in addition to meeting the needs of individual victims.[57] The potential wealth of defendants (or, alternatively, ability to provide compensation due to insurance cover) has at least an unconscious influence on the willingness of the courts to extend the doctrine of vicarious liability. Extensions of liability would be pointless if compensation could not be paid.[58]

Yet, there is a danger of placing too much faith in the general panacea of insurance cover. The imposition of liability will, at some point, have an impact on premiums[59] and insurance cover is not limitless.

---

[55] G. Viney and P. Jourdain, *Traité de droit civil: les conditions de la responsabilité*, 3rd edn (Paris: LGDJ, 2006), N° 791-1 and N° 808. See also Jourdain, 'La responsabilité du fait'.

[56] See Viney and Jourdain, *Traité de droit civil*, N° 791-1 and N° 808.

[57] Viney and Jourdain, on this basis, question the logic of imposing a heavy burden of strict liability on parents without legislation requiring insurance to cover such losses: *Traité de droit civil*, N° 892 (discussed in more detail in Ch. 7).

[58] See Lord Denning in *Morris v Ford Motor Co.* [1973] 1 QB 792 at 798: 'The damages are expected to be borne by the insurers. The courts themselves recognise this every day. They would not find negligence so readily – or award sums of such increasing magnitude – except on the footing that the damages are to be borne, not by the man himself, but by an insurance company.'

[59] See P. Jourdain D 2003 Jur 231 at 234: 'Increasing excessively parental liability ... risks creating a serious increase in insurance premiums.' The UK government also justified its refusal to intervene to extend recovery for psychiatric injury claims on the basis that expanding the class of persons who can recover damages for psychiatric illness would lead to a significant increase in insurance premiums: Department for Constitutional Affairs, *The law on damages*, CP 9/07 (2007), para. 87, and Annex B: Regulatory Impact Assessment.

Extending liability must therefore be balanced against the practicalities of insurance provision and the ability of the market to absorb or distribute costs. Further, as seen in Chapter 6, the notion of risk is also more difficult to apply beyond the profit-making corporation to small charitable organisations seeking to assist the public and often the most disadvantaged in society. Liability may threaten the continued operation of these organisations and at the very least add to their operational costs.[60]

More fundamentally, the concept of risk fails to reflect the current legal position in any system. In French law, a notion of risk arising from the activities of an enterprise fails to explain the breadth of the relationships giving rise to liability, described in Chapter 5, which go beyond business interests to include liability for family members and friends. More generally, if we accept that an enterprise creating risks to innocent third parties through the acts of its employees in the course of their employment should be held strictly liable as one of the costs of the business, there is no real reason why this should not extend to *all* harmful acts, including the acts of independent contractors working on its behalf.[61] Chapter 7 highlights recognition of the logic of this argument in the context of Article 1384(4) of the French Civil Code which imposes strict liability on parents for the harmful acts of their children.[62] The culpability of the child is deemed irrelevant – in the *Fullenwarth* decision of 1984, the court held that 'it is sufficient that the [child] has committed an act which is the direct cause of the damage suffered by the victim'.[63] It is unclear how a rationale based on risk would limit liability to 'tortious' acts by 'employees' which cause harm to innocent victims: both wrongful and non-tortious acts derive from the risks arising from the defendant's enterprise. As noted in Chapter 7, not all commentators have welcomed the removal of the tort requirement

---

[60] See, for example, Binnie J in *Jacobi v Griffiths* (1999) 174 DLR (4th) 71 at para. 68 and C. R. Tremper, 'Compensation for harm from charitable activity', *Cornell Law Review*, 76 (1991), 401 at 426–8.

[61] Arlen and MacLeod argue that by not extending liability to the torts of independent contractors, vicarious liability insulates principals even when they are better able to regulate independent contractor care-taking than the courts: J. H. Arlen and W. B. MacLeod, 'Beyond master-servant: a critique of vicarious liability' in M. S. Madden (ed.), *Exploring tort law* (Cambridge University Press, 2005), pp. 111–42.

[62] 'The father and mother, in so far as they exercise "parental authority", are jointly and severally liable for the damage caused by their minor children who live with them.'

[63] Ass plén 9 May 1984 (2nd case) D 1984.525 concl J. Cabannes, note F. Chabas, (1st case) JCP 1984 II 20255 note N. Dejean de la Bâtie.

under Article 1384(4), and the proposed reforms of the French Civil Code include a provision which would reintroduce an element of fault.[64]

The risk rationale also throws doubt on the issue of the employers' indemnity, examined in Chapter 2. If it is rational to render employers liable for their employees' torts, why should the employer be able to undermine this allocation of risk by claiming reimbursement from the employee himself? La Forest J, in his powerful dissenting judgment in the Canadian case of *London Drugs Ltd v Kuehne & Nagel International Ltd*,[65] suggested that, in most cases, the logic of risk liability compelled the elimination of the possibility of the employee bearing the loss (although such a view has not generally found favour in Canada).[66] Such arguments have raised a lively debate in France, being seen by many as the basis for the notorious *Costedoat* decision of 2000, which stated that an employee, acting within the limits of the task assigned to him, would no longer be liable to the third party victim.[67] Although, as seen in Chapter 2, most legal systems limit the employee indemnity, it is still generally available in relation to intentional torts and has yet to be abolished.

8.2.3.2 Deterrence

The deterrence argument requires us to predict human behaviour on an objective basis. Logically, it is assumed, the threat of paying compensation under a strict liability regime will encourage employers to take steps greater than those demanded by the negligence standard, criminal law and/or statutory requirements. McLachlin J in *Bazley v Curry* held that:

The second major policy consideration underlying vicarious liability is deterrence of future harm. Fixing the employer with responsibility for the employee's wrongful act, even where the employer is not negligent, may have a deterrent

---

[64] See Article 1355 ('A person is liable strictly for harm caused by persons whose way of life he governs or whose activity he organises, regulates or controls in his own interest. This liability may arise in the situations and subject to the conditions provided for by Articles 1356 to 1360. It rests on proof of an action of a kind which would attract liability in a person who caused the harm directly') in P. Catala, Avant-projet de réforme du droit des obligations et de la prescription (Paris: La Documentation française, 2006): translation by S. Whittaker and J. Cartwright: www.justice.gouv.fr/art_pix/rapportcatatla0905-anglais.pdf

[65] [1992] 3 SCR 299, (1993) 97 DLR (4th) 261 at 284.

[66] See L. Klar, *Tort law*, 4th edn (Toronto: Carswell, 2008), p. 648.

[67] Ass plén, 25 February 2000 Bull Ass plén N° 2; JCP 2000 II 10295 concl R. Kessous, note M. Billiau.

effect. Employers are often in a position to reduce accidents and intentional wrongs by efficient organization and supervision.[68]

Deterrence is interrelated with the notion of risk. It is the introduction by the employer of the risk (or the material increase of an existing risk) which implies the possibility of employer intervention to manage the risk in question.[69]

However, a number of concerns may be raised in relation to the deterrence argument. The existence of insurance will inevitably cushion the impact of paying compensation. If insurance is compulsory and, due to market forces, premiums are not directly related to the number of claims against a particular employer, why should an employer incur costs implementing greater preventative measures? While the insurer *may* adjust the resulting premium to reflect positive features such as a good claims record or good risk management, or negative features such as a poor claims record, much will depend on the nature of the business and the insurer's own experience in the business sector.[70] What of the risk-taker, who is fortunate and incurs limited claims? What of the inherent risks which cannot be prevented? Consider, for example, the sexual abuse cases noted in Chapter 6 where carers and teachers, despite reasonable steps to verify their reliability, intentionally abused children in their care. In such circumstances, apart from ensuring that all employees are never left alone with children or permitted to communicate with children without supervision, the possibility of abuse is not preventable and it is submitted that such steps would clearly be unworkable in practice. In *Lister v Hesley Hall*,[71] for example, the warden lived in the home with his wife – this did not prevent the abuse. One must also consider the notion of deterrence in relation to the victim and the employee himself. Risk-based reasoning, by increasing the ease by which victims obtain compensation, arguably reduces the incentive for victims to take care of their own safety. Accident avoidance may thus be seen to have two perspectives: encouraging preventative measures by employers, but also encouraging victims to avoid accidents by which they may be

---

[68] (1999) 174 DLR (4th) 45 at para. 32.   [69] Ibid., at para. 34.
[70] The UK government site, Business Links (www.businesslink.gov.uk), which gives expert advice to businesses, reports that for most small to medium-size risks, the insurer will use a book rate, or average rate, which is based on the claims they have paid out to similar businesses. For large or very large cases the insurer may, however, calculate the premium based on the claims record of the business over a number of years, if it is relatively stable.
[71] [2002] 1 AC 215.

injured. One might also express concern whether such liability, in cushioning the accountability of the employee, also reduces the incentive for employees to take responsibility for their actions. Clearly such actions risk dismissal but, in French law, a willingness to protect employees from direct claims by victims and indemnity claims from employers has raised concerns that the law has gone too far. In the context of strict parental liability for the harm caused to others by their children, some authors have challenged the desirability of viewing children as 'risk-creation' devices, rather than maturing human beings who should be encouraged to take responsibility for their actions.[72]

It may be concluded that accident prevention and deterrence should be seen as a possible beneficial consequence of vicarious liability, but not a major underlying justification for its imposition. Nevertheless, risk reasoning has grown in importance in recent years – notably as a justification for extending the scope of employment to cover inherently risky activities, as seen in Chapter 6 – but, as a general explanation, it fails to explain why vicarious liability has not taken the next logical step of extending liability to all harmful acts which cause loss to the claimant. We may also question whether risk provides sufficient certainty. Despite use of economic theory by many, usually North American, authors, the English and French courts use 'risk' in a very loose sense, not based on economic theory but a general sense that the probability of injury derives from risks associated with the workplace for which the employer logically should be held responsible.[73] By linking risk with notions of fairness, in the sense of an equitable and just result, the courts indicate clearly that risk, although influential, will not be the sole rationale for the imposition of liability.

8.3 Balancing policy objectives: the modern approach to justifying vicarious liability

The above rationales – fault; victim compensation; risk and deterrence – have featured in the case law examined in this book. These rationales not only have theoretical relevance, but also practically affect how we

---

[72] See O. Tournafond D 2001.2851 at 2856; H. Groutel Resp civ et assur 2001.chron N° 18; J. Mouly JCP 2001 II 10613.

[73] As Molfessis notes, there is not in fact any one notion of risk deriving from one's activities and commentators will therefore refer to the notions of *risqué/autorité, risqué/enterprise* and *risqué/profit* depending on the context: see N. Molfessis, 'La jurisprudence relative à la responsabilité des commettants du fait de leurs préposés ou l'irrésistible enlisement de la Cour de cassation' in *Mélanges Gobert* (Paris: Economica, 2004), para. 59.

interpret the basic elements of the vicarious liability framework. Consider, for example, the notion of control considered in Chapter 3 in the context of the employer/employee relationship. Liability may be justified where the defendant has control over the tortfeasor on the basis that, in failing to prevent the wrongful act occurring, he may be presumed to be at fault (be it a lack of supervision or simply poor choice of actor).[74] This would suggest a narrow view of the employment relationship, based on the actuality of control. Alternatively, the person controlling others may be best placed to compensate victims of their actions and distribute their losses, or liability may be said to stimulate the person in control to take greater precautions whilst forcing him to accept the risks which result from the enterprise he is controlling. These grounds suggest a broader view of the employment relationship satisfied by the mere power or right of control. The justifications given above thus influence how we interpret the conditions for vicarious liability.

Despite the multitude of rationales given, one may conclude that *no single rationale* explains the modern doctrine of vicarious liability examined in this book. As John Fleming famously acknowledged, '[V]icarious liability cannot parade as a deduction from legalistic premises, but should be frankly recognised as having its basis in a combination of policy considerations'.[75] The challenge for a legal system is therefore reaching the correct combination of policy rationales. In utilising the doctrine of vicarious liability, each legal system must decide what weight to give to the competing policies of fault, victim compensation and risk/deterrence. Diagram 3 illustrates the competing theories and their impact on victim compensation.

Fault-based liability places the greatest burden on the victim who must establish that the employer has been at fault. As we have seen, however, the courts have proven willing to presume or imply fault, rising at its highest to an irrebuttable presumption of fault. The situation in Germany and Spain is relevant here. Whilst both Civil Codes impose a rebuttable presumption of fault on employers for injuries caused by their employees, the courts have made it difficult for employers to rebut this presumption: on Diagram 3, moving liability towards the

---

[74] See, for example, *Mersey Docks and Harbour Board v Coggins & Griffith (Liverpool) Ltd* [1947] AC 1 at 18 per Lord Simonds: 'The doctrine of the vicarious responsibility of the "superior", whatever its origin, is today justified by social necessity, but, if the question is where that responsibility should lie, the answer should surely point to that master in whose act some degree of fault, though remote, may be found.'

[75] Fleming, *The law of torts*, p. 410.

BALANCING POLICY OBJECTIVES   245

```
         Fault based                    ||              Strict liability
---------------------------------------------------------------------------
  |          |          |              ||            |            |

Actual    Implied    Rebuttable    Irrebuttable    Risk liability    Risk liability
fault     fault      presumption   presumption     for torts        for harm
of        of         of fault      of fault        connected        connected
employer  employer                                 with the         with the
                                                   workplace        workplace
```

→→→→→→→→→→→→→→→→→→→→→→→→→→

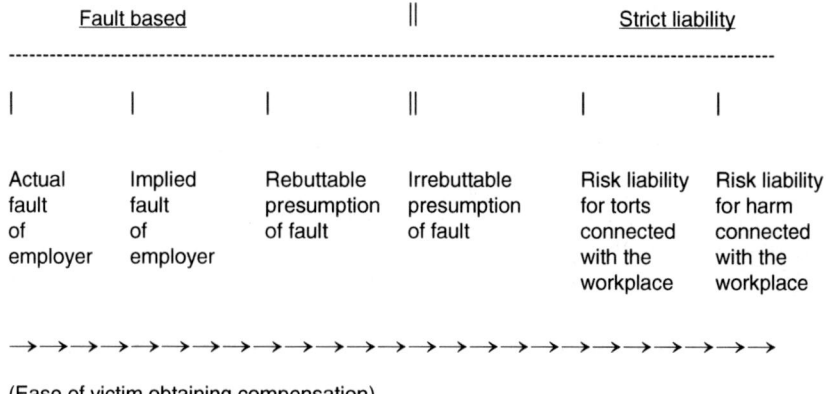

(Ease of victim obtaining compensation)

Diagram 3 Liability in tort/delict of the employer

centre.[76] What the diagram does not reveal is the alternative bases of liability in other areas of private law or by legislation; of particular significance in Germany. Most legal systems will favour the right-hand half of the diagram for which three variables are highlighted, starting with an irrebuttable presumption of fault to risk-based liability for all harms arising from workplace accidents. As stated, only the French legal system approaches the extreme right of the diagram; most legal systems are positioned more centrally.

For a more detailed understanding of the influence of policy on the law, case law must be examined. The use of policy arguments in leading common and civil law cases will be examined below.

8.3.1 *Prioritising risk: the fair allocation of the consequences of the risk and deterrence*

La Forest J in *London Drugs Ltd v Kuehne & Nagel International Ltd*,[77] in an influential dissenting judgment, found the explanation for vicarious liability to rest on a number of policy concerns: compensation, deterrence and loss internalisation. His judgment is expressly cited by McLachlin J in the leading Canadian case of *Bazley v Curry*,[78] who acknowledged that 'First and foremost is the concern to provide a just and practical

---

[76] See notes on §831(1) BGB and Article 1903 of the Spanish Civil Code in C. von Bar and E. Clive (eds.), *Principles, definitions and model rules of European private law: draft common frame of reference. Full edition* (Munich: Sellier, 2009), pp. 3464 and 3461 respectively.
[77] See [1992] 3 SCR 299 at 336.
[78] (1999) 174 DLR (4th) 45 (hereafter *Bazley*).

remedy to people who suffer as a consequence of wrongs perpetrated by an employee'.[79] In promoting a rationalisation based on risk and deterrence, the Canadian Supreme Court recognised the ongoing significance of victim compensation as a fundamental concern. A 'just and practical' remedy therefore here encompasses the notion that he who introduces a risk should incur liability to those who may be injured. This, in the view of the Supreme Court, lies at the heart of tort law.[80] The fair allocation of loss does not, however, extend to all torts, but those connected with the employment relating to the risk created by the employer and which the employer could have attempted to prevent.[81]

The primacy of risk-based reasoning has also come to dominate the approach of the French courts. The combined effect of the decisions of the *Assemblée plénière* in 1988 on *abus de fonction* (*Héro*)[82] and in 2000 on the employer indemnity (*Costedoat*),[83] is both to extend liability under Article 1384(5) and to focus liability on the employer, not the employee. In preventing a victim suing a *préposé* who is acting within the limits of the task assigned to him by the *commettant*, the employer is not merely guaranteeing the liability of the tortfeasor but replacing him as sole defendant. Equally, by rendering the employer liable for all tortious acts unless he can show that they were committed (i) without authorisation; (ii) for the employee's own ends and (iii) were outside the normal duties of his job, the French courts impose the burden on employers for risks arising from torts connected loosely with the workplace.

Nevertheless, as shown above, the role of risk in both the Canadian and French legal system has been balanced against other concerns. Chapter 2 noted that, more recently, case law has sought to extend the exceptions to the *Costedoat* ruling and that the proposals for reform of the French civil code would amend the law.[84] In neither system has

---

[79] Ibid., at para. 30. McLachlin J also expressly acknowledged the influence of John Fleming, and of A. O. Sykes, 'The boundaries of vicarious liability: an economic analysis of the scope of employment and related legal doctrines', *Harvard Law Review*, 101 (1988), 563 in which Sykes puts forward the idea of 'enterprise causation' as the key to vicarious liability, imposing strict liability where the employment relation increases the probability of each wrong.

[80] (1999) 174 DLR (4th) 45 at para. 30. [81] Ibid., at paras. 35–6.

[82] Ass plén 19 May 1988 D 1988.513 note C. Larroumet, Gaz Pal 1988.2.640 concl M. Dorwling-Carter, Def 1988.1097 note J.-L. Aubert, RTD civ. 1989.89 obs P. Jourdain. Followed by Crim 4 January 1996 JCP 1996 IV 1028.

[83] Ass plén, 25 February 2000 Bull Ass plén N° 2; JCP 2000 II 10295 concl R. Kessous, note M. Billiau.

[84] Catala, *Avant-projet de réforme*, Article 1359-1.

the right of the employer to seek an indemnity from the employee (the antithesis of enterprise liability) been abolished completely. French commentators have criticised the uncertainty caused by the 1988 *Héro* decision and, as seen in Chapter 5, the potential extension of Article 1384(1) – liability of those with the power to direct, control and manage another[85] – to all relationships where one person exercises some form of control over another has not occurred. Viney and Jourdain argue that an unwillingness to objectify the relationship giving rise to the risk of injury signifies a reluctance to embrace risk-based reasoning fully.[86] Chapter 6 highlights the fact that *Bazley* has not led to a great extension of liability in Canada and the cautious approach of the Canadian courts has prevented any greater extension of risk-based liability.[87] One may conclude that despite the primacy of risk-based reasoning in these two systems, risk alone is not accepted as the sole justification for vicarious liability and must be counter-balanced against other factors to determine when it is 'fair and just' to impose vicarious liability.

8.3.2 *A proportionate response: what is 'fair and just'?*

As Stevens has indicated,[88] to base a doctrine on reaching a balance of policy rationales is bound to lead to uncertainty. Not only will there be different views on how to balance the arguments in question, but such responses will differ over time, rendering precedents of limited utility not only due to the focus on the facts of each case, but changing perceptions of the role of vicarious liability over time. It is unclear, however, how this is to be avoided, whether one chooses to view vicarious liability as based on attribution and the fiction that the employer has committed the fault, or on the principle of liability for the faults of others. In both cases, the question arises: *when* and *under what conditions* will the employer be held liable? The current structure of vicarious liability – relationship of tortfeasor and defendant, commission of a tort, employer

---

[85] 'A person is liable not only for the damages he causes by his own act, but also for that which is caused by the acts of persons for whom he is responsible, or by things which are in his custody.'

[86] Viney and Jourdain, *Traité de droit civil*, N° 791-1.

[87] Note also express references to the danger of a flood of liability: for example, Binnie J in the companion case to *Bazley* of *Jacobi v Griffiths* (1999) 174 DLR (4th) 71 at para. 29: 'Much as the Court may wish to take advantage of the deeper pockets of the respondent to see the appellants compensated, we have no jurisdiction *ex aequo et bono* to practise distributive justice.'

[88] Stevens, *Torts and rights*, p. 274.

indemnity, connection between the tort and the relationship – indicates that no one policy is predominant. Examining the leading cases in English and Australian law one can identify a number of primary and secondary policy arguments, which continue to influence the courts.

Primary policy factors

- loss distribution
- making the risk-creator pay
- victim compensation.

Secondary policy factors

- deterrence encouraging accident prevention
- level of wrongdoing: is the employer being held liable for negligent or intentional/criminal wrongdoing?
- presumed fault by the employer.

In English law, the judgments of Lords Millett and Nicholls stand out. In seeking a justification for the imposition of vicarious liability, Lord Millett in *Lister*[89] and *Dubai Aluminium*[90] highlights the three primary policy factors outlined above. Whilst the doctrine may function as a loss-distribution device, it seeks to render the employer accountable for the risks inherent to the employment relationship. Lord Nicholls in *Dubai Aluminium* equally emphasises the significance of the risks arising from the parties' relationship and the just allocation of the risk of losses.[91] In a more recent decision of the House of Lords on vicarious liability, Lord Nicholls stated the position succinctly, noting also the additional secondary policy factor of encouraging accident prevention:

> Whatever its historical origin, this ... principle of strict liability for another person's wrongs find its rationale today in a combination of policy factors ... [T]hese factors are that all forms of economic activity carry a risk of harm to others, and fairness requires that those responsible for such activities should be liable to persons suffering loss from wrongs committed in the conduct of the enterprise. This is 'fair', because it means injured persons can look for recompense to a source better placed financially than individual wrongdoing employees. It means also that the financial loss arising from the wrongs can be spread more widely, by liability insurance and higher prices. In addition, and importantly, imposing strict liability on employers encourages them to maintain standards of 'good practice' by their employees.[92]

---

[89] *Lister v Hesley Hall* [2001] UKHL 22 at para. 65.
[90] *Dubai Aluminium Co. Ltd v Salaam* [2002] UKHL 48 at para. 107.   [91] Ibid., at paras. 21–3.
[92] *Majrowski v Guy's and St Thomas's NHS Trust* [2006] UKHL 34 at para. 9.

The High Court of Australia in its leading case of *New South Wales v Lepore*[93] adopts similar reasoning. The High Court in *Hollis v Vabu Pty Ltd*[94] commented that the modern law of vicarious liability was adopted 'not by way of an exercise in analytical jurisprudence but as a matter of policy', finding that no one policy could be identified as completely satisfactory in all cases. In *Lepore*, the majority nevertheless identified a number of relevant policy concerns: risk, loss distribution, victim compensation, and accident prevention. A further issue was raised: the degree of culpability for which the employer would be held liable.[95] Gleeson CJ, for example, sought to confine liability for intentional misconduct to relationships invested with a high degree of power and intimacy,[96] for others, such misconduct was the antithesis of what could be said to be within the functions of an employee and imposed a responsibility beyond anything an employer should reasonably bear.[97] Weight placed on this factor has led to a more restrictive approach than that adopted by the House of Lords in *Lister* and the Supreme Court of Canada in *Bazley*.[98]

What the English decisions and *Lepore* indicate is that whilst one may agree on the relevant factors, disagreement may exist on the weight to give to each factor. The English Supreme Court and the High Court of Australia have both acknowledged that 'the master is a more promising source for recompense than his servant who is apt to be a man of straw',[99] but the concept of risk is more contentious. Is it enterprise risk – rejected in *Lister* and by the majority in *Lepore*[100] – or a more general notion of taking responsibility for risks arising from one's activities? The position of the High Court in *Hollis* is, for example, more equivocal, where the majority stated:

---

[93] [2003] HCA 4, (2003) 212 CLR 511 (hereafter *Lepore*).
[94] [2001] HCA 44, (2001) 207 CLR 21 at para. 34 per Gleeson CJ, Gaudron, Gummow, Kirby and Hayne JJ.
[95] See, notably, [2003] HCA 4, (2003) 212 CLR 511 at paras. 218–21 per Gummow and Hayne JJ.
[96] Ibid., at para. 74.   [97] See ibid., at para. 342 per Callinan J.
[98] Lord Millett in *Lister v Hesley Hall* [2001] UKHL 22 at para. 79 commenting that 'it is no answer to say that the employee was guilty of intentional wrongdoing, or that his act was not merely tortious but criminal, or that he was acting exclusively for his own benefit, or that he was acting contrary to express instructions, or that his conduct was the very negation of his employer's duty'.
[99] Fleming, *The law of torts*, p. 410.
[100] See [2003] HCA 4, (2003) 212 CLR 511, notably para. 126 per Gaudron J and para. 223 per Gummow and Hayne JJ.

In general, under contemporary Australian conditions, the conduct by the defendant of an enterprise in which persons are identified as representing that enterprise should carry an obligation to third persons to bear the cost of injury or damage to them which may fairly be said to be characteristic of the conduct of that enterprise. In delivering the judgment of the Supreme Court of Canada in *Bazley v Curry*, McLachlin J said of such cases that 'the employer's enterprise [has] created the risk that produced the tortious act' and the employer must bear responsibility for it. McLachlin J termed this risk 'enterprise risk' and said that 'where the employee's conduct is closely tied to a risk that the employer's enterprise has placed in the community, the employer may justly be held vicariously liable for the employee's wrong'.[101]

It is unclear whether the majority (notably the same judges as in *Lepore*) was seeking to approve McLachlin J's reasoning or using it as a shorthand version of a general statement of risk liability.

Another issue is the extent to which the practicality of accident prevention be taken into account: Gummow and Hayne JJ in *Lepore* are particularly sceptical that, despite criminal sanctions, a school could prevent a teacher abusing his pupils.[102] The factors also interact. Increasing liability for intentional acts extends the risks for which the employer will be held liable and the ease with which the victim obtains compensation and puts corresponding pressure on loss distribution mechanisms. This is dealt with in French law by the Insurance Code which, at Article L.121-2, requires insurance companies to cover liability for both negligent and intentional misconduct arising under Article 1384 of the Civil Code,[103] but elsewhere insurance policies will generally cover negligent, not intentional, misconduct. One final additional factor may be identified. Despite our earlier doubts, the reassurance of the fiction of fault continues to play a role, seen in England and Wales in Lord Hobhouse's judgment in *Lister*. It has also been raised in the context of risk-based reasoning. As Flannigan states, 'If employer risk regulation is the correct basis for the doctrine ... it is the act or right to act of the employer, his risk contribution to the worker's activity or operation, which leads to his responsibility'.[104] In other words, the employer is at fault in failing to regulate the risks he created. It would seem that the notion of finding some (implicit) fault justification for vicarious liability continues to retain its appeal.

---

[101] See [2001] HCA 44, (2001) 207 CLR 21 at para. 42 per Gleeson CJ, Gaudron, Gummow, Kirby and Hayne JJ (references omitted).
[102] See [2003] HCA 4, (2003) 212 CLR 511 at para. 219.
[103] This provision has the status of '*d'ordre public*' and cannot be modified by agreement.
[104] Flannigan, 'Enterprise control', 36. See also Viney and Jourdain, *Traité de droit civil*, N° 791-1.

8.3.3 Conclusions

In balancing policy objectives, one sees variance between jurisdictions. The English courts, regarding risk as a 'relevant factor',[105] may be distinguished from the position seen in Canada and France above. The Australian courts place greater emphasis on the secondary concerns, resulting in a more restrictive view of the course of employment requirement in *Lepore*. This indicates that policy is not simply of theoretical significance, but a practical concern, informing how the courts interpret the building blocks of vicarious liability.

In determining, therefore, the relationships giving rise to liability, the French emphasis on risk/activity suggests a broader definition. In *Hollis*, the High Court of Australia notably used the policy ground of deterrence to argue for the existence of an employer/employee relationship where it would encourage the introduction of greater safety measures to reduce the number of accidents and the risks to the community as a whole.[106] The narrow English approach must be questioned in the light of the policy-based framework below.

In contrast, in relation to the scope of liability, the English courts have been willing to adopt a broad (too broad?) notion of 'course of employment'. All the discussions of policy cited in this chapter arise in this area of law. It does appear questionable why such policy arguments are confined to this one aspect of the doctrine. While in French law, prioritising risk has led to a generous view of the scope of liability, such risk reasoning is now subject to challenge from commentators seeking to question its dominance by raising the need to balance risk against other policy rationales.

Identification of the correct balance of policy objectives will thus depend on a number of factors. First of all, what policies are deemed socially, economically and politically appropriate in each State and the willingness of the courts to utilise tort to distribute losses and impose liability requiring one party to absorb risks. It will also be relevant to what extent victims are in fact dependent on the law of tort to provide compensation. The balance must be informed by other legal and extra-legal mechanisms providing compensation, for example, liability arising in different areas of private, public and criminal law; legislative or private schemes providing compensation (consider, for example,

---

[105] *Bernard v Attorney-General of Jamaica* [2004] UKPC 47 at para. 18 per Lord Steyn.
[106] [2001] HCA 44, (2001) 207 CLR 21 at para. 53, ground 4, relying on McLachlin J's ruling in *Bazley v Curry* (1999) 174 DLR (4th) 45 at paras. 32–3.

strict liability for motor accidents in France and Germany, no fault liability in New Zealand under the Accident Compensation Scheme,[107] and the extent to which most jurisdictions have brought workers' compensation into the social security system); the availability of insurance provision and the level of employee protection generally. What is important is that the conditions giving rise to vicarious liability are not seen in the abstract, but within a policy-based framework. This allows us to understand the differences (and similarities) between legal systems and the values they represent. This is a vital step in reaching a deeper understanding of the doctrine of vicarious liability itself.

8.4 General conclusion

The rationales underlying vicarious liability have varied over time. In the context of small, pre-Industrial Revolution businesses, the justification of fault (implied/presumed) or identification seems the strongest: the high level of control exercised over individual employees by individual employers rendering this the most logical rationale. Post-Industrial Revolution with the rise of corporations, the skilled professional and the existence of a strong insurance market, justifications change. To this must be added welfare considerations which encourage the compensation of innocent victims and use of loss distribution mechanisms to spread risk throughout society or at least a particular sector. The rationales used by systems reflect such evolving concerns, but also some conservatism: an unwillingness to relinquish any concept of fault, albeit fictional, and concern against overburdening employers. This is despite increased recognition of the social importance of responding to the risks arising from the workplace. No system has chosen to render employers liable for all harms caused by the risks of their enterprise, be they non-tortious or caused by independent contractors. In reality, the search for what is 'fair and just' represents an attempt to balance the concerns raised above according to what is deemed desirable by society at any one time. At times, law must recognise that certainty does not equate with social justice and while the aim of this book has been to give guidance and a clearer structure to the law, it cannot fail also to recognise the nuances in the law, which make tort law capable of adapting and evolving over time and changing to meet new social needs. Put simply, there is a limit to what 'vicarious liability in tort' can achieve in terms of

---

[107] Accident Compensation Act 2001 (NZ). See, generally, www.acc.co.nz/.

risk distribution and victim compensation and, as Atiyah recognised in 1967, other mechanisms exist which deal more efficiently and effectively with victim needs. Vicarious liability is thus a compromise: a private law mechanism which seeks to provide some resolution to the needs of victims and reflects increasing awareness of the need to respond to the risks posed to society by industrialisation and technological advances. It is a compromise which reflects the variety of policy justifications utilised by the courts and will inevitably result in variations between different legal systems.

What may be recognised, however, are the similarities which exist between legal systems and that, despite its uncertainties, the doctrine continues to play a significant role in modern legal systems today. This book has identified the common general framework across legal systems and that the same basic questions are asked in both civil and common law systems: what relationships give rise to liability? What connection must exist between the person harming the victim and his relationship with the defendant? On what basis may such liability be justified? In Chapters 3–5, we demonstrated that, although the employer/employee relationship is the primary relationship in all legal systems, *all* systems go beyond this relationship. In Chapter 5, we strongly argue that common law systems should include the so-called 'dependent contractor' within the doctrine of vicarious liability and thereby extend the doctrine to include temporary and agency workers who are economically dependent on the employer. This would give conceptual clarity and remove once and for all the questionable assumption that the definition of 'employee' should be the same in all areas of the law. Equally, resort to non-delegable duties and agency principles is both unhelpful and counter-productive and should be avoided whenever possible. As doctrines based on primary liability, they do not advance our understanding of vicarious liability, but represent in many cases an historical device designed to circumvent the limitations of the vicarious liability doctrine. The answer is obvious: once the narrow definition of the relationship giving rise to vicarious liability is removed, the need for such circumlocutions will disappear. In Chapter 6, we examined the trend in modern legal systems to extend the scope of liability by means of more generous definitions of 'course of employment' or 'the functions for which the tortfeasor has been employed' which demonstrated increased reliance on risk-based reasoning, embraced to varying extents across legal systems. Such case law provides a practical example of the need to balance the policy interests identified in this chapter, including the contentious extension of liability for intentional torts. It is argued that more guidance is needed and that the common law courts should be more willing to consider the possibility of primary liability in such circumstances and focus vicarious liability on situations where the employee has wrongfully harmed persons or objects which he has been employed to protect. Chapter 7 contrasted common law adherence to negligence reasoning in relation to parental liability for the torts of their children with the position in most European States. In rejecting the possibility of risk-based reasoning or even a presumption of fault in this context, the common law courts have demonstrated an unwillingness to extend strict liability, recognising the continued importance of parental autonomy (at least in tort law) and the limitations of tort law as a mechanism for social change.

Despite such reservations, the need for vicarious liability is unquestioned. It is not a quirk of the common law but a principle which crosses legal systems in a surprisingly similar way. Different terminology and legal structures should not blind us to the similar legal frameworks which exist across common and civil law jurisdictions. This would suggest one final conclusion to this work: vicarious liability is part of our legal systems and, whilst difficult to understand, represents a fundamental part of the ability of the law of tort or delict to respond to changing social and economic needs. It will thus continue to evolve and change in accordance with the changing values of society. Legal systems should therefore avoid rigidity and ensure that changes – we have highlighted here new employment structures – are integrated into its principles. The policy rationales described in this chapter impact on all aspects of the vicarious liability framework. Like all elements of tort law, it is not static: this is its strength, not its weakness.

9 A postscript: a harmonised European law of vicarious liability?

This chapter will consider the potential impact of proposals for the future harmonisation of European private law. From the 1980s, there has been growing support for the possibility of harmonisation of private law at a European level.[1] Although initially primarily academic initiatives, from 1989 support has also been received from the European Parliament[2] and Commission.[3] Recent years have seen three major publications of European tort law principles: the Principles of European Tort Law (PETL) (2005),[4] Principles on Non-Contractual Liability Arising out of Damage Caused to Another (the SGECC principles) (2006),[5] and the Draft Common Frame of Reference (DCFR) (2009).[6] These projects go

---

[1] The prime motivator was Ole Lando, who, in 1982, established the Commission on European Contract Law, leading to the publication of the Principles of European Contract Law (PECL): see O. Lando and H. Beale, *Principles of European contract law: Parts I and II* (The Hague: Kluwer Law International, 2000) and O. Lando et al. (eds.), *Principles of European contract law: Part 3* (The Hague: Kluwer Law International, 2003).

[2] See the resolutions of the European Parliament of 26 May 1989 (OJ C 158, 26.6.1989, p. 400), 6 May 1994 (OJ C 205, 25.7.1994, p. 518), 15 November 2001 (OJ C 140 E, 13.6.2002, p. 538) and 2 September 2003 (OJ C 76 E, 25.3.2004, p. 95) that a uniform internal market cannot be fully functional without further steps towards the harmonisation of civil law.

[3] Notably Communication from the Commission to the Council and European Parliament on European Contract Law of 11 July 2001, COM (2001) 398 final.

[4] European Group on Tort Law, *Principles of European tort law* (The Hague: Kluwer, 2005); www.egtl.org/principles/

[5] Non-Contractual Liability Arising out of Damage Caused to Another: www.sgecc.net/.

[6] Note also the work of the Trento Common Core project, which seeks to identify 'the common core of the bulk of European private law, i.e., of what is already common, if anything, among the different legal systems of European Union member states': The Common Core of European Law: see www.common-core.org/theproject.html and publications such as M. Bussani and V.V. Palmer (eds.), *Pure economic loss in Europe* (Cambridge University Press, 2003) and F. Werro and V. V. Palmer (eds.), *The boundaries of strict liability in European tort law* (Durham, NC: Carolina Academic Press, 2004).

beyond a summary of existing law, but seek to establish a set of principles for future European private law. In the words of one of the project groups:

> The aim of the Study Group is to produce a set of codified principles for the core areas of European private law (patrimonial law). Although the foundation for our work is detailed comparative law research, the principles which we are fashioning will represent more than a mere restatement of the existing law in the various EU jurisdictions from the standpoint of the predominant trends among the diverse legal regimes. Instead the Study Group seeks to formulate principles which constitute the *most suitable* private law rules for Europe-wide application.[7]

The most significant proposal to date is that of the DCFR. In October 2009, the Study Group on a European Civil Code (SGECC) and the Research Group on EC Private Law ('Acquis Group') published a six-volume work entitled *Principles, definitions and model rules of European private law: draft Common Frame of Reference. Full edition*,[8] replacing earlier outline editions published in 2008 and early 2009. This represents the result of a three-year research project, requested and funded by the European Commission,[9] and supported by the European Parliament.[10] The idea of a Common Frame of Reference was raised by the Commission in its 2003 Communication, 'A more coherent European contract law – an action plan',[11] in which it envisaged a publicly accessible document

---

[7] SGECC Aims: www.sgecc.net/ (emphasis added).

[8] C. von Bar and E. Clive (eds.) (Munich: Sellier, 2009).

[9] Reflecting the work of the Joint Network on European Private Law (CoPECL: Common Principles of European Contract Law) funded as a 'Network of Excellence' under the European Commission's sixth Framework Programme for Research and Technological Development, Priority 7 – FP6-2002-Citizens-3, Contract N° 513351.

[10] See, for example, European Parliament resolution on European contract law and the revision of the *acquis*: the way forward of 23 March 2006: P6_TA(2006)0109, and European Parliament resolution on European contract law of 7 September 2006: P6_TA(2006)0352.

[11] See European Commission, 'A more coherent European contract law – an action plan' February 2003 COM (2003) 68 final, OJ C 63, 15. 3. 2003, p. 1, calling for comments on three proposed measures: increasing the coherence of the *acquis communautaire*, the promotion of the elaboration of EU-wide standard contract terms, and further examination of whether there is a need for a measure that is not limited to particular sectors, such as an 'optional instrument'. The second measure of EU-wide standard contract terms was not being taken forward: see European Commission, 'First Progress Report on the Common Frame of Reference' COM (2005), 456 final, p. 10. The nature of the CFR is further elaborated in the subsequent Communication: 'European Contract Law and the revision of the *acquis*: the way forward' COM (2004) 651 final, 11 October 2004, in which it was described as 'a tool box for the Commission when preparing proposals, both for reviewing the existing *acquis* and for new instruments': Annex 1.

providing best solutions in terms of common terminology and rules, which would assist Community institutions in revising the existing and future *acquis communautaire*, act as a possible point of reference for legal development by national legislators and provide the basis for further reflection on an optional instrument[12] in the area of European contract law.[13]

The final version of the DCFR consists of 6,563 pages and goes far beyond the harmonised principles and rules of contract law requested by the Commission.[14] It contains 'principles, definitions and model rules' of European private law (together with copious comparative notes and comments on the model rules) and takes the form of ten books, including General principles (Book 1), Contracts and other juridical acts (Book II), Obligations and corresponding rights (Book III), Specific contracts and the rights and obligations arising from them (Book IV), Non-contractual liability arising out of damage caused to another (tort law) (Book VI), Unjustified enrichment (Book VII) and Trust law (Book X). The aim of the drafters of the DCFR is clear: 'If the content of the DCFR is convincing, it may contribute to a harmonious and informal Europeanisation of private law'.[15] Vicarious liability (or, to use the terminology of the DCFR, 'Accountability for damage caused by employees and representatives') is found in Book VI, Article 3:201.

This brief chapter will examine two proposals for a common European law of vicarious liability provided by PETL and the DCFR (the wording of the DCFR is the same as that of the SGECC principles).[16] It will consider to what extent harmonisation of the principles of vicarious liability is possible using these models and what this signifies in terms of the future of vicarious liability at a European level.

---

[12] That is, a set of general principles on European contract law, which would place at the disposal of parties an additional contract law regime.
[13] European Commission, 'Action plan', 4.1.1.
[14] A fact acknowledged by the drafters in von Bar and Clive (eds.), *Principles, definitions and model rules*, Introduction, paras. 30–1: 'The coverage of the DCFR is thus considerably broader than what the European Commission seems to have in mind for the coverage of the CFR ... The "academic" frame of reference is not subject to the constraints of the "political" frame of reference ... The correct dividing line between contract law (in this wide sense) and some other areas of law is in any event difficult to determine precisely. The DCFR therefore approaches the whole of the law of obligations as an organic entity or unit.'
[15] See ibid., Introduction, para. 8.
[16] See www.sgecc.net/media/downloads/updatetortlawarticles_copy.doc.

9.1 Two frameworks for liability: Article 6:102, PETL (liability for auxiliaries) and Book VI, Article 3:201, DCFR (accountability for damage caused by employees and representatives)

Although this book has identified differences between European Member States, for example, the retention of fault-based reasoning in systems based on German law, the extremely generous interpretation of liability for others adopted in French law and the confinement of English law primarily to employer/employee relationships, common trends may be found across legal systems. Chapter 6 noted that courts in civil and common law jurisdictions were increasingly willing to adopt an extensive interpretation of the 'course of employment' or the 'functions for which they have been employed' tests. Equally, Chapter 8 identified growing consensus as to the significance of risk-based reasoning. It is possible, therefore, to find commonalities between legal systems, indeed a common general framework for vicarious liability.

It is this general framework which the two leading examples of harmonised principles seek to expound.

Article 6:102, PETL: liability for auxiliaries
 (1) A person is liable for damage caused by his auxiliaries acting within the scope of their functions provided that they violated the required standard of conduct.
 (2) An independent contractor is not regarded as an auxiliary for the purposes of this Article.

VI, Article 3:201, DCFR: accountability for damage caused by employees and representatives
 (1) A person who employs or similarly engages another is accountable for the causation of legally relevant damage suffered by a third person when the person employed or engaged:
   (a) caused the damage in the course of the employment or engagement; and
   (b) caused the damage intentionally or negligently, or is otherwise accountable for the causation of the damage.
 (2) Paragraph (1) applies correspondingly to a legal person in relation to a representative causing damage in the course of acting as such a representative. For the purposes of this paragraph, a representative is a person who is authorised to effect juridical acts[17] on behalf of the legal person by its constitution.

Although the terminology used differs, a common framework may be identified:

---

[17] A juridical act is defined in Book II, Article 1:101 as a statement or agreement which is intended to have legal effect as such.

- liability is strict;
- a person is held liable for damage caused by his 'auxiliaries' or 'employees, similarly engaged others and representatives';
- the latter must be acting 'within the scope of their functions' or 'in the course of the employment or engagement';
- the latter must also 'violate the required standard of conduct' or 'cause damage intentionally or negligently or be otherwise accountable';
- independent contractors are not included.

As such, this resembles the general framework for liability established in Chapter 2 of this book. Two preliminary comments may be made, however. First, neither set of principles accepts the fault basis of the German Civil Code, § 831 BGB. Both favour the dominant model embraced by the common law and French legal system. Modern European tort law therefore recognises that strict, not fault-based, liability is most appropriate in this area of law. Secondly, both sets of principles, by requiring the commission of a tort and utilising a tort framework, retain the mixed policy approach identified in Chapter 8 and do not, therefore, go a step further and fully embrace risk-based reasoning.

Yet, despite the general similarities in structure, a number of terminological questions arise. Whilst one might query the meaning of the tests identifying wrongful conduct, the term 'juridical act' in the DCFR (a concept alien to common law systems)[18] and the decision of PETL not to include express reference to corporations on the basis that it might cause too much interference with company law,[19] the real interpretative concerns for vicarious liability are two-fold: the definition of the relationship giving rise to liability and the test for determining the extent of liability. A common European law must present definitions which are capable of consistent interpretation across Member States, otherwise harmonisation will be illusory. Member States will need guidance to ensure that a uniform approach is adopted, regardless of pre-existing legal traditions and national laws. To what extent do Article 6:102 of PETL or Article 3:201 of the DCFR achieve this goal?

9.1.1 The relationship giving rise to liability: for whom is the employer liable?

Neither PETL nor the DCFR use the term 'vicarious liability', but prefer broader terminology: liability for 'auxiliaries' (PETL) or 'employees,

---

[18] See the book review by H. Collins *Modern Law Review*, 71 (2008), 840.
[19] O. Moréteau, *Principles of European tort law* (The Hague: Kluwer, 2005), p. 113.

similarly engaged others and representatives' (DCFR). For the common lawyer, accustomed to the terms 'master/servant' and 'employer/employee', the term 'auxiliary' will be particularly troubling. The European Group on Tort Law in its commentary fully accepts that Article 6:102 does not reflect the common law tradition; 'auxiliary' being defined as 'an employee, but also anyone willing to help, acting under the supervision of the liable party'.[20] In this sense, it resembles the broader French position which includes relationships where one person can be said to supervise, direct and control another, for example, an electoral candidate being held liable as *commettant* (employer) when one of his supporters entered into a fight with a supporter of another candidate, which led to the latter's death.[21] Liability is expressly said to apply beyond the business sphere and to include domestic relationships such as the occasional helper, whether acting gratuitously or not.[22] The terminology of the DCFR will be more familiar to the common lawyer, notably the terms 'employee' and 'representative',[23] but although the Article is primarily concerned with the traditional employment relationship, the notes to Article 3:201 (and indeed the wording 'similarly engaged others') indicate that liability is more extensive. The notes conclude that 'The requisite for liability for another is always the minimum abstract possibility of directing and supervising their conduct through binding instructions ... The only decisive factor is that there is a relationship of instructional dependence (or superiority and inferiority), out of which flows an authority on the part of the liable person to control the conduct of the relevant acting party.'[24]

In harmonising the relationships giving rise to liability, clearly the civilian approach is predominant.[25] This will raise difficulties for common lawyers both in terms of interpretation and in achieving

---

[20] Ibid., at p. 115.
[21] Crim 20 May 1976 Gaz Pal 1976.2.545 note YM, RTD civ. 1976.786 obs G. Durry.
[22] See Morétean, *Principles*, p. 116.
[23] Defined in von Bar and Clive (eds.), *Principles, definitions and model rules*, Annex to the DCFR: 'A "representative" is a person who has authority to affect the legal position of another person, the principal, in relation to a third party by acting in the name of the principal or otherwise in such a way as to indicate an intention to affect the principal's legal position directly.'
[24] Ibid., 3455. Confusingly, the introductory comment at 3453 refers to 'employees and auxiliary persons placed on an equal footing to them', here equating 'auxiliaries' with non-employees.
[25] The DCFR explanatory notes and comments include examples of cases illustrating how its provisions will work in practice. It is noticeable that no common law case is cited in relation to the provisions dealing with 'employees etc.' under Article 3:201.

consensus to an extension in liability. An associated difficulty is in defining *what* relationships, beyond the employment contract, will be included. The current German approach (using the terms *Geschäftsherrn* and *Verrichtungsgehilfen* (translated as principal and vicarious agent)) also includes non-employment relationships,[26] but is not as extensive as that seen in French law.[27] The German test is predicated on the right to give instructions (*Weisungsrecht*),[28] whilst French law prefers a test of subordination:[29] both discussed in Chapter 3. Article 3:201 highlights instructional dependence, but also mentions subordination. In contrast, PETL defines an auxiliary as requiring some form of subordination or integration, suggesting again a far more extensive definition.

This may lead us to question whether, whichever provision is chosen, interpretative consistency may be found. As highlighted above, common lawyers will find the provisions problematic. The term 'auxiliary' and the tests of instructional dependence or subordination are unfamiliar and encapsulate a doctrine distinct from the common law perception of vicarious liability. Even the reference to 'independent contractor' must be approached with caution: clearly, under these definitions, parties classified as independent contractors in English law might be seen as 'auxiliaries' or 'similarly engaged others'.[30] Whilst civil lawyers may be more familiar with the terminology, this raises dangers of its own. A German lawyer seeing a test of instructional dependence will assume that no interpretative change is needed. As will, of course, a French lawyer seeing the term 'subordination'. In view of the distinctions between French and German law, this is problematic. In agreeing a set of principles, there is a danger of smoothing over differences which become significant at the point of application by the court (and

---

[26] See BGH 15 February 1957 LM § 823 BGB (Hb) 5 (client is *Geschäftsherr* of lawyer whom he instructs). For a comparative discussion, see W. van Gerven, J. Lever and P. Larouche, *Cases, materials and text on national, supranational and international tort law* (Oxford: Hart, 2000), 5.1.

[27] See Ch. 5 of this book; J. von Standinger, D. W. Belling and C. Eberl-Borges, *Kommentar zum Bürgerlichen Gesetzbuch* (Berlin: De Gruyter, 2008).

[28] See MünchKommBGB/Wagner, 5th edn (Munich: C. H. Beck, 2009), § 831, Rn 14 § 831, Rn 59ff.

[29] G. Viney and P. Jourdain, *Traité de droit civil: les conditions de la responsabilité*, 3rd edn (Paris: LGDJ, 2006), N° 792; F. Terré, P. Simler and Y. Lequette, *Droit civil: Les obligations*, 10th edn (Paris: Dalloz, 2009), N° 829.

[30] The DCFR notes, however, that the term 'similarly engaged' is capable of resolving the temporary employee problem, outlined in Ch. 4 and arising in all legal systems, by resolving that they have been similarly engaged by the client company: see von Bar and Clive (eds.), *Principles, definitions and model rules*, 3456.

interpretation by lawyers). It is submitted that the exact breadth of the relationship giving rise to liability is unclear at present.

9.1.2 'Within the scope of their functions' and 'course of employment or engagement': to what extent is an employer liable?

Similar questions may be raised in relation to the terms 'within the scope of their functions' (PETL) and 'course of employment or engagement' (DCFR). Chapter 6 of this work highlighted the difficulties experienced by all modern legal systems in applying these tests in a manner consistent with societal values and the goals of the law of torts, and the variance in practice between not only common and civil law, but different common law and civil law jurisdictions.[31] To attempt to codify this requirement in view of the different approaches across legal systems is ambitious at the very least.

The notes to PETL indicate that an approach is proposed which would be similar to that of the French courts, whereby liability should arise where there is some form of 'linkage' between the task undertaken and the tortious act in question.[32] The wording of the test equally suggests the influence of the French test (*dans les fonctions auxquelles ils les ont employés*). Such a test contrasts significantly with the common law 'close connection' test and its unanimous rejection of a test based on the mere opportunity to commit the tort. In contrast, the DCFR test of 'course of employment or engagement' may be more familiar to the common lawyer, but again caution is needed. The comments to Article 3:201 point to a narrower test than that advocated by PETL: 'The demarcation depends on whether the person acting was working within the employer's sphere of influence or was exclusively pursuing personal aims ... Damage only lies outside the context of accountability ... where the employee pursues entirely personal interests on occasion.'[33] The English case of *Mattis v Pollock*[34] (considered in this book to amount to a very generous interpretation of the English test) is said to be consistent with

---

[31] As seen in the leading cases noted in this book: *Lister v Hesley Hall Ltd* [2001] UKHL 22, [2002] 1 AC 215 (England and Wales); *Bazley v Curry* (1999) 174 DLR (4th) 45 (Canada); *New South Wales v Lepore* (2003) 212 CLR 511 (Australia); Ass plén 19 May 1988 D 1988.513 note C. Larroumet (France); BGH 20 September 1966 VersR 1966, 1074 (Germany).

[32] See Moréteau, *Principles*, p. 116.

[33] See von Bar and Clive (eds.), *Principles, definitions and model rules*, 3457.

[34] [2003] EWCA Civ 887 (illustration 11), discussed and criticised in Ch. 6. The following case is excluded: where a doctor is on holiday far away from home and negligently treats a fellow holiday-maker (illustration 9: Bírósági Határozatok (BH) 1996/89).

this. Actions contrary to instructions will not be excluded.[35] No further guidance is given.

Again one sees greater emphasis on more generous civil law provisions and certainly the PETL provisions would surprise the common lawyer and require a revision of the rationale underlying the common law doctrine of vicarious liability. The DCFR provision is more restrictive and greater guidance is given, but again it is difficult to predict how national courts would interpret this provision and whether a common interpretation could be achieved without difficulty. It is unhelpful, for example, that the term 'sphere of influence' is not defined and, in practice, case law guidance would be needed to discern how this term should be interpreted. Equally, one might question when an employee would be deemed to be exclusively pursuing personal aims. One might argue that sexual abuse is a classic example of deviant behaviour for personal gain: does this mean that *Lister v Hesley Hall Ltd*[36] would no longer give rise to liability?

9.2 Conclusion: practicality and principle

A number of conclusions may be drawn as to the possibility of harmonisation in this context. Any harmonisation provisions must bring together divergent legal systems and provide a common legal framework in which a mutual understanding and interpretative consensus is reached. This raises problems of translation, conceptual clarity and application. It will also involve, as Hesselink recognises, choices between different ideologies, cultural norms, economic structures and competing interests.[37] As acknowledged by the nineteen pages of notes to the DCFR which outline national provisions in this area of law,[38] the practice of the legal systems of European Member States differs, despite their similar legal framework. This is also the conclusion of this book. The challenge is to overcome such barriers and achieve mutual agreement as to the scope and application of the legal doctrine.

Despite the guidance indicated above, a number of hurdles may be identified which must be overcome before a common European law of vicarious liability may be said to exist. The first derives from the nature

---

[35] Illustration 10: BH 2001/56.   [36] [2001] UKHL 22, [2002] 1 AC 215: discussed in Ch. 6.
[37] M. W. Hesselink, 'The European Commission's action plan: towards a more coherent European contract law?', *European Review of Private Law*, 12 (2004), 397 at 404–5.
[38] See von Bar and Clive (eds.), *Principles, definitions and model rules*, 3459–77. The notes give a fascinating snapshot of modern European private law.

of tort law itself. Tort law is inherently vague. It has not only a predilection for value-laden terms such as the 'standard of the reasonable man' and ambiguous terms such as 'cause', but it is an area of law in which the courts are frequently active in terms of legal development. Judicial intervention within the *national* context will inevitably be influenced by socio-political and economic factors, but also legal training and cultural values. At a basic level, it is often difficult to translate value-laden terms from one system to another. A simple example may illustrate the potential difficulties in reaching a common understanding and interpretation of legal rules. It is usual to translate the term 'negligence' in English into the French word '*faute*'. However, a French lawyer would interpret '*faute*' as signifying both intentionally wrongful and negligent behaviour, which is not the sense which an English lawyer would seek to impart.[39] Further, in interpreting what would amount to fault-based behaviour, despite using a test similar to that of the reasonable man (*l'homme raisonnable et avisé*, or, more traditionally, *le bon père de famille*),[40] French law will often impose a higher standard of care than that used in the common law due to concerns for victim protection and accident prevention. Such internal socio-political concerns impact on the interpretation of basic legal terminology.

This leads to the second hurdle which is the influence of policy on legal development. In interpreting the constituent elements of the vicarious liability test, it is not simply a question of applying mechanically the appropriate definition, but applying the test to the actual facts of each case in a way which reaches a fair and just result. The definitions provided by PETL and the DCFR give limited guidance as to their application. Harmonisation of legal principle will only operate successfully where there exists a common understanding and interpretation of unified principles. The crucial issue is not whether the ideology of a particular system dominates the principles – as stated earlier, they do not seek to identify the existing state of European private law, but what it should be – but whether the principles are likely to be acceptable to all European legal systems and interpreted in the same manner.

---

[39] German law, in contrast, uses both terms in § 823(1) (*Schadensersatzpflicht*): 'Wer *vorsätzlich oder fahrlässig das Leben, den Körper, die Gesundheit, die Freiheit, das Eigentum oder ein sonstiges Recht eines anderen widerrechtlich verletzt...*' (A person who, intentionally or negligently, unlawfully injures the life, body, health, freedom, property or another right of another person is liable to make compensation to the other party for the damage arising from this.)

[40] Viney and Jourdain, *Traité de droit civil*, N° 463.

Despite the obvious scholarship underlying both PETL and the DCFR, Articles 6:102 and 3:201 are problematic in terms of their generality and inability to address the differences which exist between the operation of different European systems despite their similarities in terms of structure. More guidance is needed. The wording of the tests may be similar, but the balance of policy rationales utilised in each system reflects national perceptions of risk, fault, victim compensation and loss distribution. It is difficult to reflect the subtleties of such an exercise through a general codified principle of law. Whittaker, commenting on the DCFR, remarks on 'the extraordinarily open-textured nature of the propositions – be they values behind the law, or principles overriding or underlying the model rules'.[41] Whilst such open-textured principles permit tort law to operate flexibly and permit judicial creativity, they do not necessarily give sufficient clarity to ensure a common interpretative framework. In view of the mixed reception, particularly from common lawyers,[42] to the DCFR, the drafters' own admission that the inclusion of tort principles goes beyond the requirements of the European Commission and the fact that the DCFR is not structured on an 'everything or nothing' basis,[43] a common European law of vicarious liability is unlikely to be implemented in any form in the near future.

---

[41] S. J. Whittaker, 'A framework of principle for European contract law?', *Law Quarterly Review*, 125 (2009), 616 at 647. Note also Professor Whittaker's criticism of the DCFR in his report for the UK Ministry of Justice: *Draft Common Frame of Reference: an assessment* (Ministry of Justice): www.justice.gov.uk/publications/eu-contract-law-common-frame-reference.htm.

[42] See, for example, J. Cartwright, 'Interpretation of English law in light of the Common Frame of Reference' in H. Snijders and S. Vogenauer (eds.), *Content and meaning of national law in the context of transnational law* (Berlin, New York: Sellier de Gruyter, 2009).

[43] See von Bar and Clive (eds.), *Principles, definitions and model rules*, Introduction, at para. 74: '... it would be a quick and simple task to adjust the draft to apply only to contractual rights and obligations.'

Appendix: Key provisions of the French and German Civil Codes

In this annexe, to assist the reader unfamiliar with French and German law, I list the key provisions of the French and German Civil Codes referred to in this book. The translations of the French Civil Code are taken from *Légifrance*: www.legifrance.gouv.fr and the translations of the German Civil Code and Basic Law are taken from the German Ministry of Justice site: www.gesetze-im-internet.de/englisch_bgb/englisch_bgb.html.

France: French Civil Code/Code civil (C civ)

Article 371-1
(Act No 2002-305 of 4 March 2002)
Parental authority is a set of rights and duties whose finality is the welfare of the child.

It is vested in the father and mother until the majority or emancipation of the child in order to protect him in his security, health and morality, to ensure his education and allow his development, showing regard to his person.

Parents shall make a child a party to judgments relating to him, according to his age and degree of maturity.

Article 372
(Act No 2002-305 of 4 March 2002)
The father and mother shall exercise in common parental authority.

Where, however, parentage is established with regard to one of them more than one year after the birth of a child whose parentage is already established with regard to the other, the latter alone remains vested with the exercise of parental authority. It shall be likewise where parentage is judicially declared with regard to the second parent of the child.

Parental authority may however be exercised in common in case of joint declaration of the father and mother before the chief clerk of the *tribunal de grande instance* or upon judgment of the family causes judge.

267

Article 388
(Act No 74–631 of 5 July 1974)
A minor is an individual of either sex who has not yet reached the full age of eighteen years.

Article 489-2
A person who has caused damage to another when he was under the influence of a mental disorder is nonetheless liable to compensation.

Article 1147
A debtor shall be ordered to pay damages, if there is occasion, either by reason of the non-performance of the obligation, or by reason of delay in performing, whenever he does not prove that the non-performance comes from an external cause which may not be ascribed to him, although there is no bad faith on his part.

Article 1382
Any act whatever of man, which causes damage to another, obliges the one by whose fault it occurred, to compensate it.

Article 1383
Everyone is liable for the damage he causes not only by his intentional act, but also by his negligent conduct or by his imprudence.

Article 1384(1)
A person is liable not only for the damages he causes by his own act, but also for that which is caused by the acts of persons for whom he is responsible, or by things which are in his custody.

Article 1384(2)
(Act of 7 Nov. 1922) However, a person who possesses, regardless of the basis thereof, all or part of a building or of movable property in which a fire has originated is not liable towards third parties for damages caused by that fire unless it is proved that the fire must be attributed to his fault or to the fault of persons for whom he is responsible.

Article 1384(3)
(Act of 7 Nov. 1922) This provision may not apply to the landlord and tenant relationship, which remains governed by Articles 1733 and 1734 of the Civil Code.

Article 1384(4)
(Act No 70–459 of 4 June 1970)
The father and mother, in so far as they exercise 'parental authority' (Act No 2002–305 of 4 March 2002), are jointly and severally liable for the damage caused by their minor children who live with them.

Article 1384(5)
Masters and employers, for the damage caused by their servants and employees in the functions for which they have been employed.

Article 1384(6)
Teachers and craftsmen, for the damage caused by their pupils and apprentices during the time when they are under their supervision.

Article 1384(7)
(Act of 5 April 1937) The above liability exists, unless the father and mother or the craftsmen prove that they could not prevent the act which gives rise to that liability.

Article 1384(8)
(Act of 5 April 1937) As to teachers, the faults, imprudence or negligent conducts invoked against them as having caused the damaging act must be proved by the plaintiff at the trial, in accordance with the general law.

Article 1385
The owner of an animal, or the person using it, during the period of usage, is liable for the damage the animal has caused, whether the animal was under his custody, or whether it had strayed or escaped.

Article 1386
The owner of a building is liable for the damage caused by its collapse, where it happens as a result of lack of maintenance or of a defect in its construction.

Germany: German Civil Code/Bürgerliches Gesetzbuch (BGB)

§ 2 (Beginning of majority)
Majority begins at the age of eighteen.

§ 30 (Special representatives)
It may be provided by the articles of association that, in addition to the board, special representatives are to be appointed for particular transactions. In case of doubt, the power of agency of such a representative extends to all legal transactions that the sphere of business allocated to him normally entails.

§ 31 (Liability of an association for organs)
The association is liable for the damage to a third party that the board, a member of the board or another constitutionally appointed representative causes through an act committed by it or him in carrying out the business with which it or he is entrusted, where the act gives rise to a liability in damages.

§ 89(1) (Liability for organs)
The provision of § 31 applies with the necessary modifications to the treasury and to corporations, foundations and institutions under public law.

§ 253II (Intangible damage)
If damages are to be paid for an injury to body, health, freedom or sexual self-determination, reasonable compensation in money may also be demanded for any damage that is not pecuniary loss.

§ 276 *(Responsibility of the obligor)*
  (1) The obligor is responsible for intention and negligence, if a higher or lower degree of liability is neither laid down nor to be inferred from the other subject matter of the obligation, including but not limited to the giving of a guarantee or the assumption of a procurement risk. The provisions of sections 827 and 828 apply with the necessary modifications.
  (2) A person acts negligently if he fails to exercise reasonable care.
  (3) The obligor may not be released in advance from liability for intention.

§ 278 *(Responsibility of the obligor for third parties)*
The obligor is responsible for fault of his legal representative and of persons whom he uses to perform his obligation, to the same extent as for fault on his own part. The provision of § 276(2) does not apply.

§ 823 *(Liability in damages)*
  (1) A person who, intentionally or negligently, unlawfully injures the life, body, health, freedom, property or another right of another person is liable to make compensation to the other party for the damage arising from this.
  (2) The same duty is held by a person who commits a breach of a statute that is intended to protect another person. If, according to the contents of the statute, it may also be breached without fault, then liability to compensation only exists in the case of fault.

§ 826 *(Intentional damage contrary to public policy)*
A person who, in a manner contrary to public policy, intentionally inflicts damage on another person is liable to the other person to make compensation for the damage.

§ 828 *(Minors)*
  (1) A person who has not reached the age of seven is not responsible for damage caused to another person.
  (2) A person who has reached the age of seven but not the age of ten is not responsible for damage that he inflicts on another party in an accident involving a motor vehicle, a railway or a suspension railway. This does not apply if he intentionally caused the injury.
  (3) A person who has not yet reached the age of eighteen is, to the extent that his responsibility is not excluded under subsection (1) or (2), not responsible for damage he inflicts on another person if, when committing the damaging act, he does not have the insight required to recognise his responsibility.

§ 829 *(Liability in damages for reasons of equity/Billigkeit)*
A person who, for reasons cited in sections 827 and 828, is not responsible for damage he caused in the instances specified in sections 823 to 826 must nonetheless make compensation for the damage, unless damage compensation can be obtained from a third party with a duty of supervision, to the extent that in the circumstances,

including without limitation the circumstances of the parties involved, equity requires indemnification and he is not deprived of the resources needed for reasonable maintenance and to discharge his statutory maintenance duties.

§ 831 *(Liability for vicarious agents)*
(1) A person who uses another person to perform a task is liable to make compensation for the damage that the other unlawfully inflicts on a third party when carrying out the task. Liability in damages does not apply if the principal exercises reasonable care when selecting the person deployed and, to the extent that he is to procure devices or equipment or to manage the business activity, in the procurement or management, or if the damage would have occurred even if this care had been exercised.
(2) The same responsibility is borne by a person who assumes the performance of one of the transactions specified in subsection (1) sentence 2 for the principal by contract.

§ 832 *(Liability of a person with a duty of supervision)*
(1) A person who is obliged by operation of law to supervise a person who requires supervision because he is a minor or because of his mental or physical condition is liable to make compensation for the damage that this person unlawfully causes to a third party. Liability in damages does not apply if he fulfils the requirements of his duty to supervise or if the damage would likewise have been caused in the case of proper conduct of supervision.
(2) The same responsibility applies to any person who assumes the task of supervision by contract.

§ 833 *(Liability of animal keeper)*
If a human being is killed by an animal or if the body or the health of a human being is injured by an animal or a thing is damaged by an animal, then the person who keeps the animal is liable to compensate the injured person for the damage arising from this. Liability in damages does not apply if the damage is caused by a domestic animal intended to serve the occupation, economic activity or subsistence of the keeper of the animal and either the keeper of the animal in supervising the animal has exercised reasonable care or the damage would also have occurred even if this care had been exercised.

§ 839 *(Liability in case of breach of official duty)*
(1) If an official intentionally or negligently breaches the official duty incumbent upon him in relation to a third party, then he must compensate the third party for damage arising from this. If the official is only responsible because of negligence, then he may only be held liable if the injured person is not able to obtain compensation in another way.
(2) If an official breaches his official duties in a judgment in a legal matter, then he is only responsible for any damage arising from this if the

breach of duty consists in a criminal offence. This provision is not applicable to refusal or delay that is in breach of duty in exercising a public function.
(3) Liability for damage does not arise if the injured person has intentionally or negligently failed to avert the damage by having recourse to appeal.

§ 840 (Liability of more than one person)
(1) If more than one person is responsible for damage arising from a tort, then they are jointly and severally liable.
(2) If besides the person who is obliged to make compensation for damage caused by another person under sections 831 and 832 the other person is also responsible for the damage, then in their internal relationship the other is obliged alone, and in the case specified in section 829 the person with a duty of supervision is obliged alone.
(3) If besides the person who is obliged to make compensation for damage under sections 833 to 838 a third party is responsible, then the third party is solely obliged in their internal relationship.

§ 1626(1) (Parental custody)
(1) The parents have the duty and the right to care for the minor child (parental custody). The parental custody includes the care for the person of the child (care for the person of the child) and the property of the child (care for the property of the child).

§ 1631(1) (Contents and limits of care for the person of the child)
(1) The care for the person of the child includes without limitation the duty and the right to care for, bring up and supervise the child and to specify its abode.

§ 1672 (Living apart where the mother has parental custody)
(1) If the parents live apart for a period that is not merely temporary and if, under section 1626a (2), the mother has parental custody, the father, with the approval of the mother, may apply for the family court to transfer to him alone the parental custody or part of the parental custody. The application is to be granted if the transfer serves the best interests of the child.
(2) To the extent that a transfer has occurred under subsection (1), the family court, on the application of a parent with the approval of the other parent, may decide that the parents should have joint parental custody, if this is not inconsistent with the best interests of the child. This also applies to the extent that the transfer has later been cancelled under subsection (1).

Index

accident prevention, 193, 242, 243, 248, 250
Ackner, Lord, 190
administrative law, 50–3
agency, 131, 132, 176
   and motor vehicles, 110–16
      conceptual difficulties of, 114, 141, 253
      common law, in, 12, 13, 47, 102, 144
      definition, 109
      scope of the agent's authority, 110
Atiyah, P.S., 4, 42, 98, 159, 228
   compensation, 253
   control test, 59
   dual liability of employers, 81, 89–90, 93
   inclusion of all workers in vicarious liability, 140
   independent contractors, 125
   insurance, 237
   risk, 194
Australia, 71, 123
   agency, 102, 129–31
   course of employment test, 172–4, 191
   Hollis v Vabu, 74–5, 76, 249
      control, 75, 127–9, 143
      policy concerns, 249, 251
   Insurance Contracts Act 1984, 33
   Ipp Report, 117
   legislation for vicarious liability, 105
   motor vehicle legislation, 115
   New South Wales v Lepore; Samin v Queensland; Rich v Queensland, 161, 249, 251, 262
   parental responsibility, 200–1
   policy factors, 249, 251
   prohibited conduct, 155
   right to an indemnity, 34
authority
   ostensible, 176, 178, 179, 181
   parental, 220

Baty, Thomas, 228, 230
Bazley v Curry, 2, 19, 76, 92, 161, 174, 194, 249
   McLachlin J, 162–6, 189, 191, 194, 238, 241–2, 246, 247
Blackburn, Lord, 116–17
Blackstone, Sir William, 57
Blieck case, 20, 30, 133–40, 186, 223
borrowed servant problem, 56, 83–93, 142
Brüggemeier, G., 10, 103

Callinan J, 115, 173, 174
Canada, 42, 72, 92–3, 132, 260
   671122 Ontario Ltd v Sagaz Industries Canada Inc., 69, 71, 72, 79
   Bazley v Curry, 2, 19, 76, 92, 161, 162–6, 174, 189, 193–4, 241–2, 246, 247
   McLachlin J, 162–6, 189, 191, 194, 238, 241–2, 246
   control test, 162
   course of employment test, 155, 191
   enterprise risk, 169
   extension of liability, 247
   Jacobi v Griffiths, 161, 163
   legislation for vicarious liability, 105
   motor vehicle legislation, 115
   right to an indemnity, 35
   risk, 194, 251
Cane, P., 89, 112, 179, 237
Chabas, François, 233
children, capacities of, 212
civil law systems, 2, 229; *see also* French Civil Code, German Civil Code
   and common law systems, 5
   control, 86
   employer/employee relationship, 65, 78
   extension of vicarious liability outside the employment context, 106–8, 263
   independent contractors, 125

273

INDEX

civil law systems (cont.)
  intermediate category of employee, 131
  principles of fault, 2
  professionals, 156
  terminology used in, 26
Clyde, Lord, 189
common employment, doctrine of, 119
common law systems
  administrative law, 50–1
  agency, 108–16, 144
  civil law systems and, 5
  close connection test, 262
  company law and, 47
  concurrent liability, 44
  connection between the tort and the parties' relationship, 145
  contract of employment, 56
  course of employment test, 157–81, 193
    close connection test, 189
    deliberate wrongdoing, 160–2
  development of vicarious liability in, 12–13
  employer/employee relationship, 65, 79, 143
  equality before the law, 44
  exemplary damages, 17, 22, 39–43
  extension of vicarious liability outside the employment context, 26, 108–26, 116–26
  functional limit on liability, 148
  legislation for vicarious liability, 103–5
  master's responsibility for actions of servants, 232
  motor vehicle legislation, 141
  parental liability, 196, 223–6
  parental responsibility in, 197–203, 254
    duty of care owed to children, 199
    fault-based liability, 206–10
    framework for in tort law, 203–17
    models of, 205–13, 223
    preventing children from causing injury to another, 198, 200–3
    proof of fault, 202
    protection of children, 197, 198–200
    standards expected, 201, 206
    standards of care, 226
    vicarious or strict liability, 210–13
  professionals and, 62–3
  responsibility in, 1
  rigidity of, 122
  strict liability, 6, 223–6
  system of precedent, 166
  tort law and social change, 226
company law, 46–50
compensation, 209, 230, 234–7, 246, 251, 252, 253
  and the course of employment test, 146, 153

contract law, 43–54, 44–6, 97
  and doctors, 63
  liability in, 5, 67
contract of employment, 23, 55–79, 82, 101, 128, 142
  and temporary workers, 96
  contract for services, 23, 58, 71
  definition, 79
  control, 55, 87, 99, 128, 140, 244, 252
Cooke J, 70–1
corporations, 7, 47, 252
course of employment test, 150–88, 251, 253
  appraisal of the situation, 188–95
  authority of the employee, 178, 179
  case law, 192
  close connection test, 162–3, 165–6, 167, 169, 172–4, 178, 180–1, 188–95, 262–3
  common law system, in the, 160–2
  connection between the risk and the wrong that results, 162–6
  composite test, 70–3, 75, 131, 133, 193
  strong connection test, 164
  European law in, 258
  factors in, 191, 195
  Salmond test: *see* separate entry
  significance of policy in, 150–3
courts, discretion given to, 2, 73, 76, 106, 107, 195
craftsmen liability, 24
criminal law, 53–4, 160, 202
culpa in eligendo/in vigilando, 231–4

damages, exemplary, 17, 22, 39–43
de Greuille, Bertrand, 25, 59, 229
Denning Lord, 14, 69, 113, 118, 155
  Cassidy v Ministry of Health, 61, 62, 69, 118, 122
  Denham v Midland Employers' Mutual Assurance Ltd, 98
dependent contractors, 127, 143, 144, 253
deterrence, 42, 43, 76, 163, 172, 241–3, 245–7
  Hollis v Vabu, 129, 251
doctors, 13; *see also* professionals
  contract law and, 63
  control and negligence, 61–5
Draft Common Frame of Reference (Europe), 255, 256, 257
  Book VI, Article 3:201, 258–63
  course of employment test, 262
  terminology used in, 260, 264

employees, 140; *see also* independent contractors, temporary workers
  accountability of, 39, 243
  intermediate category of, 131

INDEX

employer/employee relationship, 7, 23, 31, 55–79, 120, 230, 253
  agency relationships, 56, 82, 94, 143, 253
  borrowed servant problem, 83–93, 142
    dual liability, 89–93
    triangular relationship, 83
  changes in, 60, 65, 76, 77, 93, 142
  composite test, 70–3, 75, 131, 133
  considering the totality of the relationship, 70–3, 78, 97
    application of the test, 73–7
    bicycle couriers, 74–5, 79
    distinguishing factors, 75–7
    owner-drivers, 73–4, 79
  contracting-out of core tasks, 99, 126, 143
  control, 55, 87, 99, 128, 244, 252
  control test, 57–9, 75, 78, 244
    alternative approaches to, 66–73, 69–73, 78
    composite test, 70–3, 75, 131, 133
    doubts about, 60–5
    interpretation of, 66–8
    limitations of, 74
    response to doubts about, 65
  dual liability of employers, 98
  employer as bearer of risk, 37
  employer as guarantor, 37
  entrepreneur test, 70–3
  flexible interpretation of, 128, 131, 141, 143, 144
  independent contractors, 23, 58, 62, 72, 126, 140
  organisation (integration) test, 69–70, 69–73, 141
  the parent/child relationship and, 196, 211
  partners in a firm, 56, 104
  power to organise, direct and control the activities of another, 133–40
  professionals and, 60, 61–5, 78, 85, 118
  reasonable care towards employees, 119
  right to an indemnity, 38, 241, 247
  shared control, 91
  special cases, 81
  temporary workers 56, 81, 93–8, 143, 253
    alternative approaches to, 97–8
    casual workers, 95
    finding liability, 95–6
    triangular relationship, 94
  triangular relationship, 150, 234
  vertical integration of, 82, 93
England and Wales
  motor vehicle legislation, 115–16
  parental liability, fault-based, 206–10
  parental responsibility in, 210–13, 218–19, 224
  parenting orders, 203, 204, 219
  risk, 251
English Law Commission, 40
enterprise risk, 163, 164, 165, 169, 238, 247, 249
Eörsi, G., 21
Europe, 5
  differences in legal systems, 265
  Draft Common Frame of Reference, 255, 256, 257
    Book VI, Article 3:201, 258–63
    course of employment test, 262
    terminology used in, 260, 264
  European Group on Tort Law, 260
  harmonised law of vicarious liability, 255–65
    control test, 261
    course of employment test, 258, 262–3
    fault-based principles, 258
    independent contractors, 261
    interpretation of liability, 258
    relationship giving rise to liability, 259–62
    scope of an employer's liability, 262–3
    terminological questions, 259
  parental liability, 196
  presumption of fault, 254
  Principles of European Tort Law
    Article 6:102, 258–63
    terminology used in, 264
  Research Group on EC Private Law, 256
  Study Group on a European Civil Code, 256
European Centre of Tort and Insurance Law, 208–9
European Commission, 255, 256
European Group on Tort Law, 260
European Parliament, 255
exemplary damages, 17, 22, 39–43

Fabre-Magnan, M., 139
fairness, 243, 252; *see also* justice
Fedke, J., 209
Feliu, J.S., 211
Flannigan, R., 126, 250
Fleming, J.G., 122, 150, 238, 244
France
  administrative courts, 134
  Assemblée plénière decisions, 181–8, 216–17
  Bertrand case, 215–16, 219, 221, 223
  Blieck case, 20, 30, 133–40, 186, 223
  case law on *dans les fonctions auxquelles ils les ont employés* test, 181–8, 188–9
  Code of Criminal Procedure, 53
  command and control, 232
  company law, 44, 47, 48–9
  contract law, 44, 63, 64
  Costedoat case, 36–8, 241, 246, 247
  course of employment test, 181–8

France (cont.)
  criminal law, 53–4, 156
  division between civil and criminal chambers, 182, 183
  dual liability of employers, 91
  faute de service, 36, 52
  faute personnelle, 36, 38
  faute séparable ou détachable, 49
  Fullenworth decision, 214, 240
  insurance, 33, 35, 103, 220, 250
  loi Badinter, 183
  parental liability, 135
    objective standard of care for, 212
    strict liability, 213–17
    vicarious or strict liability, 210–13
  public sector employees, 24, 36, 44, 52
  right to an indemnity, 34, 35–8
  right to give instructions, 58–9, 63, 102
  risk, 246, 251
  temporary workers, 97
fraud, test for, 175–81
French Civil Code, 2, 8–9, 23, 103, 267–9
  § 1384 (5), 25–6, 27–8, 52, 103, 107, 145, 213, 232, 238
  extension of, 138–40, 247
  foundations of, 147
  functions of the *commetant* and *préposé*, 35, 180
  interpretation of, 45, 53–4, 108, 138–40
  limitations of, 139, 141, 180
  parental authority, 216
  abus de fonctions, 181, 182, 185–8, 246
  administrative courts, 44, 52–3
  Assemblée plénière decisions, 184
  borrowed servant problem, and the, 86
  breadth of vicarious liability in, 3
  categories of liability, 9
  commettant and *préposé*, 25, 57, 139
  connection between the risk and the wrong that results, 262
  contrat de travail, 107
  contrat d'entreprise, 107
  control test, subordination and authority, 261
  doctrine of *apparence*, 180
  employer as guarantor, 236
  extension of vicarious liability outside the employment context, 106, 139
  fairness and social justice, 234
  fault, 8, 9, 264
  force majeure, 215, 216, 221
  les fonctions auxquelles ils les ont employés, 150–8, 181–8, 188–95, 262
    connection between the employer and the employee's duties, 186
    limiting the scope of liability, 183–4

liability
  for the acts of others, conditions for, 185
  of physicians, 67
  no-fault liability, 186
  presumed liability, 23–4
  strict liability, 6, 23, 25
parental liability, 24, 29, 135, 219–20, 222–3, 240
  and domicile of the children, 217
  faute de surveillance or d'éducation, 213, 214
  limitations of the system, 223–4
  presumption of liability, 214
  strict liability, 218
  policy considerations, 152
  reform of, 29–30, 37–8, 78, 138–40, 217, 241, 246
  requirement for a wrongful act, 29
  right to give instructions, 66
  risk, 194, 239, 251
  serious misconduct, 36
  standard of care, 264
  subordination and authority, 68, 137
Galand-Carval, S., 196, 221
Gaudu, F., 88, 91
German Civil Code, 2, 269–72
  §§ 276–278, 63
  § 278, 45
  § 823(1), 11, 12, 28, 46, 49, 232, 264
  § 831, 9–10, 11, 26, 103, 148, 231, 232
    fault, 28–9
    reform of, 46
  § 832, 206–7
  § 839 (liability for officials), 51–2
  § 1626(1), 207
  § 1631(1), 207
  in Ausführung der Verrichtung, 150–88
  borrowed servant problem, 88
  contract law and company law, 43, 45, 47
  contract of employment, 57
  control test, right to give instructions, 261
  course of employment test, substantive connection, 153
  doctrine of decentralised exoneration, 11
  fault-based principles, 4, 5, 19, 146, 259
  Geschäftsherr and *Verrichtungsgehilfe*, 26, 64–5, 261
  parental liability
    emphasis on the facts of the case, 208
    fault-based, 206–10
    reverse burden of proof, 206–7
  policy considerations, 152–3
  presumption of fault, 29, 103, 231

INDEX

public sector employees, 51–2
reform of, 11, 46, 232
requirement for a wrongful act, 29
right to give instructions, 66–7
tort law, 45
Germany
   company law, 47, 49–50
   contract law, 43, 45
   criminal courts, 156
   employer/employee relationship, tests for, 97
   fault-based principles, 103
   Imperial Law of Liability, 232
   presumption of fault, 244
   right to give instructions, 59, 63
Gummow J, 114–15

Haldane LC, Viscount, 47–8
Hallet LJ, 85
Hesselink, M.W., 263
Heuston, R.F.V., 157
Hobhouse, Lord, 166, 175–81
Hollis v Vabu, 74–8, 143, 249–56
   control, 75, 127–9, 143
   policy concerns, 249–51
Holt CJ, 12–13
hospitals, liability of, 62, 118–21, 236

Ibbetson, D.J., 12, 229
identification, theory of, 228, 231–4
indemnity, right to, 30–9
   limiting the application of, 32
independent contractors, 58, 62, 74, 79, 81, 93
   case law on, 107
   in European law, 261
   justifications for vicarious liability, 125
   non-independent, 127, 143, 144, 253
industrial revolution, 7, 55
insurance, 20, 188, 235, 237, 239, 242, 252
   employer insurance, 236
   in England, 152
   in France, 33, 221, 250
   motor insurance, 112, 115, 141
Ipp JA, 174
Ipp Report, 117
Irish Law Reform Commission, 224

Johnston, David, 147
Jourdain, P., 219, 238, 247
   Bertrand case, 219
   control test, 68, 88
   risk, 107, 137, 238, 247
justice, 8, 153, 163, 166–72, 247–50, 252
   corrective, 1, 16–17, 31, 233, 239
   distributive, 16–17, 212, 239

parental liability and, 212, 220
responsibility and, 39, 136, 230
right of indemnity, and the, 31, 38
risk and, 247
social, 234, 252

Kahn-Freund, O., 60
Keith, Lord, 177–8

La Forest J, 35
Larouche, P., 67
Laski, Harold, 238
Latin maxims, 14, 19, 228, 232, 233
Lawson, F.H., 7
Legeais, R., 67
Lever, J., 66
liability, 21–54, 138
   authority, 58
   company law in, 43–54
   concurrent, 44
   conditions for, 58
   contract law in, 43–54, 67
   control test for, 57–9
   craftsman liability, 24
   delictual liability, 57, 223
   direction, 58
   dual liability, 81, 89–93, 98
   fault-based principles, 22, 59, 198, 230, 244
   joint and several, 49, 89–93
   primary, 16–18, 41, 43, 132, 253
   public law in, 50–3
   rationale for imposition of, 16
   strict liability, 22, 230
Lister v Hesley Hall Ltd, 3, 160–2, 169, 189–90, 193, 242, 263
   Lord Hobhouse, 175, 233, 250
   Lord Millett, 158, 159–60, 166–72, 248
   Lord Steyn, 132, 166–72, 191
   scope of vicarious liability, 19–20
loss distribution, 107, 113, 172, 193, 234–7
   and risk, 36, 220, 239, 252
Lunney, M., 89, 112, 132, 179, 191
Luntz, H., 91

MacGuigan JA, 60
MacKenna J, 73–4
Magnus, U., 209
Markesinis, B.S., 11, 45, 208
Martin-Casals, M., 211
Mason J, 120
master's responsibility for actions of servants, 12, 22, 109
master's tort theory, 13–15, 232
Mazeaud, H.L., 233
McCarthy, L., 132

McHugh J
    Hollis v Vabu, 76, 128, 131–2, 133, 143
    Northern Sandblasting Pty Ltd v Harris, 140
McKee v Dumas, 84
McKendrick, E., 120, 126, 141
McLachlin J, 162–6, 189, 191, 194, 245, 252
    Bazley v Curry, 238, 241–2
    Jacobi v Griffiths, 163
Millett, Lord, 158
Morton, Lord, 15
motor vehicle legislation, 115–16, 252
Mouly, J., 141

negligence, 9, 179–80, 216, 232, 254, 264
New South Wales v Lepore, 2, 19, 120, 124, 161, 172–4, 249, 250, 251, 262
New Zealand, 102, 129–31
    Accident Compensation Scheme, 252
Newark, F.H., 14
Neyers, J.W., 92
Nicholls, Lord, 2
    Dubai Aluminium Co Ltd v Salaam, 3, 167, 171–2, 194, 248
non-delegable duties, 13, 17, 102, 116–26, 141, 144, 253
    and hospitals, 62, 118–21
    categories of, 118
    collateral negligence, 122–6
    limitations on, 122–6
    other duties, 121–2
    policy considerations, 121
    schools of, 124, 173

Oliphant, K., 191, 219, 224
organisational fault, 46

parent/child relationship
    and the employer/employee relationship, 196, 211
    standard of care, 217
parental autonomy, 205, 218, 219, 222, 225
parental liability, 24, 135, 196–225, 240, 254
    and schools, 204
    and tort law, 218
    for the torts of the child or the acts of the child, 210
    in common law systems, 206–10, 223–6
    objective standard of care for, 208
    parent–child–victim triangular relationship, 225
parental responsibility
    at common law, 197–203, 208, 210–13, 218–19, 224
        liability to parties injured by the child, 200–3
        liability to the child, 198

in tort law
    choice of model, 217–23
    fault-based, 206–10
    framework for, 203–17
    models of, 205–13
    vicarious or strict liability, 210–13
parenting orders, 203, 204, 219
Phegan J, 94–5
Phillips MR, Lord, 119
police officers, liability for actions of, 42, 103, 170–1
Pollock, F., 12, 229
Pothier, R.J., 147, 231
primary liability and vicarious liability, 16–18, 41, 43, 132, 175, 193
Principles of European Tort Law, 255
    Article 6:102, 258–63
    terminology used in, 264
professionals, 78, 118, 252
    autonomy and discretion of, 61, 78, 85
public bodies, claims against, 53
public law, 50–3
public safety, 121
public sector employees, 24, 36, 44, 52
punishment, 40; see also justice

qui facit per alium facit per se, 14, 228, 232

Rebut, D., 237
reform on vicarious liability law, 4, 224
    in England and Wales, 32, 33
    in France, 29–30, 37–8, 78, 138–40, 217, 241, 246
    in Germany, 11, 46, 232
Reid, Lord, 14, 198
representative agents, 127–33, 140
res ipsa loquitur, 234
Research Group on EC Private Law, 256
respondeat superior, 228, 233
responsibility, 1, 15, 243, 249
    and tort law, 1
    apportionment of, 92, 131
    individual, 136, 224, 230
    of parents, 204
Ribot, J., 211
risk, 29, 34–6, 121, 237–41, 242–3, 245–7, 249–50
    and justice, 239, 243, 247
    and uncertainty, 243
    enterprise risk, 9, 37, 163, 164, 165, 169, 238, 247, 249
    social risk, 223
Roman law, 6–7, 147, 149
    paterfamilias' liability, 7, 147

Sachs LJ, 123
Salmond test, 157, 159, 160, 161, 162, 169, 181

INDEX

in Australia, 172, 174
risk-based reasoning, 36, 39, 173, 188, 238, 250
Scott, Lord, 40
servant's tort theory, 13, 15
sexual abuse, 124, 161, 164, 173, 242
Slynn, Lord, 51
Smith, Y.B., 235
Spain, 210–13, 244
Stevens, G.M., 77
Stevens, Robert, 233, 247
Steyn, Lord, 168, 194
Lister v Hesley Hall Ltd, 166–72, 191
strict liability, 22, 230
Study Group on a European Civil Code, 256

temporary workers, 56, 81, 93–8, 143, 253
alternative approaches to, 97–8
casual workers, 95
finding liability, 95–6
triangular relationship, 94
Terré, F., 185
tort law
and changing social and economic needs, 254
and responsibility, 1
Principles of European Tort Law, 255
role of in society, 239
vagueness of, 264
Trindade, F., 89, 112, 132, 179

Unberath, H., 11, 45
uncertainty about the law, 18, 20, 79, 171, 243, 247
and risk, 243
and the close connection test, 171, 263
in common law, 4, 13, 89
United States
doctrine of the 'family car', 113
economic reality test, 70–3, 74
employer/employee relationship, economic reality test, 74
parental liability, 225
Restatement of Agency, 58, 70, 71, 98, 108, 157, 192
right to an indemnity, 35

van Gerven, W., 66, 68
vicarious liability, 22, 26, 101, 230, 247–51
agency and motor vehicles, 110–16
civil law systems in, 229
common factors in, 22
common law in, 12–13
course of employment test, 12, 23, 150–88
common law systems in, 157–81
deliberate wrongdoing, 160–2
economic reasoning, 166
fraud and, 175–81
significance of policy in, 150–3
tests for, 162–81
courts' considerations of, 2
criteria for, 227
definition, 1–9
exemplary damages and, 17
extension of, 2, 3, 26, 101, 140–3, 146, 240
case law, 106–26
in civil law systems, 106–8
in common law systems, 108–26
rational for, 229
representative agents, 127–40
statute by, 103–6
harmonised law of, 255–65
consensus on, 263
policy considerations, 264
practicality and principle, 263–5
social, political, economic and cultural factors, 264
historical overview, 6–13
Latin maxims and, 14, 19, 228, 232, 233
legal basis for, 13–18
master's tort theory, 13–15, 232
parental liability, 218
policy and principle, 227
policy considerations, 81, 93, 97, 102, 129, 150–3, 264
balancing, 243–52, 253, 265
case law examples, 151–3
deterrence, 76, 172
fairness and justice, 247–50
loss distribution, 172
primary policy factors, 248
prohibited conduct, 153
public safety and risk, 121
risk: allocation of consequences, 245–7
secondary policy factors, 248
primary liability and, 16–18, 41, 43, 132, 193, 233–4, 253
rationale for imposition of, 36, 98, 107, 126, 194
changing perceptions of, 252
deterrence, 43
relationship giving rise to, 26, 101–44
case law, 106–26
statute, 103–6
requirement for a wrongful act, 27–30
right to an indemnity, 30–9
role in post-industrialised States, 5, 247
Salmond test, 157–81
in common law systems, 159
weakness of, 161
wrongful act authorised by the employer, 158

vicarious liability (cont.)
  wrongful and unauthorised mode of
    doing an authorised act, 158–62
scope of, 1, 15, 20, 145–95, 251
  limiting the scope, 147–9
  role of policy in, 162
servant's tort theory, 13
specific legislation for, 101, 103–6
  terminology, 22–7
  theoretical coherence of, 13, 19, 113
  theoretical justifications, 228
    deterrence, 241–3
    fault, 231–4
    risk, 237–41
    victim compensation and loss
      distribution, 234–7
  triangular relationship, 150, 192
  uncertainty about: *see separate entry*
victims, 177
  and parental liability, 202
  protection of, 99, 107, 193, 205, 242

  in French law, 37, 38, 180, 182, 219, 221
  in German law, 45
  reliance by, 177, 178, 179–80, 181
Vines, P., 124, 174
Viney, G., 45, 107, 186, 219
  relationship of subordination and
    authority, 68, 88, 137
  risk, 219, 238, 247
Voer, Johannes, 147

Wagner, Gerhard, 11, 46, 207
Waller, P.L., 224
Weekes, R., 169
Weinrib, Ernest, 233
Whittaker, S.J., 265
Williams, Glanville, 13, 16, 32, 126, 140, 229, 234
Wright, Lord, 72

Zimmermann, R., 11, 147
Zweigert and Kötz, 10

CAMBRIDGE STUDIES IN INTERNATIONAL AND COMPARATIVE LAW

Books in the series

Vicarious Liability in Tort: A Comparative Perspective
Paula Giliker

Legitimacy and Legality in International Law: An Interactional Account
Jutta Brunnée and Stephen J. Toope

The Public International Law Theory of Hans Kelsen: Believing in Universal Law
Jochen von Bernstorff

The Concept of Non-International Armed Conflict in International Humanitarian Law
Anthony Cullen

The Challenge of Child Labour in International Law
Franziska Humbert

Shipping Interdiction and the Law of the Sea
Douglas Guilfoyle

International Courts and Environmental Protection
Tim Stephens

Legal Principles in WTO Dispute
Andrew D. Mitchell

War Crimes in Internal Armed Conflicts
Eve La Haye

Humanitarian Occupation
Gregory H. Fox

The International Law of Environmental Impact Assessment: Process, Substance and Integration
Neil Craik

The Law and Practice of International Territorial Administration: Versailles, Iraq and Beyond
Carsten Stahn

Cultural Products and the World Trade Organization
Tania Voon

United Nations Sanctions and the Rule of Law
Jeremy Farrall

National Law in WTO Law: Effectiveness and Good Governance in the World Trading System
Sharif Bhuiyan

The Threat of Force in International Law
Nikolas Stürchler

Indigenous Rights and United Nations Standards
Alexandra Xanthaki

International Refugee Law and Socio-Economic Rights
Michelle Foster

The Protection of Cultural Property in Armed Conflict
Roger O'Keefe

Interpretation and Revision of International Boundary Decisions
Kaiyan Homi Kaikobad

Multinationals and Corporate Social Responsibility: Limitations and Opportunities in International Law
Jennifer A. Zerk

Judiciaries within Europe: A Comparative Review
John Bell

Law in Times of Crisis: Emergency Powers in Theory and Practice
Oren Gross and Fionnuala Ní Aoláin

Vessel-Source Marine Pollution: The Law and Politics of International Regulation
Alan Tan

Enforcing Obligations Erga Omnes in International Law
Christian J. Tams

Non-Governmental Organisations in International Law
Anna-Karin Lindblom

Democracy, Minorities and International Law
Steven Wheatley

Prosecuting International Crimes: Selectivity and the International Law Regime
Robert Cryer

Compensation for Personal Injury in English, German and Italian Law
A Comparative Outline
Basil Markesinis, Michael Coester, and Guido Alpa, Augustus Ullstein

Dispute Settlement in the UN Convention on the Law of the Sea
Natalie Klein

The International Protection of Internally Displaced Persons
Catherine Phuong

Imperialism, Sovereignty and the Making of International Law
Antony Anghie

Necessity, Proportionality and the Use of Force by States
Judith Gardam

International Legal Argument in the Permanent Court of International Justice:
The Rise of the International Judiciary
Ole Spiermann

Great Powers and Outlaw States: Unequal Sovereigns in the International Legal Order
Gerry Simpson

Local Remedies in International Law
C. F. Amerasinghe

Reading Humanitarian Intervention: Human Rights and the Use of Force in
International Law
Anne Orford

Conflict of Norms in Public International Law: How WTO Law Relates to Other
Rules of Law
Joost Pauwelyn

Transboundary Damage in International Law
Hanqin Xue

European Criminal Procedures Edited by
Mireille Delmas-Marty and John Spencer

The Accountability of Armed Opposition Groups in International Law
Liesbeth Zegveld

Sharing Transboundary Resources: International Law and Optimal Resource Use
Eyal Benvenisti

International Human Rights and Humanitarian Law
René Provost

Remedies Against International Organisations
Karel Wellens

Diversity and Self-Determination in International Law
Karen Knop

The Law of Internal Armed Conflict
Lindsay Moir

International Commercial Arbitration and African States Practice, Participation and Institutional Development
Amazu A. Asouzu

The Enforceability of Promises in European Contract Law
James Gordley

International Law in Antiquity
David J. Bederman

Money Laundering: A New International Law Enforcement Model
Guy Stessens

Good Faith in European Contract Law
Reinhard Zimmermann and Simon Whittaker

On Civil Procedure
J. A. Jolowicz

Trusts: A Comparative Study
Maurizio Lupoi

The Right to Property in Commonwealth Constitutions
Tom Allen

International Organizations Before National Courts
August Reinisch

The Changing International Law of High Seas Fisheries
Francisco Orrego Vicuña

Trade and the Environment: A Comparative Study of EC and US Law
Damien Geradin

Unjust Enrichment: A Study of Private Law and Public Values
Hanoch Dagan

Religious Liberty and International Law in Europe
Malcolm D. Evans

Ethics and Authority in International Law
Alfred P. Rubin

Sovereignty Over Natural Resources: Balancing Rights and Duties
Nico Schrijver

The Polar Regions and the Development of International Law
Donald R. Rothwell

Fragmentation and the International Relations of Micro-States: Self-determination and Statehood
Jorri Duursma

Principles of the Institutional Law of International Organizations
C. F. Amerasinghe